UNIVERSITY OF OKLAHOMA PRESS : NORMAN

of A

RESEARCH AND TRAINING IN THE UNITED STATES

In Pursuit of American History

Research and Training
in the United States

Walter Rundell, Jr.

FOREWORD BY JAMES B. RHOADS

BY WALTER RUNDELL, JR.

Probing the American West (with others) (Santa Fe, 1962)

Black-Market Money: The Collapse of U.S. Military Currency Control in World War II (Baton Rouge, 1964)

Holidays: Days of Significance for All Americans (with others) (New York, 1965)

Bibliography and the Historian (with others) (Santa Barbara, 1968)

In Pursuit of American History: Research and Training in the United States (Norman, 1970)

International Standard Book Number: 0-8061-0868-1

Library of Congress Catalog Card Number: 69-16725

For Deanna

FOREWORD

EARLY in 1965, Wayne C. Grover, then Archivist of the United States and chairman of the National Historical Publications Commission, selected Walter Rundell, Jr., to direct a survey of the use of original documentary source materials in the teaching of American history at graduate levels in our institutions of higher learning. Professor Rundell, who since 1961 had been serving as assistant executive secretary of the American Historical Association and director of its successful Service Center for Teachers of History, already had a wide acquaintance with the subject of the inquiry and with teaching methods and materials. He was, consequently, challenged by the assignment, accepted the appointment, and began his work in September, 1965.

This survey was financed with funds made available as a result of a generous gift of two million dollars by the Ford Foundation to the National Archives Trust Fund Board in 1964 in support of efforts of the National Historical Publications Commission to encourage and promote the publication of valuable documentary source materials for American history. The principal was to be used over a period of years to finance the collecting and editing for publication of the papers of Benjamin Franklin, Thomas Jefferson, Alexander Hamilton, James Madison, and the Adams family. The Foundation and the Commission further agreed that interest earned by the principal over this period would be used in the training of editors for this kind of scholarly work and for a survey of the need for, and the use of, such source materials in graduate teaching and study.

The Commission did not direct Professor Rundell in his work, but left him full latitude in planning his approaches to the subject, in determining methods of gathering and recording information, and in deciding how to organize and present his findings. In other words, it was felt that he should be given the same degree of freedom that the Commission allows scholars who edit the documentary publication projects it endorses and supports. Although several present and former members of the Commission have, at Professor Rundell's request, read all or portions of his manuscript and given him their comments, the finished product is his own. This book, therefore, should not be considered a report of the Commission. It is rather a survey sponsored by the Commission of professional practices and opinion and is presented for the information it contains.

It is the sincere hope of the National Historical Publications Commission that this book will stimulate discussion and careful thought by members of the historical profession, and that this in turn will lead to improvement in the historical training given to younger generations and thus in time enhance the meaning of history in American life.

JAMES B. RHOADS
Archivist of the United States

January 25, 1969

Preface

FOR decades professional historians in the United States have pursued their tasks of research and writing, usually sharing certain basic assumptions about the nature of their craft. They have incorporated these assumptions into their training of graduate students. Despite reservations expressed by some social scientists toward the historical method—or lack thereof—most historians have plowed their own furrows, largely unconcerned with criticism from allied disciplines. With the substantial growth of the profession, as evidenced by the increasing number of universities offering a doctorate in history and the ever growing publication of serious historical studies, the time has come to inquire specifically into the research training given Ph.D. candidates in United States history.

The Survey on the Use of Original Sources in Graduate History Training resulted from a stipulation the Ford Foundation made in its grant of two million dollars to the National Historical Publications Commission. The principal of this grant, made in November, 1964, is being spent over a decade to assist five letterpress publications of edited documents—the Jefferson, Adams, Madison, Hamilton, and Franklin papers. The Foundation specified that some of the interest be used for the survey, assuming that if further grants were made to bolster graduate research in history, it would be well to have some reaction from the profession concerning its practices and needs. Before the survey began, the Council of the American Historical Association endorsed its aims. The purpose of the survey, a two-year project which began on September 1, 1965, was to investigate those parts of graduate training in United States history related to research, with emphasis on source materials.

The survey was limited to United States history, as useful as it might have been to extend the investigation into other areas, since the National Historical Publications Commission and the National Archives, its parent organization, are concerned with American materials. For the purposes of the survey, however, United States history was interpreted as broadly as possible, including the colonial period and any aspects of American foreign relations.

In seeking its data, the survey relied substantially on personal interviews, arranged at universities by departmental chairmen. It endeavored to include a cross section of institutions offering the Ph.D. in history—private universities, state universities, those with well-established doctoral programs, those with new programs, and some with highly specialized emphases. Of the 114 institutions offering the Ph.D. in history, the survey director visited 70; he also called on 2 universities with a terminal M.A. in history. He interviewed professors directing dissertations, graduate students doing research for or writing dissertations, and librarians. Forty other institutions visited included private libraries, independent and state historical societies, state archives, a presidential library, and federal records centers. At each of these the director interviewed staff members concerned with graduate students' investigation of primary sources. The interviews at 112 institutions, listed in Appendix A, totaled 557. The director also conducted interviews with a number of individuals whose universities he did not visit.

This kind of research project has obvious imperfections. Working within a two-year limit, the director had to devote a certain amount of time to gathering data and a certain amount to organizing them and writing the book. He chose to divide the time equally, the first year going to research and the second to writing. The year's limitation for research obviously imposed some other limitations, since all institutions could not be visited at the most advantageous time. Sometimes key professors were unavailable during visits at certain universities, but to have built the travel schedule around such individuals would have been impossible. If, because of the lack of their testimony, the program at any university is not represented adequately, the regrettable result can only be attributed to the nature of the research. The hope of the survey is that the total number of interviews at representative institutions across the country will reflect an accurate picture of research training in United States history. Nonetheless, the survey's findings rest upon and cannot transcend its method of research.

The survey sought to systematize information gathered orally by preparing three interview schedules—one for professors, one for graduate students, and one for librarians, archivists, and historical society staffs. Appendix C contains lists of the three types of interviewees. Since such interview schedules obviously could not apply to each institutional situation, questions were modified or omitted as appropriate. The comprehensive questionnaire on which all interview schedules and other questionnaires were based is in Appendix B. The director took notes on each interview and dictated from them for transcription. His research assistant, Alison Wilson, typed nearly two thousand pages of these transcriptions and mailed them to interviewees. Each interviewee was asked to examine and comment on the transcription so that his views would be represented accurately. It was also stated that the return of the corrected transcript signified the interviewee's willingness to be quoted. It was further specified that if the transcript was not returned, it would be assumed that the interviewee had no objections to the use of the material. Consequently, this book is based on information that interviewees have approved, either specifically or tacitly. A few professors interviewed are not specialists in United States history, but their comments on matters unrelated to sources for American history often proved helpful.

In addition to seeking information through personal visits, the director sent questionnaires similar to interview schedules to unvisited institutions that could furnish pertinent data. These included departments of history with doctoral programs, departments with terminal master's programs, libraries of universities with graduate history programs, state archives and libraries, and state and private historical societies. The response from these institutions was exceptionally good, and categorized lists of respondents appear in Appendix D.

Hoping to relieve monotony of terminology in the text, the director has used some short forms that require explanation. Since history is the exclusive focus of the book, any time the word "department" appears, it means department of history unless specified otherwise. Similarly, since the preponderant concern of the survey is graduate training, when the designation "student" is unmodified, it should be understood as graduate student. While interchanging "student" with "graduate student" for stylistic variation, the book is precise about undergraduates. Since graduate students and post doctoral researchers often work alike, "historian" or "researcher" may be interpreted inclusively, depending on the context. Following a majority usage of the profession, the survey refers to master's *theses* and doctoral *dissertations*, and for the sake of clarity does not interchange the terms. But, again to minimize rigidity, the book employs the term "original sources" loosely. To avoid monotony, it uses the terms "primary sources," "primary materials," "sources," and "materials" in the same sense, with the belief that the context makes the intent clear throughout. "Original sources" encompass manuscripts, archives, printed material, or photocopy—anything a student might use in basic research. The book refers to "photocopy" generically, thus covering any form of photoduplication: microfilm, microfiche, microcard, and such facsimile reproductions as Thermofax, photostat, and Xerox. "Microform" is often used as a general term for the variety of microcopies. The terms "United States history" and "American history" are used interchangeably, "American" in this book referring only to this nation and its colonial antecedents.

Because the interviews and questionnaires dealt with many aspects of graduate history training and the book is organized topically, information from any individual may be cited at various places in the volume. No attempt is made to cross-reference these citations, for each type of information is treated within its topical context. For those who wish to see what a given person said about different topics, the index shows each citation.

The survey dealt with many problems of general concern in higher education, but its emphasis was on research training in history. *In Pursuit of American History* therefore attempts to present its information within that framework. Many of the topics treated could be—and have been—approached entirely differently. The informing principle of this volume is, on the basis of facts garnered by the survey, to report the profession's experiences as they related to graduate training. It must be remembered that comments by graduate students reflected their current involvements and were understandably not so tempered as those of mature scholars. The purpose of the book is not to pass judgment on the quality of relevant reactions but to record them as part of the total condition of graduate history training.

Since most citations are to interviews, an explanation of the method of documentation is necessary. Rather than clutter each reference with full information—name of interviewee, his institution, and the date of the interview—the footnotes simply direct the reader to the appendix in which that information is found. The appendix listing interviews is divided into four parts: Appendix C1, Professors; Appendix C2a, Academic Librarians and Archivists; Appendix C2b, Non-academic Librarians, Archivists, and Directors of Historical Societies; and Appendix C3, Graduate Students. If the interviewee's name appears in the text, the citation refers to the appropriate appendix. Successive references to interviews from the same category are identified by the name of the interviewee, followed by *ibid*. When the text does not identify the source, the citation lists the name and refers to the appropriate section of Appendix C, either by name or with *ibid*. Citations to questionnaire responses are self-explanatory.

As in any undertaking of this nature, the survey received able assistance from many quarters. The director wishes to thank those members of the staff of the National Archives and Records Service who facilitated the work with their counsel and logistical support, especially Robert H. Bahmer, Oliver Wendell Holmes, James B. Rhoads, and Walter Robertson, Jr. Though not a member of the National Archives staff, Ernst Posner deserves special appreciation for his advice and encouragement. Four members of the National Historical Publications Commission, L. H. Butterfield, Henry F. Graff, Whitfield J. Bell, Jr., and David C. Mearns, evaluated the manuscript, and the director profited greatly from their comments. His indebtedness to them and to John L. Snell and to his father, Walter Rundell, who also criticized the manuscript, is genuine. While acknowledging this helpful criticism, the director takes responsibility for the book's judgments and whatever limitations it may contain.

Without the splendid co-operation of the 557 interviewees and respondents to the questionnaires, the survey could have accomplished little. To each contributor and his institution, the survey expresses the sincerest gratitude. For her diligent and expert work in transcribing interview notes and tabulating questionnaire results, as well as for her efficient maintenance of his office during the director's long absences, Alison Wilson must be given special commendation. Edward F. D'Arms, the Ford Foundation official responsible for the grant to the National Historical Publications Commission, encouraged the survey with his interest. His support and that of the Foundation are gratefully acknowledged. The Faculty Research Fund of the University of Oklahoma provided aid for the index.

The dedication of this volume to my wife is small token of her contribution.

WALTER RUNDELL, JR.

Norman, Oklahoma
September 3, 1968

CONTENTS

In Pursuit
of American
History

RESEARCH AND TRAINING IN THE UNITED STATES

I. Historical Method

A N issue of some consequence in the historical profession is its methodology. A historian's views on the nature of his discipline inevitably influence the manner in which he teaches future practitioners about the structure and methodology of that discipline. Those instructors who view history from the humanistic standpoint, who emphasize the uniqueness of the historical event, may be less likely to feel the need for systematic methodological training than those with an orientation toward the social sciences. Merle Curti thought that the lack of a general methods course was a weakness in his department,[1] and Gabriel Kolko said that for American historians an insufficient background in methodology is "a real weakness."[2] Representing the opposite view, Shaw Livermore, Jr., discounted methodological training, for he was more interested in students' knowing how to formulate important questions than in their knowing method.[3] George W. Pierson doubted that history has very much "method."[4] Although these four professors did not express their opinions within the social science versus humanities framework, their orientation does seem

[1] Interview, see Appendix C1.
[2] Kolko, *ibid*.
[3] Livermore, *ibid*.
[4] Pierson, *ibid*.

representative of the respective stands. Nonetheless, it would be a mistake to assume that the viewpoints were mutually exclusive.

The uncertainty of the profession toward methodological training has obvious implications for the kind of history being written. This uncertainty has been generated by many factors, some of which were inherent in the development of the profession in this country. In the late nineteenth century when history was becoming established as a discipline in American higher education, the pioneering professors sought to imitate the Germanic system in which many of them had received their graduate training. An integral part of this training in scientific history had been a course in historical method, with strong emphasis on the critical evaluation of evidence. The assumption was that, by studying original sources, historians could best recover and understand the past. If the evidence withstood the most rigorous critical examination, it then could be pieced together to re-create history exactly as it happened—*"wie es eigentlich gewesen."* As Samuel Eliot Morison commented, we American historians remember this phrase from Ranke "when we have forgotten all the rest of our German."[5]

The methods course became a staple in those departments of history offering the Ph.D., and the textbook was either Ernst Bernheim's *Lehrbuch der historischen Methode und der Geschichtsphilosophie*[6] or its Gallic counterpart, *Introduction aux ètudes historiques*, by Langlois and Seignobos. Since their publications in 1931 and 1955, respectively, Homer Carey Hockett's books, *Introduction to Research in American History* and *The Critical Method in Historical Research and Writing*, have enjoyed great vogue.

For decades the value of a classical course in historical method was not questioned, but today the profession is uncertain of its worth. Many departments still offer a methods course because they feel that students who do not meet the formal requirements

[5] "Faith of a Historian," *American Historical Review*, Vol. LVI, No. 2 (Jan., 1951), 262.

[6] Publication data on all books mentioned in the text are listed in the Bibliography.

4

of such a course may be slighted in their training. Even where the course exists, however, critics frequently raised doubts about its utility, and many professors were explicit in their distaste for teaching it.[7] The reasons for this insecure and uncertain status may be found partly in changing historical fashions. The influence of the historical relativists and presentists—the Beards, the Beckers, and the Croces—has done much to undermine our concept of scientific history. With the basic assumptions concerning the nature of history removed or altered, the mode of arriving at the historical fact or generalization was likewise changed. The individual building blocks of history, the particular facts, no longer assumed the importance they had held when they were being assembled to render an exact reproduction of the past.

THE METHODS COURSE

Despite criticisms leveled against the methods course, it remained an important part of the graduate history program in a significant number of universities. Generally these institutions had taken the various criticisms into account in trying to fashion the course to meet the needs of their students. Although the nature of such courses varied according to the institution and the professor, the general objective of this type of training may be discerned from a discussion of some typical methods courses. Universities other than those cited provided similar courses, and the following examples are offered as representative, not exclusive, illustrations.

At Vanderbilt University, Henry L. Swint's course was designed to acquaint students with meaning in history and with problems related to studying and writing about it, to familiarize them with historical research techniques through precept and practice, and to promote critical evaluation and respect for accuracy. Textbooks for the course included *Historian's Handbook*, edited by Wood Gray; *The Modern Researcher*, by Jacques Barzun and Henry Graff; and *A Manual for Writers*, by Kate

---

[7] Interviews with Donald D. Johnson, Paul W. Glad, and J. Leonard Bates, see Appendix C1.

5

Turabian. Also recommended as valuable tools were the University of Chicago Press's *A Manual of Style*, the Government Printing Office's *Style Manual*, Porter G. Perrin's *Writer's Guide and Index to English*, and H. W. Fowler's *A Dictionary of Modern English Usage*.

To achieve the first objective of his course, Swint required students to read W. Stull Holt's "The Idea of Scientific History in America,"[8] Lloyd R. Sorenson's "Historical Currents in America,"[9] Theodore C. Smith's "The Writing of American History in America, 1884–1934,"[10] Charles A. Beard's "Written History as an Act of Faith" and "That Noble Dream,"[11] Charles A. Beard and Alfred Vagts's "Currents of Thought in Historiography,"[12] Chester M. Destler's "Some Observations on Contemporary Historical Theory,"[13] Perez Zagorin's "Historical Knowledge: A Review Article on the Philosophy of History,"[14] and portions of Allan Nevins' *The Gateway to History*, Cushing Strout's *The Pragmatic Revolt in American History*, and Carl L. Becker's *Detachment and the Writing of History*.

After the class studied these theoretical writings, it considered general bibliographies such as Constance Winchell's *Guide to Reference Books* and the *American Historical Association Guide to Historical Literature*. To gain some knowledge of the profession's serial literature, students examined at least five volumes of a state historical journal and five volumes of one of the following: *American Historical Review, Journal of American History, Journal of Modern History, Journal of Southern History, Journal of the History of Ideas, Journal of Negro History, Hispanic-American Historical Review, History,* or *Revue Historique*. (The list included publications outside United States history, for the course was not limited to students specializing in this area. The major

---

[8] *Journal of the History of Ideas*, Vol. I, No. 3 (June, 1940), 352–62.
[9] *American Quarterly*, Vol. VII, No. 3 (Fall, 1955), 234–46.
[10] *American Historical Review*, Vol. XL, No. 3 (Apr., 1935), 439–49.
[11] *American Historical Review*, Vol. XXXIX, No. 2 (Jan., 1934), 219–31, and Vol. XLI, No. 1 (Oct., 1935), 74–87.
[12] *American Historical Review*, Vol. XLII, No. 3 (Apr., 1937), 460–83.
[13] *American Historical Review*, Vol. LV, No. 3 (Apr., 1950), 503–29.
[14] *Journal of Modern History*, Vol. XXXI, No. 3 (Sept., 1959), 243–55.

professors of those not seeking a degree in United States history graded the formal bibliographical exercise required in the course.) One object of this examination was to help students formulate standards for reviewing books. Editing a document was the next logical assignment since many of the state journals publish such documents. The assigned document was in its original state, and the student had to identify each person, place, or other obscure item mentioned. A classmate checked the annotation for accuracy.

The course included a visit to the Tennessee State Library and Archives in downtown Nashville, where the staff explained archival practices, including the preservation and reproduction of documents, and introduced students to the research facilities.

The major assignment of the course was the preparation of a bibliography, usually connected with the student's dissertation topic. For this project, students were expected to exhaust the bibliographical resources of the Joint University Libraries, whether or not the items listed in the bibliographies were available there. Students were required to keep a record of the finding aids used in preparing the bibliography and to explain procedures followed in compiling it. In conjunction with instruction in bibliography preparation, the course dealt with footnote form.[15]

Like the Vanderbilt course, that at Georgetown University was established for students in American and non-American fields. It was required of beginning graduate students. Professors with various specialties lectured on the historiography and methodology of their fields and graded the students' research papers, but the professor in charge gave the course grade.[16] In its methods course Saint Louis University also relied on specialists to discuss appropriate methodology and materials; similarly, in its American Studies Program members of ten co-operating departments lectured on the methods and bibliographies of their various disciplines.[17]

For many years the University of Chicago has offered a course

[15] Interview with Henry L. Swint, see Appendix C1; syllabus for History 300.
[16] Interview with Joseph T. Durkin, S.J., *ibid.*
[17] Interview with Martin F. Hasting, S.J., *ibid.*

in historical method, one notable by-product of which was Louis Gottschalk's *Understanding History*. The course, required of all beginning graduate students, was under the direction of one professor but was split into European and American history sections. The American section dealt with internal and external criticism of evidence along with the analysis, synthesis, interpretation, and editing of documents. Each student wrote a paper on a minute topic that demanded intense research into original—and often diverse—sources. Examples of such topics, which were usually posed as historical questions, included "Which Way Was the Wind Blowing During the Chicago Fire?" and "When Did the First Auto Appear on the Streets of Chicago?"[18] Historians involved in the course over the years have included Gottschalk, William T. Hutchinson, William H. McNeill, and Walter Johnson.

The University of Texas, Rice University, and Louisiana State University offered courses that dealt largely with bibliographical guides. At the first institution, Barnes F. Lathrop developed the course as "a matter of annoyance and principle." He thought that too many historians did not know the basic tools of the profession. His elaborate "Checklist of Bibliographical Guides to the Sources and Literature of United States History" covered these items: current historical bibliography; general aids; British historical bibliographies; general bibliographies of United States history; dissertations; subject bibliographies; regional bibliographies; state bibliographies; library catalogs; United States national bibliographies; checklists of imprints; foreign national bibliographies; travel and exploration; periodicals; United States government publications; state government publications (including colonial and territorial); international and foreign government document bibliography; newspapers; maps and geography; manuscript collections (nonarchival); federal archives; state, county, and town archives; foreign archives; microfilms; microcards; microprints; and Texas bibliography.

---

[18] Interview with William T. Hutchinson, *ibid.*; interview with Keith McClellan, see Appendix C3.

8

During the course students examined and annotated approximately 150 items from the various categories, basing the annotation on questions asked of each finding aid. These questions dealt with its size, scope, inclusiveness, exclusiveness, annotation, and the like. Students' card-file annotations then could become the basis for their continuing efforts to keep up with bibliographies in their special fields. Lathrop also required students to write a paper on the use in historical research of a particular type of original source such as maps, newspapers, or county records. A former student termed this "the most valuable course in my whole doctoral program."

The course did not involve training in historical method, although Lathrop recognized this need. "As far as methodological training in seminars goes, I don't do anything except assign papers and make faces over the results." The fact that a methods course has been offered at the University of Texas only three times in the last thirty years indicates a general lack of interest in it.[19]

The Louisiana State University course in bibliographical guides differed from the one at the University of Texas in that it included methodology as well as the philosophy of history and the orientation of the profession. The emphasis of the course, nonetheless, was on historical materials. Students examined a variety of original sources and bibliographies and wrote critiques of them.[20] In a similar course at Florida State University, students reported orally on library holdings, emphasizing bibliographical guides to major collections. All members of the class did not handle every guide, but they took notes on reports by classmates, thereby acquiring second- if not firsthand knowledge of a variety of finding aids.[21]

At Texas Christian University, which offers one of the newer doctoral programs in history, the course incorporated historiography, bibliography, and methodology. After students reviewed research collections in various fields, they were given an exercise to acquaint them with a wide variety of reference works. This

19 Interviews with Barnes F. Lathrop and Robert L. Peterson, see Appendix C1.
20 Interview with John L. Loos, *ibid*.
21 Interview with William I. Hair, *ibid*.

"search and seizure" taught students to find the lonely fact. In another project students were given a document, sometimes written by the professor, to authenticate. They had to check the document in every possible way to prove its validity. "When they are through with this kind of exercise, they are in about as good shape to do thesis research as possible." Such training is important, for it can save students from false starts. The course also placed heavy emphasis on the development of writing skills and dealt with the different problems involved in writing articles and books.[22]

Recently Columbia University has had a compulsory course— "an uneasy balance between methodology, historiography, and the philosophy of history"—but in earlier years there was apparently no uneasiness, for the course was straightforwardly devoted to either methodology or historiography.[23] James T. Shotwell, along with others, organized the methods course. Sometimes a panel taught it, but the results were less satisfactory than when one man handled it. Allan Nevins was responsible for the course for many years, and his book *The Gateway to History* developed from it.[24] Similarly, Fritz Stern's *The Varieties of History* grew from the course, as did *The Modern Researcher*, by Jacques Barzun and Henry Graff.[25]

Reflecting the professional canons of the day when it inaugurated graduate study in history, Johns Hopkins University has retained a strong emphasis on historical method. During the first term in 1965–66, Frederic C. Lane taught a course on historiography and historical method; during the second he dealt with the methods of economic history. This sequence of courses encompassed both American and European history. At the meetings of "The Seminar," begun by Herbert Baxter Adams, history faculty members and students discussed their research concerns.[26]

[22] Interview with Donald E. Worcester, *ibid*.
[23] Interview with Robert D. Cross, *ibid*.; letter, Henry Graff to author, Apr. 26, 1967.
[24] Interview with Allan Nevins, see Appendix C1.
[25] Letter, Graff to author, above.
[26] Interview with Charles A. Barker, see Appendix C1.

History students at the University of Kentucky took a course in historical criticism at the beginning of their graduate work. Usually they read Nevins' *The Gateway to History*, Gottschalk's *Understanding History*, Langlois and Seignobos' *Introduction to Historical Study*, or other such works. The course involved the nature of both history and historical criticism and the use of documents. For one project students dissected an article in a historical periodical, checking footnotes, consulting the same sources the author used, and evaluating his application of the sources. Then they incorporated their findings in a paper. When James F. Hopkins taught the course, his students chose documents from the Clay papers to edit. These class exercises were not formally tied in with *The Papers of Henry Clay*, edited by Professor Hopkins, but they did acquaint students with an important facet of professional activity and gave them some appreciation of the major editorial projects in process throughout the country.[27]

While some departments have found the methods course too expensive to maintain, the University of Maryland has not. There were six sections of the course in the fall semester of 1965 and three the following spring, each section limited to twelve students.[28] When teaching this course, Aubrey C. Land told students that "methodological training is like playing the scales," an essential prerequisite to performing as historians. "No one would ever come to hear a concert consisting solely of technical exercises, but unless the musician has technical mastery, he cannot perform adequately, and so it is with historians." Land extended methodological training into his seminar, which he considered a methods experience related to practical research problems rather than an exposition of subject matter. "I'm interested in how graduate students synthesize sources into a historical product."[29]

In the 1940's after Yale University discontinued the course in historical method as futile, it relied on seminars to give this training and also instituted a course in the literature of American history.

27 Interview with James F. Hopkins, *ibid.*
28 Interview with David A. Shannon, *ibid.*
29 Land, *ibid.*

The department thought that excessive concentration on original sources in the seminars might lead to neglect of the important secondary works, and it wanted students to gain an overview of such material. The course met twice a week for two-hour sessions. At one session a professor discussed the literature related to a particular topic; at the other session two or three students discussed books they had been assigned to read. When Leonard W. Labaree participated in the course and dealt with the American Revolution, he discussed such sources as Peter Force's *American Archives* and the *Journals of the Continental Congress* and mentioned various categories of secondary literature such as the treatment of the Revolution by military, political, and social historians. For each lecture the professor distributed a mimeographed list of the books under discussion so that students did not have to copy all the citations. Occasionally the entire class read and discussed one of the landmark books such as Beard's *An Economic Interpretation of the Constitution of the United States*. The course required each student to write a paper on a master historian, which entailed reading all his works.[30]

The nature of the classical methods course, as much as changing historical fashions, was responsible for its deletion by many departments of history. Assuredly, the assumptions usually made in the classical methods course did impair its usefulness. The historical methodologists assumed that their guidelines and dicta were applicable to all types of history, that the course was equally useful to the student of Babylonian history and the student of the mountain men. Even when the course was devoted to comparatively discrete areas such as the history of the United States or Europe, many instructors still thought it too general and artificial. A teacher of the course explained: "There was too much variation in student interest to make a single course of general utility. . . . It was a series of examples and they didn't hang together very well."[31] In short, the classical methods course lacked specificity and applicability, and the exercises it demanded became drudgery,

---

30 Interviews with Labaree and John Morton Blum, *ibid.*
31 Interview with Clark C. Spence, *ibid.*

thereby destroying students' enthusiasm for research. This viewpoint is reflected in the comment of a professor who described himself as "not too strong on historical method" because he considered it a mistake to overburden graduate students with research "to the point where they lose enthusiasm."[32]

Where professors and students found the course sterile and irrelevant, the departments of history dropped it. Other departments deleted the course for different reasons. Although at the University of Wisconsin the course broke down under the weight of an increasing enrollment of graduate students, it has been revived, with the expectation that many students in library science and education will take it to get training in historical method and bibliography.[33] The University of Illinois recently abandoned the methods course, which had been required of all graduate students. When enrollment became too large to handle in one course, it had to be split into American and European sections and thus became too expensive to staff. One complicating factor at Illinois was that the course was attracting students from all over the campus.[34]

Whether knowledge of Clio's ways and means should be vouchsafed only to sworn votaries is moot. If there is sufficient demand for training in historical method whether within or outside the department, it seems that the institution should be willing to support such a course. Certainly the profession benefits from widespread interest in its standards and procedures.

METHODOLOGICAL TRAINING IN SEMINARS

Abandoning the course in historical method did not indicate that the practitioners felt that no methodological training was necessary, but rather that there is a better way to transmit it— through topical seminars. The great merit of the seminars, its supporters contend, is that the training it provides is directly applicable to the problems at hand. No longer does the professor

---

32 Interview with John R. Alden, *ibid.*
33 Interviews with Merrill Jensen, John A. DeNovo, and Merle Curti, *ibid.*
34 Interviews with Robert W. Johannsen and J. Leonard Bates, *ibid.*

speak theoretically and generally about the ways historians approach their materials; he deals with immediate factors. No longer does one course try to deal with methods applicable to the entire sweep of American history. The needs of students studying the colonial era and of those delving into World War I no longer have to be satisfied by a single course, which quite obviously might be strained to encompass the two areas. The great advantage of incorporating methods with subject matter in seminars is that graduate students can easily understand the interrelationship of the two types of training. The relevance of this kind of methodological training seems superior to the abstractions of the course. Furthermore, the student has the advantage of direct supervision by his professor in the seminar. Everything considered, methodological training appears manifestly more satisfactory in topical seminars than in a separate course.[35]

These theoretical advantages notwithstanding, some historians were still uneasy about the kind of methodological training given in seminars. This uneasiness over the the training could be ascribed to the profession's persistent questioning about the very nature of its method.[36] Not surprisingly, within departments committed to giving methodological training in seminars, professors disagreed on the effectiveness of this mode.

Richard S. Dunn said it was difficult for his department at the University of Pennsylvania to agree on a definition of historical method and that the department had discussed instituting a methods course—perhaps in an effort to define this training. Whatever training students received in historical method was "largely through osmosis."[37] Because graduate students at the University of Iowa had such a wide range of interests, Stow Persons thought that seminar training in historical method was the only practical solution. In satisfying these diverse interests, a methods course would waste time and students would have to undertake projects

---

[35] Interviews with Oscar Handlin, Wood Gray, Stow Persons, Robert W. Johannsen, John E. Wiltz, and Richard P. McCormick, *ibid.*

[36] Interviews with George W. Pierson and Richard S. Dunn, *ibid.*

[37] Dunn, *ibid.*

unrelated to their major interests. Malcolm J. Rohrbaugh, however, said that the seminar was strained to encompass the methodology related to diverse research interests. Consequently, he suggested the development of special seminars or short courses for methodological training.[38] When professors hold widely divergent views on methodological training, the danger exists—in the absence of a formal requirement—that some students may escape this training altogether.

Reflecting the changing notions of the profession, the University of Minnesota made its course in bibliography and criticism a requirement only for master's candidates under the nonthesis plan, a change from the earlier requirement that all graduate students take the course. The department now expects directors of theses and dissertations to train students in the methods peculiar to each field. In his proseminar Clarke A. Chambers spent one-third of the time on historical method and the remainder on a critical examination of the historiography of social welfare. Ph.D. candidates at Minnesota were exposed to methodology in four or five such seminars.[39]

Even at institutions with formal training in historical methods, individual professors usually gave students instruction in the methodology of their specialties. Marvin R. Zahniser held private sessions with his graduate students at Ohio State University, discussing both materials that must be consulted before selecting a topic and the mechanics of gathering sources for a paper.[40] John Hope Franklin said that in his seminar at the University of Chicago he "inevitably" discussed some methodological considerations. During the first few weeks he probed to see how well grounded students were in historical method. He then tried to correct any weaknesses he discovered.[41]

As the classical means of giving research training in history, the seminar has taken many forms and served different purposes. Most frequently seminar directors selected some theme or topic around

[38] Persons and Rohrbaugh, *ibid.*
[39] Chambers, *ibid.*
[40] Zahniser, *ibid.*
[41] Franklin, *ibid.*

which students did their research and writing. Sometimes, however, because of the nature of the university or of the students, the seminar was general and a student could do research on any subject within the area of United States history.[42] At those institutions which forwent the methods course, seminar directors were obliged to incorporate this training into their seminars, if indeed the students were to have any such formal help. The kind of training depended on the professor's interests and inclinations and the needs of the students. The following examples illustrate various methodological objectives professors wished to accomplish in their seminars.

Since the first-year seminars at the University of Wisconsin had to teach research methods from scratch and because of the great variations in students' abilities, the seminars experienced "considerable strain." To determine the competence of students in locating primary and secondary sources, Merle Curti assigned a bibliographical problem during the first week of the semester. He also devoted some time to historical theory, but in recent years this aspect of training has suffered because of the pressure on students to complete their master's theses and to prepare for qualifying examinations by the end of their second year of graduate work.[43]

The phase of methodological training most professors stressed was bibliographical. When he was teaching the seminar at Northwestern University, Ray A. Billington gave twelve hours of lectures on bibliographical guides. He said: "To neglect historical methodology in a seminar is to neglect a major obligation. . . . It's surprising how little you can know unless you are told. Professors should tell students about the guides and methods historians use."[44] The advanced seminar in historiography at the University of California at Riverside was a materials course which dealt with original and secondary sources by periods. Then in the topical seminars professors explained specialized finding aids, such as the

---

[42] Cf. Walter Prescott Webb, "The Historical Seminar: Its Outer Shell and Its Inner Spirit," *Mississippi Valley Historical Review*, Vol. XLII, No. 1 (June, 1955), 3–23.

[43] Interview, see Appendix C1.

[44] Billington, *ibid.*

Wagner-Camp and Winther bibliographies for the westward movement.[45] At the University of Minnesota, Paul L. Murphy devoted the first six weeks of his seminar in American legal history to the study of methods and sources. Because legal reference tools are organized for lawyers, not historians, he paid special attention to the use of legal encyclopedias, *Corpus Juris*, and *American Jurisprudence*.[46]

In addition to devoting half his seminars to a discussion of bibliography, government documents, criticism of evidence, citation, note taking, and quantification, Lawrence E. Gelfand of the University of Iowa also considered the construction of a book review. He chose a book that was central to the seminar's theme, had each student read it and write a review, and then criticized the results.[47] The department at the University of Iowa pioneered in incorporating social science techniques in historical research. Another department with similar concern is that at Washington University. Although the mechanics of its two graduate colloquia were left to individual instructors, the thrust of the colloquia was to develop analytical sophistication. Expressing distaste for abstract methodology, William N. Chambers said that a student should assume the responsibility for a problem and work at solving it with the help of his instructor.[48]

In both seminars and lecture courses at the University of Kansas, graduate students were expected to write research papers. George L. Anderson required students to submit their research notes with the papers. He made the appropriate methodological and stylistic comments on the papers and returned them for final revision.[49] George Washington University followed a similar procedure of having students learn methodology through their own research projects. *Historian's Handbook*, prepared by members of the department, replaced a formal methods course. Wood Gray expected students to read the *Handbook* and be responsible

---

[45] Interviews with Robert V. Hine, Hal Bridges, and Edwin S. Gaustad, *ibid.*
[46] Murphy, *ibid.*
[47] Gelfand, *ibid.*
[48] Chambers, *ibid.*
[49] Anderson, *ibid.*

for knowing its content. All seminars at George Washington incorporated methodological training, and students followed the suggestions of the *Handbook* in their own research.[50] W. Stull Holt of the University of Washington also advocated learning historical method by doing rather than through reading books. "It is better to do the work, with the professor challenging and pointing the way." At the University of Washington, seminars concentrated on a research topic rather than trying to promote general knowledge of a period.[51]

The University of Delaware, in co-operation with the Eleutherian Mills-Hagley Foundation, offered a master's program with special emphasis on methodological training in the history of American industry and technology. In this two-year program students spent half of each week at the Hagley Museum, where they received training in museum work, and at the Eleutherian Mills Library, doing research in its primary sources. Case Institute of Technology, with its doctoral program in the history of science and technology, naturally attracted graduates of this master's program.[52] At Case the historical methods course was tailored for students working in these specialized fields. For instance, students were trained in the interpretation of patent records, old scientific journals, and scientific transactions. Moreover, Case's Archive of Contemporary Science and Technology afforded graduate students firsthand acquaintance with manuscript work.[53]

UNDERGRADUATE METHODOLOGICAL TRAINING

Assuming that undergraduate history majors should know something of the profession, as well as the subject matter, many departments offered methods courses for juniors and seniors. The Santa Barbara, Los Angeles, and Berkeley campuses of the Uni-

[50] Gray, *ibid.*
[51] Holt, *ibid.*
[52] Interviews with Edward C. Ezell and Bruce Sinclair, see Appendix C3. After the survey gathered its data, Case Institute of Technology and Western Reserve University merged into Case Western Reserve University. To avoid confusion and to reflect conditions at the time of its investigation, the survey maintained the distinction between the two.
[53] Interviews with Melvin Kranzberg and Edwin T. Layton, see Appendix C1.

versity of California were among those institutions. At Santa Barbara the department assumed that all graduate students had had methodological training; if one had not, he took the undergraduate course.[54] The number of history majors at Los Angeles necessitated the department's offering twenty-eight sections of the methods course in 1965–66.[55] At Stanford University all history majors were trained in methods in the basic seminar for undergraduates, and the University of Hawaii offered a methods course for its junior history majors.[56]

Some institutions such as the University of Nebraska and Rice University had five-year programs leading to the M.A. Nebraska career scholars were admitted to seminars for methodological training in their senior year.[57] The Rice program, financed by the Ford Foundation, was an attempt to accelerate production of graduate degrees and stressed such professional concerns as historiography, methodology, and interpretation. Students usually enrolled in the program at the beginning of their junior year.[58]

Undergraduates at Brown University acquired methodological training only through experience on research papers. After they prepared an outline and a bibliography, they were often "just thrown into the original sources to sink or swim," according to William G. McLoughlin, Jr. To prevent their going under completely, Professor McLoughlin interviewed them at various stages of their work to give advice. He found that in the long run such interviews saved time, for without them the students were "pretty much at sea."[59]

While Duke University offered no graduate methods course, its undergraduate honors seminar placed considerable emphasis on methodology, as did other undergraduate seminars. In these seminars students wrote research papers, often based on the extensive manuscript collection in the university library. Both pro-

54 Interview with Alexander DeConde, *ibid*.
55 Interview with George E. Mowry, *ibid*.
56 Interviews with David M. Potter and Cedric B. Cowing, *ibid*.
57 Interview with James A. Rawley, *ibid*.
58 Interview with Sanford W. Higginbotham, *ibid*.
59 McLoughlin, *ibid*.

fessors and the manuscripts staff assisted students by suggesting topics for the papers.[60]

Undergraduates at Yale University had occasion to work in manuscripts on class assignments. In his course on the history of the South, Staughton Lynd had his students conduct research in the Ulrich B. Phillips papers to test concepts in secondary literature against information in the Phillips documents. Such class projects put some strain on the manuscript collection, for the students disorganized the papers. The Yale librarian of historical manuscripts found that young professors assigned manuscript research earlier than their older colleagues.[61]

The responsibility for training undergraduates in historical research methods was not borne alone by departments with graduate programs. At Macalester College, which offered no graduate work in history, the department spent considerable effort in acquainting students with research techniques and varieties of original sources. Each year some history majors from Macalester spent a month working on the staffs of such repositories as the National Archives and the Manuscript Division of the Library of Congress.[62]

CURATORS' VIEWS ON METHODOLOGICAL TRAINING

The issue of how best to teach historical method is by no means settled, despite the edge that seminar training seems to enjoy over the special course in methodology. The important question is whether students are receiving adequate instruction in historical method, irrespective of means.

What have been the fruits of the profession's transmission of its methodology to graduate students? Judging by the response of librarians and archivists—those who have the best firsthand knowledge of how well students put their training into practice, of how effectively they cope with the sources available to them—

[60] Interviews with Richard L. Watson, Jr., *ibid.*, and Mattie Russell, see Appendix C2a.
[61] Interview with Judith Schiff, see Appendix C2a.
[62] Letter, Boyd C. Shafer to author, Jan. 17, 1967.

the fruits have been largely displeasing. Librarians and archivists commented on a number of areas in which graduate history students and many professors demonstrated inadequate preparation for research. These included unfamiliarity with the facilities of a research library, inadequate training in using manuscripts, using secondary works instead of available original sources, intimidation by archives, insufficient grounding in secondary literature, and general bibliographical weakness, particularly with government documents and related finding aids. A few typical reactions illustrate these points.

The fundamental ignorance of graduate history students concerning research procedures disturbed many librarians. The librarian of the Library Company of Philadelphia commented: "We find . . . that little thought has been given to training in the methodology of research in a library. We try to make our resources fully available but we do not feel that it is our job to train researchers in their use."[63] The head of special collections at the Newberry Library lamented: "It is terribly discouraging to work with new professors and graduate students. They often disregard valuable materials, probably because they are too inexperienced to be able to make judgments. Ninety per cent of the graduate students have had so little preparation in the use of rare materials they don't even have the sense to keep their hands clean. They don't know the amenities of research—the basic, physical problems that arise in handling rare materials."[64] At the University of Chicago the director of the library said: "We know that the research potential in the University of Chicago library system is greater than its actual use. The library could be used more skillfully and purposefully. Students need better training in the use of a research library."[65]

At one time training in the use of manuscripts was thought to be the foundation of historical research, but in many places such training has fallen into neglect. The manuscripts curator at the

[63] Letter, Edwin Wolf II, Library Company of Philadelphia, to author, Sept. 19, 1966.
[64] Interview with Colton Storm, see Appendix C2b.
[65] Interview with Herman H. Fussler, see Appendix C2a.

University of Kentucky, a Ph.D. in history, questioned the department's training of graduate students in the effective use of manuscripts. "We teach the students what we can, but the question is whether it should be the library's responsibility or that of the Department of History. Much of the impetus for the use of original sources has come from the library, not the Department of History."[66] The librarian of the Library Company of Philadelphia said that the ability of students using manuscripts has varied tremendously. "A surprising number of graduate students are completely unprepared to handle the sometimes difficult hand of the 18th century."[67] "We don't have what I would call effective use of our manuscript materials," commented the head of special collections at the Newberry Library. "There are three major universities in the Chicago area and none of the history departments has made consistent use of the Newberry Library in training graduate students in historical research. The professors have paid little attention to our extraordinary original sources. It is so much more fun to go to London or Madrid or even California than to work in a humdrum place like Chicago—close to home."[68] At the New York Public Library, the keeper of manuscripts complained that he sometimes had "to give basic instruction on the use of manuscripts, such as telling users to keep the manuscripts in order and not to lean on the volumes. Occasionally we have professors who think they know best. One professor working in a collection of Madison material wanted to remove a letter that James Monroe had written to Madison and put it in the Monroe collection."[69]

The experience of researchers often is no index of their ability to keep collections in order, for "distingushed professors on down to undergraduates" may be remiss. But researchers are frequently helpful in discovering errors in arrangement and cataloging.[70] Despite curators' instructions, researchers are likely to get unbound manuscripts out of order. A salient feature in manuscript research

---

[66] Interview with Jacqueline Bull, *ibid*.
[67] Letter, Edwin Wolf to author, above.
[68] Interview with Colton Storm, see Appendix C2b.
[69] Interview with Robert W. Hill, *ibid*.
[70] Interview with Mattie Russell, see Appendix C2a.

was identified by the director of libraries at the University of Kansas. He said that graduate students appeared intimidated by or impatient with manuscripts.[71] Even students reconciled to working in manuscripts rather than printed sources seemed to want to find a neat collection of papers that would constitute most of the research for their dissertations, according to the curator of manuscripts at Duke University. She added, "Who would not want to do that if he could, considering the limited factors of time and inadequate financial resources?"[72]

A criticism akin to that leveled against restricting research to a single manuscript collection, but more telling in that it indicates even less initiative, dealt with graduate students' preference for using secondary works when original sources were available. The liaison librarian for history and the reference librarian at Indiana University concurred that graduate history students preferred "to use secondary works and crib the references. They . . . frequently depend upon the secondary work's use of references and won't check them."[73] The assistant director of libraries at the University of Utah complained that graduate history students were content to use secondary sources when the library had appropriate primary material. He noted that the library was dissatisfied with the response of graduate history students to several major sets of documents and pointed out that the *American State Papers* were used more by the English department than the history department. The heavy use of *Writings on American History* indicated that history students were more concerned with secondary materials than with original sources.[74] The state archivist of Colorado said: "Run-of-the-mill historians don't know how to cope with primary archival sources. They are prone to rely on secondary sources when the original sources are available. Historians are among the minority of the users of our state archives."[75]

Closely related to the problem of intimidation by manuscripts

[71] Interview with Thomas R. Buckman, *ibid.*
[72] Interview with Mattie Russell, *ibid.*
[73] Interviews with Irvin Welsch and E. L. Craig, *ibid.*
[74] Interview with Richard W. Boss, *ibid.*
[75] Interview with Dolores Renze, see Appendix C2b.

is the even greater difficulty graduate history students have with archival records. Unless a student has been warned that research in manuscripts or archives is different, slower, more painstaking, and consequently more demanding than research in any kind of printed material—primary or secondary—he may be confounded and overwhelmed when immersed in archives.[76] At the Kansas City Federal Records Center, the regional director and the chief of the reference service branch commented on the unwillingness of graduate history students to wade through great quantities of archival material. "They seem to want short cuts to research and don't have the time necessary to do systematic work in federal records."[77] The acting director and the curator of manuscripts of the Minnesota Historical Society pointed out that graduate students were not trained to cope with the proliferation of modern original sources.[78] The South Caroliniana Library director thought graduate history students from the University of South Carolina were reluctant to work in state manuscripts because they feared being charged with provincialism. They preferred to work with such sources as New York newspapers on microfilm or the *Congressional Record*, which also took less time than archival sources.[79]

A further deficiency in methodological training was reflected in evidence that some graduate students began research in manuscripts without sufficient preparation. The manuscripts curator at Indiana University thought that major professors should ascertain that their students had sufficient grounding in secondary literature pertaining to their subjects before beginning manuscript research. Otherwise, students were likely to be confused, to flounder, and to waste both their own time and that of the curators. For example, one student had to go through the Upton Sinclair papers three or four times because he did not know in

[76] Interview with Sherrod East, acting assistant archivist for the National Archives, *ibid*.

[77] Interviews with Benjamin F. Cutcliffe and Frank Lilly, *ibid*.

[78] Interviews with Robert C. Wheeler and Lucile M. Kane, *ibid*.

[79] Interview with E. L. Inabinett, see Appendix C2a.

24

advance what he was looking for.[80] Staff members at the National Archives did not find this inadequacy to be general, at least in recent years. Most graduate students who do research there have read the appropriate secondary works before coming so that they can make the most effective use of government records. Moreover, students benefit from the research experience their professors have had in the National Archives.[81] "You can always tell graduate students of professors who have worked here themselves; they reflect their professors' own knowledge of the material."[82]

Another important reservation expressed by librarians and archivists regarding training in historical method concerned bibliography, including finding aids, and printed government documents. The manuscripts librarian at the American Philosophical Society found that lack of training in bibliography was a major factor in graduate students' being "abysmally ignorant of research procedures." He gave half the graduate history students coming to the American Philosophical Society an hour's lesson on using finding aids.[83] The head of special collections at the Newberry Library referred to the "appalling lack of preparation in bibliography" which graduate students in American history brought to their researches. He asked professors, "How do you dare turn out graduate students who profess that they have never heard of Sabin or Evans or Streit or Wroth or Vail or Winsor?"[84] According to the director of libraries at Emory University, the "average history and English student knows little about bibliographical tools." This ignorance reflected an apparent weakness in seminar training.[85] The reaction of the Indiana University library staff to the ineptness of graduate students with government documents

[80] Interview with Elfrieda Lang, *ibid*.

[81] Interview with Jane Smith, acting director of Social and Economic Records Division, see Appendix C2b.

[82] Interview with Julia B. Carroll, reference specialist and consultant on State Department Records, *ibid*.

[83] Interview with Murphy D. Smith, *ibid*.

[84] Colton Storm, "Needs and Opportunities for Research at the Newberry Library," p. 11, paper presented at the meeting of the Western History Association, Oct. 15, 1966.

[85] Interview with Guy R. Lyle, see Appendix C2a.

was typical. The liaison librarian for history said that the students were frightened by government documents, for they did not know how to use the serial set or related indexes. He attempted to dispel some of the fear through lectures in seminars in American colonial and European history, which were obviously not prime targets for information pertaining to United States government publications. History professors had not asked the documents librarian to discuss her specialty with their graduate students, although she was "always happy to supply such reference information to students as much as possible."[86] The director of the Illinois Historical Survey at the University of Illinois observed that students needed a great deal of help with finding aids. "Students normally don't know how to go about using many of the printed original sources."[87] Graduate students, lacking much understanding of bibliography, sometimes blindly followed suggestions about which sources were reliable and unreliable and what was original and secondary source material. The chief of the American History Division of the New York Public Library often disagreed with the students' superficial judgments on sources.[88] Librarians at Tufts and Stetson universities said that because their graduate history students were trained in bibliography and government documents they made fairly effective use of original sources. At Tufts this training came in a required historiography course; but at Stetson, which offered a terminal M.A. in history, individual teachers handled this instruction in a "spotty manner." The Stetson librarian thought a general course in bibliography would strengthen the program.[89]

As explicit and basic as some of the foregoing criticisms are, it would be misleading to accept them without evaluation. Librarians and archivists have their own perspective, as surely as historians do. They ordinarily are proud of the material in their domain and are eager to see it used fully and properly. Custodians of orig-

---

[86] Interviews with Irvin Welsch and Helen Lightfoot, *ibid.*
[87] Interview with Robert M. Sutton, see Appendix C1.
[88] Letter, Gerald D. McDonald to author, June 28, 1966.
[89] Questionnaires returned by Joseph S. Komidar, Tufts University, and Charlotte A. Smith, Stetson University.

inal sources, being emotionally identified with their holdings, may overvalue them. When historical researchers fail to share this opinion and do not mine a vein thoroughly, the custodians feel that the historians are remiss. Similarly, librarians and archivists have much more occasion to use bibliographies and finding aids than historians and naturally should be more familiar with them. When historians do not share this immediate familiarity and skill, custodians are quick to find fault. While the criticisms librarians and archivists level against the technical equipment of historians are well founded, they should be tempered with these qualifications of perspective.

GRADUATE STUDENTS' VIEWS ON METHODOLOGICAL TRAINING

Whereas the reaction of librarians to the methodological training of graduate history students was largely unfavorable, that of graduate students themselves was mixed. Many found that their methodological training, either in a formal course or in seminars, was effective and stood them in good stead. Some said it was the most valuable part of their graduate experience or that all graduate students should take a course similar to theirs.[90] A student at Washington University said the course in historical materials he took at the University of Denver provided the background and framework for his further graduate study. He subsequently made a point of knowing bibliographical aids and recommended that more emphasis be put on them in formal training.[91] Other students who had specific training in historical bibliography testified to its great worth, especially in terms of their own research projects.[92]

At the University of California at Berkeley, the seminars incorporated training in historical method and, according to one student, did it excellently. "The professors are hypercritical in teaching us how to use original sources. This is what graduate work is all about here: learning to criticize the evidence systema-

[90] Interviews with John L. Gaddis and William A. Baughin, see Appendix C3.
[91] Interview with Bernard Axelrod, *ibid.*
[92] Interviews with Ronnie Tyler, Macel D. Ezell, and Burton I. Kaufman, *ibid.*

tically."[93] A student at the University of Kansas said: "The best methodological training has come from the seminars. I had to do one paper three times, with careful corrections at each juncture. The seminar entailed a discussion of hows and whys in the use of original sources."[94] Another graduate student at Kansas made practical use of his theoretical training in evaluating evidence. He discovered a document relating to the celebrated Populist Mary Elizabeth Lease and, in analyzing it, established that she worked with the Republican party in 1894.[95] Similarly, a student at the University of Cincinnati learned of Columbia University's Oral History Collection and subsequently discovered an interview with her thesis subject, Samuel Dickstein, while preparing a bibliography for a methods course. The course required students to compile bibliographies on subjects outside their field to familiarize them with a variety of original sources.[96]

A recent Ph.D. from Princeton University called his research seminar "perhaps the most valuable training I've had in the use of original sources. . . . There were three students in the seminar, so we received individual attention. . . . The seminar dealt with the critical use of sources, memoirs, and the integration of published material and manuscripts. All told, it was invaluable training."[97] Seminar training at the University of Nebraska included on occasion a trip to the Truman Library, where students spent an entire day learning about the library and its use. The library staff explained the correct form for citing its records as well as how to use its filing system. In addition to the outing, the seminar offered thorough methodological training, including the use of government documents and finding aids.[98]

Students who had been employed in a manuscripts collection or on a documentary editorial project testified uniformly to the immense contribution their work made to their understanding of

[93] Interview with Lisle A. Rose, *ibid.*
[94] Interview with John D. Unruh, Jr., *ibid.*
[95] Interview with Orval G. Clanton, *ibid.*
[96] Interview with Constance B. Schulz, *ibid.*
[97] Interview with William M. Leary, Jr., *ibid.*
[98] Interviews with William D. Rowley and Milton O. Gustafson, *ibid.*

historical method. At the University of North Carolina, a student working on the project supported by the National Historical Publications Commission to microfilm important records from the Southern Historical Collection said that he learned 95 per cent of what he knew about the use of original sources from the project.[99] Graduate students working in the Michigan Historical Collections, Division of Manuscripts of the University of Oklahoma Library, and the Maryland Hall of Records were enthusiastic about the insights their work gave them. One discovered that in manuscript collections there is often good material in unexpected and obscure spots, and another learned to read colonial handwriting.[100] A student at Brown University who worked as a research assistant on the project of editing the Isaac Backus papers found that in locating, arranging, and indexing the documents, he learned much about historical method.[101]

Many graduate students have had less enthusiasm about their training in historical method than those cited above. Usually the complaints concerned not the quality of that training but the absence of it. From the University of California at Riverside came this comment: "Methods are discussed obliquely in seminars and in dissertation research. I think more training would be useful."[102] From the University of Pennsylvania: "I've had virtually no formal training in the use of original sources. I feel strongly that I should have had more. . . . Our training is informal or presumed."[103] From Western Reserve University: "We have some seminar training in historical method, but much of it is on a hit-or-miss basis, according to the professor's individual interests. We pick up methodology on our own—we struggle through."[104] A student of colonial history at the University of California at Los Angeles said he had had no systematic training in the use of primary sources and felt that such training would have been "abso-

[99] Interview with Clyde E. Pitts, *ibid.*
[100] Interviews with Richard M. Doolen, Robert C. Carriker, and Douglas A. Scott, *ibid.*
[101] Interview with John M. Bumsted, *ibid.*
[102] Interview with Richard A. Fitzgerald, *ibid.*
[103] Interview with David R. Kobrin, *ibid.*
[104] Interview with James T. Kitson, *ibid.*

lutely helpful. Training in calligraphy would be valuable to any colonial historian. The professors assume that you can learn historical method on your own—catch-as-catch-can."[105] At Columbia University, according to doctoral candidate Eric Foner, methodological training was left to individual supervisors and varied accordingly. He sometimes felt a lack of such training.[106]

A student at the University of Southern California remarked: "I have been to several universities of good standing and found that very few have any kind of methodological training on the graduate level. . . . We need more of this. With inadequate formal methodological training, we develop techniques on our own that aren't the best."[107] Anne E. Hughs of the University of Hawaii alleged that the methodology course had changed little in thirty-five years. "Here we take a course in historical method, which is an attempt to acquaint graduate students with the way to do research. But I have not found this course satisfactory." As an undergraduate at New Mexico State University, she became acquainted with a variety of library resources, including many finding aids, while doing exhaustive research on an obscure problem assigned by one of her professors. Mrs. Hughs is one of many students who felt that their undergraduate training in historical method was superior to that which they received as graduate students.[108]

From Michigan State University came the comment: "Professors have not given enough attention to bibliographical techniques and finding aids. I went a long time without knowing that this library had the Evans [Early American Imprint] Series. The only bibliography I picked up was from bits and snatches in seminars, and this was inadequate."[109] Dorothy Day, Social Studies librarian at Brown University, reported that a Ph.D. candidate

[105] Interview with James Zeidman, *ibid*.

[106] Interview, *ibid*.

[107] Interview with Kenneth Smith, *ibid*.

[108] Interview with Anne E. Hughs, *ibid*. Corroboration of this view came from interviews with graduate students Ronald L. Jones, Duke University; Philip Racine, Emory University; and Roy Bird, University of California at Santa Barbara, *ibid*. They were undergraduates at Vanderbilt, Bowdoin, and UCSB, respectively.

[109] Interview with Ronald S. Wilkinson, see Appendix C3.

writing a dissertation on Cotton Mather also knew nothing of the Evans series.[110] Frequently students who have had sound bibliographical training commented that without accompanying instruction in the evaluation of evidence, once that evidence was found, they felt only half-prepared for their assignments as research historians.[111] One Stanford University graduate student reported: "My training in the use of original sources is mostly what I picked up myself. . . . A graduate student is on his own when he starts doing research here. We need more instruction in the use of the library. Instruction in various bibliographical tools and systematic use of these tools is very much needed."[112] Another Stanford comment was: "I have received very little training in the use of original sources. We have had general comments in the historiography courses on how to use original sources, but this comment is minimal. . . . This is one of the weaknesses in our training program: not enough systematic training in the use of original sources. Perhaps the graduate school assumes that you get this training as an undergraduate. . . . The professors assume too much knowledge on our part."[113]

One Princeton University student commented: "We've had no formal training in the use of original sources. . . . I wish I had learned something about historical method properly. Too much time has been wasted in learning by doing. I think graduate students should have specific instruction."[114] That the reaction of two other Princeton students differed sharply points up the obvious fact that where there was no general requirement for methodological training, a student's experience depended largely on the inclinations of individual professors. At Yale University the director of graduate studies for the history department reported that the department insisted that the old methods course was not a success. He explained that despite the methodological training

110 Interview, see Appendix C2a.
111 Interviews with Raymond Pulley, John L. Gaddis, and Jon L. Wakelyn, see Appendix C3.
112 Interview with Lynn Hales, *ibid.*
113 Interview with Jean Gould, *ibid.*
114 Interview with Robert D. Cuff, *ibid.*

provided by professors in classes and seminars, the graduate students were "agitating for a methods course." His colleagues, however, maintained that there was no need for one.[115]

While the foregoing comment might be reminiscent of Milton's line in *Lycidas*, "The hungry sheep look up, and are not fed," the methodological situation probably is not so bleak as this testimony indicates. In fact, some graduate students preferred not having any specific training in historical method. Whether their attitude reflects antinomian proclivities, innate distrust of professors, a sense of masochism, or fresh, creative impulses should be left for psychologists to determine. Whatever the disposition, these students thought that they learned more working without direction than with the help of professors. The *Harvard Guide* and various manuals on research gave sufficient assistance, asserted an Emory University graduate student, that formal methods training would be only duplicative.[116] Labeling himself a "Deweyite when it comes to research," a student at Ohio State University found that his practical experience was of more benefit than the methods course. But he added that he had profited from the course, for it gave him a knowledge of bibliographical indexes.[117]

A student at George Peabody College for Teachers reported that a lack of guidance reflected that institution's philosophy, belief in "the discovery method, not show and tell."[118] Quite likely, this belief represented Peabody's involvement in the curricular revision that has been under way in secondary schools since the mid-1950's and which may ultimately affect graduate training in history.

The first beachhead of revision was secured by the Physical Science Study Commission (PSSC), which spawned Education Services, Incorporated. The PSSC, inspired by Jerrold Zacharias, revamped the high school physics course so that students operated as research physicists, making their own discoveries rather than being told didactically about the work of others. The physicists

115 Interview with Howard R. Lamar, see Appendix C1.
116 Interview with Richard M. McMurry, see Appendix C3.
117 Interview with John S. Beltz, *ibid*.
118 Interview with Glen L. Nutter, *ibid*.

were so encouraged that the PSSC decided to extend similar experiments to other areas of the school curriculum. The commission drew in experts from other disciplines and formed Educational Services, Incorporated. Much of the inspiration for the activities of the revisionists has been the educational theories of Jerome Bruner, as stated in *The Process of Education*. Bruner argued that a child of any age can be taught the method of any discipline. Those who have sought to revolutionize history teaching have therefore concentrated on introducing children to primary sources and teaching them to reason as historians do in reconstructing the past. These educational theorists maintain that what a child does not work out for himself has little relevance and will be quickly forgotten, but that the historical conclusions he draws himself, after examining the original evidence, will stay with him. If this inductive philosophy dominates history teaching in the schools, the implications for the profession in both undergraduate and graduate instruction are manifest.[119]

The critical statements of graduate students concerning faulty training in historical method should not be accepted without evaluation, for it is possible that their opinions do some injustice to the quality of training at various universities. The human mind, being what it is, often does not absorb material lacking immediate relevance. Quite likely, professors at the universities mentioned have discussed historical method, but graduate students have not been receptive. Perhaps at the time of the discussion, students thought methodology was a side issue, not of immediate concern, and therefore did not assimilate the information. If a professor mentioned a particular finding aid or documentary series without

[119] I have entered my reservations toward reckless revision of the history curriculum and teaching methods in "History Teaching: A Legitimate Concern," *Social Education*, Vol. XXIX, No. 8 (Dec., 1965), 521–24, 528; and in a review of Edwin Fenton, *Teaching the New Social Studies in Secondary Schools: An Inductive Approach* in the *Journal of American History*, Vol. LIV, No. 1 (June, 1967), 93–95. Similar cautions have been issued by Mark Krug, "Bruner's New Social Studies: A Critique," *Social Education*, Vol. XXX, No. 6 (Oct., 1966), 400–406, and Gerald Leinwand, "Queries on Inquiry in the Social Studies," *Social Education*, Vol. XXX, No. 6 (Oct., 1966), 412–14. The February, 1967, issue of *Social Education* (Vol. XXXI, No. 2, 122–24) carried laudatory letters in response to Krug's article.

going into detail, students might well have failed to recognize the importance of the reference. Indeed, a student could even have taken notes and then forgotten all about them. Later, when the need arose for this particular information, the student had no memory of it and might even feel that his instruction had not been adequate.

It is desirable always to remember the very real limitations we experience in the learning process, without attempting to assess credit or blame. Few things are taught or learned once and for-ever. The ideal situation exists when methodological training coincides with a specific problem, but we cannot always rely on having ideal situations. Moreover, students perhaps expect some types of aid that no professor can extend. These qualifications of graduate students' complaints notwithstanding, the frequency and intensity of the criticism should give the profession concern.

If historians have been as unsuccessful in introducing the tools of the craft to their apprentices as librarians, archivists, and many of those apprentices contend, what explanations can be offered for this lack of success, other than the qualifications previously stated concerning differing perspectives and the human learning process? These explanations are threefold and simple. The first is that professors simply have not made the effort to teach historical method, either through lack of interest or inclination or through preoccupation with other things. These "other things" are what many a professor refers to as "my own work."

The second explanation, and one that can be elaborately docu-mented, is that professors themselves were sometimes ignorant of many types of original sources, bibliographies, and finding aids. Custodians of special collections at such places as the Newberry Library, University of Kentucky, Federal Records Center at Kansas City, University of Chicago, California State Archives, Texas State Library, Colorado State Historical Society, Brown University, John Carter Brown Library, University of Virginia, Chicago Historical Society, South Caroliniana Library, State His-torical Society of Wisconsin, New York Public Library, South Carolina Archives Department, and Library Company of Philadelphia have commented on history professors' lack of knowledge of their holdings.[120] Although the survey did not investigate training in fields other than United States history, the research of graduate students in twentieth-century German history displays these same deficiencies, according to Robert Wolfe, the National Archives specialist in archives relating to European history.[121] (Its holdings of over 25,000 reels of microfilmed German documents make the National Archives the foremost center outside Germany for research in this field.)

While common, this ignorance is certainly not universal, for staff members at the Rutgers—The State University Library and the Michigan Historical Collections at the University of Michigan indicated that their history professors had good knowledge of local original sources and that such knowledge was reflected in the way their graduate students used the collections.[122] The great burden of comments by such custodians, however, was that too many professors were unfamiliar with and/or uninterested in, collections directly related to the research their graduate students were conducting. Not knowing institutional resources themselves, these professors were not well qualified to direct graduate students to the materials.

Aside from professorial shortcomings, there is yet another reason for lapses in methodological training. Historians do not ensure sufficiently close co-ordination with librarians and archivists, who usually are competent in the technical areas where professors are weak. Library staffs stand willing to meet with seminars to discuss their specialties and to give general orientation lectures on the use of a research library, but often are not invited by professors. Such lack of communication on the campus does little credit to those responsible for graduate training.

120 Interviews with Colton Storm; Stuart Forth; Benjamin F. Cutcliffe; Robert Rosenthal; W. N. Davis, Jr.; Dorman H. Winfrey; Enid T. Thompson; Christine D. Hathaway; Thomas R. Adams; Anne Freudenberg; Clement Silvestro; Claramae Jacobs; Leslie H. Fishel, Jr.; Robert W. Hill; and Charles E. Lee, see Appendices C2a and b; and letter, Edwin Wolf, to author, above.

121 Interview, see Appendix C2b.

122 Interviews with Donald A. Sinclair and Robert M. Warner, see Appendix C2a.

35

The evidence indicates that our profession needs more and better training in historical method. It is of genuine importance that this training, whether in a methods course or in seminars, be taken seriously by both professors and students and that it be relevant. Whether the issues in methodological training are directly related to each student's research problem should not be a matter of great concern. When students are trained only in terms of their immediate research interests, they often are unable to break out of their specialty—either in publication or in directing research. Some historians, as Roy Nichols pointed out in his presidential address before the American Historical Association, continue to write doctoral dissertations all their lives.[123] Such historians are likely to perpetuate the kind of training with graduate students that makes it difficult for them to move from the specific area of the dissertation to more general studies.[124] If professors could impart to graduate students the idea that acquaintance with a wide variety of methodological and bibliographical tools can give them greater perspective and scope in their own scholarship and in the graduate teaching they in turn may do, the benefits would be appreciable. But if methodology is taught without imagination and a conviction of its worth, no enthusiasm will be generated among students. Once again they will be burdened and bored and will consequently learn little. Thus, they will probably continue to muddle along as historians have done too often. Those who have had sound training in historical method have usually been eager to testify to its worth, even if it seems better retrospectively than at the time of the training.[125] Such testimony considered in conjunction with previously cited complaints about inadequate methodological training should leave little doubt about the work that needs to be done. Educators currently responsible for training Ph.D.'s in United States history should restudy their obligations in dealing with Clio's ways and means.

[123] "History in a Self-Governing Culture," *American Historical Review*, Vol. LXXII, No. 2 (Jan., 1967), 423.

[124] Interview with Stuart Forth, see Appendix C2a.

[125] Interviews with Philip D. Jordan, see Appendix C1; Henry Feingold and Burton I. Kaufman, see Appendix C3.

II. Social Science Tools

CHANGING modes in historical thinking inevitably affect the way graduate students are trained. Just as the rise and predominance of scientific history led to careful and explicit methodological training, so its waning influence has been reflected in the profession's frequent indifference to methodology in the graduate education of historians. Now that the social and behavioral sciences are making an obvious impact on historical investigation, however, the techniques of these sciences must be taught if they are to be used effectively. Consequently, some of the most vigorous proponents of methodological training are historians who want students to be capable of using these techniques. A preference for offering this training separately or for combining it with the more conventional type dealing with the evaluation of evidence is a matter of individual disposition. If professors are opposed or indifferent to social science training, they are likely to ignore it. Thus the extent to which the profession moves toward the social sciences depends significantly upon the attitudes of the individuals responsible for graduate training. In its assessment of the impact of the social sciences on historical research, this chapter examines those attitudes and discusses factors outside the discipline that have kindled graduate students' interest in the social sciences.

37

It also deals with specific programs for teaching social science techniques and their concrete applications, the educational program of the Inter-University Consortium for Political Research, the use of computers, the problems of interdepartmental communication between the social sciences and history, and the need for specialized interdisciplinary courses.

HISTORIANS' ATTITUDES TOWARD THE SOCIAL SCIENCES

United States historians express a wide range of reactions to the utility of the tools and techniques of the social and behavioral sciences in historical investigation.[1] The attitudes, ranging from enthusiasm to disdain or contempt, are important to the extent that they influence graduate training. Such influence need not be explicit to make its mark. Despite the generally conservative nature of their profession, historians recognize the impact on and contributions to historical writing that the social and behavioral sciences are making. Many historians feel sheepish about their inadequate knowledge of the new approaches, and perhaps this sense of inadequacy causes them to express more enthusiasm for the new approaches than they otherwise would. These enthusiastic expressions may subconsciously be compensation for reluctantly expressed ignorance. Alert historians, like other academics, do not want to appear indifferent to technological or methodological progress. Whatever the motivation, the following comments illustrate the range of historians' reactions to such techniques as sampling, career-line analysis, reference-group theory, Guttman scale analysis, content analysis, and such concepts as type, role, image, and class.[2]

The most favorable response historians make to the social and behavioral sciences is to teach their techniques to graduate stu-

[1] The April, 1968, issue of the *Journal of Contemporary History* (Vol. III, No. 2) devoted several articles to the relationship between the social sciences and history. See especially C. Vann Woodward's caveat, "History and the Third Culture," pp. 23–35.

[2] These and other devices are described and discussed in Edward N. Saveth (ed.), *American History and the Social Sciences* and in Werner J. Cahnman and Alvin Boskoff (eds.), *Sociology and History: Theory and Research.*

dents. The sophistication of this teaching depends, naturally, on the historian's own preparation. Those in the front ranks of quantitative historians have estimated that probably only about three dozen of their colleagues are conversant with statistics through multiple correlation and regression analysis.[3] Consequently, while these men are only securing beachheads, they still exert considerable influence. One such professor is Allan G. Bogue, who found that graduate students enrolled in his seminar at the University of Wisconsin to become familiar with quantitative techniques.[4] The history department at the University of Pennsylvania had no unified position on the use of social and behavioral science techniques in historical research, but the influence of those members favorably disposed to the techniques made itself felt throughout the profession. Thomas C. Cochran, Charles Rosenberg, Lee Benson, Gabriel Kolko, Anthony N. B. Garvan, Murray G. Murphey, James J. Flink, and Seymour Mandelbaum "all emphasized the social science approach."[5]

An attitude of cautious hospitality toward the social science approach characterized many history departments. At the University of Notre Dame, despite some sardonic reference to "Cliometricians," there has been no last-ditch opposition to quantification. Because of J. Philip Gleason's interest in the social sciences, he informed his seminar of their conceptual and methodological approaches relative to historical research. He thought historians should be aware of how social scientists establish hypotheses and criteria of verification.[6] Charles G. Sellers, Jr., of the University of California at Berkeley similarly expressed caution and hospitality toward the social science techniques. His students made considerable use of these techniques, but not so deliberately as social scientists. "It probably would be useful if the students were more systematic and self-conscious concerning the use of these tools. I have the typical historian's wish that the evangelists weren't so

[3] Allan G. Bogue, "United States: The 'New' Political History," *Journal of Contemporary History*, Vol. III, No. 1 (Jan., 1968), 10.

[4] Interview, see Appendix C1.

[5] Interview with Thomas C. Cochran, *ibid.*

[6] Gleason, *ibid.*

fervent about the social sciences."[7] The Vanderbilt department was becoming more involved with social science procedures because of their potential value. "We want to be cautious, but you'd be putting your head in the sand to ignore these important tools."[8]

Allan Nevins, described in the dedication of *American History and the Social Sciences* as a "distinguished narrative historian," said that when he directed graduate work at Columbia University, neither his students nor he realized "how much statistics could contribute to their work—how important a scientific handling of statistics can be. Computers have revolutionized our handling of statistics." While he acknowledged the contribution of computers to scholarship, Nevins felt somewhat hostile toward the intrusion of econometrics into economic history because "economic history based on written sources and econometrics based on statistics often seem to be working at cross purposes."[9]

Some historians who were favorably disposed toward the social sciences expressed more interest in their concepts than in their techniques. Robert R. Dykstra stressed the importance of a sociological orientation, even if historians fail to use specific social science techniques: "Historians should understand society as sociologists have suggested it. They should be aware of the dynamics of status, power structure, and the like."[10] Barry D. Karl considered the information obtainable from quantitative techniques less useful than the generalizations that can be made from sociological analysis. He found demographic insights helpful to the historian.[11] Stow Persons, who had been dealing with the relationship of nineteenth-century institutions, such as the changing family structure, to intellectual history, commented that his "concern with the social sciences is less with technique than concept." Of his department at the University of Iowa, another well known for its hospitality toward the social sciences, he said: "Someone not so favorably disposed would be terribly on the

[7] Sellers, *ibid.*
[8] Interview with Herbert Weaver, *ibid.*
[9] Nevins, *ibid.*
[10] Dykstra, *ibid.*
[11] Karl, *ibid.*

defensive in this department. There is some lack of full and complete sympathy with the social science approach, however."[12]

A sure sign of the recognition of the importance of the concepts and techniques of the social and behavioral sciences in historical research is their formal incorporation in graduate instruction. Sometimes such inclusion has been difficult in departments with influential professors protesting. Where there has been no cake of custom to be broken, however, the new approaches can be easily instituted. For example, in inaugurating its doctoral program in American urban history, the University of Toledo provided specific training in quantitative techniques.[13]

Because of the unfortunately deep-seated antagonism between the social sciences and the humanities, with history having a foot in each camp and therefore being caught in the cross fire, and because of the relatively recent efforts in incorporating the social and behavioral science concepts and tools in historical study, the profession still expresses many reservations toward the new approaches. These reservations range from indifference to outright hostility. The chairman of the department at the University of Illinois characterized the department as "very conservative and traditional with reference to using social and behavioral science techniques in historical research."[14] Other professors in the department spoke of its passive attitude toward, and ignorance of, the social and behavioral science techniques.[15] "I leave the door open for students to work with the social science tools if they want," said J. Leonard Bates, "but I can't help them much, except in suggesting reading."[16]

Social science techniques hold no interest for Frank Freidel and have not made much impact on his students. Although he said that he was glad to have his students use those techniques, he could not give them good advice. "In training students, I encourage diversity

---

[12] Persons, *ibid.*
[13] Questionnaire returned by Noel L. Leathers, chairman, Department of History.
[14] Interview with Robert W. Johannsen, see Appendix C1.
[15] Interviews with Clark C. Spence and Robert M. Sutton, *ibid.*
[16] Bates, *ibid.*

and independence. I don't want students to do something exactly the way I would do it."[17] Although dubious about the various social science tools, Don Higginbotham nevertheless thought that his students at Louisiana State University should know something about them. Consequently, he discussed sampling, career-line analysis, type, role, image, and class in his seminars.[18] The Claremont Graduate School tolerated such methods but never encouraged them.[19]

Many historians who were impressed with the contributions the social and behavioral science techniques can make in historical research maintained that their attitude was one of caution or cautious co-operation. Others used "caution" to indicate basic hostility toward the possibility of such social science contributions. Both collectively and individually, historians have expressed distaste for quantitative methods. An indicator of such distaste has been apparent when departments were given the opportunity to vote on their organizational affiliation. At the University of Kentucky the department voted to be in the College of Letters and Languages rather than in the School of Social and Behavioral Science.[20] In 1964, when the department at Michigan State University had the option of being part of either arts or social sciences when the College of Arts and Sciences split, it voted nineteen to one for the arts college.[21]

About 60 per cent of the department at Ohio State University, according to John C. Burnham, was hostile to the social sciences. The hostility was directed not so much toward the techniques as toward the "neglect of standard analysis accompanying the techniques." Burnham found that his students were familiar with the ordinary social science techniques. One of his master's candidates used a scalogram for work on the science lobbying of the 1940's.[22] At the University of Minnesota there was an even and conspicuous

[17] Freidel, *ibid.*

[18] Higginbotham, *ibid.*

[19] Questionnaire returned by John Niven.

[20] Interview with Paul C. Nagel, dean of the College of Arts and Sciences, see Appendix C1.

[21] Interview with Gilman M. Ostrander, *ibid.*

[22] Burnham, *ibid.*

42

split in the department over the application of social and behavioral science techniques to historical study.[23] The history faculty at the City University of New York was "most unreceptive to the behavioral sciences," according to Julius M. Bloch. Probably the reason was that their training had been conventional and they did not understand the new social science tools.[24] At the University of Wisconsin the department was in both the humanities and the social studies divisions, and professors were consciously in each camp. Some made significant use of social science techniques, but many considered themselves to be working in the humanities. "Some think the social science tools are nonsense—a passing fad."[25] The departments at the University of Colorado and the College of William and Mary reported, respectively, that their attitudes toward social science techniques varied from "indifferent to hostile" and from "enthusiasm to cold disdain."[26]

Some historians have found the premises of various social science research techniques objectionable, or at least unhistorical. Sampling has drawn heavy fire. James W. Patton, director of the Southern Historical Collection at the University of North Carolina, said: "Sampling makes me see red. You can't do historical research with sampling."[27] Frank O. Gatell of the University of California at Los Angeles described himself as "probably the world's greatest enemy of sampling." In theory he favored the use of quantitative techniques in historical research, but he was repelled by the "botch" so many historians make in using them. "Those with a social science orientation are usually quantifiers looking for short cuts. They let the method take over. They want to encompass more data but to handle them with mechanical ease. I have no objection to any technique—multivariant analysis or any other tool—but . . . these techniques involve more, not less, work."[28] Ernest Wallace of Texas Technological College thought that the

23 Interview with Allan H. Spear, *ibid.*
24 Interview with Bloch, Dorothy Ganfield Fowler, Howard L. Adelson, and Sidney I. Pomerantz, *ibid.*
25 Interview with Irvin G. Wyllie, chairman, *ibid.*
26 Questionnaires returned by Daniel M. Smith and William W. Abbot.
27 Interview, see Appendix C1.
28 Gatell, *ibid.*

social science tools were not applicable to the kind of research that he and his students did. He wanted exhaustive and definitive research on a topic rather than a mere sample of the data.[29]

The social science techniques, many have commented, are no substitute for the historian's judgment, intuition, or common sense. The historian who writes biography does not need to be immersed in psychological theory, but he does need to be curious about, and to try to understand, human nature. He needs to be able to see things through his subject's eyes. The better historians have "intuitive insight into these problems."[30] Gabriel Kolko found that social science tools are no substitute for historical perception. "I don't think historians are getting much from these, and I've had a good bit of experience with them. One good document can give you more insight than a thousand chi square correlations—and I say this with some knowledge of the material." Some of his students were more enthusiastic about the tools at the beginning of their study than at the end. "Students should know of these techniques, if only to avoid them when inappropriate."[31] The most skeptical statement is George W. Pierson's: "I hope the profession will use these social and behavioral science tools, but only with the greatest reservations. I'm afraid that mediocre and poor graduate students will leap toward the social science techniques. The more you are a historian, the less content you are with ideal types and models. If these tools are abused, they are worse than no tools at all. The kinds of things these tools will tell the historian often aren't worth knowing. They tell you things that you've already established by extrasensory perception. Future graduate students in history should know about the social science tools, but ought to be warned that they are basically antihistorical."[32]

Further comments on the limitations of social science tools in historical research fell into these categories: quantification merely documents the obvious; the techniques become ends in themselves; and the techniques cannot measure nuances to which

29 Wallace, *ibid.*
30 Interview with T. Harry Williams, *ibid.*
31 Kolko, *ibid.*
32 Pierson, *ibid.*

historians must be sensitive. One specific complaint about the difficulties with quantifying was that it is an expensive way of proving what is already known.[33] Vernon L. Carstensen, who was fundamentally dubious about the social science techniques, complained that quantifiers establish what has often been evident from common-sense logic. Nonetheless, quantification can lend exactness and specificity that is helpful in historical studies.[34] Social scientists, commented John R. Alden, seem to come out with the same results scholars were reaching before the elaborate techniques were applied. Wallace Brown's *The King's Friends* has "the same conclusions I've reached. But it's good to have this statistical confirmation of common-sense logic."[35] The views of professors obviously have made their impact on graduate students. For example, one student at Emory University thought that historical judgment seems to boil down to the same decision whether or not tempered by the social sciences.[36]

Some historians using social science techniques tended to let the techniques dominate the problem or become the end of their research.[37] Graduate students often wanted to undertake projects in which they could employ such techniques, and they were prone to make the techniques the most obvious part of their work.[38] The results of this kind of research have been foolish and ludicrous.[39] While research should not be shaped by social science techniques, it is "stupid" for historians not to be familiar with them. "Historians should not rely on intuition when the techniques can provide more concrete data."[40]

The fact that social science techniques cannot cope adequately with the individual differences significant in history detracts from their general utility. These tools have often been used with great disregard for historical data. Scholars who employ precise mathe-

---

[33] Interview with Frank Freidel, *ibid.*
[34] Carstensen, *ibid.*
[35] Alden, *ibid.*
[36] Interview with Philip Racine, see Appendix C3.
[37] Interview with Maurice G. Baxter, see Appendix C1.
[38] Interviews with David A. Shannon and Shaw Livermore, Jr., *ibid.*
[39] Livermore, *ibid.*
[40] Interview with Donald Meyer, *ibid.*

45

matical devices to data not susceptible to quantitative measurement have produced skepticism.[41] Historians were suspicious of the way quantifiers have distorted historical evidence by too narrow base samples and of the way they have often made firm generalizations based on unreliable information.[42] A further deterrent is that the tools do not get at causation and motivation.[43] For instance, the inability of public opinion polling to reflect the intensity of feeling that leads to action is its great weakness. Consequently, graphs and statistics related to such polling are not particularly helpful because they miss nuances and intensity of feeling.[44] Quantitative devices miss the nuances precisely because they are hard to measure.[45] Social science techniques are limited in historical research because historical research and synthesis require much more than a digestion of demographic and political data. Historians need to engage in the subtle analysis beyond quantification.[46]

In many cases, the attitudes of historians toward the social and behavioral science techniques were tinctured by their sense of inadequate preparation and ignorance. Failure to apply the techniques may have sprung from lack of awareness rather than rejection after deliberate consideration.[47] Even historians interested in, and receptive toward, the techniques face the problem of obtaining proper training. Frustration arises from not having the tools and from the difficulty of acquiring them through reading.[48] Realizing this inadequacy, historians feel safer employing techniques already mastered.[49] Although professors might have used the techniques in their own research, they sometimes have not felt equipped to teach them to their students.[50] Recognizing the importance or usefulness of these techniques, some departments have

[41] Interview with Donald D. Johnson, *ibid.*
[42] Interviews with Frank W. Klingberg and John E. Wiltz, *ibid.*
[43] Interview with Harold D. Langley, *ibid.*
[44] Interview with Robert A. Divine, *ibid.*
[45] Interview with Baxter, *ibid.*
[46] Interview with Harold W. Bradley, *ibid.*
[47] Interview with Thomas N. Bonner, *ibid.*
[48] Interview with Dewey W. Grantham, Jr., *ibid.*
[49] Interview with Bayrd Still, *ibid.*
[50] Interview with David D. Van Tassel, *ibid.*

been unable to do anything significant with them because the faculty was either untrained or uninterested.[51] A few professors who said they were too far along in their careers to retool were still willing for students to undertake new methodological ventures.[52] For instance, Merrill Jensen commented: "I don't sniff at the social sciences. They can save a tremendous amount of routine work. . . . If you know what kind of questions to ask of vast quantities of data, the social sciences can be helpful."[53]

If historians are generally unwilling to study the social science techniques, it may be because of the type of graduate students who have been attracted to the discipline. Substantiation of this viewpoint might be unquantifiable, but it has its advocates, who were among those convinced of the importance of social science techniques. Elisha P. Douglass of the University of North Carolina contended: "Many graduate students in history don't have the drive of students in other professions. They are not interested in learning special techniques. They don't know foreign languages and are often unwilling to learn them."[54] Sam B. Warner, Jr., of Washington University remarked: "Most historians kind of escape into history—they don't like math, they find science too hard, and English is too literary. Therefore they go into history somewhat by default."[55]

STUDENTS' AWARENESS OF SOCIAL SCIENCES

Inadequate preparation and ignorance of social science techniques seem to have deterred historians from using them; it follows then that the profession must look to its younger members for effective employment of these tools. Usually younger professors are more interested in these tools than their elders.[56] Similarly, graduate students have often exhibited more interest in the social

[51] Questionnaires returned by Loren Baritz, University of Rochester, and Gilbert L. Lycan, Stetson University.
[52] Interviews with Robert E. Burke and Merrill Jensen, see Appendix C1.
[53] Ibid.
[54] Douglass, ibid.
[55] Warner, ibid.
[56] Interview with George E. Mowry, ibid.; questionnaire returned by Harris G. Warren, Miami University.

47

science tools than have their professors. Although graduate students tend to imitate their professors' methodology, the reliance on such imitation seems to be decreasing.[57] While it has ordinarily been the case that history students have not had time to acquire social science skills after entering graduate school,[58] many have been learning whatever they could through such means as taking courses in computer programming, auditing courses in other departments, reading independently, and attending guest lectures.

At Rutgers—The State University graduate students were more interested in social science techniques than the faculty and took the initiative in learning about them.[59] Feeling the need for more social science orientation, the president of the graduate history association organized a series of lectures on quantification in history.[60] Similarly, at Georgetown University a graduate history student arranged to have a political scientist discuss computer research at a meeting of Phi Alpha Theta. Although the Georgetown department did not discuss the social science tools extensively, it was aware of their importance, as indicated by the university's sponsoring a conference on quantification in history, at which Lee Benson and Samuel P. Hays spoke.[61] Yale University graduate students were "terribly interested" in these social and behavioral science techniques and were "running much faster than the faculty. There is almost a fault line between the members who will have nothing to do with these social science techniques and those who will go along with them." Many of the Yale graduate students were inspired by David M. Potter's *People of Plenty* to investigate the social science approach.[62]

Since historians have only very recently made much attempt to apprise their graduate students of the uses of social and behavioral science techniques, students interested in or knowing something of these techniques have usually acquired their interest

[57] Interview with Arrell M. Gibson, see Appendix C1.
[58] Interview with W. Stull Holt, *ibid*.
[59] Interview with Richard M. Brown, *ibid*.
[60] Interview with George W. Franz, see Appendix C3.
[61] Interview with John D. Finney, *ibid*.
[62] Interview with Howard R. Lamar, see Appendix C1.

48

or knowledge outside of history courses. Graduate history students with undergraduate majors or graduate minors in sociology, political science, and education expressed most interest in the social science tools. At the University of Wisconsin, Merle Curti found that most of his students were somewhat familiar with the social sciences and that they were very much interested in role theory. To fulfill the department's requirement for an outside minor, his graduate students sometimes took sociology but more often chose American literature or philosophy.[63] Michael Wallace, a graduate student at Columbia University, learned many of the social science techniques through minoring in political sociology. Familiarity with the philosophy of the social sciences gave him new approaches to his material. He was not so much interested in the techniques themselves as in the new perspectives and new ways of presenting historical findings.[64] John M. Bumsted, a 1965 Ph.D. from Brown University, majored in sociology as an undergraduate at Tufts University. In a sociology course in research method, he learned how to use various measurement tools which were later helpful in historical research. His professors at Brown were willing for him to be one of the "new wave" of sociologically oriented historians. Bumsted preferred using sociological tools in a historical setting to using them in sociology itself. "I got tired of counting heads and doing studies which merely documented what common sense has already established," he said.[65] Fred Roach, Jr., a graduate student from the University of Oklahoma who learned the social science tools as an undergraduate sociology major at Georgia State College, planned to employ them in his dissertation study of Will Rogers.[66]

At the University of Texas some graduate history students acquired knowledge of the social sciences through osmosis. Teaching assistants in history had offices near the sociology department and consequently heard much social science talk.[67]

[63] Curti, *ibid.*
[64] Interview, see Appendix C3.
[65] Bumsted, *ibid.*
[66] Roach, *ibid.*
[67] Interview with Dwight F. Henderson, *ibid.*

One of these graduate students, Marilee S. Clore, married a psychologist, who directed her reading in the social and behavioral sciences. Her initial interest in this field came, however, through the work of Thomas C. Cochran. Several professors in the history department of the university encouraged her in her social science interests.[68]

Graduate history students have been introduced to social science techniques through work in political science as much as through sociology. Paul L. Murphy found that many political science majors at the University of Minnesota chose his field of constitutional history as a logical minor. These students were usually familar with various measurement techniques. He did not encourage his majors to use these tools but did insist that they be familiar with them and with their limitations for history. Robert F. Berkhofer, Jr., also said that his students at Minnesota were aware of measurement techniques from courses in political science and sociology. The students might not have been skilled in using the tools, but they had a general orientation in the social sciences. Berkhofer and Murphy agreed that it is more important for the historian to understand the social science concepts and systems than to be expert in the specific tools.[69]

Although graduate students had become familar with the tools through political science courses, they were often cautious about applying the tools to their historical research.[70] One such student at the University of Illinois was not "confident that the political scientists understand the limits of their techniques."[71]

Just as some political science or sociology majors wanted to use measurement tools in their history minor, so it has been with education majors or those with some background in education. Because of the importance of statistics relating to student performance and attitudes, training in quantitative tools has become common in education courses. Consequently, students in this field,

[68] Clore, *ibid.*
[69] Interviews, see Appendix C1.
[70] Interviews with Barry Knight and Lloyd E. Ambrosius, see Appendix C3.
[71] Ambrosius, *ibid.*

like those from other disciplines, have wished to apply their special training to historical problems.[72]

Since history has varied appeals, some students have come into the discipline from diverse quarters, which often have supplied social science training. A graduate student at Case Institute of Technology, who had also been an undergraduate there, said it was impossible to finish a technological undergraduate program without doing work in sampling and statistics.[73] Arthur M. Johnson of the Harvard Graduate School of Business Administration discovered that his students often had good backgrounds in statistics and accounting. Nevertheless, as a qualitative historian, he tried to keep the social science techniques in proper perspective.[74] Air Force officers involved in graduate history study found that their service training in social science techniques gave them general familiarity with the measurement devices.[75]

Recognizing the need for historians to be trained in fields difficult to comprehend through unassisted reading, many professors urged students to take courses in fields not closely related to history. The problem has been in reaching students early enough in their graduate careers to offer this counsel. John W. Caughey said that even when he succeeded in directing students into such outside fields, "on the whole, I don't think they come out being any more scientific than I am."[76] At the University of Michigan some historians thought that graduate students should study a cognate field in sociology, economics, psychology, or anthropology rather than one as closely related to history as literature or government.[77] Graduate history students at the University of Texas seldom ventured away from traditional minors. They usually took the minimum hourly requirement in a minor field

[72] Interviews with Paul W. Glad, see Appendix C1; George E. Frakes and David Goodman, see Appendix C3.

[73] Interview with Harry Eisenman, see Appendix C3.

[74] Interview, see Appendix C1.

[75] Interviews with Paul A. Whelen, see Appendix C3; and Theodore R. Crane, see Appendix C1.

[76] Interview, see Appendix C1.

[77] Interview with William B. Willcox, ibid.

closely related to history, such as government or American literature. Very few went into economics and sociology.[78]

TEACHING SOCIAL SCIENCE TECHNIQUES

The truest gauge of the profession's attitude toward the social
and behavioral sciences was not in what it has said but in what it
has done about them. An important aspect of this "doing" was
the actual application of the techniques in historical writing, but
the most direct influence was likely exerted through formal training in the social science methods. Quantitatively, these formal
training programs have been small. They have, however, exerted
appreciable influence, and all indications are that this influence
will increase.

At Johns Hopkins University, the wellspring of graduate history training in this country, David Donald devoted a large part
of his seminar to training students to use social and behavioral
science techniques in historical research. Donald's own interest
in this area began during his first year as a graduate student at the
University of Illinois. That year he took a course in statistics,
much to the consternation of his department, for it had never
before had a graduate student who wanted to venture into that
alien area; his second year he took as much sociology as history.
Because of his own sense of the importance of such disciplines as
statistics, sociology, and political science for historical study, he
has offered his students considerable exposure to them. Since
insufficient time and background have been severe handicaps to
historians when they used social science techniques, Donald has
not expected students to leave his seminar as masters of the techniques; but they were at least familiar with them.[79]

Donald's seminar blended conventional historical method and
the methodology of the social and behavioral sciences. He divided
the twenty-four meetings into six equal parts. Each part of the
seminar devoted two meetings to readings and two meetings to
discussion of papers students had prepared on the topic. The first

[78] Interview with David D. Van Tassel, *ibid.*
[79] Donald, *ibid.*

52

part dealt with such traditional considerations as the use of the library, the knowledge of literary form and style, and the evaluation of conflicting evidence. The reading assigned for the other five parts reflected the seminar's orientation toward the behavioral sciences and dealt with biography; social classes, social mobility, and elites; content analysis; political parties; and elections. However innovative Donald's approach in exploring new dimensions of problems and ways the social sciences can aid historians in solving them, he cautioned that "method ultimately is only the servant of insight."[80] Appendix E lists the readings related to these topics.

In addition to acquainting students with behavioral science techniques in historical research, the seminar was designed to help them identify dissertation topics. The writing assignments were therefore an application of the techniques to individual research projects, all of which were in the period of the Civil War and Reconstruction. For instance, papers dealt with an aspect of the dissertation involving the use of content analysis, the structure and behavior of a political party, and so on.[81] This device of specifying that seminar projects employ some measurement tool was also used by Professors Richard P. McCormick, Richard S. Kirkendall, and Alfred A. Cave, of Rutgers and the Universities of Missouri and Utah, respectively.[82]

For more than two decades Thomas C. Cochran of the University of Pennsylvania has been in the forefront of American historians using and urging the use of social science concepts in historical writing. His clarion call protesting the traditional conception and presentation of our national history came in "The 'Presidential Synthesis' in American History."[83] Through the years his writings have influenced younger historians to investigate the past from fresh angles. In 1964 he published *The Inner Revolution*, a collec-

[80] Interview with Sydney Nathans, see Appendix C3.

[81] David Donald, Syllabus for History 643–644, Johns Hopkins University.

[82] Interviews with McCormick and Cave, see Appendix C1; and James R. Sharp, see Appendix C3.

[83] *American Historical Review*, Vol. LIII, No. 4 (July, 1948), 748–59.

tion of essays demonstrating the impact on historical writing of the social and behavioral sciences.

To acquaint his seminar students with the social science approach to history, Cochran discussed Bulletins 54 and 64 of the Social Science Research Council, *Theory and Practice in Historical Study* and *The Social Sciences in Historical Study*, and similar publications. He considered basic methods of quantification and the formation of categories and hypotheses. Whenever possible, he used illustrations of various social and behavioral science techniques in teaching but warned students that the techniques might not be applicable to individual problems. His instruction amounted to "a series of admonitions to graduate students not to forget to look at problems from various social and behavioral science angles." Nonetheless, he cautioned against distorting problems with techniques.[84]

Cochran urged American history students at Pennsylvania to take Murray G. Murphey's seminar in American civilization. (In the American Studies program at the University of Texas, William H. Goetzmann also devoted a seminar to the social sciences in American culture.[85]) Describing Murphey as a "brilliant, mathematically inclined American historian," Cochran said that Murphey gave excellent methodological training in the social and behavioral science techniques. Unless students have had such training, Cochran felt it a mistake for teachers of advanced seminars to assume too much. Professors must be explicit in teaching these techniques. In teaching the procedures himself, Cochran encouraged students to learn what techniques they would need for solving particular problems.[86]

David M. Potter's teaching and writing have been similarly instrumental in orienting history students toward the social sciences. His influential *People of Plenty* was an attempt to find specific ties between history and the social sciences. In his teaching at Stanford University, he tried to "acquaint students with the

---

[84] Interview, see Appendix C1.
[85] Interview with Joseph M. Hawes, see Appendix C3.
[86] Interview, see Appendix C1.

54

range of possibilities so that they would know where to go when confronted with a particular problem that might be susceptible to some social science approach." He warned, though, that a professor cannot possibly anticipate the techniques a student might need in his research. Students should identify a particular need and then attempt to equip themselves to meet that need. Learning to use specific tools "is much better than trying to acquire a broad range of knowledge in all the social science techniques."[87]

Many other historians who have been influential in sensitizing the profession to the contributions of the social sciences to historical writing emphasized the point Cochran and Potter made about students learning techniques applicable to individual problems. For example, a biographer should know psychology and a student of the corporation should know sociology and economics.[88] Bernard Bailyn and Oscar Handlin commented that graduate students should investigate the successful ways in which mature historians have used particular devices. "We should approach our research problems from the historical, rather than social science, standpoint," Bailyn contended. "It is much more useful for a graduate student to try to emulate the skillful use some historian has made of social or behavioral science techniques than for him to try to ground himself thoroughly and systematically in the various social sciences he thinks he might find a need for."[89] Handlin pointed out that the profession has been unresponsive to decades of exhortation to use social science methods. It is when students observe older and respected historians using the tools meaningfully that they will equip themselves similarly. Since social science tools become obsolete, students must have sufficient consciousness of what will be useful for a particular problem.[90]

At the University of Washington, Thomas J. Pressly took a middle position on the use of social science techniques in historical

---

[87] Potter, *ibid.* This view was also expressed by David Alan Williams, Donald Meyer, Frank O. Gatell, Howard S. Miller, Lawrence E. Gelfand, and Sam B. Warner, Jr., *ibid.*

[88] Interview with Alfred D. Chandler, Jr., *ibid.*

[89] Bailyn, *ibid.*

[90] Handlin, *ibid.*

research since he did not "want to get too far away from the common-sense approach and common language." He was attracted as much to literary sources as to statistics. To acquaint his students with representative social science devices, he referred them to such works as *Handbook of Social Psychology*, edited by Gardner Lindzey; "Who Were the Senate Radicals?" by Edward L. Gambill;[91] and "The Civil War Synthesis in American Political History," by Joel H. Silbey.[92] In dealing with social science techniques, Pressly urged students to apply analytical judgment. They should be aware, for instance, of the difference between leaders and followers. Just because a leader like Carl Schurz took a position did not indicate that his followers agreed with him.[93]

As a reflection of student interest and faculty concern, Princeton University in 1965–66 inaugurated a course to acquaint students with the social and behavioral sciences. The course, now required of all first-year graduate students, has been taught by Lawrence Stone, Arno Mayer, and Stanley Coben. Whenever appropriate, visiting lecturers discussed their specialties with the students. With this full-year course, Princeton is doing "as much to train students in the use of social and behavioral science techniques . . . as any other institution."[94] Princeton discontinued the traditional methods course "because graduate students didn't need it."[95]

When the new course was first offered, the topics covered were social sciences and history; historical methods and philosophy; methodology in the social sciences; psychology and biography; social psychology; national character; social structure, elites, and social mobility; community studies; education; and kinship, marriage, and the family. Under consideration during the second semester were the state, power, politics, revolution, mass society and totalitarianism, demography, economic growth, religion, and quantitative methods. The organization of the

91 *Civil War History*, Vol. XI, No. 3 (Sept., 1965), 237–44.
92 *Civil War History*, Vol. X, No. 2 (June, 1964), 130–40.
93 Interview with Pressly, see Appendix C1.
94 Interview with W. Frank Craven, *ibid.*
95 Interview with Jerome Blum, chairman, *ibid.*

course was altered somewhat for the fall, 1966, term, primarily by the substitution of two units on the sociology of religion (millenarianism and puritanism) for units on national character and education.[96]

Both Duke and Columbia universities inaugurated programs to apprise graduate history students of the methods of the social sciences. The social science seminar at Duke acquainted students in each discipline with the techniques and skills of the other social sciences. There has been no opportunity yet to determine the effect of this seminar.[97] The Columbia colloquium, designed more specifically to train historians in measurement techniques, was financed by a National Institutes of Health grant to promote training in social history.[98]

The departmental organization at the Case Institute of Technology has been particularly conducive to interchange between historians and social scientists. Because of the major thrust of the institute in scientific and technical fields, the humanities and social studies were combined in one department, making close communication possible. The department gave courses in historical methods and social research methods. Robert C. Davis, who taught the latter, also lectured on social psychology and content analysis to the former. Graduate history students whose dissertation projects were oriented toward social research took that methods course. It dealt with surveys, problems of measurement, interviews, and content analysis—topics a sociology major would study in the introductory course.[99]

Davis was eager for graduate history students to become more exposed to the social sciences; yet he pointed out the danger of their thinking that methodology will supplant reflection. "I would hate to see historians fall into this trap. We must all realize that methods are only tools and do not substitute for creative thinking." Davis contended that historians attempting to use the social and behavioral science techniques "often borrow the metaphor,

[96] Syllabuses and bibliographies for History 500, Princeton University.
[97] Interview with I. B. Holley, Jr., see Appendix C1.
[98] Interview with Robert D. Cross, *ibid.*
[99] Interviews with Melvin Kranzberg, Edwin T. Layton, and Robert C. Davis, *ibid.*

but not the concept. Hofstadter deals with status revolution and Benson with reference group theory, but neither uses these techniques in the way in which a behavioralist would. Saveth's book *American History and the Social Sciences* is a horrible example of how historians borrow social science techniques and distort them."[100]

Despite whatever shortcomings *American History and the Social Sciences* has, professors discussed it in seminars to show how historians employed social science techniques. W. Stitt Robinson and Aubrey C. Land used the book in their seminars at the Universities of Kansas and Maryland, respectively. Although Land has always required his students to examine their material from the viewpoints of content and form analysis, he systematically dealt with quantitative tools for the first time in this seminar. Each student reported on a chapter in the book. Land thinks that "the future of historical research lies in the incorporation of these social and behavioral science techniques."[101]

Although *American History and the Social Sciences* facilitates the investigation of the use of various tools by historians in bringing examples together between two covers, it has been common practice for history professors to introduce their students to such examples in the more fragmented forms of individual articles and books. Usually such introduction has not been accompanied by explicit instruction in the use of the tools. The historians whose writings were cited most often as examples are Lee Benson, Thomas C. Cochran, Merle Curti, David Donald, Stanley Elkins, and Samuel P. Hays.[102] One student complained that even though his interest in social science techniques had been genuinely whetted by such examples, he was so caught up with deadlines in other parts of his graduate program that he did not have time to read deeply about the procedures.[103]

100 Davis, *ibid.*

101 Robinson and Land, *ibid.*; interview with Douglas A. Scott, see Appendix C3.

102 Interviews with Edward Younger, Gene M. Gressley, and John L. Loos, see Appendix C1; Lynn Hales, Jean Gould, and Standley W. Claussen, see Appendix C3.

103 Interview with James R. Sharp, see Appendix C3.

Whether historians had formal training in the use of social science techniques or picked them up through reading no doubt influences the way these techniques are used. One professor's basic pessimism about the use of quantitative devices by historians probably resulted from his belief that their training was inadequate. "I don't think you can cure most historians' lousy sampling techniques. They don't establish control of their samples and don't lay out any kind of project on a statistical basis. . . . I get sarcastic about our lack of sophistication in these areas sometimes. Sophomores in psychology are taught to use coefficient correlations, but historians seem to be unaware of them."[104] Arthur Bestor is also "bothered with the crudity with which historians handle statistics."[105] This pessimism notwithstanding, historians have obviously made increasing use of social science techniques. The following samples—random, to be sure—at least reflect some of the recent projects involving quantitative measurement.

APPLYING SOCIAL SCIENCE TECHNIQUES

Concepts and tools from sociology are among those historians frequently employ. Historians at the Harvard Graduate School of Business Administration have used the concepts of type, role, image, and class extensively in trying to understand how businessmen see themselves. They also discovered that comparative study of administrative decision-making in such various fields as government, business, and religion was helpful, since these decisions were based on similar factors. Along with these concepts, the business historians most frequently used the tools of sampling and statistics.[106] A graduate student at the University of Utah, writing a dissertation on that state's National Guard, employed behavioral concepts to assess the factors responsible for maintaining enlistments in different towns and found an apparent correlation between enlistment rates and the active role the National Guard played in the community's life.[107] At the University of Oklahoma

[104] Interview with Barnes F. Lathrop, see Appendix C1.
[105] Bestor, *ibid.*
[106] Interview with Ralph W. Hidy, *ibid.*
[107] Interview with Richard C. Roberts, see Appendix C3.

a graduate student with a sociology background wrote a dissertation on the status of women, making considerable use of type, role, image, and class. According to his supervising professor, he also did some primitive work with career-line analysis and reference-group theory.[108] Marilee S. Clore planned a dissertation on the organization of the League of Women Voters, based on league records and papers of suffragettes. Depending on the quantity of sources available, she considered exhausting a narrow sample with quantitative techniques and then generalizing on the basis of correlation devices.[109]

The techniques of content analysis, developed to interpret or clarify meaning in writing, has interested many historians. When James Harvey Young was doing research on nineteenth-century proprietary drugs, he talked with Seymour Lipset about using content analysis on patent medicine advertisements. After trying the device for a while, he gave it up in preference for generalizing.[110] A graduate student at the University of Pennsylvania used content analysis on the sermons of Charles G. Finney. After she carried out this project without formal guidance, she came under the supervision of Lee Benson, who restrained her from using further quantitative tools until she had appropriate training.[111] At the University of Chicago, John K. Alexander had the advantage of discussing various quantitative devices with L. J. Lemisch, both in seminars and on the job as his research assistant. Alexander used content analysis to identify a plagiarist of some eighteenth-century documents related to American prisoners of war during the Revolution.[112] Roy A. Kotynek, who wrote a dissertation on Alfred Stieglitz, used content analysis to study the recurrence of words and concepts in Stieglitz' correspondence. His extensive reading of Freud sensitized him to the problems of personality, and his study of role concept enabled him to evaluate Stieglitz' ideas on the artist's role in society.[113]

[108] Interview with John S. Ezell, see Appendix C1.
[109] Interview, see Appendix C3.
[110] Interview, see Appendix C1.
[111] Interview with Dale Holman, see Appendix C3.
[112] Alexander, *ibid.*   [113] Interview, see Appendix C3.

Scaling devices have been used with some frequency to identify particular groups. Historians at the University of Iowa have probably employed the Guttman scale analysis more extensively than those elsewhere. For example, Malcolm J. Rohrbough had a graduate student who applied this device in his dissertation on Jacksonian democracy in Illinois, and Edward L. Gambill used the method to establish an attitudinal scale for Congress in the Reconstruction era.[114] Graduate students of William R. Hutchison at American University conducted some sampling and tried to discover social and other characteristics of liberal Protestants by using a form of career-line analysis.[115] Richard A. Fitzgerald employed career-line analysis in an effort to understand American literary radicals. For the structural framework of his dissertation, "Comparison of the Social Background of American Literary Radicals, 1910–1940, *The Masses, New Masses*, and *The Liberator*," Fitzgerald relied on the work of Talcott Parsons, Edward Shils, Robert E. Lane, Harold Lasswell, and psychoanalyst Herbert E. Krugman.[116] Sydney Nathans' dissertation, "Daniel Webster and the Whig Party," involved Massachusetts election statistics and analyzed roll-call votes in the national Congress.[117]

In his doctoral program at the University of Wisconsin, Kenneth R. Bowling took a minor field in political science, where he learned to use computers. He decided that automatic data-processing techniques could be applied to his dissertation research on the first Congress. He employed cluster-block analysis, a type of roll-call analysis developed by David B. Truman. In this process he compared the roll-call votes of each member of the first Congress for each session, registering *yes, no*, and *zero* votes. With a matrix, he established the percentage of agreement among members. He also dealt with votes on amendments to the Constitution, since he believed that roll-call analysis was invalid unless surrounding evidence was incorporated.[118]

[114] Interview with Rohrbough, see Appendix C1; interview with Gambill, see Appendix C3. Cf. n. 91, above.

[115] Interview, see Appendix C1.

[116] Interview, see Appendix C3.

[117] Nathans, *ibid*.

[118] Bowling, *ibid*.

A student writing a dissertation on Populist leadership in Kansas approached his problem by compiling a composite profile. His charts showed such factors as age, previous political background, and time of arrival in Kansas. Donald R. McCoy, his major professor, encouraged students to apply measurement tools whenever applicable.[119] George L. Anderson, chairman of the department at the University of Kansas, said: "We try to pursue the cultural-anthropological approach that Professor James C. Malin pioneered in. . . . We try to train students to find out all they can about people."[120]

Two graduate students at Emory University used statistical devices in their research. Edward L. Weldon's thesis was a historiographical evaluation of Mark Sullivan's *Our Times*, and his dissertation was an intellectual study of Sullivan as a Progressive. In his seminar with James Harvey Young, Weldon wrote a paper on quantification, content analysis, and covert culture, with an eye toward using one of these tools on his thesis. One chapter was devoted to a quantification of topics Sullivan covered in *Our Times*.[121] Elizabeth M. Lyon's dissertation, "A History of Commercial Architecture in Atlanta, 1865 to the Present," fell within the American Studies field of Emory's Institute of the Liberal Arts. She used statistics in calculating the relationship of Atlanta's population to the square footage of office space and correlated the type of firms with their various building structures.[122]

Alan Calmes, a graduate student at the University of South Carolina, brought a rich social science background to his dissertation research on the economic history of the eighteenth-century rice plantation in South Carolina. His thesis on an anthropological topic, "Acculturation of Cusabo Indians," treated a South Carolina tribe. He had taken a course in research archaeology, worked for the state archaeologist, and participated in excavations with the university's archaeology department. In the summer of 1965 he directed excavations. Part of his interest in the excavation of

[119] Interview with Orval G. Clanton, *ibid.*
[120] Interview, see Appendix C1.
[121] Interview, see Appendix C3.
[122] Lyon, *ibid.*

historical sites was stimulated by Colonial Williamsburg's seminar in historical administration. As a case study for his dissertation research, he hoped to choose a rice plantation with good records and an excavatable site.

In the course of his research, Calmes used economic techniques to establish the ability of South Carolina to bear financial burdens during the eighteenth century. "I reduced a vast quantity of accounts over a seventeen-year period to graphs of expenditures and showed how extraordinary expenses were sunk at various times. I have worked out the relationship of paper money to taxation. This was a matter of giving monetary evaluation to vouchers South Carolinians had received for their material contributions to . . . the French and Indian War and [showing] how the vouchers served as tax payments. [Lawrence H.] Gipson asserts in his grand history that South Carolina was unable to bear the burden of the French and Indian War, but from my research I find that not only were they able to make their material contributions, but they were enjoying a period of prosperity. . . . The province of South Carolina could have pursued a much more vigorous war effort. Instead, the royal government in England bore the brunt of the expenses while personal fortunes were made in the colony."[123]

ICPR PROGRAM

Since 1965 the summer programs of the Inter-University Consortium for Political Research (ICPR) have promoted considerable awareness among historians of the uses of quantification and computer research.[124] Both professors and graduate students have enrolled for courses in research design, data analysis, and applications of mathematics to political research. The large instructional staff frequently provided participants with individual guidance and tutelage, making particular efforts to aid graduate history students in employing quantitative techniques to historical problems. The staff of the ICPR, located in the Survey Research

123 Calmes, *ibid.*

124 For a discussion of the work of the ICPR, see Jerome M. Clubb and Howard Allen, "Computers and Historical Studies," *Journal of American History*, Vol. LIV, No. 3 (Dec., 1967), 599–607.

Center at the University of Michigan, thought that graduate history students need much more training in statistics, mathematics, research design, and the logic or philosophy of science to use quantitative methods effectively. Ideally such training should begin early in the students' graduate careers or even in undergraduate years. Because so many historians receive this training toward the end of their graduate work or have to get it independently after their formal schooling, they are unable to make optimum use of quantitative methods or data. One advantage of having such training is that these skills are applicable to virtually the whole range of historical research, according to Jerome M. Clubb, director of data recovery for the ICPR.[125]

Frequently professors who recognized the value of quantitative techniques but felt unequipped to give such training were eager for students to participate in the ICPR program. Richard L. Watson, Jr., formerly chairman of the history department at Duke University, said that the department was conscious of the need for the social science tools. He brought in political scientists, sociologists, and psychologists to discuss their tools with his seminar.

The department at Duke also sent students to Ann Arbor for more formal training.[126] One who went in 1965 was Lawrence H. Curry, Jr., who said that the program was designed not so much to teach mastery of quantitative techniques as to give a general introduction to techniques for manipulating political data and their broad applicability. Despite having studied calculus as an undergraduate, Curry found that the sophisticated correlations and factor analysis were too complicated for him to undertake. He could, however, use roll-call analysis and other scaling analyses without "intricate" training. Since his background in statistics was too weak to enable him to absorb much of the ICPR program, he recommended that other graduate history students at Duke take a basic course in political science methods before going to the ICPR summer session.[127] Richard S. Kirkendall of the University

[125] Interview, see Appendix C1.
[126] Watson, *ibid*.
[127] Interview, see Appendix C3.

of Missouri also attended the 1965 program and subsequently promoted the use of scale analysis, which his students have found helpful.[128]

Marilyn A. Domer, a graduate student from Ball State University who participated in the ICPR program in 1966, acquired her interest in the social sciences through preparation for social work. As part of her graduate minor in sociology, she took a course on the structure of mathematics, probabilities, and mathematical statistics. This background notwithstanding, she was more enthusiastic about using social science concepts than the tools in historical research. Quantification is merely "one tool among many" to her. "I think we are moving in the direction of using quantitative data in historical research and I want to be able to understand the assumptions behind this use," she said. [129]

While serving member universities across the country, the ICPR also tries to propagate the faith in Ann Arbor, but with qualified success. Richard M. Doolen, a graduate history student at the University of Michigan, wrote a dissertation on "The Greenback Party in the Middle West, 1874–1886." To determine party leadership, he employed career, ethnic background, income, and age factors. The ICPR invited him to program these data on a computer, but he was not "impressed" with this approach and felt that he did not have time to divert to learning programming.[130]

Apart from the ICPR program, several history departments have either had students using computers for dissertation research or had planned such use. The University of California at Los Angeles has established a survey research center where faculty members can learn the techniques of machine research. While still at UCLA, George E. Mowry, professor of history and dean of the division of social sciences, said that the center should reflect the interest and needs of the faculty and the graduate students. The survey research center will have one-third of the time on the machines in the university's computer center. Mowry tried to interest more students in

---

[128] Interview, see Appendix C1.
[129] Interview, see Appendix C3.
[130] Doolen, *ibid.*

social science techniques as the "only way to keep from being smothered with twentieth-century documents. Unless students are able to sample the mass of research data intelligently, they will be overwhelmed."[131] J. Rogers Hollingsworth of the University of Wisconsin took a course in computer programming to learn the language. He hoped to use the computer to handle census data, voting statistics, and legislative voting—things an individual researcher could not do efficiently. He said, "Our computer center could do more to meet the needs of the social sciences, especially since we've come into the field late."[132]

Possibly university computer centers have not encouraged historians to use their machines because they have been unaware of the desire of historians to do so. Hitherto, the computer centers have largely been the domain of those disciplines with large research grants. At the University of Pennsylvania, for instance, it was not easy for historians to use the computer since grant money is required.[133] Only recently have historians been recipients of the kind of grants necessary to enable them to make appreciable use of computers. With more money available, perhaps historians will now find increasing opportunity to use automatic data processing. Even without large grants, graduate students at the University of Notre Dame and Northwestern University have used their institutions' computers to handle commercial statistics for dissertations on the colonial period.[134]

One historian who took a year off to study quantification was dissatisfied with the results. Daniel R. Beaver of the University of Cincinnati wanted to see if computer research could be an aid in handling data on military administration. During his study and association with social scientists, he found that his particular interests defied the use of the broad categories and generalizations the social scientists espoused. Beaver could derive no standard practices of military administration, for he concluded that it is often a matter of individual personalities influencing and develop-

[131] Interview, see Appendix C1.
[132] Hollingsworth, *ibid.*
[133] Interview with Richard S. Dunn, *ibid.*
[134] Interviews with Marshall Smelser and Clarence L. Ver Steeg, *ibid.*

ing their jobs according to their interests and inclinations. "Our historical methods," asserted Beaver, "are more sophisticated than the quantitative methods. Nothing substitutes for finely trained judgment."[135]

Further disenchantment with quantitative methods was expressed by Robert H. Ferrell of Indiana University. When he, Maurice G. Baxter, and John E. Wiltz did research for their book, *The Teaching of American History in High Schools*, they used a computer to code questionnaire responses from teachers. "We used the computer merely to give a scientific aura to what we could have done by hand, and what we already knew through conversations and hunches. I can assure you that our computer operation was something less than effective."[136]

If historians think computer research or quantification will supplant conventional research in original sources, they are mistaken, according to Allan G. Bogue. In his opinion, empirical data will only supplement manuscript research.[137] Historians should always remember, however, that manuscripts are often no more than random fragments from the past. It is shocking to discover how little some manuscript collections reveal about individuals. "In addition, any manuscript collection is at best an accidental historical accretion, pointing perhaps to conclusions that are completely different than those we would derive if all of the related manuscript collections had been preserved."[138]

SOCIAL SCIENTISTS' ATTITUDES TOWARD HISTORY

Problems historians have had in "getting time" on computers at their universities often reflected poor communication among various disciplines. This poor communication showed up repeatedly when historians sought the co-operation of colleagues in providing training in social science techniques for history students. Julius M. Bloch of the graduate history faculty of the City University

[135] Beaver, *ibid*.
[136] Letter, Ferrell to author, Oct. 6, 1966.
[137] Interview, see Appendix C1.
[138] "United States: The 'New' Political History," *loc. cit.*, 22.

of New York admitted frustration when he saw how little his students knew of the social and behavioral sciences. Interested primarily in their own students, professors in these areas seemed unconcerned about graduate history students being apprised of their techniques. "Too little is being done to break down the artificial barriers between the disciplines."[139] Wood Gray said that the department at George Washington University was eager to become involved with social science techniques. It would like to have a paperback manual on the use of these techniques in historical research, similar to *Historian's Handbook*, which Gray produced in collaboration with other members of the department. Gray asked the university's psychology department for suggestions on training historians to use psychological insights, but without positive response. "They don't want to get involved with training historians. . . . They prefer to remain more theoretical."[140]

Some members of the history department at the University of Hawaii felt that they were slighted by the university's Social Science Research Institute because they were not behavioristically oriented. Cedric B. Cowing said, "Many of us are interested in the social sciences and don't want to be eliminated from [this] area just because we aren't behaviorists." He contended that historians can use social science tools better than social scientists, if not with their precision. Cowing gave a humanistic orientation to his interdisciplinary course on man in society.[141]

The reaction of professors at Columbia University to the question of communication between historians and social scientists proved the danger of generalization. Students of Alden T. Vaughan who took courses in statistics and sociology usually were not pleased with the results, for the courses were not geared to historians.[142] Conversely, students of Frederick D. Kershner, Jr., at Columbia's Teachers College profited from sociology and psychology courses and found that the behaviorists were hospi-

---

[139] Interview, see Appendix C1.
[140] Gray, *ibid.*
[141] Cowing, *ibid.*
[142] Vaughan, *ibid.*

table.[143] James P. Shenton reported that his students were very much interested in and familiar with the social sciences techniques. Since they gained this familiarity on the undergraduate level at Columbia, there was obvious co-operation among the disciplines. With the National Institutes of Health grant for the study of social history, the history department has explored deeply the application of social science concepts and techniques to historical research.[144]

In a department as large as that at the University of Wisconsin, the cleavage between humanists and social scientists was apparent. About one-fourth of the approximately fifty members of the department encouraged students to acquire competence in the social sciences. J. Rogers Hollingsworth expected that those with an inclination to the social sciences would "probably find some difficulty in communicating with historians with a purely humanistic bent. More students are taking a different tack from their major professors today than before." Their interest in problems their mentors were unconcerned with also caused communication difficulties.[145]

The willingness of social and behavioral scientists to work with historians in the Inter-University Consortium for Political Research reflected the most positive co-operation among the disciplines to date. The establishment by the American Historical Association of the Committee to Collect the Basic Quantitative Data of American Political History signified the profession's concern for communication. From its beginning in January, 1964, this committee has worked closely with the ICPR in gathering state and county voting and demographic statistics.[146] Further evidence of the desire for communication was the creation by the Mathematics Social Science Board (MSSB) of a history committee in 1964. (The MSSB itself was spawned by the Social Science Research Council and the Institute for Advanced Study

143 Kershner, *ibid.*
144 Shenton, *ibid.*
145 Hollingsworth, *ibid.*
146 *Annual Report of the American Historical Association, 1965, Volume 1, Proceedings,* pp. 62–63.

in the Behavioral Sciences.) This MSSB committee has tried to develop ways by which historians can acquire competence in mathematics and statistics. It has had some funds to encourage the application of quantitative methods to historical research as well as to assemble historians, social scientists, and statisticians so that such application may be evaluated by quantitative experts.[147]

   While the social and behavioral sciences have their vocal partisans among historians, the majority of the profession is too inexperienced with and ignorant of measurement techniques to express significant approval of them. Nonetheless, historians normally feel that any device which can deepen the understanding of the past should be employed. There have been sufficient indications that quantitative techniques may promote such understanding to cause most historians to want to know more about them. They especially think that graduate students should have the opportunity to investigate these techniques systematically. Because of academic departmental divisions, it frequently has been difficult for graduate history students to acquire quantitative skills, and national organizations like the ICPR can train only a limited number. It would therefore be most beneficial if universities would establish formal interdepartmental programs in quantitative methodology so that a student's training in this area would not be a matter of chance or whim. Some institutions have already provided these programs. The University of Notre Dame's sociology department and business school have established a social science laboratory, which has generated interest throughout the campus.[148] At the University of Iowa, Deil S. Wright of the political science department taught a general course in social science methodology.[149] In the history department at San Francisco State College, even the nonbehaviorists agreed on the importance of the social science techniques and incorporated them into the department's two methods courses.[150] Although historians at Rutgers—The State University discussed the desirability of giving

[147] "United States: The 'New' Political History," *loc. cit.*, 14.
[148] Interview with J. Philip Gleason, see Appendix C1.
[149] Interview, see Appendix C1.
[150] Questionnaire returned by John L. Shover.

more formal training in social science techniques, no professor wanted to undertake the responsibility. Departmental reluctance may have been occasioned by the fact that students there do not have the opportunity to take a general course in social science tools. Richard P. McCormick, chairman of the department, foresaw increasing likelihood of co-operation between historians and political scientists. "If the current trend in political science continues, political history will probably be lost to history departments. This means that we will have more interdisciplinary work. Historians will join political scientists and use their tools."[151] Some historians at Indiana University called for an interdepartmental methodological minor field for the Ph.D. to train students in the range of quantitative techniques.[152]

There is no question that the historical profession is expressing more interest in social science concepts and tools than ever in the past. Since the days when Frederick Jackson Turner began training graduate students, historians have been incorporating some quantitative techniques in their research. It has been largely within the last decade, however, that enthusiasm for this approach has pervaded the profession, perhaps because of the great possibilities opened by computers. Now most historians who know little or nothing about these methods express some sense of inadequacy. They think the profession should not be caught napping while significant methodological advances are being made. As a consequence, there is a general willingness to allow graduate students to learn the quantitative techniques and to see the results of this methodology that is essentially new to historians. Those who are leading the profession toward quantitative methods are quick to state the limits of these methods in historical investigation. The methods cannot supplant the trained judgment of a historian, and the tools should never determine the problem under scrutiny. Whether full-scale use of quantitative methods will materially alter the course of United States historiography remains to be seen.

[151] Interview, see Appendix C1.
[152] Questionnaire returned by Walter T. K. Nugent, director of graduate studies in history, Indiana University.

The experiments now under way will indicate the contribution the quantitative methods can produce.

If quantifiers should dominate the profession, the future use and growth of repositories of original sources may be fundamentally affected. Historians' traditional research emphases on literary sources have created a premium on manuscript collections and archives. But latter-day quantifiers comment, with some accuracy, that manuscript collections themselves often represent no more than a random sample of the written record of the past. If the profession experiences a major shift in research methods toward social and behavioral science techniques, it will obviously use literary records less and private repositories will probably modify their collecting policies. Governmental agencies may not be so quick to alter their archival programs, and the profession may indeed increase its use of archives containing quantitative data such as census reports, election returns, and other technical items. While the new approaches may drastically alter research patterns, repositories would do well to remember that in dialectical terms, the quantitative synthesis is unlikely to endure. The new antithesis may well be a return to a humanistic approach to the study of history, for, whatever its limitations, it alone can furnish what Benedetto Croce called "words that nourish and keep warm the minds and souls of men."[153] Against the day of this return, and perhaps discounting some of the quantifiers' current claims, repositories should hesitate to discard established acquisition policies. It is hoped that they will also be receptive to new needs of the profession by collecting quantitative data wherever practicable.

[153] Benedetto Croce, *History: Its Theory and Practice* (New York, Harcourt, Brace and Co., 1921), 27.

III. Collecting Original Sources

UNTIL graduate historical studies were begun in the United States in the last quarter of the nineteenth century, universities made no systematic attempt to collect manuscripts. Many had kept their own archives—often with no sense of stewardship for the future, but because less decision was required to retain the material than to discard it. When these archives contained papers of administrators and faculty who were instrumental in both education and religion, the papers have subsequently proved invaluable for research in these areas. During the time institutions of higher learning were not actively collecting manuscript sources, the job fell mostly to private and state historical societies. To cite notable examples, the Massachusetts Historical Society (founded in 1791) and the State Historical Society of Wisconsin (founded in 1846) performed this task industriously and imaginatively. Nonetheless, around the country great troves of original sources lay unknown, for scholars had expressed little need for them. James Ford Rhodes, for instance, spoke contemptuously of the "source-fiend."[1] The number of graduate history students doing original

[1] James Ford Rhodes, Introduction to *A List of Books and Newspapers, Maps, Music, and Miscellaneous Matter Printed in the South During the Confederacy, Now in the Boston Athenaeum*, p. v.

research toward the end of the century had not yet made much impact on collecting institutions. The Library of Congress' comparative inattention to its manuscripts serves as a case in point.[2]

Toward the turn of the century, the picture began to change. Publications identifying and locating original sources aroused historians' awareness of research possibilities. Justin Winsor, whose own career typifies the transition from antiquarianism to professionalism, issued the first guide to Harvard's primary sources, and Volume VIII (1889) of his *Narrative and Critical History of America* contained a fifty-six-page inventory of manuscript sources. His "Manuscript Sources of American History" remains a landmark description of American manuscripts.[3] Unlike other Boston curators, Winsor was no pack rat trying to conceal his resources. He preferred to inform people of what was available and direct them to the material.[4] Early in the twentieth century, Charles M. Andrews and some gentlemen scholars started to utilize the British Public Record Office for research. J. Franklin Jameson began calling attention to original sources through the influential guides published by the Carnegie Institution of Washington. Reflecting Jameson's leadership, the *American Historical Review* and the *Annual Reports* of the American Historical Association contained edited sources. Jameson, who constantly called for more published documents and guides to archives and manuscripts, had always wanted a national archives created. Although his persistent lobbying for the establishment of the archives did not bear fruit until 1934, his constant pressure awakened historians to their responsibilities for the bibliographical and archival foundations of the profession. With his urging, historians began working as bibliographers, archivists, and documentary editors. "Jameson's example and initiative must have counted for more than anyone now can measure."[5] The danger is that the altogether

[2] Fred Shelley, "Manuscripts in the Library of Congress: 1800–1900," *American Archivist*, Vol. XI, No. 1 (Jan., 1948), 3–19.

[3] Justin Winsor, "Manuscript Sources of American History," *Papers of the American Historical Association.*

[4] L. H. Butterfield, "Bostonians and their Neighbors as Pack Rats," *American Archivist, Vol.* XXIV, No. 2 (Apr., 1961), 141–59.

[5] John Higham with Leonard Krieger and Felix Gilbert, *History*, 24. Cf. Eliza-

salutary influence of Jameson may wear thin with the passage of years. If the profession is to maintain its intellectual prosperity, it cannot afford to neglect its foundations.

Although universities responded slowly to the idea of collecting sources which graduate students could research, they did respond. In 1905, the University of California bought the library of Hubert Howe Bancroft, which became the cornerstone of its research collection; in 1916, Yale University acquired Henry Wagner's prestigious Texas and Middle West Collection. After World War I it had become *de rigeur* for graduate history students to base their research on original sources, and most universities were making efforts to supply these needs.

This chapter deals with the ways various universities have tried to provide primary sources as the basis for their graduate research. It is by no means a catalog of all the resources available at institutions granting the Ph.D. in history, for such information has been published elsewhere, notably in the Hamer *Guide to Archives and Manuscripts in the United States* and the *National Union Catalog of Manuscript Collections*. Rather, it uses selected institutions to illustrate various policies and needs for collecting primary sources. The predominant collecting pattern, especially among state-supported institutions, is regional, but sometimes the region extends far beyond state boundaries. Easily the greatest percentage of repositories in the country contain documents relating to their respective geographical areas. Two other motivations are responsible for the development of source collections: interests of private institutions and research interests of individual professors (which also may be regional).

REGIONAL COLLECTING

When a passenger "deplanes" at the Raleigh-Durham, North Carolina, airport, one of the first signs he sees welcomes him to the "Research Triangle." The name of the airport identifies two of the triangle's points, and Chapel Hill is the third. One suspects

beth Donnan and Leo F. Stock (eds.), *An Historian's World: Selections from the Correspondence of John Franklin Jameson.*

that the boosters and developers responsible for this nomenclature are touting the area's research activities in hopes of luring more industry to North Carolina. Whatever research capacity the triangle boasts in the scientific and technical areas could hardly be surpassed by its resources for the United States historian. The three points of the historians' research triangle are the Southern Historical Collection, at the University of North Carolina at Chapel Hill; the manuscript division of the Duke University library, at Durham; and the North Carolina Department of Archives and History, at Raleigh, the state capital. While these resources have a strong regional emphasis, they include some important material unrelated to southern history.

The University of North Carolina established the Southern Historical Collection to gather manuscripts from fourteen southern states (including Maryland, Kentucky, and Missouri). It took this step in 1930 because no other agency was making a systematic effort to preserve the manuscript sources of southern history, many of which had already been destroyed. Since the university appealed to the entire South for manuscripts, it has always encouraged wide use of this regional resource.[6] An important aspect of the utilization of the collection by historians is the close relationship it has maintained with the university's department of history. The long-time director of the collection, James W. Patton, held a professorship in the department, as did his energetic predecessor, J. G. de Roulhac Hamilton. J. Isaac Copeland, who became director in September, 1967, also is a professor of history. This close relationship, the familiarity of other professors with the manuscripts, and the department's emphasis on southern history have resulted in its graduate students using the collection extensively.[7]

Appraising the use of manuscripts presents difficult qualitative problems, especially when considered in connection with standard library reports. According to Patton, many librarians not

---

[6] J. G. de Roulhac Hamilton, "The Southern Historical Collection," *Library Resources of the University of North Carolina*, (ed. by Charles E. Rush), 39–46.
[7] Interview with Patton, see Appendix C1.

familiar with manuscript research are likely to underestimate manuscript use. They can easily count the number of books checked out, and these statistics appear far more impressive than the number of researchers who might use manuscripts during any given period. Historians understand, of course, that mere numbers have little relationship to the importance of research in manuscripts. For record-keeping purposes, the Southern Historical Collection reports the number of researchers who have come in each day and the collections each has consulted. It makes no effort to assess the extent of use of any particular collection.[8]

The Duke University manuscript collection, described by a professor as "rich beyond belief," constitutes the second major resource for historians in the research triangle. Like the Southern Historical Collection, it has attracted scholars from the entire nation. More important, it has furnished an excellent resource for Duke students, and all history professors at the university have urged their students to use the local manuscripts as much as possible. One professor, I. B. Holley, Jr., has developed a resourceful method of determining the value of individual collections for supporting graduate research projects. He has carefully selected undergraduate honors students not planning to pursue graduate work in history and has used them as "front runners." In the course of their research, they have been able to "dig into a collection" and produce entirely suitable undergraduate term papers. According to the results of each paper, the professor can readily assess whether the manuscript collection warrants further exploitation for either a thesis or a dissertation. This device has served two ends: undergraduates had an opportunity to work in depth with manuscripts, and graduate students avoided working on materials which did not justify their effort. "It is important," Holley declared, "not to run graduate students up blind alleys that might waste a year of their time."[9]

The third point of the triangle, the North Carolina Department of Archives and History, contains manuscripts, microfilm,

[8] *Ibid.*
[9] Holley, *ibid.*

and printed documents related to the state and, to a lesser extent, to the Southeast. In addition to having responsibility for state, county, and municipal records and newspapers, the agency also holds records dealing with various organizations, churches, businesses, and private citizens. H. G. Jones, the state archivist, felt that graduate students concerned with North Carolina history have been generally aware of his resources and have used them effectively, but in a limited way.[10]

Within this research triangle, students have access not only to state documents but to printed federal government documents as well, both at the University of North Carolina and at Duke. Most universities offering the Ph.D. in United States history are equipped with the standard government documents. Because many of the institutions that have recently entered the doctoral field began as land-grant colleges and as such were official depositories for government documents, their holdings in these materials are good, despite frequent deficiencies in other types of primary sources.

State universities with manuscript collections have usually made an effort to acquire material related to the state or region in which they are located. The collection at the University of Kentucky is fairly typical in this respect. It consists, in part, of records from the Kentucky iron and Burley tobacco industries as well as papers of notable Kentucky business and political leaders.[11] The acquisitions policy of Wayne State University in Detroit has been geared to the area's economic activity. The most important component of its collection is the Labor History Archives, although no member of the history department has specialized in labor history. Included in this collection are the papers of James Carey and Walter, Victor, and Roy Reuther, as well as records of the Industrial Workers of the World. In addition, the collection is the official depository for the United Automobile Workers (UAW) and the Congress of Industrial Organizations (CIO). Since the Labor History Archives does have formal connections with the UAW

[10] Questionnaire returned by Jones.
[11] Interview with Thomas D. Clark, see Appendix C1.

and other labor organizations, the history department has chosen to avoid the field of labor history and thereby deflect any suspicion of being an official spokesman for organized labor. As a consequence of this position, graduate students at Wayne State have made less use of the university archives than students from the University of Michigan, Harvard, and Columbia.[12]

As an outgrowth of regional research needs, archival collections have been developed by several institutions such as Texas Technological College, the University of Houston, and the University of Wyoming. The first of these recognized that its region was "short on both rainfall and Anglo-American history" and has tried to do something about the latter by establishing the Southwest Collection to preserve historical records of the area. The collection contains personal papers, business records, and various association and institution records. The business records reflect the region's economic pursuits: cattle, land companies, and farming. Many southwestern authors, including Walter Prescott Webb, Allan Bosworth, Ramon Adams, and Carl Coke Rister, have donated manuscripts to the collection.[13] The University of Houston, through the Texas Gulf Coast Historical Association, has concentrated on gathering business records of its region. Included in its collection are records from the petroleum, lumber, and sugar industries.[14] The Western History Research Center of the University of Wyoming has similarly stressed business and economic records in its collecting program. Its materials relate to cattle, oil, wool, antitrust investigations, reclamation and irrigation, and transportation (especially air mail). The center, the depository for the Western Writers of America, is building a collection of Western American fiction.[15]

The attitudes of many colleges and universities concerning the collection of original sources to support their graduate work in

[12] Interview with Philip P. Mason, professor of history and Wayne State University archivist, *ibid.*

[13] Roy Sylvan Dunn, "The Southwest Collection at 'Texas Tech,'" *American Archivist*, Vol. XXVIII, No. 3 (July, 1965), 413–19.

[14] Interview with James A. Tinsley, see Appendix C1.

[15] Interview with Gene M. Gressley, *ibid.*

history frequently have been influenced by the proximity of research repositories and their mutual relations. When the repositories are tax supported, universities usually rely on them considerably. This reliance is probably nowhere more evident than in the District of Columbia area. Because of the immense riches of the Library of Congress and the National Archives, some universities in the immediate area have neglected acquiring original as well as secondary sources.[16] Professors at American University and the University of Maryland have made it clear to their graduate students from the outset that they are expected to make the Library of Congress their base of operations and to use the National Archives when appropriate.[17] Some history professors at Johns Hopkins University, dissatisfied with the original sources there, sent their students to nearby Washington for research.[18]

Although the University of Virginia, at Charlottesville, has a manuscript collection of considerable scope, it naturally cannot meet the research needs of all members of the department. Fortunately, historians in Charlottesville are close enough to Washington repositories to consider them a part of their own resources. In addition, the Virginia Historical Society and the Virginia State Library, both in Richmond, and Colonial Williamsburg offer abundant material at comparatively close range. Colonial Williamsburg's comprehensive photocopy collection of eighteenth-century primary sources relating to Virginia makes it an ideal research center for students of the period. These photocopies were acquired from such other depositories as the John Carter Brown Library, the Library of Congress, and Duke University. The MacGregor Collection of printed works at the University of Virginia library constitutes a valuable source for scholars interested in early American history. Since historians working in the early nineteenth century copied original documents extensively, by current canons their history is defective; but since some of these

16 Cf. Allan M. Cartter, *An Assessment of Quality in Graduate Education,* 114–15.

17 Interviews with Roger H. Brown and Horace S. Merrill, see Appendix C1.

18 Interviews with David Donald and Stephen E. Ambrose, *ibid.*

documents now are unavailable elsewhere, their compilations have obvious rewards for today's researchers.[19]

Most universities located in metropolitan centers rely to some extent on the resources of other repositories in the area. In Philadelphia, the University of Pennsylvania has not actively developed a manuscript collection in American history, but its students have a number of alternatives at the American Philosophical Society; the Historical Society of Pennsylvania; the municipal reference library; the Customs House; Swarthmore, Haverford, and Bryn Mawr colleges, which have Quaker and other material; the Library Company of Philadelphia; and a number of religious denominational libraries. The university maintains the union catalog of books for the greater Philadelphia area.[20]

Although there are fewer repositories in Cleveland than in Philadelphia, graduate students at Western Reserve University, Case Institute of Technology, and Kent State University nonetheless have ample sources to draw on. To prevent duplication, the Cleveland Public Library, which contains three million volumes, and the Western Reserve Historical Society collaborate with the universities in ordering original sources. The Western Reserve University library houses the regional union catalog. As an example of the co-ordination in acquisitions between Western Reserve University and the Cleveland Public Library, the two have provided between them the full printed diplomatic correspondence on the origins of World Wars I and II.[21] The resources of the Cleveland area are obviously available to all its graduate students; but because of the specialization of the doctoral program at the Case Institute of Technology and the newness of that at Kent State University, students at these schools have not used the Cleveland repositories as extensively as have students from Western Reserve University.

New York City offers graduate history students extraordinary research opportunities apart from whatever original sources its

19 Interview with David Alan Williams, *ibid.*
20 Interviews with Thomas C. Cochran and Richard S. Dunn, *ibid.*
21 Interviews with Carl H. Cramer and Marion C. Siney, *ibid.*

universities possess. Among the institutions granting the Ph.D. in history in the New York metropolitan area, Columbia University has the largest collection of primary sources, although, according to one of its professors, these lack focus. Its range of photocopied material reveals no systematic procedure of collection, and the manuscripts resemble a "random harvest." The difficulty is that the library has not developed a way to inform people of its collecting procedures and has not made clear the goals and limits of the manuscript collection. The Oral History Collection is another resource at Columbia that students have difficulty using, obviously because of the nature of the material rather than its administration. Students have no way of knowing the scope or worth of an oral history interview without examining it closely, which is true of other types of uncalendared sources.[22]

At New York University space limitations in the library have prevented the development of a major manuscript collection. Although the history department makes certain that the library gets all the current significant secondary works, it has not yet resolved the problem of determining which research collections should be developed when the university occupies its new Bobst Library. At that time the university will be "committed to developing an independent, significant research collection in various areas." A departmental committee has been trying to decide which areas should be stressed. One of these will surely be urban history, now well represented at the university by good secondary and excellent printed sources from the Tamiment Collection. This collection, which came from the now-defunct Rand School of Social Science, includes labor, leftist, and socialist material. The university also will attempt to acquire significant documents relating to New York and other selected cities. It was aided in this effort by the history department, which was involved in the task force established to salvage the New York City municipal archives. The department also has been active in the project sponsored by the Institute for Early American History and Culture to preserve municipal archives. As the history department studied

22 Interview with James P. Shenton, *ibid*.

the problems of building a manuscript collection at the university, one of its major concerns was to avoid duplicating areas already covered by the New York Public Library and the Columbia University library.[23] Historians from Columbia and New York Universities acknowledged the importance of the New York Public Library to their graduate research programs, and the City University of New York emphatically signified its reliance on that institution by locating its graduate studies division across Forty-second Street from the library.

Chicago is another metropolitan area munificently endowed with a wide range of original sources which graduate students from the area may exploit. The most extensive academic collection is housed at the University of Chicago, which has nearly three million manuscripts, seventy-one thousand sheets of microprints, and about forty thousand reels of microfilm in addition to extensive printed sources. Although a few universities in the East that are considerably older than the University of Chicago, founded in 1891, have more manuscripts, its collection of primary sources is "impressive in both quality and quantity." Also available in the city are the significant holdings of the Newberry Library, the Chicago Historical Society, and the John Crerar Library, now located at the Illinois Institute of Technology.[24]

Adjacent to the University of Chicago is the Center for Research Libraries (CRL), which began in 1949 as the Midwest Inter-Library Center. A grant of $250,000 from the Rockefeller Foundation enabled the CRL to erect its building on land donated by the university. Basically, the CRL lends to other libraries; but scholars, who need not be associated with a member institution, may do research at the center if that is more convenient. Ten to twelve researchers, mostly graduate students, use the CRL each week. Originally, when membership in the organization was limited to midwestern institutions, ten universities with large research libraries belonged. In 1962 the CRL lifted all geographical restrictions on membership and now hopes that all seventy to eighty major research libraries in

[23] Interview with Bayrd Still, *ibid*.
[24] Interview with William T. Hutchinson, *ibid*.

the United States will join. Dues are based on a formula geared to a member library's acquisitions budget and currently run between $4,000 and $16,000 annually. The basic purpose of the CRL is to augment resources of member libraries, especially those with infrequently used materials. Its collection developed through the deposit of such materials from members and through the direct acquisition of broader research materials. The economic sound-ness of co-operatively maintaining a repository of such items is borne out by the findings that for some subjects as much as 25 per cent of the holdings of research libraries are used no oftener than once every one hundred years. The Northwestern University library made a study which showed that 75 per cent of the scien-tific and technical material in that library could be removed from the shelves and the remaining holdings would satisfy 99 per cent of the requests. Gordon Williams, director of the CRL, pointed out that if libraries would co-operate in purchasing infrequently used material, they could use the money saved to provide multiple copies of books generally in demand. "Libraries might then be able to offer their users *everything* they need within three to five days, instead of as now, some within a few minutes and others not for weeks or months." One of the difficulties with the interlibrary loan system is that the participating institutions are frequently not geared to it, and loan requests cannot be filled promptly. Whereas it may take universities from two to three weeks to fill a loan request, the CRL can do it within a day, since it was established to handle mail orders.[25]

Among the important holdings in the more than 2,000,000 volumes belonging to the CRL are over 600,000 foreign disserta-tions, of which 250,000 came from the Library of Congress. The CRL currently acquires printed foreign dissertations. It plans to add at least 4,500,000 volumes to its total holdings. Perhaps its best known collection is the one containing runs of 146 micro-filmed foreign newspapers, most of which date back to 1956, and some to 1938. The CRL tries to have a complete collection of documents from the fifty states from 1952 to the present. High

25 Interview, see Appendix C2b.

84

on the CRL's list of priorities for future acquisitions are copies of foreign archives, both governmental and private. It would also like to obtain copies of older books available only in European libraries. When the CRL gets new material, members are apprised of the acquisitions. Monographs and serials are cataloged, and members as well as the National Union Catalog receive copies of the cards. The CRL does not catalog materials which it collects comprehensively and which can be identified by form such as foreign dissertations. Members are expected to be aware of the CRL's distinctive collecting programs.

The CRL council is composed of two representatives from each member institution. The director of libraries is automatically a representative unless the president of the institution specifies otherwise. The other member is not a librarian, and the CRL prefers an administrator acquainted with budgetary matters. The council elects a fifteen-man board of directors, approves the budget and assessments, and makes necessary changes in the by-laws.[26]

Despite the comparative newness of Los Angeles as both a city and a center for higher education, the metropolitan area boasts some outstanding research facilities. The newness has also seemed to increase the dependence of the universities on the resources of each other and on those of nonacademic institutions. The University of California at Los Angeles, which awarded its first history Ph.D. in 1938, had no systematic program for acquiring manuscripts until approximately twenty years ago. Its collection is now adequate for research in local history, but the history department does not stress this area. Each year only one or two UCLA graduate history students have used its manuscripts for dissertation research, although three to five students from each seminar have worked in the collection. Master's candidates from state colleges in the area and students from the University of Southern California (USC), Occidental College, Pomona College, and the University of Redlands seem to have made greater use of the facilities. The UCLA library, as a state institution, has not dis-

[26] *Ibid.*

couraged any scholarly use of its original sources.[27] In fact, a USC professor said frankly: "We've relied on the materials available in the UCLA library. . . . UCLA understands our problems and is most helpful."[28]

Graduate students from UCLA, USC, the Claremont Graduate School, and other nearby institutions have relied heavily on several libraries in the metropolitan area when they needed primary sources not available at the academic institutions. The William Andrews Clark Library has a great deal of Montana material and offers fellowships to foster research in Montana history.[29] In San Marino the Huntington Library has splendid collections for American colonial history and the westward movement. Some historians in the area such as John A. Schutz, a colonial specialist at USC, and Claremont doctoral candidates make the Huntington their base of research.[30] The Los Angeles County law collection is the best west of the Hudson. This eminence results from the fact that since 1902 every filing fee in the county has gone to the law library. The public library in Los Angeles has an excellent collection of local sources as well as newspapers, and the County Museum and Southwest Museum also maintain research collections. Students have had free access to the Latter-day Saints genealogical library in the Los Angeles Mormon Temple.[31]

Cincinnati is similar to Los Angeles, but on a smaller scale, in that historical researchers there, too, must rely on a network of repositories for their original sources. Although the University of Cincinnati holds the standard printed sources, it has no manuscripts of any importance since the Cincinnati Historical Society was located in the basement of the university library until 1965. Daniel R. Beaver's seminar in local history therefore had to rely on the resources of the Cincinnati Historical Society and the

[27] Interview with James Mink, UCLA archivist and historical manuscript librarian, see Appendix C2a.

[28] Interview with Russell L. Caldwell, see Appendix C1.

[29] Interview with Mink, above.

[30] Interview with Schutz, see Appendix C1; questionnaire returned by John Niven, Claremont Graduate School.

[31] Interviews with George E. Mowry, Frank O. Gatell, John W. Caughey, Howard S. Miller, and John A. Schutz, see Appendix C1.

Cincinnati Public Library. "Many of our local manuscript collections," said Beaver, "are virginal and need to be ravished."[32] According to the university librarian, the director of the Cincinnati Historical Society agreed that university students had not used the society's collections as much as they should.[33] Nonetheless, most of the graduate students doing research at the society have come from the University of Cincinnati.[34] Students from Xavier University usually have relied on the research facilities of the society, the Cincinnati Public Library, and the University of Cincinnati.[35] Besides the foregoing repositories, the city boasts the nation's finest assemblage of sources relating to American Jewish history. The American Jewish Archives was established as a research center for Hebrew Union College, a postgraduate institution for training Reformed rabbis. All students at the college must take Jacob R. Marcus' course in American Jewish history, which requires a paper based on the archives or printed sources in the college library. Located near the University of Cincinnati, the American Jewish Archives, along with the historical society, serves as a manuscript center for the university; and university students constitute the archives' largest body of users.[36]

Both Seattle and Denver offer similar research facilities to graduate students in their areas. Each has a Federal Records Center and a large public library. (The National Archives and Records Service has Federal Records Centers in Boston; New York City; Philadelphia; Suitland, Maryland; Atlanta; Chicago; Kansas City, Missouri; Fort Worth; Denver; San Francisco; Los Angeles; and Seattle. These centers contain the records of governmental agencies operating within ten regions of the country. The records are generally of less historical value than those in the National Archives, but they may pertain directly to many research projects involving the national government. Historians should become

[32] Beaver, *ibid.*
[33] Interview with Arthur T. Hamlin, see Appendix C2a.
[34] Interview with Lee Jordon and Virginia Jergens, see Appendix C2b.
[35] Questionnaire returned by Paul L. Simon.
[36] Interview with Marcus, see Appendix C2a. See also his "The American Jewish Archives," *American Archivist*, Vol. XXIII, No. 1 (Jan., 1960), 57–61.

aware of the research potentialities of the Federal Records Centers.)[37] The Colorado State Archives and the State Historical Society are across the capitol grounds from each other in Denver, while the state archives of Washington is in Olympia and the State Historical Society is in Tacoma. Since the University of Denver has no manuscripts, its students have made heavy use of the Western History Department of the Denver Public Library as well as other collections in the city.[38] Graduate students from the University of Colorado, located only twenty miles from Denver, frequently have used both the city's repositories and the university's western manuscript collection.[39] The manuscript section of the University of Washington library is "alert and one of the very best," and the library has all the government documents a researcher would need.[40]

Even when universities make little or no attempt to provide manuscripts for graduate research, resourceful students can make the most of what is at hand. Fortunately, primary sources are available in nonacademic repositories located throughout the country, as the following examples illustrate. Students at the University of Richmond have done research in the state library and archives, the Virginia Historical Society, and the Valentine Museum, all in Richmond.[41] Those at the State University of New York at Buffalo have access to the Buffalo Historical Society,[42] and those at Bowling Green State University (Ohio) sometimes use the Rutherford B. Hayes Memorial Library.[43] Kansas State University is situated close to Abilene, home of the Eisenhower Library, and the Kansas State Historical Society in Topeka. Its graduate students use these depositories along with the Truman Library in Independence, Missouri.[44] In Salt Lake City, home of

[37] Cf. Gerald T. White, "Government Archives Afield: The Federal Records Centers and the Historian," presented at the meeting of the Organization of American Historians, Apr. 27, 1967.

[38] Interview with Theodore R. Crane, see Appendix C1.

[39] Questionnaire returned by John A. Brennan.

[40] Interview with Arthur Bestor, see Appendix C1.

[41] Questionnaire returned by R. C. McDanel.

[42] Questionnaire returned by John T. Horton.

[43] Questionnaire returned by William R. Rock.

[44] Questionnaire returned by Joe W. Kraus.

the University of Utah, the best original sources are in the Office of the Latter-day Saints Church Historian, the Utah State Historical Society, and the Latter-day Saints Genealogical Society.[45] At Boston University there are just enough original sources to give students practice in handling them. Practice research projects have been devised to acquaint students with the problems faced in actual research.[46] For these projects graduate students in the Boston area are blessed with the resources of the Massachusetts Historical Society, the Houghton and Baker libraries of Harvard University, the Boston Public Library, the Boston Athenaeum, the Commonwealth Archives, and other smaller, but often highly specialized and therefore important, collections.

In many instances state universities, along with other state agencies, have been placed in state capitals. When the agencies included state historical societies and archives, graduate students were often the chief beneficiaries. Quite commonly, especially in the Midwest with its tradition of strong state historical societies, ties between state universities and historical societies are intimate. Probably the most notable example of this closeness is found in Madison, where the state historical society is located on the campus of the University of Wisconsin. The society, begun in 1846, serves as the research center for the university's graduate students in United States history and contains the celebrated Draper Collection, among other valuable resources.[47] Merrill Jensen commented that the society "frankly has one of the best working libraries in the country."[48] Like the State Historical Society of Wisconsin, the Ohio Historical Society is located on a college campus. Plans are under way, however, for constructing a new building approximately one and one-half miles from Ohio State University.

[45] Interview with Brigham Madsen, see Appendix C1.
[46] Interview with Robert E. Moody, *ibid.*
[47] On Draper's influence, cf. Reuben Gold Thwaites, *Lyman Copeland Draper: A Memoir*; William B. Hesseltine, *Pioneer's Mission*; Lester J. Cappon, ed., "Correspondence between Charles Campbell and Lyman C. Draper, 1846–1872," *William and Mary Quarterly*, 3rd Series, Vol. III, No. 1 (Jan., 1946), 70–116; Josephine L. Harper, "Lyman C. Draper and Early American Archives," *American Archivist*, Vol. XV, No. 3 (July, 1952), 205–12; Donald R. McNeil (ed.), *The American Collector.*
[48] Interview, see Appendix C1.

Described by Francis P. Weisenburger as "an adjunct to the university," the society includes the papers of Washington Gladden and Warren G. Harding among its holdings.[49]

The Nebraska State Historical Society, in Lincoln, adjoins the campus of the University of Nebraska, whose history department considers the society's holdings part of its resources for graduate work.[50] In addition to Nebraska material, the society has a good collection of printed sources because of its program of exchanging publications with other historical societies. In this manner the Nebraska and Texas state historical societies and other such organizations have acquired the East Coast societies' extensive publications of colonial and revolutionary documents.[51] Aside from its printed sources for early American history and the manuscripts indirectly related to Nebraska, the society has little non-Nebraska material for the nineteenth century. The university's principal holdings in primary sources for this period are printed government documents. As a result of these limitations, James A. Rawley, a specialist in nineteenth-century history, tried to tailor his students' topics to fit the available resources. He preferred to have graduate students work on Congressional and presidential subjects.[52]

Although the capital of Missouri is Jefferson City, the state university and historical society are both in Columbia. In fact, the State Historical Society of Missouri is housed in the university library, along with the Western Historical Manuscripts Collection. These two collections provide graduate students with important Missouri and western sources.[53] The Harry S Truman Library in Independence, Missouri, is easily accessible to scholars at the Universities of Missouri and Kansas. Like the Franklin D. Roosevelt Library in Hyde Park, New York; the Herbert Hoover Library in West Branch, Iowa; and the Dwight D. Eisenhower Library in Abilene, Kansas, it houses the former President's papers and those of many officials related to his administration.

[49] Interview, *ibid.*
[50] Interview with James C. Olson, *ibid.*
[51] Interviews with Jack M. Sosin and David D. Van Tassel, *ibid.*
[52] Rawley, *ibid.*
[53] Interview with Richard S. Kirkendall, *ibid.*

These presidential libraries are operated by the National Archives and Records Service. To promote more systematic research in its collections, the Harry S Truman Library Institute appointed Donald R. McCoy of the University of Kansas its director of studies in April, 1967.

In Columbia, South Carolina, the state university and the archives are separated by only one block. Charles E. Lee, the state archivist, has been among the most active of his profession in promoting academic use of state archives. Students of George C. Rogers, Jr., a specialist in South Carolina history, worked at the archives constantly.[54] With the Tennessee State Library and Archives in Nashville, Vanderbilt University until just recently has not felt the necessity for obtaining manuscripts. Because the university was not involved in collecting, papers that ordinarily might have been sent to Vanderbilt went to the state archives. Graduate students at Vanderbilt have had no problem in gaining access to the state archives because the two institutions always have maintained a close relationship.[55] This relationship has been engendered by the fact that virtually all the professional staff at the archives, the Tennessee Historical Society, and the Tennessee Historical Commission are either graduates of or former professors from Vanderbilt. These agencies, incidentally, are intertwined in an astoundingly complex network.[56]

Universities that rely considerably on the resources of state historical societies are fortunate when these agencies' acquisitions art not limited to the state. For instance, the wide-ranging collecting program of the State Historical Society of Wisconsin enables graduate students at the university to do research on many topics unconnected with the state. But most state historical societies do, in fact, acquire only state-related material and consequently can support manuscript research only to this extent. When universities such as Vanderbilt have to depend on the manuscript sources of this kind of state historical society, they must, of course, use other types of original sources for research unrelated to the state. Dewey

[54] Rogers, *ibid.*
[55] Interview with Herbert Weaver, *ibid.*
[56] Cf. Ernst Posner, *American State Archives*, 255–61.

W. Grantham, Jr., described Vanderbilt as a good example of an institution that has relied perforce on printed original sources for topics not dealing with the state. Printed government documents have formed the basis for his students' research on non-Tennessee topics. Vanderbilt is too far from the great mass of manuscripts for its students to have easy access to them, so they use what is at hand.[57]

Many colleges with terminal M.A. programs in history have manuscript collections to support research by graduate students. These collections are usually regional in nature, with frequent emphasis on regional industry. The following examples illustrate such collecting policies. Stephen F. Austin State College, in Nacogdoches, Texas, has records from the East Texas lumber and oil industries and holds the Nacogdoches Archives, which includes the official records of the Republic of Texas. (It must be remembered that Texans have always taken their archives seriously. They fought the Archives War in 1842 when President Sam Houston tried to remove the Republic's records from Austin to Washington-on-the-Brazos.)[58] The college is also the depository for the East Texas Historical Association.[59] On the other side of the state, the Panhandle-Plains Museum, on the campus of West Texas State University, contains manuscripts related to that region.[60] In New Mexico, both New Mexico State University and New Mexico Highlands University have regional records. The latter's Arrott Collection emphasizes military records of the area.[61] Wichita State University and Western Michigan University likewise have regional manuscript collections.[62]

COLLECTING BY PRIVATE UNIVERSITIES

Just as state universities and colleges ordinarily gather material

[57] Interview, see Appendix C1.

[58] Dorman H. Winfrey, "The Archive Wars in Texas," *American Archivist*, Vol. XXIII, No. 4 (Oct., 1960), 431–37.

[59] Questionnaires returned by C. K. Chamberlain, chairman, Department of History, and Mildred Wyatt, librarian.

[60] Questionnaire returned by Lowell H. Harrison.

[61] Questionnaires returned by Sigurd Johansen and Lynn I. Perrigo.

[62] Questionnaires returned by William E. Unrau and Alan S. Brown.

related to the state or region in which they are located, private universities are likely to reflect their own particular interests or sponsorship in their collections. At Saint Louis University, a Jesuit institution, the collecting program has stressed materials related to the Roman Catholic church. It has records of Catholic missions to the Indians, including letters of Father Pierre DeSmet, and microfilms of Jesuit records from all over the United States as well as some from Rome.[63] The Vatican Film Library constitutes Saint Louis University's richest resource, although little of its material is related to United States history. Only a few of the university's doctoral students in United States history have based their research on microfilm from the Vatican.[64]

Just as Saint Louis University has Roman Catholic sources, other church-related institutions likewise have denominational material. The University of the Pacific and the University of Richmond have Methodist and Baptist records, respectively, and Brigham Young University has papers of prominent Mormons such as Senator Reed Smoot.[65] Similarly, institutions with a predominantly Negro student body such as Fisk University, Howard University, and Virginia State College hold manuscripts related to various phases of Negro history.[66]

University manuscript collections sometimes reflect the acquisition policy of the library more than the research interests of the department, as at Yale. This is especially true when libraries have independent endowments, which often obligate the institution to follow the collecting interests of the endower. Yale's Western Americana collection, the finest on the East Coast, comprises one of its greatest manuscript strengths. It includes the Wagner, Coe, and Streeter collections. The university also has significant manu-

[63] Interview with Martin F. Hasting, S.J., see Appendix C1.

[64] Interview with Lowrie J. Daly, S.J., director of the Vatican Film Library, see Appendix C2a.

[65] Interview with Leland D. Case, director, California Historical Foundation, University of the Pacific, *ibid*.; questionnaires returned by R. C. McDanel, University of Richmond, and Donald T. Schmidt, Brigham Young University.

[66] Interview with Henry L. Swint, see Appendix C1; questionnaires returned by Joseph H. Reason, Howard University, and Edgar A. Toppin, Virginia State College.

93

scripts for research in colonial history and twentieth-century American diplomatic history, including the papers of Colonel Edward M. House and Henry L. Stimson.[67]

√ The Princeton University library has a fairly large collection of historical manuscripts from the colonial period to the present, including papers of religious, educational, literary, political, and legal figures. Its great emphasis is currently on collecting papers for the Center for the Study of Twentieth Century American Statecraft and Public Policy. The center already has the papers of Adlai Stevenson, John Foster Dulles, and Bernard Baruch.[68]

Because of its specialization in the history of science and technology, the Case Institute of Technology defined its policy of collecting original sources along these lines. The most important component of Case's collection is the Archive of Contemporary Science and Technology, which aspires to contain pertinent material from the entire country. The institute supplements its manuscript holdings with microfilms of scientific papers from other depositories.[69]

Possibly America's most distinctive contribution to the world of music has been Dixieland jazz, coming originally from New Orleans. So that the historical record of this American musical idiom would be preserved, William R. Hogan, chairman of the department at Tulane University, obtained a Ford Foundation grant to establish the Archives of New Orleans Jazz at the university. The staff of the archives has interviewed between five and six hundred musicians and has collected approximately two thousand photographs and between six and eight thousand phonograph records. The manuscript aspect of the archives is limited, since most of the early jazz musicians were illiterate.[70] In the more

[67] Interviews with Leonard W. Labaree and Howard R. Lamar, see Appendix C1.

[68] Alexander P. Clark, *The Manuscript Collections of the Princeton University Library: An Introductory Survey* (Princeton, N.J., Princeton University Library, 1960).

[69] Interview with Melvin Kranzberg and Edwin T. Layton, see Appendix C1.

[70] Interview, *ibid.*

conventional realm of original sources, the university has strong collections relating to medical and southern history.[71]

COLLECTING DETERMINED BY RESEARCH INTERESTS

Frequently a university has a particular collection of papers because they relate to the research interest of a professor. In preparation for writing *Pills, Petticoats, and Plows: The Southern Country Store*, Thomas D. Clark accumulated extensive store records, which he later turned over to the University of Kentucky manuscript collection.[72] On a broader scale, the holdings of the Bancroft Library of the University of California at Berkeley reflect the research interests of Herbert E. Bolton, its director from 1916 to 1940. The library is especially strong in manuscripts and printed sources relating to the West Coast and the Spanish borderlands, where Bolton's research interests lay. Since the university bought the original collection from Hubert Howe Bancroft, the library's strengths were fairly well defined from the start. Under Bolton's guidance, however, many important acquisitions fortified its holdings pertaining to Western America and the Spanish borderlands. In addition to the material in the Bancroft Library, the Berkeley campus has manuscripts in the medical and law schools as well as in the archives on water resources.[73]

Established by Clarence W. Alvord as an outgrowth of his research interests, the Illinois Historical Survey at the University of Illinois, at Urbana, contains European documents dealing with the North American colonies and the diplomatic rivalries in the Mississippi Valley. These documents include manuscripts, printed and photocopied material, and typescript. Between the time of statehood and the Civil War, the survey material focused on Illinois, representing the research interests of Theodore Pease.

[71] Interviews with John Duffy, *ibid.*, and Connie G. Griffith, director, Manuscript Division, see Appendix C2a.

[72] Interview, see Appendix C1.

[73] Interview with A. Hunter Dupree, professor of history and former director of the Bancroft Library, see Appendix C1.

Because little has been added to the survey in recent years, Robert M. Sutton, its current director, recommended undertaking a new collecting venture within the established period of the survey. There are no immediate plans to extend its holdings beyond the Civil War.[74] Of the university's thirteen or fourteen manuscript collections, its most extensive is its archives, which relates entirely to university operations.[75] Professors frequently require that seminar students write papers based on materials located in these archives. In J. Leonard Bates's seminar in the spring of 1966, two out of thirteen students were using the archives. One was gathering information on civil rights in Urbana and the other on late nineteenth-century religious revivals. Both students used printed sources in addition to the archival material. Winton U. Solberg's seminar on higher education in the United States, 1850–1950, focused on the University of Illinois, and most of the students consequently did their research in the university archives. Among its printed sources, the university's collection of trade journals is outstanding.[76] Graduate students from Illinois have easy access to another important manuscript depository, the Illinois State Historical Society, in Springfield. Its 1,500,000 manuscript items relating to Illinois history are contained in 135 large collections, 2,000 small collections, and 808 bound manuscript volumes. The society also has 30,000 microfilm reels of newspapers and 400 reels of manuscripts. Half the society's researchers have been graduate students, two-thirds of whom are from the University of Illinois.[77]

Further evidence of how important collections of original sources sometimes have resulted from the research interests of various professors was found in the Social Welfare History Archives Center of the University of Minnesota. When Clarke A. Chambers conducted research for *Seedtime of Reform: American Social Service and Social Action*, he discovered that repositories were

[74] Sutton, *ibid*.

[75] Interview with University of Illinois library staff: R. B. Downs, dean of Library Administration; Thomas E. Ratcliffe, reference librarian; John Littlewood, documents librarian; and Maynard Brichford, university archivist, see Appendix C2a.

[76] Interviews with Bates and Solberg, see Appendix C1.

[77] Questionnaire returned by Paul Spence.

collecting two kinds of material—papers of famous men and papers of active reform groups. No agency was involved in collecting records of social service organizations, and these records were in places inaccessible to researchers. Chambers thought that these materials should be collected and cared for properly. His proposal that the University of Minnesota undertake such an archives project met with favor, and the university began approaching foundations. After receiving some negative responses, the institution tried a new tack. Miss Helen Hall, widow of Paul U. Kellogg, editor of *Survey* and *Survey Graphic*, leading organs of social reform and social service, interceded with the Russell Sage Foundation. It made an initial grant, and subsequently the National Institute of Mental Health allocated $135,000 to be spent over three years, beginning September 1, 1965. To qualify for this grant, the applicants had to prove that mental health was connected with social work, social work with history, and history with archives. The university provided the archives with space, supplies, personnel, overhead, and half-time graduate research assistants. Maxine B. Clapp, university archivist, directed the trained staff in processing the collections. An indication of the expense involved in establishing this center is the fact that it cost approximately $20,000 to process the *Survey* collection (125 linear feet).[78]

Some universities acquire important sources because the research interests of their professors are channeled into large-scale documentary editorial projects. The manuscript division of the Princeton library will be further enriched by the photocopies from the editorial work on the Woodrow Wilson papers. Arthur S. Link, editor-in-chief of *The Papers of Woodrow Wilson*, planned to turn over the first installment of photocopies after the fifth volume was published. The editorial project has relied primarily on photocopies of the original Wilson material.[79]

Similar editorial projects at other universities will provide or are providing original sources for graduate research. As the Dwight D. Eisenhower papers are published at Johns Hopkins, the de-

[78] Interview with Chambers, see Appendix C1.
[79] Link, *ibid*.

classified files at the presidential library in Abilene, Kansas, will be completely open to researchers. The editorial staff, headed by Alfred D. Chandler, Jr., has been making a detailed index and evaluation of the papers, which should prove a great help when finished. Microfilmed by the staff, the core of the Eisenhower collection is the files of both Ann Whitman, the former President's secretary, and Brigadier General Robert L. Schultz, his military aide at the White House and a personal aide later.[80] William G. McLoughlin, Jr., editor of the Isaac Backus papers, published at Brown University, has discouraged major research in these papers until the editorial work is done, but he has permitted students with minor projects to dip into the material.[81] At the University of Kentucky, where the papers of Henry Clay are being edited, students have had access to all available Clay material for their research. James F. Hopkins, editor of the papers, tried to assemble a comprehensive collection on microfilm and acquired copies from as far away as Switzerland, Hawaii, and Canada. In some of Hopkins' seminars, all students have worked on the Clay material.[82]

The foregoing projects involved letterpress publication, but at New York University the microfilm publication of the Albert Gallatin papers likewise provided original sources for graduate research. This project, cosponsored by the National Historical Publications Commission, involved in its initial stage a gathering of the extant photocopied Gallatin material, since the university had no originals.[83]

ALTERNATIVES TO MANUSCRIPT COLLECTING

Many universities, because of their location or the newness of their doctoral programs in history, have made little or no attempt to build significant manuscript collections. Rather, they have relied locally on printed and photocopied sources and have expected students to travel to use manuscripts, if necessary. David M.

[80] Chandler, *ibid.*
[81] McLoughlin, *ibid.*
[82] Hopkins, *ibid.*
[83] Interview with Bayrd Still, *ibid.*

Potter, chairman of the Stanford history department, said that his university became involved in the "big circle of research institutions too late to give priority to a major manuscript collection." Therefore, the department has advocated the university's developing a microfilm collection and not competing for scarce manuscripts. Its collecting program has stressed the acquisition of original sources such as newspaper files and census material to contribute to its general strength. Potter expected to have a good newspaper file on microfilm within a decade.[84]

Both the Los Angeles and Santa Barbara campuses of the University of California, being comparatively young, have better collections of printed and photocopied sources than manuscripts and will continue to emphasize acquiring the former. Like Stanford, UCLA has developed large files of microfilmed newspapers.[85] UCSB has emphasized acquiring photocopy rather than manuscripts to support its research program. Alexander DeConde, chairman of the UCSB department, said: "I am really not concerned with manuscript collecting here. I'd rather have thousands of letters on microfilm than a few rare items. I like material that can be used and is as accessible as possible to scholars and graduate students." As a result of this policy, UCSB acquired such photocopied series as the presidential papers from the Library of Congress, much of the National Archives microfilm, the Adams papers, and the Evans Early American Imprint Series. What enabled UCSB to offer a doctoral program, according to DeConde, was its specialization and its access to the library resources of other branches of the university. The Santa Barbara campus has a union catalog of holdings in the entire university system, can order material by wire from Berkeley and Los Angeles, and runs a bus to the latter city daily. Its graduate students have access to the library on any campus of the university. DeConde applauded the fact that copies of centralized library holdings, particularly microfilms, are available throughout the university system.[86]

84 Potter, *ibid.*
85 Interview with Theodore Saloutos, *ibid.*
86 DeConde, *ibid.*

The University of Connecticut has concentrated on building a collection of photocopied source materials to support its doctoral program in history, begun in 1961. In addition to having the Evans Series and the American Periodical Series (1800–1850), the library hoped to build a balanced microfilm collection of newspapers, state archival series, and presidential papers. Although the university has no manuscripts, it was organizing an archives for future acquisitions. Its printed sources consist of the standard government publications, a large portion of the Congressional serial set, recent publications of edited documents, and some out-of-print diaries, memoirs, and travel accounts.[87]

The new Ph.D. programs at Northern Illinois University and the State University of New York at Albany have similarly relied on photocopy and printed sources to support their graduate research.[88] One difficulty in inaugurating doctoral programs has been that libraries often were not geared to graduate research. While a university can get large quantities of photocopy quickly, a deficit in printed sources is difficult to overcome. For instance, Michigan State University was not a full government documents depository until 1947, and its collection of documents before that time is poor. It has no Congressional hearings before 1947 unless a professor made a special effort to get them. Madison Kuhn called this "our greatest lack of printed material. Our nineteenth-century periodicals are very poor, and we have come late into book buying. Until ten years ago, we bought only on an undergraduate college level, not as a major research library."[89]

Conversely, some institutions offering a terminal M.A. in history have systematically built research collections of photocopy and printed sources. Utah State University, an example of such institutions, has been a government depository since the 1890's and consequently has a full run of federal documents. Among its collection of photocopy are the Evans Series and national and Utah newspapers. For Utah and surrounding states, it has the

---

[87] Questionnaire returned by Robert W. Lougee.
[88] Questionnaires returned by Emory G. Evans and Kendall A. Birr.
[89] Interview, see Appendix C1.

photocopied *Early State Records*, territorial papers from the National Archives, and census papers.[90]

At the University of Hawaii there are insufficient original sources for research in "mainland" United States history. Hence, Herbert F. Margulies, departmental chairman, tried to impress his graduate students with the sense, rather than the substance, of scholarly research. Even if the original sources are "inadequate to arrive at definitive judgments, they can at least be suggestive if properly handled." He urged the use of biographies, autobiographies, and articles in scholarly journals. The thrust of the university's doctoral program is in Oriental and Pacific history, with American and European history offered as secondary fields. Any dissertations in the latter fields would probably have a Pacific focus. The university's first Ph.D. in United States history was awarded for a dissertation on the social and cultural history of Honolulu. For scholars doing research on Hawaiian topics, the state offers ample resources—the state archives, the Hawaiian Mission Children's Society, and the university library.[91]

SOME SPECIALISTS NOT DEPENDENT ON MANUSCRIPTS

Specialists in certain areas of American history, such as the colonial period and intellectual history, encounter comparatively little difficulty in obtaining original sources. The consensus that colonialists have a greater percentage of their primary sources available in print and photocopy than specialists in any other period holds because the great body of political literature has been published, largely by the historical societies of the East Coast. Some of the material was poorly edited, but old institutions, such as the University of Pennsylvania, that have had standing orders for these documentary publications are optimally equipped for research in the period. Richard S. Dunn pointed out that because the University of Pennsylvania acquired all such available material in the nineteenth century, it had a comparatively better collection then than now.[92]

[90] Questionnaire returned by S. George Ellsworth.
[91] Interview, see Appendix C1.   [92] Dunn, *ibid.*

Students at East Coast universities naturally have easier access to colonial manuscripts than those in other parts of the country, for only in isolated instances have tramontane repositories such as the Huntington Library acquired significant colonial manuscripts. The Huntington's Brock Collection contains important material on colonial Virginia.[93] Even if students of the colonial period are "on the wrong side of the mountains" to have manuscripts available locally, they suffer few handicaps, as professors at Vanderbilt University, Louisiana State University, and the University of Washington testified.[94] Various photocopy projects, such as the Evans Early American Imprint Series, published by the American Antiquarian Society; the Adams papers, published by the Massachusetts Historical Society; the American Periodical Series, sponsored by the William L. Clements Library and the Department of English at the University of Michigan; and the recent microfilm publications cosponsored by the National Historical Publications Commission and individual repositories, have enabled institutions anywhere in the country to conduct serious research in early American history.

Possibly students of intellectual history are in an even more fortunate situation, for "practically anything printed is an original source for them."[95] David W. Noble, a specialist in this field at the University of Minnesota, said that his students are lucky since the university has good printed holdings. The first dissertation he directed was based on novels of the Progressive period. Correspondence of the novelists under consideration had been published, so the student could do all his research on campus. Another of Noble's doctoral students used only materials available in the university library in writing on the attitude of radical Republicans toward labor. Two other students, writing on Walter Lippmann and William Allen White, respectively, did 90 per cent of their research in the published materials by the authors that were available at the university; the remaining research was based on per-

---

93 Interview with David Alan Williams, *ibid*.
94 Interviews with Douglas E. Leach, Don Higginbotham, and Max Savelle, *ibid*.
95 Interview with David W. Noble, *ibid*.

sonal papers housed at Yale and the Library of Congress.[96] Stow Persons, who agreed that "printed sources are the central material of intellectual history," noted the University of Iowa's large collection of printed material in American history. He considered books and journals most important.[97] David D. Van Tassel extended the purview of intellectual and cultural history by saying, "Practically everything is an original source."[98]

Closely akin to intellectual history in this respect is social history, but the types of sources used vary with the interests of individual practitioners and sometimes prove hard to come by. At the University of Texas, Robert C. Cotner devoted a seminar in social history to southern cities during the depression. Students did considerable research in newspapers, but the library's lack of the *New Orleans Times-Picayune* and the *Atlanta Constitution* since the 1920's precluded serious investigation of those cities. The library, instead of building to the strength of its southern newspaper collection, bought in new and diverse fields.[99] The seminarians collected data through interviews when appropriate, and if a student exhibited a flair for interviewing, Cotner invited him to participate in the university's oral history project dealing with the pioneers of Texas oil. This project, financed by the Walter B. Sharp Fund, contains more than 150 tape recordings.[100] Cotner had some success in getting undergraduates involved with research in their hometown data such as minutes of city council meetings, court records, newspapers, church records, and family memorabilia. If students found sources of more than routine value, the university encouraged the owners to permit it to photocopy the material for permanent retention.[101]

[96] *Ibid.*
[97] Persons, *ibid.*
[98] Van Tassel, *ibid.*
[99] Cotner, *ibid.* Professor Cotner wrote on Mar. 4, 1967, that since the interview, the library has purchased the *Atlanta Constitution* to 1951 and promises to complete the run. It has also brought its file of the *Wall Street Journal* up to date and made a large addition of Los Angeles newspapers.
[100] Robert C. Cotner and Peyton E. Cook, "Dudley Crawford Sharp—Secretary for Air," *East Texas Historical Journal*, Vol. II, No. 2 (Oct., 1964), 99.
[101] Interview with Cotner, above.

PROBLEMS OF COLLECTING

For those wishing to take new approaches to historical phenomena, the availability of original sources can pose serious problems. Donald Meyer has tried using psychological tools in historical analysis in the belief that they offer the only new insights, but he ascertained that few libraries have good resources for such an approach. The possibility of investigating the history of women and child rearing, a subject to which Meyer has devoted seminars, is good, since little has been done in this field so far. But for such research, historians need new types of materials such as letters of ordinary, undistinguished people and nonmetropolitan newspapers. In such newspapers "you get naïve raw material" that explains popular culture. Because original sources related to popular culture are fugitive or excessively local, Meyer wished that money could be spent to photocopy local newspapers on a mass basis.[102]

Since the accumulation of original sources is obviously based on conventional methods of research, any new approach is likely to be handicapped by the existing arrangement of material. Even if posing new questions causes problems, greater difficulty ensues when researchers and custodians of original sources are not agreed on the collecting policy of an institution. Allan G. Bogue commented that "the refusal of a perverse librarian to provide an adequate flow of manuscript accessions to support a respectable program of conventional graduate research helped to change the research orientation of two graduate seminars in the direction of quantification, given the local availability of state and federal legislative and election records."[103] At the University of Iowa the department urged the library to launch a systematic program for collecting historical manuscripts. "The department wants a full-time manuscripts man in the library, someone to seek out actively and aggressively, collate, and arrange manuscripts."[104]

[102] Meyer, *ibid.*

[103] "Fission or Fusion? Historians, Political Scientists and Quantification," paper delivered at the 1966 meeting of the American Political Science Association, pp. 10–11. A revision of the paper was published as "United States: The 'New' Political History," *loc. cit.*

Another type of collecting problem facing university libraries involves the rapid expansion of photocopy projects. Historians at Rutgers—The State University were divided in their opinions on the policy the library should follow. Richard P. McCormick, chairman of the department, posed the question of whether Ph.D.-granting institutions should try to acquire all the major photocopy publications or should rely on borrowing them through inter-library loan. "It doesn't seem to make lots of sense," he contended, "for all universities to acquire all the big photocopy sets. It would be more sensible to get these through interlibrary loan."[105] His colleague Lloyd C. Gardner countered that the university should not rely on borrowing original sources that would be used more efficiently if available on campus—even with the best of mailing and lending facilities.[106] Richard M. Brown found that the Rutgers library was reluctant to borrow material for seminar research, so he preferred having original sources at hand.[107]

Space limitations have been a factor in Northwestern University's program for collecting primary sources. Richard W. Leopold, departmental chairman, opposed the university's acquiring further manuscripts until the completion of its new library. The school purposely lagged behind in procuring photocopied material because of the lack of storage space in the library, both for material and for mechanical readers. These limitations will be overcome upon completion of the new library. The university's principal collections are the Charles G. Dawes and the Manasseh Cutler papers.[108]

Even when space or funds have not been factors, some departments have not encouraged the purchase of photocopied sources. Robert H. Ferrell, diplomatic historian at Indiana University, was opposed to his university's buying microfilmed State Department documents from the National Archives, for he thought any serious research in this material must be done in Washington. Because of

[104] Interview with Malcolm J. Rohrbough, see Appendix C1.
[105] McCormick, *ibid.*
[106] Gardner, *ibid.*
[107] Brown, *ibid.*
[108] Leopold, *ibid.*

the expense entailed in purchasing big runs of microfilm that may be used only once or twice a year, he preferred spending the money to send students to Washington. Ferrell particularly questioned the wisdom of buying the voluminous twentieth-century State Department files on film.[109]

Historians, faced with significant changes in their profession and society, should work closely with curators to see that appropriate original sources are being collected. As research needs and emphases change, as society demands new answers from the past in an effort to understand current involvements, historians and curators must ensure that basic research materials are available. Repositories should be systematically collecting data related to urban history and the Negro revolution sweeping the country. Such subjects offer good opportunities to institutions with new collecting programs. Historians using social and behavioral science techniques should make their needs, in terms of primary sources, known to curators. Many students of American political history are aware that the Inter-University Consortium for Political Research maintains data archives, but this centralized collection is merely a beginning. Sources susceptible to quantification abound throughout the country, often crudely organized and cared for. Researchers and curators must co-operate to ensure their preservation.

The great abundance of original sources in hundreds of repositories across the country should leave no resourceful, energetic graduate student wanting for research material. What he needs often might not be handy, but the Hamer *Guide* and the *National Union Catalog of Manuscript Collections* have vastly facilitated locating manuscripts. Except for students of colonial and intellectual history, who can rely largely on printed and photocopied sources, most doctoral students in United States history would not expect to find all their research material in their university libraries. Their use of nonacademic repositories has demonstrated

109 Ferrell, *ibid.*, and letter to author, Apr. 24, 1967. If researchers do come to the National Archives to consult records that have been filmed, the Archives expects them to use the film rather than the originals. This prevents further wear and tear on material that in some cases is quite fragile.

both their need for knowledge of the holdings of these repositories and the mutual dependence of the research community. As more institutions offer the doctorate in history and as the number of candidates increases, universities generally are giving serious attention to the adequacy of original sources to support the research of their doctoral candidates. The relationship between the availability of original sources and dissertation topics is the concern of the next chapter.

IV. Dissertation Topics

AN issue almost as troublesome to United States historians as the effectiveness of methodological training concerns the starting point for historical investigation. Ideally a person should approach a dissertation topic while simultaneously shaping the historical question and searching for sources holding the answers. But, in practice, students frequently begin the search from one point or the other—the question or the sources. Through the years many doctoral candidates have chosen their dissertation topics on the basis of available original sources. Whether this has been the traditional or conventional mode is debatable, but the criticism of this path of inquiry is pointed. Historical research, the critics say, should begin with the framing of important questions. Only after the historian has determined questions needing answers should he think about where he might find those answers. To choose a body of data as the basis for a dissertation without ascertaining whether it will answer relevant and meaningful questions is to blunt or pervert the thrust of historical research.

The inclination of historians to proceed from sources to topic quite likely reflects archival influences on the profession. This in turn would reflect the canons of scientific history: that the sources can be analyzed, evaluated, and meshed to re-create what actually happened. The great respect for and reliance on custodians of original sources by scientific historians lent weight to the former's evaluation of their material. Hence, if an archivist recommended material for research, historians were wont to be receptive. As the influence of Germanic history passed, historians became less inclined to make the location of a body of data their first step in research, although this procedure is by no means extinct.

Two comments precisely illustrate the conflicting viewpoints on the best method for beginning a dissertation. Thomas R. Adams, librarian of the John Carter Brown Library, stated: "My position is that the John Carter Brown Library collects printed material related to the history of America up to 1800 and that this material frames the historical questions to be asked. The vogue today seems to be for historians to frame their questions and then try and find sources that will answer these questions. I think it is a sounder procedure to locate a body of research material and then put questions to it."[1] Robert F. Berkhofer, Jr., of the University of Minnesota said: "My whole approach is to have students come up with a problem and then figure what they need to know to prove or disprove the problem. Then the evidence is marshalled. The material shouldn't determine the problem. The problem should come first. The search for original sources should come only after a meaningful problem has been identified. Fresh new material is not the place we need to begin—we should begin with significant questions."[2]

Closely related to this problem of where historical investigation should begin is the question of who should initiate it—the professor or the student. In one of his more cynical moments, Walter Prescott Webb advised prospective historians never to take an idea into graduate school.[3] His sarcasm found its target in the conventional practice of professors' assigning dissertation topics. However conventional this practice might have been in the 1920's when Webb was in graduate school, it is no longer necessarily the

[1] Interview, see Appendix C2a.
[2] Interview, see Appendix C1.
[3] "History as High Adventure," *American Historical Review*, Vol. LXIV, No. 2 (Jan., 1959), 265–81.

rule. While a graduate student naturally looks to his supervisor for guidance and direction and ordinarily works with a specialist because of his field, many professors are loath to assign exact topics for dissertations. They prefer that students work out their topics on the basis of their own interests and inclinations, and it is usually as a last resort that a professor specifies the subject. Some professors are philosophically opposed to assigned subjects, sometimes as a result of personal experience. Gilman M. Ostrander of Michigan State University encouraged graduate students to choose their own topics, largely because his assigned subject had taken two years out of his life.[4] Shaw Livermore, Jr., of the University of Michigan would not assign a dissertation topic, believing a student should determine his own research interests. "The dissertation is too important to a man's career to be chosen by a professor. I am happy, however, to talk at length about a dissertation topic with students."[5]

Certainly the choice of a dissertation topic is one of the most important decisions the graduate student faces, for it usually plays an important role in his subsequent professional life. Because of the specialty it represents, it can determine where the writer receives an appointment to teach, since departmental vacancies are normally in specified areas. Then if the dissertation can be converted into a book quickly, the man's career is off to a good start. Allan Nevins and Charles A. Barker emphatically recommended that their students conceive of dissertations as books, and "an astonishing number" of these have been published.[6] Usually a person's career travels in the direction indicated by his choice of a dissertation topic. A historian can, of course, work successfully in areas other than that of his dissertation, but such a change frequently demands extensive retooling. The delays and frustrations involved often work to the professional disadvantage of the man

4 Interview, see Appendix C1.

5 Livermore, *ibid.*

6 Nevins and Barker, *ibid.* Cf. J. Franklin Jameson's comments on the limitations of dissertations as books in Elizabeth Donnan and Leo F. Stock (eds.), *An Historian's World*, 221.

changing his tack. The importance of the choice of a dissertation topic should not, then, be underestimated.

Obviously many students depend on their supervisors to suggest dissertation topics. They choose to work with a professor because of interest in his field and because of his own investigations. Frequently these investigations reveal further areas needing inquiry—areas to be covered by dissertation research. Consequently students in Professor X's seminar choose a dissertation topic related to the theme of the seminar, as Webb once had students write on various aspects of the Great Frontier. With what one suspects to be increasing frequency, however, graduate students now are marching to a different drummer—they are deciding their own topics. These decisions seem to be based on one of two factors: the student's own background and experience or his access to original sources.[7]

TOPICS RELATED TO WRITER'S EXPERIENCE

The fact that students choose dissertation topics related to their personal experience is perhaps a sign of encouragement in the face of arguments by some social scientists that history has no utility. As long as students discern historical meaning in personal terms, the discipline should retain its vitality. And when history teachers—at all levels—can promote this discernment, there should be no fear for the place of history in the school curriculum.

Springing directly from her personal involvement in the New York City public schools was Selma C. Berrol's dissertation topic, "Immigrants at School: The Impact of the Immigrants upon the Public School System of New York City, 1898–1914." Mrs. Berrol's emotional interest in this problem resulted from being the child of immigrants, a product of the public schools, and a teacher in the city school system. One of the initial group of doctoral candidates at the City University of New York, Mrs. Berrol became aware of the sources for this subject through a paper she

[7] Graduate students did not enunciate the problem-before-sources philosophy held by many professors, although their failure to do so does not necessarily indicate their position in the matter. The interview technique may not have encouraged a response from students on this issue.

III

wrote on the topic for the 1840–60 period. Her most important sources included records of the Board of Education, to which she had easy access; annual reports and correspondence of the super-intendent of schools; and the Dillingham Report, consisting of some forty volumes resulting from the federal government's in-vestigation of immigrants between 1907 and 1911. Mrs. Berrol also explored the popular press and contemporary periodicals such as the Muckraker literature.[8]

With similar motivation, Gloria Creutz chose "Italian Immi-grants in California" as her dissertation topic at the University of Southern California. A descendant of Italian immigrants, she learned of the sources for her research through family conversa-tions. She used immigrant statistics, both American and Italian; immigrant correspondence; Roman Catholic church records; diaries, and such Italian-language newspapers as *La Chronica de San Francisco* and *L'Italo Americano*.[9]

Marilee S. Clore's dissertation at the University of Texas dealt with the organization and early activity of the League of Women Voters. Because of her interest in "the problem of women," she planned originally to study the image of women in Hollywood films, but abandoned that for a more manageable topic. Interest in the issue of women's suffrage, engendered by her suffragette grandmother, led to Mrs. Clore's topic. She researched the papers of famous suffragettes such as Florence Kelley and Jane Addams in addition to league papers at various state headquarters.[10]

Marilyn A. Domer, a student at Ball State University, in Muncie, Indiana, wanted a dissertation topic for which she could use her experience in social work and her background from a minor in sociology. She chose "The Development of Social Wel-fare and Social Planning in Middletown" as her subject because it incorporated her interests and because the necessary material was handy and available. Muncie is the Middletown of Robert S. and Helen M. Lynd's famous studies, which Miss Domer used

[8] Interview, see Appendix C3.
[9] Creutz, *ibid.*
[10] Clore, *ibid.*

as a point of departure. Her original sources included welfare department records, minutes and reports of Muncie agencies involved with welfare, and local newspapers.[11]

Graduate history students who had been in the armed forces frequently chose dissertation subjects related to that experience. Ronald L. Jones wrote a master's thesis on United States military aid to Latin America from 1945 to '59 and projected his dissertation as "The Problem of Uruguayan Military Technology." He became interested in the master's topic while on exchange naval duty with Brazil and Chile, which entailed training Brazilian and Chilean crews on destroyers that the American government was turning over to their countries. This training made him aware of the following sources for the thesis: printed records of the Lend-Lease Board and of the State Department's Munitions Office and Foreign Liquidation Commission; Congressional hearings of the foreign relations, appropriations, and defense committees; the *Congressional Record*; various State Department publications; and the Truman and Eisenhower volumes of *The Public Papers of the Presidents*.[12]

An Air Force officer on active duty, Major Paul A. Whelan, chose "The History of the Third Air Division in World War II" as his dissertation topic at Saint Louis University. He selected this subject in consultation with Albert J. Simpson, chief of the Air Force historical division, who thought it logical for Air Force officers working on doctorates in history to use such topics for dissertations. The individual would benefit by getting a topic and the Air Force would recover a segment of its past. Whelan had his pick of the air divisions and chose the Third because it has the most dramatic history. Its records fill thirty-five file cabinets in the archives of the Air University at Maxwell Air Force Base, Alabama. Whelan put the division in its command perspective by doing research in the records of the Eighth Air Force Headquarters and the British bomber command.[13]

11 Domer, *ibid.*
12 Jones, *ibid.*
13 Whelan, *ibid.*

Graduate history students with legal training often want to bring that training and interest to bear on their dissertation subjects. While studying law in Japan, Yasuhide Kawashima became attracted to legal history. As a doctoral candidate at the University of California at Santa Barbara, he wrote his dissertation on "Massachusetts Law and the American Indians, 1689–1763." Most of his primary sources consisted of Massachusetts county court records, and he visited courthouses and microfilmed appropriate material.[14]

While taking a law degree at Stanford University, Robert M. Ireland became familiar with the original sources he later employed at the University of Nebraska in writing his dissertation. As his topic, Ireland selected the legal career of William Pinckney because he wanted to study an early lawyer, an area in which little research has been done. Ireland agreed with David Alan Williams that certain nineteenth-century biographies that quote important documents related to this subject are faulty by current standards but valuable since they reproduce many of the primary sources.[15] Ireland consulted two such books about Pinckney and also considered as one of his best sources those reports of the Maryland courts located in the University of Nebraska library. Like so many other early political and legal documents, they are printed. The Pinckney manuscripts consist of eight to ten pieces in each of these repositories, all of which Ireland visited: the Maryland Hall of Records, the Maryland Historical Society, the Historical Society of Pennsylvania, Harvard University, the Massachusetts Historical Society, and the New-York Historical Society.[16]

It should be no surprise when graduate history students at the University of Utah select dissertation topics related to Mormonism, since the Church of Jesus Christ of Latter-day Saints has been the dominant factor in the history of the territory and state. Even the title of Floyd A. O'Neil's dissertation, "The Non-Mormons in Utah," indicated the dominance of Mormon culture and the

[14] Kawashima, *ibid*.
[15] Cf. Chap. III, n. 19.
[16] Interview, see Appendix C3.

accommodation Gentiles had to make to it. Many of the non-Mormons were European immigrants who worked Utah's mines, and the study concentrated on their experience in mining communities. O'Neil grew up in a mining camp among minority groups and thereby gained firsthand knowledge of some of the sources for his study. He interviewed European immigrants and their children and examined mining journals, reports, and newspapers. Another important source was the papers of a Utah Protestant missionary society which tried to convert the Mormons. O'Neil described their effort as a "colossal failure." The records he used most extensively were those Department of Justice files in the National Archives that deal with Utah.[17]

Charles Peterson, another graduate student at the University of Utah, wrote on "The Mormon Settlement of the Little Colorado Basin in Northern Arizona." The topic was personal, since Peterson's family was involved in this settlement, and his knowledge of the original sources derived from his interest, as a Mormon, in genealogy. The sources consisted of journals and diaries of original settlers and church leaders in Salt Lake City, as well as correspondence between them and local officials. Many of his data came from the Office of the Latter-day Saints Church Historian, but he also collected much information from family genealogical societies, including his own.[18]

An amateur interest in painting led Roy A. Kotynek, graduate student at Northwestern University, to his dissertation subject, "Alfred Stieglitz and the Introduction of Modern Art to America." In the course of his master's work, he took a research seminar with Ray A. Billington, who encouraged him to write a paper on the Chicago Armory Show of 1913. While conducting this research, Kotynek found frequent references to Stieglitz, the master photographer who sponsored modern art in his gallery. His interest aroused, Kotynek consulted the Hamer *Guide* and discovered the Stieglitz archives at Yale. An article on this collection in the 1951 *Yale Library Gazette* convinced Kotynek that there was

[17] O'Neil, *ibid.*
[18] Peterson, *ibid.*

enough material on Stieglitz for his dissertation. The Yale collection proved to be the most important source for Kotynek, who also researched the Newberry Library's Sherwood Anderson collection for its Stieglitz letters.[19]

Although deciding dissertation topics on a personal basis may have utilitarian motives and rewards, it may not result in the broad cultivation optimal in graduate history training. From the standpoint of acquiring wide scholarly knowledge and experience, dissertation writers probably should not devote themselves to topics intimately related to their own experience, whether it be military, religious, economic, or whatever. This avoidance would remove the taint of parochialism and special pleading.

TOPICS RELATED TO ACCESSIBLE SOURCES

In many cases the choice of a dissertation topic has been directly related to the accessibility of original sources. Sometimes this occurred through necessity, and sometimes it was a matter of fortuity or coincidence. One reason that doctoral candidates have been inclined to choose subjects for which the sources are easily available is the pressure to finish the dissertation within a limited time. Sidney I. Pomerantz, a member of the graduate history faculty of the City University of New York, decried this approach of those "who are in a hurry to finish their degree. . . . Historical questions should be framed first and research should not be done on the basis of what sources are available."[20] With increasing concern being expressed over the length of time the average doctoral candidate takes in earning the Ph.D., it is doubtful whether general support could be mustered for any cause contributing to a more leisurely pace.[21] The correlation between

[19] Kotynek, *ibid.*

[20] Interview, see Appendix C1.

[21] Cf. Dexter Perkins and John L. Snell, *The Education of Historians in the United States*, 203–205. The Ford Foundation recently made grants to ten universities to enable them to streamline the Ph.D. program in the humanities and social sciences. The University of Chicago received an initial three-year grant of $1,045,000 and expects to get another $3,000,000 over the next seven years. It plans to concentrate support during the period when doctoral candidates are doing research and writing dissertations. (*University of Chicago Newsletter*, Vol. II, No. 2 [June 26, 1967].)

the procedure of choosing a topic on the basis of an important historical question and the time involved in writing the dissertation should not, however, necessarily generate delay.

The frequency with which dissertations and theses result from the convenient availability of a body of papers indicates that the profession, brooking the criticism, obviously countenances this approach. Many dissertations come about because of the combination of the availability of sources and some specific desire to have them used. Harry Eisenman's dissertation, "Charles Francis Brush—Pioneer, Innovator in Electrical Engineering," is an example. C. Baldwin Sawyer, a friend of Brush's son and founder of Brush Laboratories, wanted someone to write a scholarly study of Brush, inventor of the arc lamp, and established a fellowship at the Case Institute of Technology for this purpose. The fellowship included money for arranging the Brush papers and doing the research. As a Case graduate student, Eisenman fell heir to the project. His undergraduate major in electrical engineering gave him technical competence to deal with this subject.[22]

Another instance of official sponsorship of graduate research was the master's thesis Lyman Moody Simms, Jr., wrote at the University of Virginia. A faculty committee hired him to make a study of the university's du Pont endowment, and he later used this study as the basis of his thesis. Philip F. du Pont gave the University of Virginia an endowment of six million dollars in 1928, specifying that half should be used for student aid. This was the largest sum given by an individual donor to any American state university. The du Pont study had to be handled with care, for the donor had been expelled from the university for a prank. Despite the sensitive issues involved, Simms was allowed free access to minutes of meetings of the faculty and board of directors and was able to examine pertinent sources. Simms reported that he said some damaging things about the state government and the university, but "nothing was cut. I was asked to tone down three statements on du Pont, but this was constructive criticism."[23]

[22] Interview with Eisenman, see Appendix C3.
[23] Simms, *ibid.*

Sister Mary Christine Taylor is an example of a doctoral candidate who worked on a dissertation after becoming established in college teaching. She based her study on a body of records convenient to her teaching post in upper New York, far away from Saint Louis University, where she was enrolled. Her dissertation, "Foundations of Catholicism in Northern New York," derived substantially from the records of the Ogdensburg diocese, founded in 1872, and the archives of the Quebec diocese, which sent many early missionaries into the area. Having organized the Ogdensburg diocesan archives, she had good knowledge of their contents. Through the bishop, she sent a questionnaire to 118 pastors, who furnished information based on the original baptismal and marriage records of their parishes. She found the bishop extremely co-operative in helping her gather data, and she was allowed to photocopy anything she needed from the diocesan archives. To put her topic in proper perspective, Sister Mary Christine also conducted research in the archdiocesan archives in Baltimore and New York City as well as in the diocesan archives in Albany. For the historical geography of the region, she used Geological Survey records, county atlases, and county histories.[24]

A doctoral candidate unsure of where he will be when he does dissertation research should choose a topic on the basis of sources that would be generally available. This was the consideration of Constance B. Schulz, a University of Cincinnati graduate student who planned to go with her husband wherever he might be employed. Consequently, she chose a comparative study of American political deists, concentrating on Adams and Jefferson—a subject for which she could easily find the necessary printed sources.[25]

Another graduate student at the University of Cincinnati illustrated the reverse of the foregoing situation. Since James M. Morris found it difficult to travel with his five children, he wanted a topic on which he could do all the research in Cincinnati. Being interested in labor history, he chose "The History of Organized Labor in Cincinnati." With the exception of the Molders Interna-

24 Taylor, *ibid.*
25 Schulz, *ibid.*

tional, the unions co-operated in letting him use their records. He researched the local files of the Brotherhood of Railway and Steamship Clerks; the Hotel and Restaurant Employees and Bartenders' International Union; the International Union of United Brewery, Cereal, Soft Drink and Distillery Workers of America; and the Metal Polishers, Buffers, Platers, and Helpers. Local labor publications as well as newspapers also constituted important sources for him.[26]

With some students, a dissertation subject rests not upon the availability of a particular body of sources but upon the total assets of a repository. The choice of the repository, then, precedes that of a topic and is usually based on its convenience. Since the student decides to do his research in the general area which the repository's holdings would support, the actual topic is delimited by the holdings. Milton O. Gustafson, a graduate student at the University of Nebraska, had his first taste of manuscript research when David Cronon took his seminar students to the Truman Library. After Gustafson had used that library for research on his master's thesis, he decided that it would be the main resource for his dissertation. He conferred with the library director, Philip C. Brooks, about dissertation possibilities and selected "Congress and Foreign Aid, the First Phase, UNRRA, 1943–47." Although he found the bulk of his sources at the Truman Library, Gustafson also visited the United Nations archives, for the United Nations Relief and Rehabilitation Administration records; the National Archives; the Library of Congress; and the Roosevelt Library.[27]

On occasion, graduate students have chosen particular dissertation topics in the mistaken belief that they would have easy access to their sources. Such was the case of Keith Shumway, who wrote "A History of the Chicago Church Federation, 1907–1940" at the University of Chicago. Knowing some of the people in the federation, he had no trouble being allowed to use the records, but he found them in "terrible condition." He had to dig much of the

[26] Morris, *ibid.*
[27] Gustafson, *ibid.*

material out of basements, and it was completely unorganized.[28]

The problem of gaining access to sensitive materials can be highly frustrating to the researcher, but as some of the foregoing examples attest, graduate students frequently are permitted to use such sources. Sometimes they are able to do so because custodians are unwilling to take the trouble to enforce restrictions. When Bobby W. Saucier was an undergraduate at the University of Southern Mississippi, he learned that the university had the Theodore G. Bilbo papers. As a graduate student at Tulane University, he decided to write his dissertation on Bilbo's senatorial career and undertook the task of gaining access to the congressman's papers. He found that the Bilbo heirs had stipulated that before researchers could see the materials, the president of the University of Southern Mississippi had to examine the collection, consisting of about one million pieces, to remove anything that might reflect on, or cause embarrassment to, any living person. When Saucier studied the papers, he found that the president had not inspected the entire collection. Saucier was not allowed to photocopy any documents, and any time he worked in the papers a library employee had to be present. The library was willing for him to take notes by dictating documents on a tape recorder.[29]

The researcher can be hindered seriously when denied access to pertinent material in collections. For a seminar paper on Ann Arbor during the depression, David M. Katzman, a graduate student at the University of Michigan, wanted to use records of local realtors. He discovered that the realtors' sensitivity about providing housing for half the Michigan student body caused them to suspect any historical investigation. Katzman was able to use the papers of the Chamber of Commerce and the Community Fund, however.[30]

Among the greatest frustrations to researchers are restrictions on access to classified documents of the federal government. Richard Dalfiume felt that the army threw roadblocks in his way

[28] Shumway, *ibid.*
[29] Saucier, *ibid.*
[30] Katzman, *ibid.*

at every turn when he was doing research for "Desegregation of the Armed Forces, 1940–1953," his University of Missouri dissertation. Initially, the army was reluctant for him to become involved with the project. Like everyone else working in classified records, he had to be fingerprinted for a security clearance. He found that all records related to integration or segregation had been classified secret, not because national security was involved, but because they dealt with a sensitive issue. To gain access to some important files, he had to call on Missouri's Senator Edward Long for assistance. The army warned Dalfiume that he would have trouble getting the dissertation cleared by its Office of the Chief of Information, even after he had been given access to the records.[31] Such clearance is required when any portion of a secondary work is based on classified files.

SOURCES FOUND IN PREVIOUS RESEARCH

As the foregoing discussion of the ways and reasons students have chosen dissertation topics demonstrates, many choices were based on knowledge of the requisite primary sources. This knowledge can derive from the individual's background, from efforts to promote the use of a body of records, or from general awareness of accessible sources. Frequently, however, students came to identify sources for dissertations through their previous research on seminar papers and theses. Another means by which students learned of sources was through employment in research collections. When the choice of a dissertation topic was not the result of previous knowledge of sources, students used several means to investigate and locate needed material. However dedicated their professors may have been to considering the problem before considering the sources, the students' final choices of topics usually rested upon the decision that sufficient primary sources existed for their purposes. They made this determination by studying the bibliographies and footnotes in secondary works related to the subject, by consulting appropriate finding aids such as the Hamer *Guide* and the *National Union Catalog of Manuscript Collections,*

[31] Dalfiume, *ibid.*

or by consulting the supervising professor. As a rule, students ordinarily employed all these means in locating their material.

Frequently the kernels of dissertations lay in students' research papers. At Columbia University, Michael Wallace's dissertation, dealing with political parties between Jackson and the Civil War, began as a short colloquium paper on the Albany regency. He found that the subject had considerable potential, especially in the areas of two-party ideology and party loyalty, and expanded the paper into a master's thesis. With the encouragement of Richard Hofstadter, he extended the thesis into a dissertation. The history faculty at Columbia encouraged students to save time by developing research interests in this manner.[32] Two graduate students at the City University of New York similarly expanded earlier projects into dissertations. Gerald Kurland's topic, "Seth Low: A Study of the Progressive Mind," began as a seminar paper, which then resulted in a master's thesis. Vincent J. Flanagan was encouraged by his supervising professor, Hans Trefousse, to develop his thesis on Gouverneur Kemble Warren into a full biography.[33] Graduate students from universities around the country confirmed this common practice of expanding theses into dissertations and thereby taking advantage of intimate knowledge of the original sources from previous research.[34]

Another means by which graduate students became acquainted on their own with source materials they later chose for dissertations was through employment in research collections. Students who worked for the Division of Manuscripts of the University of Oklahoma, the Clements Library and the Michigan Historical Collections at the University of Michigan, and the Cincinnati Historical Society commented that they became interested in their dissertation topics by first getting to know the related original sources.[35] William A. Baughin, a University of Cincinnati

[32] Wallace, *ibid.*
[33] Kurland and Flanagan, *ibid.*
[34] Interviews with Orval G. Clanton, Carl E. Skeen, Dale Holman, Graham D. Taylor, Edward L. Weldon, Lorna Sylvester, and John D. Unruh, Jr., *ibid.*
[35] Interviews with Howard L. Meredith, Albert T. Klyberg, Richard M. Doolen, and William A. Baughin, *ibid.*

graduate student who worked at the Cincinnati Historical Society, selected his topic in a somewhat involved fashion. While helping Murray Seasongood edit his autobiography, Baughin obtained access to the Seasongood papers for his dissertation, a critical biography of the Progressive Cincinnati politician. The society subsequently persuaded Seasongood to donate the four hundred boxes of papers to it, and Baughin arranged and cataloged them.[36]

Bibliographical work also can provide students with knowledge of original sources. When Standley W. Claussen was a senior research analyst for the Hispanic-American Research Project at the University of California at Los Angeles, he compiled a bibliography of English, Portuguese, and Spanish sources related to Hispanic-American studies. From this work he grew interested in the sources and chose to write on "The Black Legend of Spain in American Thought, 1790–1830."[37] From a bibliography he developed for a methods course at the University of Illinois, Lloyd E. Ambrosius became familiar with the sources he used for his dissertation on "The United States and the Weimar Republic."[38]

SOURCES FOUND THROUGH SECONDARY WORKS

A fairly standard practice followed by graduate students in locating original sources for their dissertations has been to check the footnotes and bibliographies of secondary works related to the proposed topic.[39] The procedures used by Selma C. Berrol and Glen L. Nutter illustrate the practice. Both studied the sources cited by Lawrence Cremin in *The Transformation of the School* for their dissertations on "Immigrants at School: The Impact of the Immigrants upon the Public School System of New York City, 1898–1914," and "The *New Republic* and Its Relation to Progressive Education, 1914–30," respectively.[40]

For his dissertation on "The Origin and Passage of the Lend-

[36] Baughin, *ibid.*
[37] Claussen, *ibid.*
[38] Ambrosius, *ibid.*
[39] Interviews with James R. Sharp, Lynn Hales, Ian Mugridge, Roy Bird, Joseph Maizlish, Kenneth Smith, D. Terry Boughner, William Dirk Raat, James C. Curtis, and James L. Lancaster, *ibid.*
[40] Berrol and Nutter, *ibid.*

Lease Act," Warren F. Kimball began compiling his list of sources by going to the best secondary works such as Langer and Gleason and "pirating the footnotes."[41] George E. Frakes checked the footnotes of good secondary works on South Carolina for information on sources for his study of "The Origin and Development of the Legislative Committee System in the Royal Period of South Carolina, 1721–1776." These secondary works included books by David D. Wallace, Jack P. Greene, Hennig Cohen, and J. Harold Easterby.[42] Footnotes in the five volumes of the edited papers of William Gilmore Simms provided Jon L. Wakelyn with a starting point for compiling a list of primary sources for his dissertation, "A Political Study of William Gilmore Simms' Career." He also consulted the bibliography of Oscar Wegelin's book on Simms.[43] In departments where professors assigned written projects on similar and related topics, students searching for original sources often profited from consulting the bibliographies of dissertations previously submitted. Richard M. McMurry, writing on the "Atlanta Campaign of 1864" at Emory University, and Robert C. Carriker, working on "Camp Supply: Frontier Outpost on the Southern Plains" at the University of Oklahoma, found this to be the case.[44]

SOURCES FOUND THROUGH GUIDES

Graduate students also frequently used finding aids and subject bibliographies to discover primary sources. Until publication of Philip M. Hamer's *A Guide to Archives and Manuscripts in the United States* in 1961, there was no finding aid that achieved general, national coverage of these materials. The next year saw publication of the initial volume of the *National Union Catalog of Manuscript Collections* (*NUCMC*). Subsequently, graduate students have made extensive use of these finding aids.[45] The

---

41 Kimball, *ibid.*
42 Frakes, *ibid.*
43 Wakelyn, *ibid.*
44 McMurry and Carriker, *ibid.*
45 Interviews with Lisle A. Rose, W. Wayne Smith, Norman Crockett, Robert M. Ireland, and Richard A. Andrews, *ibid.*

guides to secondary literature that graduate history students have used most frequently are the *Harvard Guide* and *Writings on American History*.[46] For bibliographical information on specific topics in specialized fields, students turned to such publications as Henrietta M. Larson's *Guide to Business History*,[47] Monroe N. Work's *Bibliography of the Negro in Africa and America*, the United States Bureau of Labor Statistics' *Negroes in the United States*, or Paul Lewinson's *A Guide to Documents in the National Archives for Negro Studies*.[48]

SOURCES IDENTIFIED BY PROFESSORS

The influence professors exerted on graduate students was often evident not only in the choice of dissertation topics but also in the way students learned of the related original sources. Frequently a professor suggested both topic and sources. Sometimes students received such advice from professors who were not supervising their dissertations, and sometimes one professor suggested the topic and another the sources. William R. Hogan, chairman of the department at Tulane University, suggested that James Breeden, a graduate student, write a dissertation based on the papers of Joseph Jones, located in the Tulane Medical School. The resulting topic was "Joseph Jones, Confederate Surgeon, 1861–65," and John Duffy, the university's specialist in the history of medicine and public health, directed the dissertation. Hogan also informed Breeden that the archives at Louisiana State University contain approximately three thousand Jones items, and Breeden found other Jones papers at the University of Georgia through *NUCMC*.[49]

At the University of Kentucky, Robert P. Hay's dissertation was "A Jubilee for Free Men: The Fourth of July 1776–1876." His interest in the topic was stimulated by his adviser, Paul C. Nagel, who had used Fourth of July orations in his own research

[46] Interviews with W. Wayne Smith, Jon L. Wakelyn, H. Warren Gardner, and Joseph M. Hawes, *ibid*.
[47] Crockett, above.
[48] Interview with John D. Finney, *ibid*.
[49] Breeden, *ibid*.

and could therefore direct Hay to appropriate sources. These consisted primarily of newspapers and pamphlets. Patriotic orations, Hay found, were usually published in newspapers in the West and as pamphlets in the East.[50]

S. David Buice, a graduate student at the University of Oklahoma, had his topic suggested by one professor and sources by another. Arthur H. DeRosier, Jr., the supervising professor, knowing Buice's interest in southern history and reconstruction, indicated "History of Reconstruction in Indian Territory" as a suitable subject. Arrell M. Gibson pointed out some important sources at the university, and Buice found others through studying Gibson's *Guide to Regional Manuscript Collections in the Division of Manuscripts University of Oklahoma Library*. Buice then traced other material through the bibliographies and footnotes of secondary works.[51]

For his Michigan State University dissertation on Standard Oil investments in China from 1895 until 1914, Barry Knight had most of his original sources mapped out by his adviser, Paul Varg. When Varg was doing research on missionaries in China, he became interested in the impact of American investments there and learned the sources. Knight's two principal bodies of material were the Standard Oil archives in New York City and the records of the Baldwin Locomotive Company. He also consulted the major trade publications of the period.[52]

John C. James's dissertation at Johns Hopkins University on the history of financing late nineteenth-century railroads was based on private archives of various railroads, manuscripts of financiers, federal and state reports, and financial press reviews. His adviser, Alfred D. Chandler, Jr., told him the types of material to use, and James developed the project with an eye to available sources.[53]

Professors frequently have offered as much assistance to master's thesis writers as to doctoral candidates in locating original sources.

[50] Hay, *ibid.*
[51] Buice, *ibid.*
[52] Knight, *ibid.*
[53] James, *ibid.*

Students working on theses at Emory University, the University of North Carolina, the University of Southern Mississippi, and George Washington University commented that their supervisors directed them to the necessary sources. One noted that his adviser, John Gonzalez of the University of Southern Mississippi, insisted that the student try to find his own material and would make suggestions only when the researcher had gone as far as he could.[54]

As many of the foregoing examples have documented, the processes of choosing a topic for a dissertation and locating the requisite original sources were rarely compartmentalized or the result of a single line of investigation. To a large extent, a topic choice came about because of the interaction of several factors: specialties and interests of professors, backgrounds and interests of candidates, and knowledge of the accessibility of primary sources. Similarly, graduate students rarely relied on only one method of locating their sources. They did not find their original sources through just their own research, their employment, bibliographies and footnotes in secondary works, finding aids, or professors. The search became more a matter of using all available means of tracking down appropriate material. This chapter has indicated several ways students learned about sources. Although these ways overlap and supplement each other, one represented the initial mode of investigation. The others followed.

[54] Interviews with Philip Racine (thesis at Emory University under M. Eugene Sirmans on the confiscation of Loyalist property in the back country of South Carolina), Margaret L. Neustadt (thesis at University of North Carolina under George B. Tindall on Lucy Randolph Mason), Neil R. McMillen (thesis at University of Southern Mississippi under John Gonzalez on the American reaction to the rise of Nazi Germany, 1933–34), and James H. Holmes (thesis at George Washington University under Howard M. Merriman on "Naval Government of Alaska, 1879–84"), *ibid.*

V. Local Sources

FOR some years there has been a tendency to identify local sources, such as deeds, wills, and tax, court, voting, business, and church records, with antiquarianism and genealogy. Many professional historians have shunned this type of material, thinking it lacked significance. Graduate supervisors have often been reluctant for doctoral candidates to become involved with local topics because of the problems of getting such dissertations published as books.[1] However well a candidate writes on a topic of limited appeal or importance, his chances of publication remain slight; and since books are the milestones on the path to success in the profession, the graduate student should be concerned with the possibilities of publishing his dissertation.

As any thoughtful historian knows, it is a great mistake to equate local history and local sources with antiquarianism. Since the early days of the profession in this country, some historians have treated local topics with sensitivity and sophistication. Frederick Jackson Turner was fascinated with the local particulars that invested the larger historical canvas with meaning. Although serious local historians between Turner's and more recent times may have felt their work was insufficiently appreciated by the

[1] Interview with Fletcher M. Green, see Appendix C1.

profession, today they can take genuine pride in some of the contributions of this genre, such as Sumner Chilton Powell's study of Sudbury, Massachusetts, and Benjamin W. Labaree's and Stephan Thernstrom's studies of Newburyport, Massachusetts.

As historians have applied the elaborate methodology of the social and behavioral sciences to local sources, which lend themselves so well to this treatment, both the sources and the field of local history have become enhanced in the eyes of the profession. By no means, however, are these sources the special province of the quantifiers, for they can be used meaningfully by the serious humanistic historian. Representatives of the latter group seem especially sensitive to the neglect of local sources. Arthur Bestor, who expressed substantial reservations about the usefulness of quantification in history, thought that the profession has used local sources insufficiently. When he taught the methods course at the University of Illinois, he took students to the courthouse and state archives to introduce them to such material.[2] At the University of North Carolina, Fletcher M. Green and Hugh T. Lefler agreed that historians have been remiss in using local sources.[3] Lefler said that the types of sources on which Jackson T. Main based *Social Structure of Revolutionary America*—inventories of probate records, tax lists, travel accounts, account books, and diaries—have not been used enough. "Of all sources used by American historians, local records are the most neglected."[4]

In addition to the dominantly national viewpoint of American historians, a reason for the neglect of local sources, according to two state archivists, has been that professors often were unfamiliar with the sources or did not understand how they can be used. "Except for newspapers, only a few professors in California are acquainted with . . . local records."[5] According to the South Carolina archivist, a specialist in the British Empire preferred that his students use "official documents" rather than wills and land

[2] Bestor, *ibid.*
[3] Green and Lefler, *ibid.*
[4] Lefler, *ibid.*
[5] Interview with W. N. Davis, Jr., historian, California State Archives, see Appendix C2b.

grants. This professor did not seem to understand that such instruments were just as "official" as documents emanating from England and "just as important in illustrating imperial administration."[6]

Another reason for the insufficient exploitation of local sources is that they frequently are fragmented. Since the records do not reflect a coherent or unified picture, students often have difficulty filling in the gaps. A student writing a master's thesis at Ohio University undertook to use the kind of sources Merle Curti investigated in his study of Trempealeau County, Wisconsin, but the uneven coverage of records thwarted him. The records of the board of education of one town covered one time period, the vestry records from another town covered a different period, and so on.[7] This experience pointed up the necessity for the researcher to have some assurance that the sources available are commensurate with the topic. Conversely, one should feel sure that the importance of a local topic justifies working with the source material available; historians should not devote years of research to a topic of limited significance just because of an amplitude of records.

A further problem in using local sources—as the very term implies—is their location. One of the profession's most diligent advocates of local sources, Robert E. Brown of Michigan State University, said, "You can get at these sources only at the places where they exist in the original—largely in the county courthouses." He also noted that because of the special conditions any given type of local source reflects, as many different types as possible should be used so that the researcher can make the proper correlations.[8] W. Frank Craven of Princeton University also commented on the problem of reaching local sources, which his students use considerably. Since it is hard for students in seminars to leave the university for research with original local sources, he preferred that students use them after they have completed

[6] Interview with Charles E. Lee, director of the South Carolina Archives Department, *ibid.*
[7] Interview with Harry R. Stevens, see Appendix C1.
[8] Brown, *ibid.*

courses and are working on dissertations. One of his students wrote a dissertation on Dedham, Massachusetts, which had published three volumes of its town records. The student supplemented research in these printed sources with work in Dedham on church and other records.[9] Although the use of local sources may pose problems of distance on the East Coast, these are magnified when the distances increase, as in Texas. When William R. Hogan did research on the social history of the Republic of Texas, he examined records in twenty-four county courthouses, though it was difficult to visit the various locales.[10]

In addition to having to use local sources "endemically," a further problem may involve the condition of the sources. If the custodial agency has neglected its responsibilities, the sources may be unusable when found, and too often records have simply been thrown away. New York City, for example, has discarded so many of its municipal records that the researcher may be at a severe disadvantage. Moreover, according to Robert D. Cross, "The City Archives is not a co-operative agency."[11] Because of the city's attitude toward its records, several historians and other interested persons formed the Institute for Early New York City History to bring pressure for the preservation of municipal documents. The institute's work was a major factor in persuading Mayor John Lindsay to establish a task force for this purpose.[12] Irrespective of how well municipal records are kept, their mass— like that of federal government records—challenges the researcher to extract meaningful data from the chaff. Louis C. Hunter dealt with this problem directly in his American University seminar on the industrialization of the city. He discussed techniques for finding pertinent historical data in American city records, which seminar members used almost exclusively.[13]

Despite problems of accessibility and maintenance of local

[9] Craven, *ibid.*
[10] Hogan, *ibid.*
[11] Cross, *ibid.*
[12] Interview with Julius M. Bloch, *ibid.* See "Group is Formed to Save Archives," *New York Times* (July 9, 1966), p. L29.
[13] Interview with Stephen Coe, see Appendix C3.

sources and despite some professional insensitivity to them, these sources are popular in many quarters and students have used them "emphatically."[14] These sources have not only been used emphatically, but enthusiastically, as the following comments indicate. Barnes F. Lathrop described himself as a "great patriot on these local sources."[15] George C. Rogers, Jr., said: "These local sources are my favorite—I've just become wild about them." He and his students studied South Carolina wills, inventories of personal property, newspapers, tax records, church records, and similar sources. As state chairman for the collection of voting data for the Inter-University Consortium for Political Research (ICPR), he amassed considerable data, which one of his students analyzed. Rogers demonstrated to his seminar how these local sources could be utilized. His own interest in local history grew out of his writing the history of Georgetown County, a "dry run" for his history of South Carolina.[16]

Graduate history students at Yale University "just go wild with these local sources, particularly for the colonial and early national periods," declared Howard R. Lamar. Their enthusiasm has been kindled by the university's location in New England, where the sources are available and accessible.[17] William G. McLoughlin, Jr., of Brown University confirmed that in New England these sources are excellent and easy to reach. "We can get to any New England sources through the state archives and local historical societies."[18] Bernard Bailyn said that his students at Harvard have used any local sources they could lay their hands on. He saw a growing interest in demographic history, involving much detailed work in local sources, and thought that some of the most interesting dissertations were being based on them.[19]

Among the most enthusiastic champions of local sources have been the quantifiers, who ordinarily employ measurement as an

[14] Interview with Henry L. Swint, see Appendix C1.
[15] Lathrop, *ibid.*
[16] Rogers, *ibid.*
[17] Lamar, *ibid.*
[18] McLoughlin, *ibid.*
[19] Bailyn, *ibid.*

aid in understanding human behavior. Since wills, inventories, deeds, and tax, voting, and court records lend themselves to quantification and reflect important behavioral patterns, they naturally have come into vogue. J. Rogers Hollingsworth said that these local sources are the kinds of materials his students at the University of Wisconsin used most frequently. He directed students to local history because of his conviction that scholars need to understand the social structure of communities and their uniqueness before much progress can be made in grasping the larger issues of history. Nonetheless, local history should be studied within the context of the larger issues.[20] Sam B. Warner, Jr., whose work in urban history has been highly statistical, said, "In the long run we'll all be using these local sources."[21]

In areas where local sources are easily available, historians are likely to use them extensively. In addition to New England, Cincinnati and Denver are places where historians have capitalized on material at hand. Master's candidates at the University of Cincinnati have concentrated on local sources.[22] "We've had theses," said Daniel R. Beaver, "on everything from early wine growing in Cincinnati to Hiram Powers."[23] Although in Denver the local sources, especially the official city and county records, are not always well organized, students at the University of Denver have used them heavily.[24]

Several of the newer doctoral programs, in stressing regional, state, and local history, have relied almost exclusively on nearby sources. Usually these institutions are not well endowed with original sources, and their graduate students must seize any materials they can get. History departments at the University of Mississippi, Washington State University, Texas Technological College, and the University of Hawaii have all promoted research

[20] Hollingsworth, *ibid.*

[21] Warner, *ibid.*

[22] Interview with Thomas N. Bonner, *ibid.*

[23] Beaver, *ibid.*

[24] Interviews with Michael McGiffert, Allen D. Breck, and Theodore R. Crane, *ibid.*

in local sources.[25] While the emphasis has usually been related to the availability of local sources, this has not always been the case. The popularity of local history in Hawaii results from its evocation of the romance and excitement of the monarchy, international intrigue, and the state's multiracial heritage.[26] At Texas Technological College in Lubbock, physical isolation led to emphasis on regional history, but the college has made great efforts to provide its students with ample resources in the Southwest Collection. As one professor put it, Texas Tech has an anomalous situation in that most of its graduate history students, regardless of their field, wind up doing research in Southwest materials.[27]

When universities confess their limitations of inadequate research resources by emphasizing local history and relying on nearby sources, the profession can react in one of two ways. It can contend that such universities ought not attempt doctoral work in history, or it can take the position that the nation's demands for college history teachers justify the existence of these programs. In the latter case, the profession should make these confessions of limited resources the basis for urgent requests to the federal government and foundations for grants to bolster institutional holdings of original sources. If funds become available to acquire sources related to a variety of American and European and certain other non-American areas, proper training could be offered without the stringent restriction of relying on local sources for doctoral research. Surely higher education is enough of a national asset to warrant adequate support for worthy doctoral programs.

To the extent that colleges and universities offering a terminal master's degree in history are less well endowed with a variety of original sources than universities offering the doctorate, their history departments have urged graduate students to use convenient local sources. Some of these institutions, like their senior counter-

<hr>

[25] Questionnaires returned by Joseph O. Baylen, University of Mississippi, and George A. Frykman, Washington State University; interviews with Lawrence L. Graves and Cedric B. Cowing, see Appendix C1.

[26] Cowing, above.

[27] Interview with Seymour V. Connor, *ibid.*

parts, have made efforts to collect local and regional sources to facilitate students' research. Representative of such institutions is West Texas State University, whose Panhandle-Plains Museum collects local sources. Almost half the master's candidates there have used local sources in writing theses. At the College of William and Mary, whose students have access to the resources of Colonial Williamsburg, local sources have been consulted for approximately two-thirds of the theses.[28]

The following table, compiled from interviews, shows the types of local sources graduate students used in their research and the number using each type. Of the 169 graduate students interviewed, 34 reported no research in local sources.

Newspapers	78	Military records	3
Court records	22	Town records	3
Business records	20	Architectural records	2
Voting records	20	Interviews	2
Church records	18	County histories	1
Wills	12	Union records	1
Deeds	7	Photographs	1
Local censuses	3	Artistic evidence	1
Local manuscripts	3	City directories	1

GENEALOGICAL RESEARCH

Historians may not have used local sources more systematically and effectively because they felt that the materials have been pre-empted by genealogists, whose work historians are inclined to disparage. This disparagement results largely from the quality of much genealogical work and the unfortunate impressions created by those who pursue genealogy to qualify for membership in exclusive patriotic and hereditary organizations. Although many genealogists undertake their research because of a genuine curiosity about the past and with a desire to transmit family records to

[28] Questionnaires returned by Lowell H. Harrison, West Texas State University; William W. Abbot, College of William and Mary; Rupert N. Richardson, Hardin-Simmons University; Sigurd Johansen, New Mexico State University; William D. Metz, University of Rhode Island; John L. Shover, San Francisco State College.

their children, some others have engendered suspicion by their Brahmin attitudes. Moreover, historians are wont to deprecate genealogy, feeling that serious research should deal with topics demonstrably more significant than most family trees.[29]

One important exception must be made to this general attitude of historians toward genealogy, and that concerns the work of the Church of Jesus Christ of Latter-day Saints. Members of this church, the Mormons, pursue their genealogical work for theological reasons rather than to aggrandize their forebears or themselves. They believe that baptism, according to the ordinance of their church, is essential to salvation. With the great Mormon emphasis on the cohesiveness and integrity of the family unit, it becomes important to living Mormons that baptism and marriage rites be performed by proper authority to ensure the salvation of their ancestors who died outside the Mormon church, so that the entire family may be reunited in celestial glory. This salvation of the dead and other rites may be achieved vicariously. A Latter-day Saint who identifies an unbaptized ancestor may go to one of the church's temples to receive the sacrament of baptism for the ancestor. The scriptural basis for this practice is Paul's question to the Corinthians, "Why are they then baptized for the dead?" (I Cor. 15:29), indicating this as a practice of primitive Christians. So that they may identify and earn salvation for as many ancestors as possible, Mormons have been involved in vast genealogical work. In 1894 the church established the Latter-day Saints Genealogical Society in Salt Lake City to co-ordinate this work, which has entailed world-wide microfilming of local sources containing demographic data. By 1967, the society had accumulated approximately half a million rolls of microfilm. In preserving and making this material available for historical research, the Church of Jesus Christ of Latter-day Saints performs a splendid service for which historians can be thankful.

[29] For illuminating treatments of family history, see Lester J. Cappon, *Genealogy, Handmaid of History*, No. 17, Special Publications of the National Genealogical Society; and Philip J. Greven, Jr., "Historical Demography and Colonial America," *William and Mary Quarterly*, 3rd Series, Vol. XXIV, No. 3 (July, 1967), 438–54.

Among those who commented on the benefits of the Mormon genealogical projects were Clarence L. Ver Steeg and Kenneth M. Stampp. Ver Steeg's students have worked on microfilmed genealogical records from representative counties in the colonies, sometimes taking random samples. He encouraged them to use the records for specific data.[30] Stampp found the Mormons' genealogical microfilm project "most valuable."[31] Numerous repositories across the country have microfilm copies of local records because of having co-operated with the Mormons in obtaining access to the records for filming. For example, the University of Kentucky library acquired its collection of Kentucky wills, deeds, and marriage records in a co-operative project with the Mormons.[32] In Georgia the state archives sponsored the microfilming of county records by the Mormons in return for a copy of each film. Two-thirds of the county records of Georgia have now been microfilmed by the Mormons.[33] Similarly, the Mormons microfilmed most of the Virginia county records and provided the state archives with copies.[34]

Despite the profession's generally disparaging attitude toward genealogy, some historians, as the foregoing examples illustrate, are aware of the contributions genealogy can make to historical investigation and appreciate the spade work done by diligent "head-hunters." This appreciation is not limited to those who have benefited from Mormon activity. David S. Sparks, a Civil War specialist at the University of Maryland, predicted that "local history, properly construed and related to national problems, will be the emphasis of the future. I firmly believe we must learn how to use these local sources as well as genealogy. Genealogy has received a bad name from its amateur practitioners. But historians should pay far more attention to the relationships that can be

[30] Interview with Ver Steeg, see Appendix C1.

[31] Stampp, *ibid*.

[32] Interview with Stuart Forth, director; Jacqueline Bull, Manuscripts curator; Kate Irvine, Reference librarian; Rebekah Harleston, Government Documents librarian, see Appendix C2a.

[33] Interview with Ruth Corry, head of research, Georgia State Archives, see Appendix C2b.

[34] Interview with David Alan Williams, see Appendix C1.

established through a scholarly approach to genealogy."[35] Merrill Jensen urged his students at the University of Wisconsin to consult genealogies as well as town records, tax records, newspapers, and court records. He called genealogy "invaluable" for research in the eighteenth century, since it enables one to trace important family connections.[36]

Many archivists and librarians with local sources in their custody have discovered that genealogists make far greater, and often more effective, use of these sources than historians.[37] The director of the South Carolina Archives said that about nine times more genealogists than historians have used his holdings. The ratio would be reversed, however, for the man-hours spent in research.[38] Although records in the National Archives are not local sources, many of them contain demographic data valuable for genealogists. Among the State Department sources, the appointment and passport records have been studied by genealogists but not by graduate history students.[39] Sherrod East said the quality of genealogical research in the National Archives has improved considerably in the last few years. "We find that genealogists using these local records are using them in a more scholarly manner than historians using the same records. . . . There is too much deprecation of genealogists by historians."[40]

NEWSPAPERS

Newspapers constitute an important research source of both local and general information for graduate history students. While historians can use any number of metropolitan dailies as a source of national and international data, they show an understandable preference for the *New York Times*. Aside from the *Times* and a very few other large dailies, though, historians research newspapers as a local source. They have used newspapers in preference

[35] Sparks, *ibid*.
[36] Jensen, *ibid*.
[37] Interviews with Jacqueline Bull, see Appendix C2a; Colton Storm, Sherrod East, Julia B. Carroll, Charles E. Lee, and Harriett C. Owsley, see Appendix C2b.
[38] Lee, above.
[39] Carroll, above.
[40] East, above.

to other types of sources because newspapers are easily available and accessible and because of comparatively good bibliographical control over them. Although newspapers have shortcomings as historical sources, they do not present problems of legibility as handwritten documents do, and their chronological arrangement facilitates research.

The testimony of supervising professors plus the documentation in theses, dissertations, articles, and books established without question that graduate students and their seniors in the profession have researched newspapers diligently.[41] This diligence has resulted perhaps from the fact that newspapers may present the only evidence available and in a convenient form. Unless the historian has some way of evaluating newspaper data, however, he risks accepting information at face value that is likely imprecise or untrue.

Although such pitfalls confront all those employing newspapers as a local source, only a few historians commented specifically on them. When John Hope Franklin's seminar students at the University of Chicago have been unfamiliar with newspapers as a historical source, he has discussed the characteristics of nineteenth-century journalism they should know. He dealt with editorial bias, journalists' commitments, and influence of advertisers.[42] Chase C. Mooney of Indiana University termed newspapers "absolutely essential, but not for public opinion surveys. They need to be used for factual information."[43] The difficulty with writing history from newspaper sources, contended Gabriel Kolko, is that it results in refined journalism. Accordingly, he is not a "strong believer" in relying heavily on journalistic sources.[44] Morris Rieger, who for fifteen years was head of the labor and transportation

[41] Interviews with John R. Alden, Daniel W. Hollis, James Harvey Young, James Z. Rabun, Peter P. Hill, Donald F. Carmony, Carl G. Anthon, J. Leonard Bates, J. Joseph Huthmacher, David A. Shannon, Charles G. Sellers, Jr., David M. Potter, Barnes F. Lathrop, Robert F. Berkhofer, Jr., Arthur H. DeRosier, Jr., Richard D. Younger, Allen J. Going, and Robert E. Moody, see Appendix C1; Enid T. Thompson and John Knowlton, see Appendix C2b; questionnaire returned by John K. Mahon, University of Florida.
[42] Interview, see Appendix C1.
[43] Mooney, *ibid.*
[44] Kolko, *ibid.*

branch of the National Archives, testified that researchers have overemphasized newspaper accounts of strikes and union development. Newspaper reports of strikes are "highly unreliable in large part." Until the last few years, labor historians depended largely on printed sources such as the labor press and reports of union conventions, neglecting the extensive trade-union records in various parts of the country. With historians and archivists making conscious efforts to describe union archives and retire them to suitable repositories, however, researchers are relying more on these manuscript sources than on newspaper accounts.[45] James P. Shenton and Richard A. Bartlett commented that students require a different kind of caution for newspaper research. They need to establish strict limits for their research project and not follow the natural inclination to become distracted by interesting tidbits.[46]

Although the local topics for which newspapers can furnish information are limitless, some sense of the variety of uses historians have found for newspapers may be gained from the following examples. A student of Richard S. Kirkendall based a paper on city planning in Columbia, Missouri, largely on newspapers.[47] Neil R. McMillen, writing a dissertation on white citizens' councils, derived much of his data from the clipping files of the Southern Educational Reporting Service. This service, financed by the Ford Foundation, was established to collect information on race relations. Initially, it gathered journalistic reports on southern reactions to the 1954 Supreme Court decision on school integration.[48] For his dissertation on "Desegregation of the Armed Forces, 1940–1953," Richard Dalfiume researched Negro newspapers to determine Negro opinion on this topic. He used the *Pittsburgh Courier, Norfolk Journal and Guide, Chicago*

[45] Interview with Rieger, director, National African Guide Project, National Archives, see Appendix C2b.

[46] Interviews, see Appendix C1.

[47] Kirkendall, *ibid*.

[48] Interviews with McMillen, see Appendix C3; and Dewey W. Grantham, Jr., see Appendix C1.

Defender, and *Baltimore Afro-American* as well as the clipping files in the Truman Library.[49] Ronnie Tyler found that a Mexican newspaper, with all its shortcomings, gave him valuable leads for material in the Texas Archives. An account in a Mexican paper misspelled Anglo names atrociously, but when Tyler transliterated the names, he found leads to pertinent documents in the archives.[50] In his research on Frederick Law Olmsted, Charles C. McLaughlin of American University discovered that through newspapers he could often document oblique references in Olmsted's letters. He called newspapers "supremely helpful" for the Olmsted project.[51] For his dissertation on lawlessness in the West, Barton C. Olsen considered newspapers a "material source." His study of Montana newspapers revealed a great interest in that state in cultural activities. Olsen concluded that the stereotype of the wild and woolly frontier missed the mark a good bit.[52] Patrick B. Nolan's dissertation on a related subject, "Law and Order and Outlaws on the Upper Mississippi Valley Frontier," relied on newspapers as the major source.[53]

Robert P. Hay called newspapers his primary source of information on Fourth of July orations. His dissertation dealt with the celebration of the holiday during the first century of the nation's independence.[54] A dissertation dealing directly with ways the press reflected public sentiment obviously makes newspapers the basis of research. For his dissertation on "The Catholic Press Reaction to Nativism, 1840–60," Robert F. Hueston incorporated research in approximately 130 Catholic serials and found that one difficulty was that the runs were mostly fragmentary.[55] For his dissertation on "Courts for the New Nation: A History of Federal Judiciary, 1787–1800," Dwight F. Henderson was unable to examine court records for each state. To fill this research gap, he studied newspapers, but only after discussing the pitfalls of this technique with his major professor, Barnes F. Lathrop.[56]

[49] Interview, see Appendix C3.
[50] Tyler, *ibid.*
[51] Interview, see Appendix C1.
[52] Interview, see Appendix C3.
[53] Nolan, *ibid.*
[54] Hay, *ibid.*
[55] Hueston, *ibid.*
[56] Henderson, *ibid.*

COURT RECORDS

As L. H. Butterfield commented in his preface to the *Legal Papers of John Adams*, the writing of American legal history has had little relation to the social and economic affairs of the people. Except for legislative and constitutional history, legal history in a broader sense has been undernourished.[57] A recent surge of interest in legal records indicates that historians have become aware that these sources may yield data for a wide variety of subjects. The exploitation of these records by nonlegal historians may even broaden the traditionally narrow scope of legal historians.

Court records, like other types of local sources, have excited considerable emotion and enthusiasm among historians who have used them. Graduate students are not more conversant with court records, Philip D. Jordan contended, because most professors have not been inside courthouses except to complain about their taxes and most historians have a blind spot concerning legal records.[58] Among American historians, students of the colonial period are particularly aware of the value of court records. Aubrey C. Land said, "Court records probably constitute the most valuable local source we have." He thought students shun them because of their dryness, technical language, and repetitiveness. He agreed with Jack M. Sosin and Clarence L. Ver Steeg that court records can be extremely rich in social and economic information and explained that in two weeks students can learn to identify types of action, to distinguish between parts of a set of proceedings, and to find and extract historical data.[59]

Any researcher's reaction to the ease with which a particular type of record may be used obviously arises from personal experience, and experiences differ markedly when it comes to court records. Land said that these records, which have hardly been touched, are well preserved because of their official nature.[60]

[57] L. Kinvin Wroth and Hiller B. Zobel (eds.), *Legal Papers of John Adams*, I, xix.
[58] Interview, see Appendix C1.
[59] Interviews, *ibid.*
[60] Land, above.

Similarly, Yasuhide Kawashima, who derived 80 per cent of the research material for his dissertation from the Massachusetts county courthouses, found the records well organized.[61] Alden T. Vaughan was not so much impressed with the arrangement and preservation of court records he has encountered. He said that the principal complaint of his students using court records was that the records were frequently in poor condition.[62] Sydney V. James, Jr., also found fault with the maintenance of the records but was "very emotional" about advocating more work in local sources and found court records especially valuable. "There is much more in them than most historians seem to realize." Because of his involvement with Rhode Island court records, James offered suggestions about how these records—or similar ones —may best be preserved. He felt that they should be rearranged and microfilmed before they disintegrate. The film should be accompanied by a descriptive catalog with extensive cross-references. As James explained, court records, narrowly defined, give the nature of the action (shown by type of writ or indictment), the parties, the verdict, and such extras as posting bond for appeal; but they give little of the substance of the dispute, which can only be found in file papers. Those materials likely include miscellaneous documents of historical interest, which the researcher should be able to identify from a catalog without skimming the entire records. "I find myself," said James, "wishing for a printed check list of cases with simple indications of substances of dispute and notations of [unexpected] documents, accompanied by a microfilm of the formal record and file papers." Such microfilm and finding aids would make available a variety of original sources, appealing to researchers with different interests, such as legal, social, and economic historians as well as genealogists.[63]

Concern with court records is by no means restricted to colonial specialists. A graduate student whose interests in colonial and frontier history fused in his dissertation, "The Dissenting Sects on

[61] Interview, see Appendix C3.
[62] Interviews, see Appendix C1.
[63] James, *ibid.*

143

the Southern Colonial Frontier, 1720–1770," traced the litigious involvements of parsons through court records. Some of these records were printed in publications of the Daughters of the American Revolution and some in state and county historical journals.[64] John L. Loos and Clark C. Spence, both in the field of western American history, encouraged their students to use court records. Loos considered these materials an extremely rich source because they often give the historical background of a case.[65] When Spence taught the methods course at the University of Illinois, he, like Arthur Bestor, took students to the courthouse to expose them to the types of historical records available.[66] In writing his master's thesis on J. Ross Browne, David Goodman unearthed "an amazing amount" of relevant data in the Alameda, California, courthouse. He used probate records, accounts of real estate transactions, and city directories.[67] His thesis, written at the University of Arizona, was published as a book in 1966.[68] For his work in business and economic history, Vincent P. Carosso termed court records "most helpful." Important antitrust cases have been tried in the Southern District Court of New York, and these records provided valuable historical data.[69] As a practitioner of legal and constitutional history, Paul L. Murphy had his students use court records extensively. One student, following the myth-or-reality approach, wrote a dissertation about a Wyoming community. For a microcosmic study of this type, he found court records highly revealing.[70]

DEEDS

Deeds contain specific and localized information for the researcher, but have not been exploited by historians for the variety of facts they offer. In addition to being of manifest importance to

[64] Interview with H. Warren Gardner, see Appendix C3.
[65] Interview, see Appendix C1.
[66] Spence, *ibid.*
[67] Interview, see Appendix C3.
[68] David Goodman, *A Western Panorama, 1849–1875: The Travels, the Writings, and the Influence of J. Ross Browne.*
[69] Interview, see Appendix C1.
[70] Murphy, *ibid.*

the biographer, this type of legal record is valuable to the resourceful historian for worthwhile nonbiographical data. Perhaps it was no coincidence that two of the survey's three specific examples of the use of deeds involved historians with legal training. Robert M. Ireland, in his dissertation on the legal career of William Pinckney, used deeds to determine Pinckney's wealth and involvement in property litigation.[71] For his dissertation on "Massachusetts Law and the American Indians, 1689–1763," Yasuhide Kawashima established through deeds the pattern of property settlements when Indians turned land over to whites.[72] Students working on immigration activities have found deeds in the Southwest Collection at Texas Technological College highly useful.[73]

WILLS

Another kind of legal record that may reveal considerable local information, especially of an economic nature, is the will. Like deeds, wills are most obviously useful for biographical data, but the imaginative historian can derive other types of important facts from them. In his dissertation on Mormon settlement in northern Arizona, Charles Peterson employed wills as a means of analyzing Mormon attitudes toward property. Since the Latter-day Saints, along with other nineteenth-century millenialists, expected the imminent advent of Christ, this expectation was logically reflected in their views on property, which are expressed in the wills.[74] Gloria Creutz investigated wills to determine the difference between the economic activity of Italian immigrants in California and those elsewhere in the United States. Besides wills, she used deeds and records of the Garibaldina Society, an Italian fraternal organization.[75] H. Warren Gardner, a graduate student at the University of Kansas, discovered that wills can give insight into a man's philosophy of life, for example, by showing how he dealt with what might properly be left to his illegitimate children.[76] At

[71] Interview, see Appendix C3.
[72] Kawashima, *ibid*.
[73] Interview with Roy Sylvan Dunn, see Appendix C2a.
[74] Interview, see Appendix C3.
[75] Creutz, *ibid*.
[76] Gardner, *ibid*.

the Harvard Graduate School of Business Administration, which has emphasized the case study as a teaching device, a case analyzed in the business history course dealt with the will of Robert Keayne, a Boston merchant in the 1630's and 1640's. Business historians strongly believe in the use of such local sources.[77] In his own work, Thomas D. Clark has employed a variety of local sources and has encouraged his students to do likewise. One student worked with wills to construct the economic and social framework of a Kentucky county. Clark advocated that the profession make much greater use of all local sources than it has.[78]

For a project in historical sleuthing, Raymond P. Stearns asked a student at the University of Illinois to investigate wills to identify the Hugh Jones who wrote *The Present State of Virginia* in 1716.[79] As informative as wills may be, the historian researching them and other such documents in areas with any concentration of famous men is likely to be foiled by the actions of an earlier generation of autograph hunters. Richard S. Dunn commented that research with wills at the Philadelphia courthouse is difficult because many signatures have been cut out.[80] Such deletions could, of course, provide the occasion for sharpening historians' deductive powers.

TAX RECORDS

As an indication of economic activity or status, tax records furnish information related to a variety of historical interests. Researchers whose interests cover anything taxable—individual income or property, corporate activity, trade and commerce, real estate transactions, *ad infinitum*—find that tax records serve as a fairly reliable economic gauge. Researchers naturally must make allowances for inequitable tax rates and most consider the rates in conjunction with other economic indicators. Urban historians have considered tax records important in tracing the physical growth of cities, dating buildings, and reflecting economic activ-

[77] Interview with Arthur M. Johnson, see Appendix C1.
[78] Clark, *ibid*.
[79] Stearns, *ibid*.
[80] Dunn, *ibid*.

ity. Such records also establish the economic, and often social, status of individuals.[81] Students in Robert C. Cotner's seminar on the southern city in the Great Depression used tax records extensively to determine the impact of the depression on urban economies and activities.[82] For his dissertation on Portland as a case study for growth in the Far West, Paul G. Merriam derived information from city and county tax records as well as from the census and reports from the board of trade.[83]

Where taxes were intended to regulate economic activity, the records indicate fairly accurately the volume of business so controlled. Such measurement was essential in Jimmie L. Franklin's dissertation, "A History of Prohibition in Oklahoma, 1907–1959." He investigated the federal internal revenue records in Oklahoma City to determine how many persons in the state bought federal liquor stamps during state prohibition. The great number of stamp purchasers gave an index to the amount of bootlegging. After Oklahoma made the purchase of 3.2 beer legal in 1933, state tax records revealed the quantity of beer bought, and presumably consumed, by Sooners. Franklin found tax records easy to use, since they were usually printed.[84] Alan Calmes, in writing a dissertation on the economic history of rice plantations in the eighteenth century, employed tax records extensively. Such materials are a great boon to anyone doing research on that period, for "the eighteenth-century tax records itemized everything."[85]

In some cases, local sources are of obvious value in historical research, but frequently graduate students are unaware of the important information a particular type of record may reveal. At Rutgers—The State University, Donald A. Sinclair, curator of special collections, and H. Gilbert Kelley, reference librarian, noticed that students do not come to the special collections for specific sources, but with specific problems. Sinclair and Kelley suggested

[81] Interview with Bayrd Still, *ibid.*
[82] Cotner, *ibid.*
[83] Interview, see Appendix C3.
[84] Franklin, *ibid.*
[85] Calmes, *ibid.*

how local sources such as tax records can answer students' questions and how the sources can be used.[86]

VOTING RECORDS

Recently the great interest in political behavior and quantification—usually operating in tandem—has generated much research with voting records. The interest has ranged from presidential elections to Congressional roll calls down to precinct matters, so voting records of the most local nature have received their share of attention, along with those pertaining to national affairs. Around the country, many professors and archivists have cooperated to report voting statistics to the Inter-University Consortium for Political Research (ICPR) in Ann Arbor, Michigan. Each state chairman was responsible for reporting his state's voting statistics to the ICPR, which put them in its data bank. In South Carolina, George C. Rogers, Jr., had graduate students cull voting records from state newspapers,[87] and other state chairmen have done likewise. Librarians at Columbia University and the University of Michigan commented on the heavy use of their voting records by scholars associated with the ICPR. Columbia has the records of the Congressional vote analysis conducted there in the 1930's by the Works Progress Administration, and the ICPR wished to put these records on the computer.[88] Appropriately, students at the University of Michigan combed the library's collection of voting records for reports to the nearby ICPR. Agnes N. Tysse, head of the library's reference department, said, "Voting records of all kinds are much sought after and used."[89]

Research in voting records depends upon the form in which they are available. The State Historical Society of Wisconsin, which includes the state archives, has a fine set of official county returns for Wisconsin elections from 1836 onward. Scholars have easy access to these records and have used them with and without

86 Interviews, see Appendix C2a.
87 Interview with E. L. Inabinett, director, South Caroliniana Library, *ibid*.
88 Interview with Roland Baughman, head of Special Collections, Columbia University library, *ibid*.
89 Tysse, *ibid*.

computers.[90] In Ohio, where voting records are under the control of the Secretary of State, students have gotten the best service if they consulted that official to gain access to the records.[91] Donald F. Danker reported that at the Nebraska State Historical Society, where he was historian, most research in voting records was done through newspapers. Aside from this source, the society's voting records consist of the published reports of canvassing boards.[92] Students in Utah have had no difficulty securing permission to use state election returns, and many undergraduates there have made good use of voting records in honors theses.[93]

BUSINESS RECORDS

The most extensive collection of business records in the country is housed in the Baker Library of the Harvard Graduate School of Business Administration (HGSBA), and the Business History Group of the HGSBA has been responsible for much of the important writing in this field in recent years. Since the HGSBA does not offer an advanced degree in business history, the group's activities, aside from an elective course and a seminar for candidates for advanced business degrees, have most often involved visiting postdoctoral, rather than graduate, history students.[94] Aside from the considerable impact the group's program has had on the writing of business history, the most direct contribution the HGSBA has made to training graduate students in business history has been through its collection of business records, both manuscripts and printed.

To the extent that use of business manuscripts reflects the influence of the HGSBA on graduate training in business history, the following statistics indicate that this influence has been more extra- than intramural. Students in the HGSBA have constituted one-tenth of the users of business manuscripts in the Baker Li-

[90] Interview with Leslie H. Fishel, Jr., director, see Appendix C2b.

[91] Interview with Ruth Erlandson, consultant for library research, Ohio State University library, see Appendix C2a.

[92] Interview, see Appendix C2b.

[93] Interview with Alfred A. Cave, see Appendix C1.

[94] Interview with Arthur M. Johnson, *ibid.*

brary. The remainder of the Harvard community has furnished two-tenths of the researchers, and the other seven-tenths have come from elsewhere. Robert W. Lovett, the curator of manuscripts, said that Harvard students have used his material less than students from Brandeis, Boston, and Yale Universities. "We would like to have more general use of our manuscript collection, especially from the Harvard University community."[95] One of the faithful patrons of these business records has been Vincent P. Carosso, specialist in business and economic history at New York University. Since 1961 he has spent about two months each year at the Baker Library, and his students also have worked there.[96] Other scholars, graduate and postgraduate, have worked with these manuscripts under various HGSBA fellowship programs.[97]

The most obvious utility of business records is in studies focused on business history, such as Allan Nevins' works on John D. Rockefeller and Henry Ford. During the years he was writing entrepreneurial history, Nevins frequently employed graduate students at Columbia University to assist him in researching business records, usually characterized by bulk. Some of these students then went on to write dissertations in business history.[98] At the University of Missouri, Norman Crockett wrote a dissertation in the field of business history, "A Study of the Midwestern Woolen Industry." The research was based substantially on the records of three woolen companies—Watkins Mills, Appleton Mills, and Stone, Atwood, and Company. In using the Appleton Mills records, Crockett encountered a situation any researcher in business history is likely to face: the desire of company officials to review the notes and manuscript. When this desire results in censorship, the objectivity of the historian's product is impaired; but researchers frequently discover that business executives are interested in accuracy and make constructive suggestions. Crockett found the review of his material helpful. "I don't think the company

95 Interview, see Appendix C2a.
96 Interview, see Appendix C1.
97 Letter, Arthur M. Johnson to author, May 26, 1967.
98 Interview, see Appendix C1.

was trying to hide any skeletons; it was just being cautious."[99] Before a student at Emory University undertook research for a dissertation on the history of a Georgia insurance company, he had a clear understanding with the company that he could write what the evidence indicated.[100]

Even when studies have not dealt explicitly with business history, scholars have often found business records helpful in giving balance and additional dimensions to the project. Graduate students at the Case Institute of Technology have frequently consulted the records of Cleveland businesses. Although their research has been oriented toward the history of the scientific and technological phases of a company's operations, the students discovered that the purely business aspects can exert influence throughout an organization.[101] At the University of Kansas a student researched business records as well as newspapers for a history of the Kansas railroad strikes of the 1870's. Another employed the same type of sources for an economic history of Leavenworth from 1873 to 1875.[102] For a thesis on the impact of the Erie Canal on the development of Rome, New York, a student at the State University of New York at Albany investigated business records and other local sources extensively.[103] George Chalou, for his dissertation on "Indian Relations During the War of 1812," developed much pertinent information about those relations from business records. After the war both the American and the British armies bought food for the Indians in an effort to win their allegiance, and the records of these transactions constituted one gauge of intent toward the Indians. The records of smuggling activities across the New York and Vermont borders into Canada provided additional data of value for this project.[104] In his research on Alfred Stieglitz, Roy A. Kotynek discovered "most helpful" information about Stieglitz' business activities from his income tax returns.[105] Stu-

[99] Interview, see Appendix C3.
[100] Interview with James Harvey Young, see Appendix C1.
[101] Interview with Melvin Kranzberg, *ibid.*
[102] Interview with John Clark, *ibid.*
[103] Questionnaire returned by Kendall Birr.
[104] Interview, see Appendix C3.
[105] Kotynek, *ibid.*

dents at Louisiana State University working on Civil War and Reconstruction topics have occasionally used plantation records for supplementary data.[106]

The need for business records exceeds the available supply, not so much quantitatively as qualitatively. Students of diplomatic history should have access to records of businesses instrumental in foreign affairs. "We desperately need access to company records, such as those of investment banking firms."[107] Even on the quantitative level, Julius M. Bloch feared that many important business records will be destroyed because businessmen do not understand their value. Without this understanding, businessmen frequently discard records rather than incur the expense of maintaining them. Bloch advocated a "push from a high level" to inform businessmen of the historical value of their records.[108]

CHURCH RECORDS

Graduate history students seem to have used church records as extensively as any other type of local source. The most obvious employment of such sources was in church histories, either of individual congregations or parishes or of larger bodies. Many historians, however, have investigated church records for wider purposes. They have searched these records to document social attitudes and conditions, to illuminate aspects of diplomatic and medical history and biography, and to give fullness to intensive, microcosmic studies. For her dissertation on Presbyterian centers in colonial Virginia, Katherine L. Brown centered her research on the records of the Hanover Presbytery, some published in the *Virginia Magazine of History and Biography* and the remainder kept in the Union Theological Seminary in Richmond. To compare these Virginia dissenters with their coreligionists in Philadelphia and New York, Mrs. Brown researched the synodal records of these cities. To secure secular information on important laymen, she looked at court records, deeds, and wills from counties with the greatest concentration of Presbyterians. All this material

106 Interview with T. Harry Williams, see Appendix C1.
107 Interview with Lawrence E. Gelfand, *ibid.*
108 Bloch, *ibid.*

152

was on microfilm in the Virginia State Library.[109] John M. Bumsted's dissertation, "The Pilgrims' Progress: An Ecclesiastical History of the Old Colony," derived predominantly from church records. The primary emphasis of this study was the impact of the Great Awakening on the churches in Bristol, Barnstable, and Plymouth counties, Massachusetts, and in Bristol County, Rhode Island. His major sources were parish, county, and town records; the papers of Isaac Backus, an influential Baptist preacher; and the papers and publications of other ministers. For a postdoctoral project, Bumsted reconstructed the town of Norton, Massachusetts, through an intense analysis of the existing local sources. He hoped to clarify the relationships between office-holding, church membership, and landowning.[110]

In recent years the history department at Saint Louis University has had a series of theses on parish histories. To facilitate these studies, the department maintained a union list of available parish records. Most of these theses have been histories of Roman Catholic parishes, partly because parish records are usually kept systematically. One such thesis, however, was the history of a leading Saint Louis parish of the Missouri Synod of the Lutheran Church, written by a Lutheran. Some students at the university, such as Sister Mary Christine Taylor, devoted their dissertations to diocesan histories.[111] Professors at the State University of New York at Albany, Florida State University, Teachers College of Columbia University, and the University of Pennsylvania reported various church histories done as theses and dissertations.[112] At Pennsylvania, a number of clergymen have taken Ph.D.'s in history and have done research in their own church records.[113] Reflecting the research emphasis in Minnesota, the use of conference or synodal records has been much heavier than that of parish records.[114]

[109] Interview, see Appendix C3.

[110] Bumsted, *ibid.*

[111] Interviews with John F. Bannon, S.J., and Martin F. Hasting, S.J., see Appendix C1.

[112] Questionnaire returned by Kendall Birr; interviews with William I. Hair; Frederick D. Kershner, Jr.; and Thomas C. Cochran, see Appendix C1.

[113] Cochran, above.

[114] Interview with Lucile M. Kane, curator of manuscripts, Minnesota Historical Society, see Appendix C2b.

The most frequent analysis of church records for attitudes toward social problems involved the issues of slavery and race. A doctoral student at the University of Wisconsin studied church records to document antislavery sentiment in the South,[115] and a master's candidate at Ohio State University investigated the files of four Cleveland congregations to determine their attitudes toward slavery before, during, and after the Civil War.[116] At George Washington University, students have studied church records relating to the Protestant response to the race question from the Civil War to the present.[117] For his dissertation on "Southern Negroes in the Urban North: Chicago, 1915–1941," Allan H. Spear used as many church and YMCA records as he could find. These revealed the role Negro congregations played in enabling individuals to adapt to urban life.[118] A student at the University of Texas analyzed the problem of what the Presbyterian Church has done to revive its work with Negroes. To document Negroes' views of themselves, he interviewed members of six Negro Presbyterian congregations. He concluded that they were not always happy with the shouting of the Methodist and Baptist Negro churches and preferred the more restrained Presbyterian form of worship.[119] In his seminar on southern cities during the depression, Robert C. Cotner had students investigate the records of churches and civic organizations to see when welfare funds were exhausted.[120] David M. Katzman, a University of Michigan graduate student, also found that Ann Arbor church records reveal much information on civic welfare activities.[121]

Just as church records demonstrate the positions of religious organizations on important social issues, they also illuminate the influence the churches exert on various other areas of our national experience. For instance, any kind of foreign missionary work undertaken by American churches inevitably has diplomatic over-

[115] Interview with Norman K. Risjord, see Appendix C1.
[116] Interview with Marvin R. Zahniser, *ibid.*
[117] Interview with Wood Gray, *ibid.*
[118] Spear, *ibid.*
[119] Interview with Robert C. Cotner, *ibid.*
[120] *Ibid.*
[121] Interview, see Appendix C3.

154

tones, and missionary records may be helpful in the study of foreign relations. This has been the case for Harvard University students of American diplomatic history who have found that the records of the American Board of Foreign Missions in the Houghton Library reveal considerable information about this country's involvement in the Far and Middle East.[122] Approaching missionary records from a different angle, John Duffy, a medical historian, searched the records of the Society for the Propagation of the Gospel in Foreign Parts for medical data on the missionaries. For his studies of epidemics, he ascertained that to the extent churches were active in caring for the sick and burying the dead, their records provided valuable information.[123]

Church records are frequently helpful when studied in conjunction with other kinds of local sources for close investigations of communities. In his study of eighteenth-century rice plantations in South Carolina, Alan Calmes discovered that parish records were particularly helpful, for they subsumed vital statistics and voting records. These different types of data lent perspective to his economic history.[124]

Often graduate students are conditioned to investigate important original sources because they are handily situated. For this reason, history students at Vanderbilt University have made wide use of the rich collections of church records in Nashville. Moreover, the university's Divinity School has a strong church history department that generates interest in this specialty. With Methodists, Baptists, and Disciples of Christ having archives in Nashville, local historians are "blessed with a richness of sources."[125]

NONLITERARY EVIDENCE

American historians traditionally have relied on documentary sources, often neglecting artistic, architectural, or archeological evidence that could add valuable dimensions to their work. The first significant attempts to make citizens aware of their heritage

[122] Interview with Ernest R. May, see Appendix C1.
[123] Duffy, *ibid*.
[124] Interview, see Appendix C3.
[125] Interview with Herbert Weaver, see Appendix C1.

through artifacts came in the 1920's, with Henry Ford's restoration of the Wayside Inn and Dearborn Village and the Rockefeller Foundation's restoration of Williamsburg.[126] Subsequent activities of the Winterthur Museum, in Delaware, the New York State Historical Association, in Cooperstown, and the Smithsonian Institution have done much to popularize the nondocumentary approach to history.

The first serious historiographic recognition of the importance of artifacts came in the series edited by Arthur M. Schlesinger and Dixon R. Fox, *A History of American Life*. Each of its twelve volumes, published between 1927 and 1944, began its bibliographical essay with a section on "Physical Survivals." The profession subsequently has given slight attention to nonliterary evidence, however.[127] According to some leaders in the museum field, historians are still remiss in not doing more research with artifacts and artistic evidence. Mitchell A. Wilder, director of the Amon Carter Museum of Western Art, in Fort Worth, declared, "History professors haven't exercised enough imagination to use artistic evidence."[128] The director of the Colorado State Historical Society, William E. Marshall, said that neither history professors nor graduate students had made noticeable use of the artifacts in the society's museum. The problem is not just with historians, for "academics in general are not oriented toward doing research in museums." As an example, Marshall explained that for six years no student from the Colorado School of Mines asked to have any specimen from the mineral exhibit removed for detailed examination. He decried the fact that museums have not had the stature as research facilities they deserve.[129]

While these critical comments are generally valid, several theses and dissertations have employed artifacts and artistic evidence in interesting ways. A graduate student at Georgetown University

126 Cf. Roger Butterfield, "Henry Ford, the Wayside Inn, and the Problem of 'History is Bunk,'" *Massachusetts Historical Society Proceedings*, Vol. LXXVII (1965), 53–66.

127 Cf. Charles B. Hosmer, *Presence of the Past: A History of the Preservation Movement in the United States.*

128 Interview, see Appendix C2b.

129 Marshall, *ibid.*

incorporated artifacts from the Smithsonian Institution in a thesis on "Representations of Lincoln." Another Georgetown student documented a thesis on women's costumes in the nineteenth century with photographs of Smithsonian models and material from the Library of Congress' Prints and Photographs Division. This thesis showed how costumes reflected changing mores.[130] One of Avery O. Craven's graduate students at the University of Chicago documented a different kind of change with fabric artifacts. This domestic science teacher identified approximately one dozen standard quilt patterns and traced the variations they acquired as settlers moved west. She did much of her research for this "fascinating" thesis in museums.[131]

Since the historian runs certain risks in the interpretation of artistic evidence and artifacts, it is helpful to have literary documentation for reinforcement. For a seminar paper at the University of Wisconsin, Ingrid Winther used photographs of Wisconsin towns and farms to reconstruct the life of a small mining community. Fortunately, she could rely on a newspaper for basic information. Merle Curti, her professor, cautioned that artistic evidence "must be used as supplementary material and not as the main source of documentation."[132] In addition to conventional sources, Roy A. Kotynek used copies of Stieglitz' paintings and drawings to document his dissertation on "Alfred Stieglitz and the Introduction of Modern Art to America."[133] When he taught at Northwestern University, Ray A. Billington encouraged students to incorporate artistic evidence wherever possible. One of his students wrote a dissertation on the impact of the Armory Show in Chicago.[134] For a thesis at the University of Kansas on the artistic temperament of the early national period, a student studied the arts to see if they reflected the spirit of the new nation.[135] Although the artistic quality of his evidence might be suspect, Bill C.

---

[130] Interview with Joseph T. Durkin, S.J., see Appendix C1.
[131] Craven, *ibid.*
[132] Curti, *ibid.*
[133] Interview, see Appendix C3.
[134] Interview, see Appendix C1.
[135] Interview with W. Stitt Robinson, *ibid.*

Malone did research with phonograph records for a dissertation on American commercial country music, 1920–61.[136]

A few students have found architectural evidence important in their research. As documentation for her dissertation, "A History of Commercial Architecture in Atlanta, 1865 to the Present," Elizabeth M. Lyon incorporated both architectural and artistic evidence.[137] Although students of early American history at Tulane University have few architectural sources available locally, they can rely on those in Williamsburg. Hugh F. Rankin, Tulane's colonial specialist, made arrangements with Colonial Williamsburg to provide his students with architectural records and other local sources for the period. Colonial Williamsburg also makes supplemental grants that enable graduate students to travel there for research.[138]

The complaint of museum directors that historians are not sufficiently cognizant of the rewards of research among their holdings has been echoed by custodians of virtually every type of local source. That the profession is not taking advantage of the rich variety of local sources available is manifest, but this chapter's illustrations of the inventiveness and imagination some historians bring to such materials indicate that no blanket indictments may be issued. Furthermore, these illustrations should point the way to greater resourcefulness in using sources often no more distant than the county seat. Walter Prescott Webb once said that every place has a history and that a historian, if cut off from the specialized sources of his training, could make do with the material at hand if he really had the ambition for research and writing.[139] No serious student of history can complain of a dearth of research material. The challenge lies in recognizing the significance of the sometimes humble, and often neglected, local sources.

[136] Interview with Barnes F. Lathrop, *ibid*.
[137] Interview, see Appendix C3.
[138] Interview, see Appendix C1.
[139] Interview at Del Mar College, Corpus Christi, Tex., Dec. 2, 1957.

VI. Printed Sources

LONG before Johns Hopkins University inaugurated this country's doctoral training in history, a few public-minded citizens began to lay the foundation for research by printing collections of original sources. Immediately after the Revolution, Americans wishing to record the history of their fight for freedom were frustrated by the lack of any corpus of source materials. The new government provided no central repository for official documents, states had not established archives, and no private historical collections existed until after 1791, when the Massachusetts Historical Society was founded. With no organized manuscript collections, scholars with an impulse to write the history of their momentous times would have to rely on printed sources, reasoned Ebenezer Hazard, a New York bookseller who determined to collect and print colonial and revolutionary documents. His two volumes of *Historical Collections* appeared in 1792 and 1794 and served as a precursor for Peter Force's nine-volume *American Archives* (1837–53). Significantly, those who were first motivated to a systematic preservation of the documentary basis of our national history realized that in the absence of repositories, their task was to collect *and publish* sources.[1]

[1] David D. Van Tassel, *Recording America's Past*, 32–33, 87; Fred Shelley,

With documents available in print long before the originals could be consulted in a repository, scholars established research habits that have proved durable from one generation to another. When James Ford Rhodes did research for his celebrated seven-volume *History of the United States from the Compromise of 1850*, he chose to rely on the printed sources available within the comfortable confines of the Boston Athenaeum. "Source-fiends" could scour the countryside for original documents, but he prayed to "remain in my comfortable home, independent of the sleeping-car conductor and porter, hotel clerk, and librarian in a strange library, the method of which, however admirable, is not the Athenaeum method."[2] This preference for printed sources and the great number of them available are clearly reflected in the 1912 edition of the Channing-Hart-Turner *Guide to the Study and Reading of American History*. Of the sixty pages in the chapter on sources, only two deal with manuscripts. The authors obviously did not intend this *Guide* to be a manual for graduate research, but its preponderant attention to printed sources seems a fair indication of professional inclinations. The convenience of using printed sources, plus their wide availability, has ensured their enduring popularity with graduate students.

Today, as formerly, printed sources constitute an important segment of the total body of research material related to United States history. Government publications, newspapers, magazines, pamphlets, and printed editions of the papers of notable individuals offer a vast range of information. Because of the ease with which these sources may be studied, in comparison with hand-written or microcopied material, it becomes necessary to guard against their uncritical acceptance. Naturally, any source, regard-

---

"Ebenezer Hazard: America's First Historical Editor," *William and Mary Quarterly*, 3rd Series, Vol. XII, No. 1 (Jan., 1955), 44–73; Ernst Posner, *American State Archives*, 13–16; L. H. Butterfield, "Archival and Editorial Enterprise in 1850 and 1950: Some Comparisons and Contrasts," *Proceedings of the American Philosophical Society*, Vol. XCVIII, No. 3 (June, 1954), 159–70.

[2] Introduction to *A List of Books and Newspapers, Maps, Music, and Miscellaneous Matter Printed in the South During the Confederacy, Now in The Boston Athenaeum*, v.

less of form, must be evaluated, but the temptation to rely on printed sources seems greater since their very form facilitates research. For many areas of United States history, abundant printed sources exist, and sometimes dissertations have been based solely on the information they provide. Although printed sources are not available for every possible subject, their general importance should be understood by those in any way concerned with graduate training in American history.

As on so many other vital issues in graduate history training, the profession has divided views on the way students should approach printed sources. Although most historians agree that printed sources, if used with the necessary scholarly precautions, offer advantages, they disagree on the nature of these precautions. Some professors said that common sense was all a student had to have to use printed sources effectively, while others offered elaborate suggestions for the type of training needed with printed sources. These conflicting viewpoints, suggestions for training, and examples of research in major printed sources represented the profession's involvement with this extensive resource.

When information exists in only one form, all who use it, regardless of their physical location, are limited to that form. Thus, graduate students at the University of Pennsylvania and the University of Oregon consult the *Congressional Record* in the same manner. Beyond such materials that are equally available in all parts of the country, institutions offering doctoral work in history vary greatly in the resources they provide. Often the enthusiasm of professors for printed sources stems from the recognition that without these sources their institutions would be severely hampered in their graduate programs. A Vanderbilt University professor termed printed sources "absolutely invaluable in our particular situation."[3] At the University of South Carolina, George C. Rogers, Jr., said, "Since we don't have many manuscripts, how else can we do any work without printed original sources?"[4] Stephen E. Ambrose considered the easy access to

[3] Interview with Douglas E. Leach, see Appendix C1.
[4] Rogers, *ibid.*

printed sources a great advantage, especially to those on the academic periphery.[5]

ADVANTAGES OF PRINTED SOURCES

While enthusiasm for printed sources was frequently in direct ratio to the distance from manuscript centers, many historians whose universities have significant manuscript collections pointed out the advantages of printed sources. In some cases an advantage was that printed sources were available for specialized fields to which the manuscripts, however plentiful, were unrelated. Professors at the University of North Carolina, home of the Southern Historical Collection, underscored the importance of printed sources for many areas of investigation. George B. Tindall suggested that the profession may have made "too much of a fetish of manuscripts," since the form of a student's sources should depend upon what is available for the subject. For his own dissertation, "South Carolina Negroes, 1877–1900," Tindall had to rely on printed sources—newspapers and government documents—for there was nothing else.[6] Frank W. Klingberg believed that the subject should determine the form of original sources rather than vice versa. "Good manuscripts are terribly important, but low-grade manuscripts will lead students to something that might be fresh but at the same time unimportant." The growing interest in interpretative and philosophical studies among graduate students at North Carolina has caused many of them to rely largely on printed sources.[7] W. Stull Holt also commented on the profession's "fetish . . . concerning manuscripts. There is no magic in the actual document. . . . An accurate printed source is as valuable as the manuscript itself."[8] Well-edited printed sources are "more useful than the manuscripts themselves."[9]

Historians gave various reasons for preferring research with printed sources—always with the stipulation of reliable editing.

[5] Ambrose, *ibid.*
[6] Tindall, *ibid.*
[7] Klingberg, *ibid.*
[8] Holt, *ibid.*
[9] Interview with Bernard Mayo, *ibid.*

Among these reasons were easy availability and readability;[10] the assistance provided by the introduction, editorial apparatus, and index;[11] and economy of the researcher's time.[12] Printed sources are frequently preferable because in the same amount of space they contain a great deal more information than manuscripts.[13] Consequently, during a given period students can gather much more data from printed sources than from manuscripts. "There is too much emphasis on manuscripts. It's possible to do a dissertation exclusively with printed original sources."[14]

The obvious and understandable popularity of printed sources raised the question of the kind of training graduate students received—or needed—for research with such material. Many professors from institutions representing a typical cross section of those offering the doctorate in American history thought no special training was necessary. They believed that the way to learn to use printed sources was by doing so.[15] As Wood Gray put it, "The whole teaching process is geared to learning by doing rather than by precepts."[16] Most historians who saw no reason to treat printed sources differently from other original materials said that the same common-sense rules apply to any source, regardless of form, and that methodological training should comprehend printed sources. Though conceding that it is helpful for students to have some bibliographical direction with printed sources before

[10] Interviews with Bernard Bailyn, Daniel W. Hollis, James Z. Rabun, Paul H. Bergeron, and John K. Nelson, *ibid.*

[11] Interviews with Walter B. Posey, Allen J. Going, Paul H. Bergeron, Robert E. Moody, Alexander DeConde, and John R. Alden, *ibid.*

[12] Interview with Elisha P. Douglass, *ibid.*

[13] Interview with Arthur M. Johnson, *ibid.*

[14] Interview with John Duffy, *ibid.* Early in the survey, I asked if a dissertation could be based solely on printed sources. With the proviso that it depended on the subject, the response was so generally positive that I dropped the question from the interview schedule.

[15] Interviews with Daniel R. Beaver, Elisha P. Douglass, Alfred D. Chandler, Jr., Charles G. Sellers, Jr., Kenneth M. Stampp, Herbert F. Margulies, Norman K. Risjord, Robert H. Ferrell, Wood Gray, Thomas L. Karnes, William R. Hogan, W. H. Masterson, Russell D. Buhite, David S. Sparks, Robert R. Dykstra, Richard Frost, Donald R. McCoy, Thomas J. Pressly, William B. Willcox, and Shaw Livermore, Jr., see Appendix C1. Questionnaire returned by J. Treadwell Davis, University of Southern Mississippi.

[16] Gray, above.

being immersed in them, some historians frankly advocated the sink-or-swim approach,[17] while others occasionally were willing to throw out a life preserver for students who cannot swim at all.[18]

Several historians believed that when dealing with printed sources, especially government documents, the best approach was to rely on a competent specialist in the library.[19] Clarence L. Ver Steeg thought it preferable for documents librarians to provide the training in printed sources because they are generally competent and because history professors have a much narrower grasp of the material.[20]

PRECEPTS FOR USE OF PRINTED SOURCES

Although many professors recognized no need to give graduate students special training with printed sources or advocated such training by library specialists, other historians have chosen to deal with the issue concretely. They contended that professors took too much for granted in students' use of printed sources, and more—not less—formal training was needed. Among the injunctions of those advocating specific training were that students should exhaust pertinent printed sources before turning to manuscripts; they should evaluate any evidence, regardless of its form, and not fall into the trap of believing something just because it is in print; they should be aware of the mechanical pitfalls related to printing; they should examine printed sources with the greatest selectivity, keeping their problem in sharp focus; and, depending on individual need, they should acquire the facility to understand technical documents.

Because of the comparative ease of using printed sources, a researcher can save a great deal of trouble and time by exhausting this material before examining other types of sources. By doing so, he eliminates the frustration and tedium of gathering information

---

[17] Interview with Dykstra, above.

[18] Interviews with Willcox, above; and Melvin Kranzberg, see Appendix C1.

[19] Interviews with Edward Younger; Sparks, above; Clarence L. Ver Steeg, Richard S. Kirkendall, and Howard M. Merriman, *ibid.*

[20] Ver Steeg, above.

from more difficult sources.[21] A mistake that graduate students and mature scholars have made, according to Allan Nevins, is assuming that printed sources have already been digested into books and therefore completely utilized. To avoid this error, historians must keep abreast of the related secondary literature. Nevins said that in doing research for *The Ordeal of the Union*, he constantly checked printed material. "I always go back and see what James Ford Rhodes has said. I often find that some insight I thought was quite original had already been stated by an older generation of scholars. It doesn't profit us much to grind away at manuscripts and keep coming up with the same answers that older historians have had."[22] The failure to investigate printed sources before using manuscripts or archives was not restricted to historians. The National Archives has had the problem of training its staff to use printed sources rather than try to ferret out the originals. "The smartest archivists know and use the published documents to a maximum extent when it is not essential to find and use original documents."[23]

Professors believed that because some beginning graduate students were inclined to accept printed sources uncritically, all must be made aware that appearance in print in no way ensures verity.[24] This point has been made so emphatically through the years that students often held the converse notion that printed sources were inherently unreliable, and they were likely to equate manuscripts with truth. To combat such ideas, Lewis E. Atherton tried to drive home to his students that original sources in any form "can lie as eloquently as a secondary source."[25] What graduate students must do is to evaluate—to apply internal criticism—to any evidence, printed or manuscript. Questions of motive should be asked of all printed sources. For instance, students need to understand that

[21] Interviews with John Duffy, Alexander DeConde, W. C. Nunn, and Arthur H. DeRosier, Jr., *ibid.*

[22] Nevins, *ibid.*

[23] Interview with Sherrod East, acting assistant archivist for the National Archives, see Appendix C2b.

[24] Interviews with Arthur S. Link, Gene D. Lewis, and Gilbert C. Fite, see Appendix C1.

[25] Atherton, *ibid.*

data from government documents are not necessarily more reliable than those garnered elsewhere. In short, "immature graduate students need discipline of the type that Langlois and Seignobos have given to many generations. . . . We probably all slight this kind of training, because it's old and boring to us."[26]

The problem graduate students face in evaluating printed sources is not a function of their form but of their type. Consequently, one would approach a magazine or newspaper editorial and the *Congressional Record* in entirely different manners. Students should be cognizant of the peculiarities of various types of printed sources and should be skeptical toward all evidence.[27] Other professors pointed out cautions to be applied to various printed sources. Thomas C. Cochran explained that Congressional committee hearings, ordinarily ex parte proceedings to prove something, nonetheless incorporate the conflicting testimony that lends some understanding to the process of lawmaking, whereas Congressional committee reports merely give the final product.[28] Students must appreciate this important difference.[29]

Harold D. Langley is one of the professors who has stressed the need to understand the subtleties and ironies of official government reports. Since these are couched in restrained, civil service language, their true message may lie beneath the actual statements.[30] Researchers should understand how the *Annals of Congress* were prepared and their notorious inaccuracies.[31] Gales and Seaton, publishers of the *Annals*, compiled their abstracts of the proceedings of the first seventeen Congresses and the first session of the eighteenth (1789–1824) from contemporary newspapers and other sources. They relied on the *National Intelligencer* from October, 1800, through 1824, and their abstractions often compounded errors in the journalistic accounts.[32] Similarly, students

[26] Interview with Thomas C. Cochran, *ibid.*
[27] Interview with David A. Shannon, *ibid.*
[28] Cochran, above.
[29] Interview with Clarke A. Chambers, *ibid.*
[30] Langley, *ibid.*
[31] Interviews with Allan G. Bogue and Peter P. Hill, *ibid.*
[32] Laurence F. Schmeckebier and Roy B. Eastin, *Government Publications and Their Use*, 121–22.

should know that the *Congressional Record* is not necessarily a verbatim account of the proceedings of Congress.[33] Speakers have the right to amend what they said on the floor of Congress, so that what is printed in the *Record* is often an expurgated, sanitized version of their actual statements. Specialists in colonial history should study the institutional framework of the period to understand the relative importance of various reports. For instance, the reports of the Privy Council were comparatively unimportant because the council was merely a rubber stamp.[34]

David Alan Williams urged students to check each type of printed source to determine if its percentage of error makes it safe to use. He thought the editor's silence on criteria for selecting documents and the faulty editorial apparatus of the recently launched *Naval Documents of the American Revolution* restricted its scholarly value.[35] James Harvey Young cautioned his students using printed documents from executive agencies of the federal government to go behind these formal statements to examine the working papers.[36]

An important fact for a graduate student to remember is that he cannot escape the responsibility for evaluating his sources, even if their printed form betokens complete respectability.[37] If a student intends to publish the results of his research, he should check the original materials and not be content with printed editions.[38] A graduate student at the Catholic University of America, D. Terry Boughner, developed a skeptical attitude toward printed sources, though he appreciated the contributions a skilled editor can make. If at all possible, he wanted to study the originals rather than rely on printed editions of manuscripts so that his writing would be a secondary, not a tertiary, source. "As a historian, I want to stand

[33] Interviews with Frank Freidel and Alfred A. Cave, see Appendix C1.
[34] Interview with Jack M. Sosin, *ibid.*
[35] Williams, *ibid.* See Williams' critique in *Virginia Quarterly Review*, Vol. XLI, No. 4 (Autumn, 1965), 624–27. In it he identified distinctive qualities of most modern documentary editing: its specified criteria of inclusion and omission and its method.
[36] Interview, see Appendix C1.
[37] Interview with Robert P. Thomson, *ibid.*
[38] Interview with Aubrey C. Land, *ibid.*

behind whatever I write. If I've seen the originals, I've gone as far as I can in tracing the facts."[39]

If our primary obligation as historians is the proper use of evidence,[40] students should examine printed sources with the same caution, suspicion, and skepticism they would apply to any other original source. Many professors thought that the development of such a general critical capacity was more important than any specific instructions for using printed material.[41] What a student needs most in using printed sources is good sense—a quality professors unfortunately cannot communicate.[42]

While many of the cautions professors give students concerning printed sources are generally applicable to other forms of original sources, these warnings are pertinent because they can help students avoid being misled by the ease of using printed sources. Other cautions relate more directly to the nature of the form. The mechanics of transforming a manuscript into type often pose scholarly problems. Printers are not immune to the errors that plague others working with words and figures—misspelling, transposition, and omission. Researchers obviously must guard against this level of error as well as subtler ones.[43] Richard J. Hopkins, a graduate student at Emory University, was particularly sensitive to the mistakes possible with printed sources, since he was once a typesetter.[44]

In his dissertation research on barbiturates and amphetamines in American society, Hopkins became aware of some limitations of printed documents of the Food and Drug Administration. These limitations would probably apply to any policy documents generated by a bureaucracy, governmental or private. What these printed sources did not incorporate were the marginal notations that often revealed how policy decisions came about. Another

[39] Interview, see Appendix C3.
[40] Interview with Barnes F. Lathrop, see Appendix C1.
[41] Interviews with James Z. Rabun, Allan H. Spear, Oscar Handlin, Lawrence L. Graves, T. Harry Williams, Robert E. Brown, Chase C. Mooney, Marvin R. Zahniser, and Richard L. Watson, Jr., *ibid*.
[42] Interview with Gabriel Kolko, *ibid*.
[43] Interviews with Arrell M. Gibson, *ibid*; Clyde E. Pitts, see Appendix C3.
[44] Hopkins, *ibid*.

clue to policy making that does not get into print is the buck slip, which records the date a bureaucrat received and transmitted the document. The time sequence thus established enables a researcher to understand the chronology of decision making. With such helpful information omitted from the printed documents, the student needs access to the file papers.[45]

Users of printed sources may face the problem of omission at various levels. The typesetter may omit a word, a line, or more. The composer may drop the type after it has been set and fail to get it all reassembled—or reassembled correctly. Also, the editor may choose to omit portions of printed documents or even entire documents without so notifying the readers. Researchers must be aware of these possibilities and not automatically assume that the printed version represents the full account. If at all possible, students should know the principles of selectivity and omission as well as any editorial prejudices involved in the process. The major pitfall created by omissions is that the researcher cannot reason from absence.[46]

A different, and comparatively minor, mechanical problem is created when various editions of printed sources are not paged uniformly. This lack of uniformity makes citation cumbersome, as evidenced in *Messages and Papers of the Presidents*, edited by James D. Richardson. In the *Messages*, both page and volume numbers differ in various editions.[47] Pagination is not the only shortcoming of the Richardson set, which also omits some early messages and the related papers that are often more revealing than the messages. Schmeckebier and Eastin warn that "the stu-

---

[45] *Ibid.* This very problem figured in the Ballinger-Pinchot controversy. Louis Brandeis, counsel for Gifford Pinchot and Louis R. Glavis (the Interior official who collaborated with Pinchot), charged that the Attorney General's report of September 11, 1909, that was the basis for President Taft's letter of September 13 exonerating Richard Ballinger and condemning Glavis, was actually prepared months later. Brandeis demanded access to the working papers so that he could reconstruct the chronology. The investigating committee voted seven to five against letting Brandeis see the documents. Cf. Alpheus T. Mason, *Brandeis: A Free Man's Life* (New York: Viking, 1946), pp. 263–64.

[46] Interviews with Martin F. Hasting, S.J.; Merrill Jensen; and Arthur Bestor, see Appendix C1.

[47] Interview with James C. Curtis, see Appendix C3.

dent who wants all the papers would do well to consult the separate documents."[48] L. H. Butterfield called it a scandal that we have nothing better than Richardson.[49] Students should also realize that discrepancies may exist between various drafts of documents and what finally appears in print and that a printed version may not be definitive.[50]

Since specialists in early American history have a larger percentage of original sources available in print than specialists in other periods, many of the technical problems they encounter with sources, irrespective of form, involve printed material. They need to understand archaic printing forms and words, such as the thorn (the *y* symbol for *th*), abbreviations, and the way colonial calligraphy was rendered in print.[51] Though not a colonial specialist, Joseph Boskin advocated training in linguistics so that students would understand word usage and the changing values of words.[52] As an example of the need for sensitivity to these changing values, Raymond P. Stearns pointed out that some colonial definitions of words no longer apply. He recently came across the phrase "oatcake and whig" but found that the political connotations of "whig" were completely inapplicable, for its contemporary meaning was buttermilk.[53]

In addition to encountering mechanical problems posed by printed sources, graduate students sometimes have had difficulty devising a reading technique appropriate for such research. Many inexperienced graduate students have not developed the skill for selective reading. Being encumbered by reading word for word, they quickly bogged down in printed sources. To enable them to overcome such deficiencies, professors have urged students to define research problems sharply and then read with this focus in mind. Researchers should study and copy only the portion of

[48] Schmeckebier and Eastin, *Government Publications*, 309.
[49] Interview, see Appendix C2b.
[50] Interview with James A. Rawley, see Appendix C1.
[51] Interview with Douglas E. Leach, *ibid.*
[52] Boskin, *ibid.*
[53] Stearns, *ibid.*

a document dealing directly with their problem, lest they be afflicted with "documentitis."[54]

For research with technical documents, students often need specialized training to enable them to comprehend the sources. Those working in business or economic history should know what to look for in an accounting report and how to evaluate similar technical information.[55] For example, Frederic C. Lane presupposed that his students in economic history at Johns Hopkins University knew double-entry bookkeeping.[56] Those working with election statistics, census materials, or other types of printed quantitative data need something more than orthodox training in evaluating literary evidence. Since these needs are not general, they are best handled in seminars dealing with such specific research problems.[57]

With the considerable attention being given to heterodox areas of historical research, there is some danger that training in conventional types of research such as evaluating literary evidence may be slighted. So that his students could evaluate printed documents, Stow Persons concentrated on textual analysis—*explication du texte*.[58] L. H. Butterfield commented that with the elimination of systematic methodological training, "we may be losing our last contact with a whole set of skills long thought essential to interpreting documentary evidence, namely paleography, diplomatics, textual criticism, and related disciplines." While students want to apply the fashionable quantitative and behavioral techniques to masses of documents, they often are unable to understand what an individual document actually says.[59] Merle Curti advised that students of intellectual history who wished to consider fiction as an original source should read monographs that have successfully

[54] Interviews with Joseph T. Durkin, S.J.; Dorothy D. Gondos; William R. Hutchison; and Howard S. Miller, *ibid.*; questionnaire returned by Kendall Birr, State University of New York at Albany.
[55] Interview with Arthur M. Johnson, see Appendix C1.
[56] Interview with Charles A. Barker, *ibid.*
[57] Interviews with Theodore Saloutos, William N. Chambers, J. Rogers Hollingsworth, Richard S. Dunn, and Richard P. McCormick, *ibid.*
[58] Persons, *ibid.*
[59] Letter, Butterfield to author, May 3, 1967.

employed this technique, such as William R. Taylor's *Cavalier and Yankee*.[60]

Students' frequent misapprehensions concerning government documents reflected another area where specific training would be beneficial. Thomas D. Clark regretted that students jump to the conclusion that government documents relate only to political history. He explained to his students the varieties of information in government documents and the kinds of research they will support.[61] Some professors felt that the research problems with printed sources were so diverse that the most effective method of giving students the necessary training was through individual conferences.[62]

EXERCISES WITH PRINTED SOURCES

Many professors have ensured their students' familiarity with various types of printed sources and their attendant problems by assigning exercises requiring their use. For example, Paul L. Murphy assigned problems involving research in the *Congressional Record* and other such printed sources. His students learned how to handle the materials in the course of solving the problems, with Murphy evaluating the worth and utility of the various types of resources.[63] The first thing Brigham Madsen taught graduate students about printed sources was the use of indexes and finding aids. He sent seminarians to the library with exercises entailing the use of indexes.[64] Wilfrid H. Callcott had students report on guides and indexes to government documents.[65] So that his students would understand editorial foibles, Seymour V. Connor made them evaluate the abstract of the *Calendar of State Papers, Colonial series*, from the Public Record Office. This exercise afforded some notion of how printed sources have been employed.[66]

In his seminar in colonial history, Sydney V. James, Jr., assigned

[60] Interview, see Appendix C1.
[61] Clark, *ibid*.
[62] Interviews with William G. McLoughlin, Jr., and Donald F. Carmony, *ibid*.
[63] Murphy, *ibid*.
[64] Madsen, *ibid*.
[65] Callcott, *ibid*.
[66] Connor, *ibid*.

an elaborate bibliographical problem to acquaint students with a variety of printed sources and the difficulty of locating them. Each student examined and described a major collection in which the documents were not in logical sequence, such as the publications of the Massachusetts Historical Society, the Essex Institute, the Pennsylvania Archives, or the Maryland Archives. After the documents were located, their interpretation could be discussed.[67] Since students of diplomatic history must understand government documents, John A. DeNovo assigned exercises involving the government documents catalog. His students consulted the Department of State *Register* for such items as biographical information and lists of ambassadors, and he taught them to search multiple entries to obtain desired information.[68] In an effort to acquaint students with the edited papers of notable Americans, John K. Nelson had his students compare the papers with biographies of the subject, thus enabling them to evaluate how effectively the biographer studied his sources.[69] Norman A. Graebner concentrated on training his students in the use of newspapers. His classes studied the journalistic reaction to certain events, such as the American declaration of war on Spain. Students have written publishable essays on the basis of research in twentieth-century New York newspapers, and through the years Graebner has acquired much information from such projects.[70] Doctoral candidates at Northwestern University had an incentive to become familiar with important documentary publications because questions related to them are incorporated into the final oral examinations.[71]

CONGRESSIONAL PUBLICATIONS

The major sets of documentary publications presented graduate students with ample opportunity to apply their training with printed sources. These sets, along with newspapers, were the

[67] James, *ibid.*
[68] DeNovo, *ibid.*
[69] Nelson, *ibid.*
[70] Graebner, *ibid.*
[71] Interview with Richard W. Leopold, *ibid.*

printed sources historians consulted most in their research. Receiving heaviest use were the Congressional publications: (1) the *Congressional Record* and its predecessors, the *Annals of Congress*, the *Register of Debates*, and the *Congressional Globe*; (2) the Congressional serial set, identified by serial numbers and variously called the Congressional serials, the Congressional series, and the Congressional set, encompassing the Senate journal, documents, reports, executive documents, and miscellaneous documents and the House journal, documents, reports, executive documents, and miscellaneous documents; and (3) Congressional committee hearings. The considerable confusion that exists about the nomenclature and scope of Congressional publications results largely from both the many changes Congress itself has made in the system and the system's imprecision from the beginning. One of the more reliable guides, though itself inconsistent in terminology, is Laurence F. Schmeckbier and Roy B. Eastin's *Government Publications and Their Use*.[72] Other sets of printed sources popular with historians were *Foreign Relations*, edited papers of famous Americans, *Official Records of the War of the Rebellion*, the *Territorial Papers*, and state series.[73]

Most libraries catalog these printed sources and shelve them with other cataloged material. Consequently, there is no accurate way to measure how much historians use them—especially when the materials are kept in open stacks. University librarians were confident, however, that all types of government documents, cataloged and uncataloged, received extensive use. A significant indication of this use was that when students were unable to find particular documents, they turned to librarians for help. The library staff at the University of Illinois was "preoccupied with rendering such aid," and this experience seemed to be general.[74]

While no precise gauge exists for determining how much his-

[72] Rev. ed., 1961.

[73] An excellent list of documentary publications of the federal government is in Appendix D of *A National Program for the Publication of Historical Documents: A Report to the President by the National Historical Publications Commission.*

[74] Interview, see n. 75, Chap. III.

torians use Congressional publications, the following illustrations show the varied kinds of information available therein and some divers ways in which they have been employed. For his dissertation on "The Non-Mormons in Utah," Floyd A. O'Neil consulted the *Congressional Globe* and *Record* for the important nineteenth-century Congressional debates over the Mormons.[75] Because the fluoridation issue elicited Congressional comment, Eugene Watts studied the *Congressional Record* in connection with his master's thesis, "Fluoridation Controversy in Atlanta, 1950–60."[76] In an effort to understand the structure of politics in the first federal Congress, the subject of his dissertation at the University of Wisconsin, Kenneth R. Bowling made "moderately heavy" use of the *Annals of Congress*. He found the *Annals* and journals satisfactory for roll-call votes but thought newspapers were more accurate than the *Annals* for the actual debates.[77] The contention of David M. Katzman, who researched the *Congressional Record* for a seminar paper on politics of the New Deal, indicates that the passage of time has not altered this situation. "The coverage by the *New York Times* of Congressional activities is often better than that in the *Congressional Record*."[78]

Henry Feingold investigated Congressional publications for information on legislation that estalished rescue agencies for refugees from Nazi Germany and for statements from Congressmen on the subject. His dissertation was "The Politics of Rescue: Government Action and Reaction to the Jewish Refugee Problem, 1938–44."[79] In his dissertation on outlaws on the upper Mississippi Valley frontier, Patrick B. Nolan considered counterfeiting as part of the outlawry. Since counterfeiting is a federal crime, information concerning it appeared in the Congressional serial set, which Nolan consulted.[80] James Breeden used the *Congressional Globe* as a research source for his dissertation on Joseph Jones, a Con-

[75] O'Neil, see Appendix C3.
[76] Watts, *ibid.*
[77] Bowling, *ibid.*
[78] Katzman, *ibid.*
[79] Feingold, *ibid.*
[80] Nolan, *ibid.*

federate surgeon. Several of Jones's medical essays were printed in the *Globe*, as was his testimony at the trial of Major Henry Wirz, commandant at Andersonville prison.[81]

Martin Van Buren was a central figure in Michael Wallace's dissertation on political parties between the age of Jackson and the Civil War, and Wallace located a great number of Van Buren's statements on party doctrine and loyalty in the *Congressional Globe*.[82] James Lane's master's thesis at the University of Hawaii dealt with the administration of Territorial Governor Joseph Poindexter, from 1934 until 1942, during which there was a contested election. The House of Representatives investigated and published its report in the *Congressional Record*, which Lane used.[83] Indicating that for decades research in the Congressional proceedings has been a stable element in the study of the American past was Hugh T. Lefler's use of the *Congressional Record* as his major source when writing a dissertation in the 1920's on "Pig Iron" Kelley. Kelley served thirty years in Congress, so much of his activity was reflected in the *Record*. Letters in newspapers constituted another important source for Lefler.[84]

A great frustration researchers have experienced in using all types of government documents, both federal and state, is inadequate indexing.[85] The Brown University library staff believed that the Congressional serial set and *American State Papers* were inadequately used because of difficulty researchers encountered with the indexes.[86] The staff of the General Reference and Bibliography Division of the Library of Congress called the Congressional set "as complicated a set of government publications as we have." One difficulty is that there are several different index approaches to the set—Ames, Poore, the *Monthly Catalog*, and the

81 Breeden, *ibid*.

82 Wallace, *ibid*.

83 Lane, *ibid*.

84 Lefler, see Appendix C1.

85 Interviews with Madison Kuhn, *ibid*.; Joseph Maizlish and David M. Katzman, see Appendix C3.

86 Interview with Christine D. Hathaway, Special Collections librarian; Helen G. Kurtz, Documents librarian; Elizabeth Wescott, Reference librarian; Dorothy Day, Social Studies librarian; see Appendix C2a.

Checklist. "The whole indexing system to the Congressional set needs to be worked over and simplified drastically." [87]

Because of their focus, Congressional committee hearings are popular sources for historical researchers. They contain a great deal of information on a given subject and can easily be the chief resource for a project or can often be used as a supplementary source even when they do not deal directly with the research topic. Thomas C. Cochran, whose students at the University of Pennsylvania regularly consulted hearings as well as other Congressional publications, said that some of his doctoral candidates have based dissertations almost entirely on the hearings.[88] An example of a project for which hearings were central was a paper on the McCarthy-Army controversy.[89] Another Congressional investigation—that of Senator Theodore G. Bilbo—provided valuable information for Bobby W. Saucier, whose dissertation dealt with Bilbo's senatorial career.[90]

Hearings of the House Un-American Activities Committee (HUAC) furnished John S. Beltz with helpful data on American engineers who worked in Russia in the 1920's and 1930's and whose activities were investigated by HUAC. The influence of their contribution to Soviet technology was the subject of Beltz's dissertation at Ohio State University.[91] Milton O. Gustafson considered the committee hearings related to overseas relief during and after World War II "vitally important" to his dissertation, "Congress and Foreign Aid, The First Phase, UNRRA, 1943–47." The hearings revealed the areas in which Congress was both interested and uninterested.[92] For his dissertation on the development of the midwestern woolen industry, Norman Crockett determined tariff interests through committee hearings. His topic also involved extensive use of House and Senate miscellaneous

[87] Interview with Edward N. MacConomy, assistant chief; Beverley H. Brown, senior Reference librarian; and John Ulrich, assistant head, Public Reference section; see Appendix C2b.

[88] Cochran, see Appendix C1.

[89] Interview with Martin F. Hasting, S.J., *ibid.*

[90] Saucier, see Appendix C3.

[91] Beltz, *ibid.*

[92] Gustafson, *ibid.*

documents, census reports, and United States Department of Agriculture bulletins.[93] Edward C. Ezell's research for his dissertation on the development and production of the M-14 rifle included both Congressional committee hearings and the serial set. The most important of these documents were the hearings of the House and Senate appropriations committees which dealt in depth with the financing of the rifle. The serial set had little information on policy but did contain some comment on the rifle's development. Audit documents from the General Accounting Office reviewed the costs of producing the rifle and were therefore "most helpful."[94] Committee prints as well as hearings and the serial set provided John D. Holmfeld with valuable information on policy formulation for his dissertation, "The History of the Development of the Liquid Rocket Engine Combustion Problem."[95]

FOREIGN RELATIONS

Although *Foreign Relations of the United States* is more limited in its appeal than Congressional publications, it is indispensable to students of American diplomatic history and foreign policy.[96] Frequently, scholars with different specialties have discovered there material related to their interests, and the testimony of university librarians around the country substantiated the fact that the volumes are used regularly. In some instances, as at the University of Kentucky, a sufficient number of the volumes have been stolen to indicate their popularity and irregular use.[97] The reactions of historians to *Foreign Relations* as a research tool varied, some thinking the editors of the set do as well as possible and others contending that certain changes would enhance its utility.

Obviously, the *Foreign Relations* volumes include only a small

[93] Crockett, *ibid.*

[94] Ezell, *ibid.*

[95] Holmfeld, *ibid.*

[96] For the background of the series, see Richard W. Leopold, "The *Foreign Relations* Series: A Centennial Estimate," *Mississippi Valley Historical Review*, Vol. XLIX, No. 4 (Mar., 1963), 595–612. A more recent discussion of the difficulties besetting the series is the "Report of Advisory Committee on 'Foreign Relations,' 1964," *American Journal of International Law*, Vol. LIX, No. 4 (Oct., 1965), 914–18.

[97] Interview, see n. 32, Chap. V.

fraction of the official records related to American diplomacy. The sheer bulk of documents has dictated this. Omissions being imperative, the historical staff of the Department of State has compiled *Foreign Relations* following guidelines which became effective in 1925 and provide that, subject to security considerations, the volumes will include documents related to major diplomatic decisions and the formulation of foreign policy. Documents are edited with historical objectivity, texts cannot be changed, and deletions must be indicated. Editors are directed not to suppress documents that would reveal defective policies, but under some conditions regulations permit omissions. Materials that would interfere with current diplomatic negotiations or cause redundance may be omitted; and deletion of certain documents is permitted to preserve confidential information given by individuals and foreign governments, avoid needlessly offending other nationalities or individuals, or eliminate personal opinions not acted on by the Department of State.

On the issues of fidelity of transcription and inclusion of relevant but unfavorable evidence, the editors received high marks from many historians. Frank Freidel thought that *Foreign Relations* suppresses nothing of consequence to scholars.[98] Wilfrid H. Callcott, Russell D. Buhite, and Waldo H. Heinrichs, Jr., have checked original documents against their published form and discovered no discrepancies.[99] Callcott pointed out that *Foreign Relations* may omit an entire episode because of its unimportance, but not with any intent of suppression.[100] Conversely, Buhite found that *Foreign Relations* sometimes omits matters reflecting unfavorably on all parties.[101] One condition that has created an inherent distortion is that it is usually twenty years after the event before the editors apply their canons of selection.[102] Generally, however, the editors were credited with dealing honestly with State Department documents.

[98] Interview, see Appendix C1.
[99] Interviews, *ibid.*
[100] Callcott, *ibid.*
[101] Buhite, *ibid.*
[102] Letter, Henry F. Graff to author, July 12, 1967.

Possibly the most notable example of this is the revelation in *The Conferences at Malta and Yalta* of Roosevelt's concern for the Polish vote during his conversations with Stalin on the question of Eastern Europe. "The *Foreign Relations* series made no attempt to cover up FDR's vulnerability on this point."[103] Another student of diplomatic history has commented that while the record shows that Roosevelt mentioned his concern, it in no way proves that he *felt* much concern. He suggested that this issue only revealed Roosevelt's efforts to use the concept in an attempt to gain concessions from Stalin. To assume the President's vulnerability on this point, on the basis of the document, points up a pitfall in using printed sources.[104] *Foreign Relations* is a valuable tool in training historians because it enables students to develop basic judgment, even if it omits many facts. This development of judgment is more important than assembling detailed facts.[105]

Virtually all diplomatic historians, regardless of their esteem for *Foreign Relations*, asserted that their graduate students cannot rely exclusively on the series, but must consult the file documents in the National Archives.[106] Ernest R. May's students at Harvard have used *Foreign Relations* as a sample of the total documentation. They learned file numbers from the printed documents and consequently knew what to ask for at the Archives.[107]

While not denying the usefulness of the *Foreign Relations* set, several diplomatic historians felt that certain shortcomings hinder its value as a source for serious research. Since the Department of State did not impose high scholarly standards on the series before 1921, researchers studying the volumes for 1861 (the first volume) through 1913 (the last prepared under the pre-1921 standards) must be aware of their uneven and unsystematic coverage of diplomatic affairs. David M. Pletcher termed the nineteenth-century editing of *Foreign Relations* "capricious." At the

103 Interview with Norman A. Graebner, see Appendix C1.
104 Letter, John L. Snell to author, Aug. 17, 1967.
105 Interview with Graebner, above.
106 Interviews with Howard M. Merriman, R. Bingham Duncan, Marvin R. Zahniser, James F. Hopkins, Edward Younger, Ernest R. May, and John A. DeNovo, see Appendix C1.
107 May, above.

expense of more important documents, the editors published what they thought the public would like and included sentimental items such as an extensive account of the transportation back to America of the body of John Howard Payne, composer of "Home, Sweet Home." Pletcher contended that even with its current standards of textual accuracy, *Foreign Relations* is unreliable because of omissions. He preferred the Manning series for its greater accuracy and completeness.[108]

Two weaknesses identified by several historians are the failure of *Foreign Relations* to identify the individuals who prepared documents and the general ignoring of the human aspects of diplomacy. Conceding the utility of the *World War Supplements* to *Foreign Relations*, Arthur S. Link regretted the exclusion from them of "so much vital information in the [Robert] Lansing and Woodrow Wilson papers." Moreover, the supplements did not trace the evolution of foreign policy statements or show their authorship.[109] This absence of identification of document drafters has detracted from the entire series.[110] John A. DeNovo, whose students at the University of Wisconsin use *Foreign Relations* as a central source for their projects, criticized the volumes for the 1930's and early 1940's. They do not contain sufficient intra-departmental memoranda to reflect the decision-making process but merely incorporate the final decision.[111] Richard W. Leopold concurred that this failure to document policy formulation detracts from the value of *Foreign Relations*, but the work is satisfactory for data on specific negotiations such as United States–Bolivia agreements on the sale of tin.[112] In his dissertation research on Woodrow Wilson's executive agents in the Mexican Revolu-

---

[108] Pletcher, *ibid*. William R. Manning (ed.), *Diplomatic Correspondence of the United States Concerning the Independence of the Latin-American Nations*; *Diplomatic Correspondence of the United States: Inter-American Affairs, 1831–1860*; and *Diplomatic Correspondence of the United States: Canadian Relations, 1784–1860*. A grant from the Carnegie Endowment for International Peace made possible the publication of these important volumes.

[109] Interview with Link, see Appendix C1.

[110] Interview with Waldo H. Heinrichs, Jr., *ibid*.

[111] DeNovo, *ibid*.

[112] Leopold, *ibid*.

tion, Larry D. Hill found *Foreign Relations* adequate for diplomatic exchanges, but he regretted the absence of "material that might give some hint of personal feelings of diplomats and their contacts." He also discovered various differences between the wording of the original documents and the *Foreign Relations* version.[113]

Lloyd C. Gardner considered *Foreign Relations* an uneven series and labeled it "a haphazard thing" for research purposes. Because "some years are pretty good and some years are filled with trivia," he preferred the special series on World War II conferences, containing such volumes as *The Conference of Berlin (The Potsdam Conference)*. He has directed dissertations in recent diplomatic history, for which State Department files are unavailable; in these cases his students relied heavily on *American Foreign Policy: Current Documents*, the State Department *Bulletin*, and the Congressional serial set.[114]

That diplomatic historians were the greatest users of *Foreign Relations*, both for research and for teaching, was manifest. The series could be a teaching tool in a variety of ways—Gabriel Kolko exploited it by requiring all students in one of his courses to use it as the basis for their research.[115]

Whatever the preponderance of use by diplomatic historians, *Foreign Relations* has often formed a supplementary source for other specialists, as the following examples indicate. A student at the University of Illinois writing about American mining engineers in South Africa found pertinent information in the series.[116] For his dissertation on non-Mormons in Utah, Floyd A. O'Neil located in the series correspondence of consuls of immigrant minorities in Utah, primarily Austrian and Italian.[117] In his research on "The History of the Third Air Division in World War II," Paul A. Whelen investigated *Foreign Relations* to establish the areas of agreement and disagreement between the United

[113] Interview, see Appendix C3.
[114] Interview, see Appendix C1.
[115] Interview with Dale Holman, see Appendix C3.
[116] Interview with Clark C. Spence, see Appendix C1.
[117] Interview, see Appendix C3.

States and British governments over how American air power would be used in conjunction with the Royal Air Force.[118]

Since diplomatic historians have had the major stake in *Foreign Relations*, they were keenly conscious of and lamented conditions that hamper its effectiveness. R. Bingham Duncan remarked: "The *Foreign Relations* series would be improved if the Historical Office of the State Department were given sufficient monetary support so that more personnel could be used on the series." He added that in 1921 the State Department began a "solid, professional job" that won the approval of the academic community. These efforts continued until the 1950's, when the Historical Office was faced with "demands for 'special reports.' There were two volumes on Japan, which were really a white paper in the '40's. Then Secretary Dulles put on pressure for early publication of the China papers. Senator Knowland of California insisted on this. The *Foreign Relations* staff has done a fine job, even under pressures."[119] "Anything that can be done to hasten publication of the *Foreign Relations* volumes should be done. This series is falling further behind and it constitutes a handicap for those working in the area of United States diplomatic history."[120]

PAPERS OF FAMOUS AMERICANS

The publication in 1950 of Volume I of *The Papers of Thomas Jefferson* marked the beginning of an important development in the historical profession.[121] This inaugurated a series of full-scale letterpress publications of eminent Americans' papers, edited with the highest scholarly standards. Earlier projects of this nature had served a purpose, but it was not always wholly that of scholarship. The level of editing on most earlier documentary publications was

[118] Whelen, *ibid.*

[119] Interview with R. Bingham Duncan, see Appendix C1.

[120] Interview with Wilfrid H. Callcott, *ibid.*

[121] An excellent, disinterested discussion and assessment of the major publications of edited papers of famous Americans is Robert L. Brubaker's "The Publication of Historical Sources: Recent Projects in the United States," *The Library Quarterly*, Vol. XXXVII, No. 2 (Apr., 1967), 193–225. Brubaker gives a good account of the role of the National Historical Publications Commission (NHPC) in promoting these letterpress publications. For information basic to concerns of United States historians, see the NHPC's 1953 and 1964 *A Report to the President.*

such that the serious historical student could not rely on them. These publications could certainly convey impressions of a man's thinking and activities and they could be helpful as teaching tools, but the researcher had to proceed at his own risk. Since 1950, the picture has changed. *The Papers of Thomas Jefferson, The Papers of Benjamin Franklin, The Papers of Alexander Hamilton, The Adams Papers, The Papers of James Madison, The Papers of Henry Clay, The Papers of John C. Calhoun, The Letters of Theodore Roosevelt*, and similar projects have established an estate of documentary editing and publication worthy of high professional acclaim. The aim is to present definitive texts and to illuminate them with exegesis, and the severest critical test of them involves their reliability as original sources for graduate research. On this score they fare very well.

A Jefferson scholar at the University of Virginia, Merrill D. Peterson, stated that the whole point of Julian P. Boyd's edition of *The Papers of Thomas Jefferson* would be missed if students had to go behind Boyd's work to the original documents. A person studying Jefferson's thoughts "would have to go no further than the Boyd edition."[122] One of Peterson's doctoral candidates, Judith P. Pulley, used the Boyd edition as her major source for a dissertation on Jefferson's reaction to the French Revolution. Since such a use of the edition represented its most rigorous scholarly test, Mrs. Pulley's reaction was instructive. "Boyd's editorial comments are often helpful, but I am always conscious of the fact that he is editorializing. I can't take these editorial comments at face value." A distinguishing feature of Boyd's edition is the inclusion of material omitted by previous editors, and the scope of his scholarship enabled him to know what data would be beneficial. His introductory comments immediately identified for Mrs. Pulley material that would be pertinent to her study. Her other printed sources included the memoirs of both the Marquis de Condorcet and the Marquis de Lafayette and Jared Sparks's edition of the *Correspondence of the American Revolution*. She realized that the Sparks edition is unreliable but referred to it for convenience.

[122] Interview, see Appendix C1.

184

Since her focus was on Jefferson, Mrs. Pulley was not greatly concerned about the purity of the edition of documents unrelated to him, such as those in Sparks. When in doubt about Sparks, she checked some other source such as the microfilm edition of the Adams papers.[123]

Because Boyd's edition of the Jefferson papers established the canon for modern documentary editing, its critical reception— apart from its function as a source for graduate research—was significant. Bernard Bailyn explained that Boyd's analysis and interpretation of the documents, as well as his grasp of the period, which enabled him to place the documents in their historical context, elevated "a large area of historical study to a new level of comprehensiveness and exactness."[124] He has created a new genre, the exhaustive documentary biography.[125] His willingness to question all pertinent documents resulted in illuminating explanations of activities that would elude orthodox historians or biographers, simply because they usually have no need nor time for such questions. Boyd's questioning of two documents Alexander Hamilton wrote in 1790 resulted in *Number 7: Alexander Hamilton's Secret Attempts to Control American Foreign Policy*, a book seeking to demonstrate Hamilton's insatiable desire to manipulate American foreign policy. "The appearance of the same key documents in *The Papers of Alexander Hamilton* without critical commentary indicates a marked variation in depth of editing and in concept of the editorial function."[126] Boyd was well aware of criticisms that his depth of interpretation exceeded the editorial function, that he created jurisdictional disputes with historians and biographers. They have told him that his job, "as a jealous husband once said to the iceman in a Broadway show, is to deliver ice."[127] But

[123] Interview, see Appendix C3.

[124] "Boyd's Jefferson: Notes for a Sketch," *New England Quarterly*, Vol. XXXIII, No. 3 (Sept., 1960), 380.

[125] *Ibid.*, 383.

[126] Lester J. Cappon, "A Rationale for Historical Editing Past and Present," *William and Mary Quarterly*, 3rd Series, Vol. XXIII, No. 1 (Jan., 1966), 72–73.

[127] Boyd, "Some Animadversions on Being Struck by Lightning," *Daedalus*, Vol. LXXXVI, No. 1 (May, 1955), 54.

with the ice, Boyd elected to deliver those comments necessary to an intelligent explanation and presentation of the text.[128]

For her comparative study of American political deists, Constance B. Schulz called the Jefferson, Adams, and Franklin papers her principal sources. Because the Boyd edition has not yet incorporated all the material pertinent to her topic, Mrs. Schulz studied the Jefferson papers on microfilm, the Worthington C. Ford edition of Jefferson papers, and the Andrew A. Lipscomb and Albert E. Bergh memorial edition, *The Writings of Thomas Jefferson*.[129] Dwight F. Henderson found the papers of famous Americans an important source of his dissertation, "Courts for the New Nation: A History of the Federal Judiciary, 1787–1800." Since all the founding fathers had something to do with the judiciary, these printed sources were most valuable. Among the modern editions, he studied the Jefferson, Madison, Hamilton, and Adams papers and used older editions of the papers of Washington and Jay. Since these older editions omitted much important material related to his topic, Henderson thought the editorial apparatus of Julian Boyd and Harold C. Syrett (the Hamilton papers) extremely helpful. He felt it unnecessary to do any further checking on the Boyd and Syrett editions.[130] For his dissertation on "The Federal Party in the South, 1784–1804," Lisle A. Rose researched the Jefferson and Madison papers "with great profit." Despite his esteem for the respective Boyd and William T. Hutchinson editions, he believed that the research scholar should not rely exclusively on printed versions of documents. He liked to establish with printed sources the framework for further research—to stake out the problem with printed sources and then consult manuscripts only with specific questions.[131]

When James C. Curtis began using the J. S. Bassett edition of the Andrew Jackson papers in connection with his dissertation

[128] *Ibid.*, 55.
[129] Interview, see Appendix C3.
[130] Henderson, *ibid.* Cf. Richard B. Morris, "The Current Statesmen's Papers Publications Program: An Appraisal from the Point of View of the Legal Historian," *American Journal of Legal History*, Vol. XI, No. 2 (Apr., 1967), 95–106.
[131] Rose, *ibid.*

on "The Presidency of Martin Van Buren," he felt the work was satisfactory. As he became more familiar with the topic, however, he discovered that Bassett frequently left out important material. Since he had increasingly less confidence in Bassett's editing, Curtis relied more on the microfilm copies of the original letters. A printed source that Curtis used with confidence was Reginald McGrane's edition of the Nicholas Biddle correspondence. McGrane made an excellent selection of letters reflecting Biddle's national involvements.[132]

Students frequently had occasion to consult these papers of famous Americans for limited research projects. John C. Burnham had a student check *The Papers of Henry Clay*, edited by James F. Hopkins, to see if Clay linked his ideas on science to the American System.[133] In his study of American prisoners of war during the Revolution, John K. Alexander garnered some information from Leonard W. Labaree's edition of *The Papers of Benjamin Franklin* and the Fitzpatrick edition of the George Washington papers.[134] When a student of the history of science was interested in acoustics, W. Frank Craven referred him to Benjamin Franklin's letter on the subject in the Labaree edition. Craven said graduate history students at Princeton repeatedly check such references in edited papers, although they do not base major research on the volumes.[135] Arthur S. Link, editor of *The Papers of Woodrow Wilson*, hoped that both undergraduate and graduate students at Princeton would use the volumes for research as they are published. Only rarely would a student need to go behind the printed documents to check the originals.[136]

These edited documents have an obvious place in the classroom as well as on the researcher's desk. Roy Basler's edition of *The Collected Works of Abraham Lincoln* is effective with students because the editor consistently informed the reader of the conditions under which documents were written. In this case, as with

132 Curtis, *ibid*.
133 Interview, see Appendix C1.
134 Interview, see Appendix C3.
135 Interview, see Appendix C1.
136 Link, *ibid*.

Elting E. Morison's edition of *The Letters of Theodore Roosevelt*, a great advantage for students is the manageable number of volumes.[137] Alfred D. Chandler, Jr., the assistant editor of *The Letters of Theodore Roosevelt* and editor of the Eisenhower papers, felt that it was important for students to observe a man's day-to-day thinking as revealed in such projects. These observations can give insight into how pressures bearing on the subject influenced his decisions.[138] In his history of science course at the University of California at Berkeley, A. Hunter Dupree used *The Papers of Thomas Jefferson* extensively;[139] and at the University of Notre Dame, J. Philip Gleason put his senior seminar to work on *The Papers of Benjamin Franklin*.[140] The benefits of these letterpress publications extend beyond higher education, according to Kenneth S. Cooper of George Peabody College for Teachers. With the growing emphasis on inductive teaching, these volumes offer good opportunities for placing original sources in the hands of secondary students.[141]

However useful the papers of famous Americans may have been as research tools, some historians feared that the major editorial projects have moved too slowly. As long as important aspects of the individual's life are not covered by the edited publications, these sources remain limited for researchers actively working in the field.[142] "I am bothered," declared James P. Sheton, "with what is happening on the major letterpress publication projects. I will never see the end of the Thomas Jefferson papers in my lifetime." He also commented that although nearly half the Hamilton volumes were published, the most important and interesting aspect of his life was just beginning to emerge.[143]

Allan Nevins' criticism of these publications, which he termed "invaluable," was that by concentrating on the founding fathers,

[137] Interview with James P. Shenton, *ibid*.
[138] Chandler, *ibid*. Madison Kuhn made this same observation, *ibid*.
[139] Dupree, *ibid*.
[140] Gleason, *ibid*.
[141] Cooper, *ibid*.
[142] Interviews with Richard S. Dunn and Thomas D. Clark, *ibid*.; George Chalou, see Appendix C3.
[143] Interview, see Appendix C1.

188

they have led to the neglect of secondary and tertiary figures and thus tended to distort our history.[144] Moreover, by saying that these volumes "are for a gentleman's library," he raised an issue about which many historians feel strongly: that the money going into such publications might better be spent to support monographic and interpretive historical research. Raymond P. Stearns commented that it was easier to get corporations to grant hundreds of thousands of dollars for lavish letterpress publications than to get a few thousand dollars to support research on an interpretive work.[145] "I'm dubious," said Richard S. Dunn, "about the magnificent, expensive, and fancy editions of published papers."[146] Thomas C. Cochran considered the expensiveness of these editorial projects shocking.[147] Because of their cost, the editorial projects have become "a professional racket," according to Arthur M. McAnally, University of Oklahoma librarian.[148] Whatever their shortcomings, Robert E. Brown considered these edited publications "a godsend" to students without access to the originals. "They do tremendous things for lesser universities."[149]

OFFICIAL RECORDS OF THE WAR OF THE REBELLION

At a 1956 conference at the University of Kansas, William B. Hesseltine termed the Civil War the central event in human experience. Although he entertained his proposition more seriously than that particular audience did, he could have mustered considerable support elsewhere. In fact, enthusiasm for the country's centennial commemoration of the Civil War seemed to give Hesseltine's definition a prophetic quality. (Lest the mistakes and false starts of the Civil War Centennial Commission be repeated in the celebration of the bicentennial of the American Revolution, historians should exert themselves immediately to ensure that the

144 Nevins, *ibid.*
145 Stearns, *ibid.*
146 Dunn, *ibid.*
147 Cochran, *ibid.*
148 Interview, see Appendix C2a.
149 Interview, see Appendix C1.

commemoration promotes scholarly goals. For the American Historical Association's Committee on the Commemoration of the American Revolution Bicentennial, L. H. Butterfield drafted recommendations and suggestions for a publication program. See the *Annual Report of the American Historical Association, 1964, Vol. 1*, pp. 45–49.) Many historians predicted—and hoped—that when the centennial years had passed, the interest in and publications about the Civil War would subside. This has not proved to be the case, however. Despite the flood of trivia published about the Civil War, scholarly books on the subject continue to command an enthusiastic audience. As long as scholarly focus is on military aspects of the war, a printed source will constitute the major data repository. For convenience, this series is usually called the *Official Records of the War of the Rebellion*, but the full titles are *The War of the Rebellion: A Compilation of the Official Records of the Union and Confederate Armies* and *Official Records of the Union and Confederate Navies in the War of the Rebellion*.

In departments of history sponsoring research on the Civil War, the *Official Records* "are used like the Bible."[150] Although these books are kept on open shelves in the University of Oklahoma library, thereby making it impossible to obtain an exact measurement of use, the library staff knew from the number of volumes left on reading tables and the demand for an index to the army volumes (the naval volumes have one) that the series was consulted regularly.[151] The South Caroliniana Library also reported brisk use of the *Official Records* and complaints about the difficulty of working with the unindexed series.[152]

Graduate students have often employed the *Official Records* as the major source for dissertation research. When Stephen E. Ambrose (under Hesseltine's direction) gathered material for his dissertation on General Henry W. Halleck, he relied almost exclusively on the series because of the paucity of Halleck manuscripts.[153] For her dissertation, "The Gubernatorial Years of

---

[150] Interview with Frank E. Vandiver, *ibid.*
[151] Interview with Arthur M. McAnally, director, see Appendix C2a.
[152] Interview with E. L. Inabinett, director, *ibid.*
[153] Interview, see Appendix C1.

Oliver P. Morton, 1860–1865," Lorna Sylvester found much pertinent data in the *Official Records* and was able to trace involvements of Indiana's military units and their impact on state politics.[154] David Goodman, in seeking information on the activities of J. Ross Browne for his master's thesis, discovered a great deal about Browne's 1863 trip to Arizona in the *Official Records*.[155] When Robert D. Ochs was a graduate student at the University of Illinois, James G. Randall had him search the set for all Lincoln letters and compare them with the originals and other printed versions. This project of verifying Lincoln sources was connected with Randall's own research. Ochs noted a high degree of fidelity in the Lincoln letters printed in the *Official Records*.[156]

TERRITORIAL PAPERS

A set of printed documents which has won considerable praise for the quality of its editing, indexing, and contents is *The Territorial Papers of the United States*. Begun under the editorship of Clarence E. Carter in 1931, the first volume of the series was published in 1934. Before his death in 1961, Carter had edited the twenty-six volumes published so far. These dealt with territories east of the Mississippi River, as well as Louisiana, Arkansas, and Missouri. The first of the Wisconsin Territory volumes, prepared by the current editor, John Porter Bloom, was published in 1969.

The quality of the *Territorial Papers* as an original source has received mixed comments from those whose work makes them the most discriminating critics—fellow editors of documentary publications. In editing the Jefferson papers, Julian P. Boyd has consistently used the *Territorial Papers* as a reference and has determined them to be "generally reliable." When Boyd had his first occasion to test Carter's substantive scholarship, however, he discovered unexpected shortcomings. In handling the first report on the Northwest Territory that Jefferson made as secretary of state, Carter was guilty of "erroneous captions, misreadings of the texts,

---

154 Interview, see Appendix C3.
155 Goodman, *ibid.*
156 Interview, see Appendix C1.

failure to identify enclosures, and violation of the integrity of a document (i.e., treating a single document as two separate documents)."[157] Boyd admitted extreme surprise at his findings, for Carter had impressed him "as being so austere in confining himself to the single object of presenting a reliable text and eschewing as absolutely impermissible any expression of editorial judgment" that Boyd grew accustomed to accepting Carter's texts unquestioningly. "On the basis of this experience I would rank him well below [Edmund C.] Burnett in reliability and just about on a par with [John C.] Fitzpatrick."[158] James F. Hopkins, editor of *The Papers of Henry Clay*, has also consulted the *Territorial Papers* regularly. The quality of its index made it a standard reference for the Clay project,[159] and Dorman H. Winfrey found that the "marvellous" index made the *Territorial Papers* indispensable for his dissertation.[160]

Professors have expressed enthusiasm for the *Territorial Papers* as the basis for teaching assignments and dissertation research. During the twenty years William T. Hutchinson offered a course at the University of Chicago in the history of the public domain, the *Territorial Papers* were basic for his own study and that of the class.[161] Robert W. Johannsen, while teaching at the University of Kansas, based an entire seminar on this series.[162] At the University of Minnesota, Robert F. Berkhofer, Jr., sometimes assigned seminar topics for which the research had to be done in the *Territorial Papers*.[163] Farther east, a student of Bayrd Still at New York University did his dissertation research in this material,[164] as did Robert V. Haynes for his dissertation at Rice University on the Mississippi Territory.[165] Both Raymond P. Stearns and Clar-

[157] Letter, Boyd to author, June 27, 1967.
[158] *Ibid*. Cf. Edmund C. Burnett (ed.), *Letters of Members of the Continental Congress* and John C. Fitzpatrick (ed.), *The Writings of George Washington from the Original Manuscript Sources*.
[159] Interview, see Appendix C1.
[160] Interview, see Appendix C2b.
[161] Interview, see Appendix C1.
[162] Johannsen, *ibid*.
[163] Berkhofer, *ibid*.
[164] Still, *ibid*.
[165] Interview with Sanford W. Higginbotham, *ibid*.

ence L. Ver Steeg, specialists in colonial history at the University of Illinois and Northwestern University, respectively, had students use the *Territorial Papers* for projects dealing with the early history of Illinois. One of Ver Steeg's students relied heavily on the *Territorial Papers* in writing a dissertation on the beginnings of the state government.[166] In his research on the medical history of Louisiana, John Duffy discovered much pertinent information in the volumes dealing with that territory.[167]

The larger sets of printed sources have naturally afforded ample opportunity for research, but students often have had occasion to investigate some of the less ambitious series of published documents. The following instances indicate the variety of research purposes to which they were put. Donald D. Johnson assigned a University of Hawaii student the project of finding the official explanations of why the United States has declared war on various occasions. For the answers, the student based her research on *Messages and Papers of the Presidents*, edited by James D. Richardson.[168] In a senior seminar at the University of Notre Dame, Marshall Smelser sent students to the Richardson set to see official American views of the French Revolution.[169] During the fall, 1965, semester, George E. Mowry devoted a seminar to presidential uses of history, with emphasis on presidents of this century. His students made constant use of the Richardson set, *The Letters of Theodore Roosevelt*, and *Public Papers of the Presidents*.[170] The last set, published by the National Archives on a continuing basis, began with the administration of Harry S Truman and comes to the present. It incorporates every public pronouncement of the presidents.

William M. Leary, Jr., found the *Public Papers of the Presidents* especially helpful for information from Truman and Eisenhower press conferences, which he used in his biographical dissertation on H. Alexander Smith, a New Jersey senator. These volumes give

[166] Stearns and Ver Steeg, *ibid.*
[167] Duffy, *ibid.*
[168] Johnson, *ibid.*
[169] Smelser, *ibid.*
[170] Mowry, *ibid.*

the full texts of press conferences, whereas most newspaper accounts include only quotations or paraphrases. Because of Smith's different senatorial involvements, Leary also investigated *The Private Papers of Senator Vandenberg*, the special volume on China from *Foreign Relations*, the Congressional serial set, and committee hearings on General Douglas MacArthur's dismissal. He found the *Congressional Quarterly Almanac* extremely helpful because of its excellent vote tabulation.[171]

Naval documentary publications such as the *Quasi-War with France* and the *Barbary War* rest in virtual oblivion among graduate students in United States history. On the undergraduate level, a senior honors seminar under Marshall Smelser's direction worked exclusively on the *Quasi-War with France*. Assignments were made on such topics as the professional standards of naval officer Thomas Truxtun and the treatment of French prisoners.[172] At Rice University the commander of the Navy ROTC assigned research papers for the course in naval history, and the midshipmen became deeply involved in these documentary publications.[173]

Since Jon L. Wakelyn's dissertation dealt with the political aspects of the career of William Gilmore Simms, the South Carolina writer, he investigated many governmental publications. In addition to Congressional publications, *Messages and Papers of the Presidents*, and minutes of the South Carolina legislature, Wakelyn used the Calhoun papers published in the *Annual Reports* of the American Historical Association for 1899 and 1929.[174]

RECOMMENDATIONS

In the course of responding to the survey's question on the use of printed sources in graduate training, many professors made specific recommendations either for improving existing publications or for inaugurating projects which would be beneficial in that training. Following is a list of pertinent suggestions for additions that historians would like to have.

[171] Interview, see Appendix C3.
[172] Interview, see Appendix C1.
[173] Interview with Sanford W. Higginbotham, *ibid.*
[174] Interview, see Appendix C3.

1. A simplified guide to government documents.[175] The great wealth of social material in Congressional committee hearings has hardly been tapped because of the difficulty of identifying relevant data.[176] The inaccuracies in the indexing of hearings should be corrected by co-ordinating the indexes with the *Monthly Catalog* entries.[177] A descriptive guide or index to the *Official Records of the War of the Rebellion* is needed.[178] Fortunately, Dallas Irvine of the National Archives has been engaged in compiling "A Guide Index to the *Official Records of the War of the Rebellion.*"[179]

2. A comprehensive microfilm edition of Congressional committee hearings, incorporating both the unpublished and the published hearings.[180]

3. Microfilm publication of briefs filed before the Supreme Court.[181]

4. Republication of the Congressional debates from the Second Congress until the beginning of the *Congressional Globe*. The *Annals of Congress*, based as they were on the *National Intelligencer*, are inadequate for the debates.[182]

5. Publication of Congressional documents before the Fifteenth Congress, when the Congressional serial set began.[183]

6. Publication of full sets of state laws, documents, and legislative proceedings. This project should be the province of state historical societies.[184]

7. Reprinting of the Samuel I. Rosenman edition of *The Public Papers and Addresses of Franklin D. Roosevelt.*[185]

[175] Interview with General Reference and Bibliography staff, Library of Congress, see Appendix C2b.

[176] Interview with David D. Van Tassel, see Appendix C1.

[177] Interview with Jeanne B. North, chief of Government Documents division, Stanford University library, see Appendix C2a.

[178] Interviews with Avery O. Craven and James P. Shenton, see Appendix C1.

[179] Cf. *Military Operations of the Civil War: A Guide Index to the Official Records of the Union and Confederate Armies, 1861–1865.*

[180] I queried professors specifically about their interest in this and received unanimously enthusiastic reactions. The National Archives has subsequently gotten the project under way.

[181] Interview with Arthur Bestor, see Appendix C1.

[182] *Ibid.*   [183] *Ibid.*

[184] Interview with David Donald, see Appendix C1; Bestor, *ibid.*

[185] Interview with Frank Freidel, *ibid.*

8. Extension of the *Public Papers of the Presidents* from Harry S Truman back, president by president.[186]

9. Publication of full texts of press conferences of cabinet officers and other important government officials. "Press conferences are the one place these days when we can be sure that the individual government officer is speaking himself, and not relying upon a ghost writer."[187]

10. Collection in one repository of reproductions of the collected papers of many Americans from every social station, with these reproductions being made available on interlibrary loan.[188] Clarence L. Ver Steeg thought such a plan would be more beneficial than a proliferation of large-scale editorial projects. He had no quarrel with the "big five"—the papers of Jefferson, Adams, Madison, Hamilton, and Franklin—for these papers clearly merit letterpress publication. Beyond these, however, letterpress publications "can degenerate into pork-barrel projects, with each senator or congressman believing his state should be represented in the series."[189]

11. Reprinting by the National Historical Publications Commission of older publications of edited documents whose scholarly merits have been proven, but which are now scarce. James P. Shenton contended that such projects would be preferable to putting money into new letterpress editions and that they would have more utility to students doing course work than the full-scale editions. His nominations for reprinting included Milo M. Quaife's edition of the James K. Polk diary and the *Annual Reports* of the American Historical Association containing the edited papers of John C. Calhoun, Howell Cobb, and Robert A. Toombs.[190]

12. Collection of newspapers showing the diversity of American society, such as the immigrant, religious, Negro, and popular yellow press. "Almost every university library will have the *New York Times*, but it is hard to find files of the papers of Pulitzer

186 Interview with John A. DeNovo, *ibid.*
187 Interview with Ernest R. May, *ibid.*
188 Interviews with Madison Kuhn and Clarence L. Ver Steeg, *ibid.*
189 Ver Steeg, *ibid.*
190 Interview, *ibid.*

and Hearst, or tabloid papers like the *New York Daily News*. . . .
These papers reflect an important segment of American public
opinion—and at times perhaps have molded it. . . . The contemporary press of the most popular journalistic sort usually expressed
viewpoints not found elsewhere."[191] Robert D. Cross agreed with
such a collecting proposal and said that the biggest stress in the
department at Columbia University has been to get students to
treat newspapers as original sources.[192]

Since the use of original sources depends on their availability,
two suggestions on access to records in the National Archives
justify inclusion. Harold A. Bierck maintained that historians
should be able to get Congressional committee hearings for the
1800–30 period without having to request permission from the
Clerk of the House or Senate.[193] For years this matter has concerned the American Historical Association's Committee on the
Historian and the Federal Government. The *Annual Reports* for
1963, 1964, and 1965 show that the committee recommended that
the AHA Council exert pressure to get the onerous and unjustified
restriction on House records lifted. In 1965 the council passed a
resolution to this effect and the association communicated this
resolution to House members, but as of July, 1967, the House had
not changed its stand.[194] Merrill Jensen suggested that the National
Archives publish a finding aid for the early national court records,
both federal and district, and make them easily accessible to
researchers.[195]

The importance of printed sources in graduate history training
has grown for different reasons. One is that the federal government and lesser governmental units are playing increasingly larger
roles in American society and their documents reflect this greater
activity. Consequently, a larger portion of the subjects about
which historians write can be documented with government publi-

[191] Interview with William G. McLoughlin, Jr., *ibid.*
[192] Cross, *ibid.*
[193] Bierck, *ibid.*
[194] *Annual Report, 1963, Vol. 1*, p. 52; *Annual Report, 1964, Vol. 1*, p. 51;
Annual Report, 1965, Vol. 1, pp. 41, 60.
[195] Interview, see Appendix C1.

cations. Another reason for their growing importance is that the quality of some types of printed sources has improved greatly. This improvement is especially true of the current letterpress publications of edited papers of famous Americans. Furthermore, since many new doctoral programs have been initiated with-

Interviews with Professors on Students' Use of
Printed Original Sources

Printed Original Sources	Used as Appropriate	Regular Use	Extensive Use	Not Used	Not Used Regularly	Don't Know of Use
Papers of famous Americans	30	13	9	2	5	
Foreign Relations series	17	4	21	4	6	
Territorial Papers	22	5	7	5	7	2
Congressional serial set	39	12	37	1	2	
Official Records of the War of the Rebellion	22	6	8	2	5	
Early State Records (filmed)	8	2	1	3	5	
Messages and Papers of the Presidents	32	8	10	1	4	
Public Papers of the Presidents	17	4	4	3	5	
Navy publications	8	1		1	4	1
Congressional committee hearings	39	9	15		4	
Other government documents*	8	4	6		3	
Other printed sources†						

*Some other government documents mentioned: Annual Reports of the Secretaries of State, War, Health, Education, and Welfare, and Agriculture; *American State Papers*; census rolls; reports of federal agencies—Federal Reserve Bank, Federal Trade Commission, Securities and Exchange Commission, Federal Communications Commission; Labor statistics.

†Some other printed sources mentioned: Periodicals—nineteenth-century literary, political, historical societies; journals, diaries, sermons, pamphlets.

out manuscript resources, their graduate students are obviously obliged to exploit the available printed sources.

Many departments—with both new and old doctoral programs— candidly admit that without printed sources their research materials would be inadequate, and they would not be able to offer the Ph.D. In some cases, students can and do rely wholly on printed sources because of their dissertation topics, but fortunately they usually do not have to choose exclusively between these sources and manuscripts. Neither is inherently superior; each should be studied for the information it can yield most efficiently. Learning to make this discrimination is a significant part of research training in United States history.

Being unable to establish any precise method for measuring use of printed sources, the survey tried to obtain some sense of the frequency with which graduate students employed various printed sources in research. The accompanying tables indicate roughly the degrees of popularity of these sources with researchers.

Interviews with Academic Librarians on Students' Use of Printed Original Sources

Printed Original Sources	Used as Appropriate	Frequent Use	Not Used	Don't Know of Use	Not used Regularly
Papers of famous Americans	3	9		1	
Foreign Relations series		17		1	
Territorial Papers	2	7		1	3
Congressional serial set	2	14			1
Official Records	1	11	1	1	1
Early State Records (filmed)	2		1		3
Messages and Papers of the Presidents	3				1
Public Papers of the Presidents	3	3			
Navy publications	2	1	2		3
Congressional committee hearings	2	16			

Interviews with Nonacademic Librarians on Students'
Use of Printed Original Sources

Printed Original Sources	Used as Appropriate	Used Frequently	Not Used Too Effectively
Papers of famous Americans	4	4	
Foreign Relations series	3	11	
Territorial Papers	4	7	5
Congressional serial set	2	9	4
Official Records	4	7	2
Early State Records (filmed)	3		2
Messages and Papers of the Presidents	2	1	2
Public Papers of the Presidents	3	3	
Navy publications	1	1	2
Congressional committee hearings	4	12	2
Other government documents	2	2	1
Other printed sources*			

*Some other printed original sources mentioned: Annual agency reports, reports of Bureau of Indian Affairs, U.N. documents.

Interviews with Graduate Students on Their Use of
Printed Original Sources

Printed Original Sources	Use mentioned
Papers of famous Americans*	21
Foreign Relations series	24
Territorial Papers	8
Congressional serial set	67
Official Records of the War of the Rebellion	13
Early State Records (filmed)	0
Messages and Papers of the Presidents	25
Presidential papers	8
Navy publications	1
Congressional committee hearings	32
Other government publications†	12
Others	5

*Some papers mentioned: J. Adams, 1; Calhoun, 2; Clay, 2; Franklin, 1; Hamilton, 4; Jefferson, 6; A. Johnson, 1; Lincoln, 3; Madison, 3; Monroe, 3; F. D. Roosevelt, 6; T. Roosevelt, 3; Truman, 2; Washington, 1.

†Other government documents: Official statutes, 2; Indian Bureau, 2; Supreme Court, 1; Interstate Commerce Commission, 1; local state records, 1; historical statistics of the U.S.,1.

Questionnaire Responses to Students' Use of Printed Original Sources

Printed Original Sources	Ph.D. 27 respondents	M.A. 62 respondents
Papers of famous Americans	27	56
Foreign Relations series	27	62
Territorial Papers	23	47
Congressional serial set	27	58
Official Records of the War of the Rebellion	27	59
Early State Records (filmed)	15	8
Messages and Papers of the Presidents	27	62
Public Papers of the Presidents	22	52
Navy publications	19	39
Congressional committee hearings	25	47
Other government documents*	25	47
Other printed original sources	11	13

*Other government documents reported: Official records from other governments (France and England); state documents and legislative journals; colonial and historical society collections; U.N. documents.

VII. Photocopy

PROBABLY no factor has made a more significant impact upon research techniques in United States history than photocopying.[1] Distribution of photographic reproductions of manuscripts and printed sources has reduced the necessity for a scholar to conduct his research where the originals are located. Many beginning researchers now have access to sources that only the most privileged of their predecessors had a comparatively short time ago. Of course, printed editions of manuscripts and archives, long predating the advent of photocopy, also made travel to the originals unnecessary, but photocopied editions of these can be produced with far less delay and expense. Consequently, through photoduplication great quantities of material have become readily available, revolutionizing research methods in the process. With sufficient money, any institution can develop an impressive collection of photoreproduced sources, making possible research on a wide range of subjects. Moreover, possession of the major sets of

[1] "Photocopy," with its synonyms and derivatives, seems to be the best generic term to include all forms of photographic reproduction: microfilm, microfiche, microprint, photostat, Xerography, etc. Where necessary, I distinguish between microforms and facsimiles or hard copies.

[2] Interviews with Alexander DeConde and W. Stitt Robinson, see Appendix C1.

[3] *Yale Review*, Vol. XXIV, No. 3 (Mar., 1935), 519–37. The following year Binkley published the *Manual on Methods of Reproducing Research Materials*.

photocopy has enabled many universities that could not otherwise have done so to offer respectable doctoral programs.[2] Some historians and custodians of original sources are nonetheless unenthusiastic about, or antagonistic toward, research with this medium. Despite these naysayers, photocopy must now be reckoned with as an important means of studying the American past.

The changes photocopy has made in scholarly research can be traced through several publications. An early assessment (1935) was Robert C. Binkley's "New Tools for Men of Letters."[3] Since 1943, *The American Archivist* has carried an annual bibliography of "Writings on Archives and Manuscripts," containing a section on the "Application of Photographic Processes to Work with Records and Historical Manuscripts." This section is the most comprehensive listing of literature in the field. An article, "Planning for Scholarly Photocopying,"[4] summarized developments and relevant literature in the notes. A recent and comprehensive study was William R. Hawken's *Copying Methods Manual*. Financed by the Council on Library Resources and written by one of the best technicians in the field, the *Manual* contains an exhaustive glossary embracing the diverse apparatus spawned by the industry.[5] With the proliferation of mechanical equipment, most historians have been willing to leave technical aspects of the field to librarians and archivists. By not keeping current, historians have risked ignorance of developments that may pertain directly to their research needs.

ADVANTAGES OF PHOTOCOPY

Some researchers have so appreciated the possibilities afforded by photocopy that they contended its advantages far outweigh the disadvantages.[6] At many institutions, photocopy has made possible the investigation of many subjects that would otherwise have been unapproachable. Such was the case at the University of

[4] *Publications of the Modern Languages Association*, Vol. LXXIX, No. 4, pt. 2 (Sept., 1964), 77–90.

[5] See Appendix F for a selected list of finding aids for microform publications.

[6] Interviews with Bernard Bailyn, David Alan Williams, and Malcolm Moule, see Appendix C; Lisle A. Rose, see Appendix C3.

Arizona with David Goodman's thesis on J. Ross Browne. "Without microfilm, I would have been doomed," Goodman remarked.[7]

For different researchers, photocopy had various advantages over other types of original sources. Some preferred its ease of handling, especially when they were dealing with bulky items such as the *New York Times* and other newspapers.[8] Others liked to work with photoduplications because they eliminate the possibility of damage to originals and thereby speed up research.[9] Those who had to travel with research materials considered microfilm easy to transport. They also found it handy to be able to take along facsimiles of documents essential to their projects. For instance, when Sister Mary Christine Taylor went to Saint Louis University to write her dissertation on Roman Catholicism in northern New York, she took photostats of documents from the Ogdensburg diocesan archives with her.[10] If the experience of Barton C. Olsen was any indication, the hardiness of microfilm makes it an ideal way to transport documents. In doing research for his dissertation on lawlessness in the West, he made a roll of microfilm at the Montana Historical Society. En route back to Salt Lake City on his motor scooter, Olsen discovered that the film had blown away. He backtracked, found the film unwound by the roadside, and despaired. He had it cleaned, however, and discovered to his delight that it was perfectly legible.[11]

For many researchers, especially graduate students, the overriding advantage of photocopy was financial. Considering the expense of travel, in terms of time and money, great savings could be effected if one's research material were handily available on photocopy. For the growing percentage of married graduate students, many with small children, extended research trips created considerable strains. Such individuals welcomed the advantages of research with photocopy. James R. Sharp, while gathering

[7] Interview, see Appendix C3.
[8] Interviews with Constance B. Schulz, Darrel L. Ashby, and Philip Racine, *ibid.*; Charles C. McLaughlin, see Appendix C1.
[9] Interview with John Storey, see Appendix C3.
[10] Taylor, *ibid.*
[11] Olsen, *ibid.*

material for his dissertation, had a number of manuscripts micro-filmed. He estimated that using the film cut his travel time in half.[12] Kenneth R. Bowling pointed out that research away from home can be very boring. By having available on microfilm many complete editions of papers related to his dissertation on the politics of the First Congress, he saved time and money and was not separated from his family. The major editions he investigated were the Evans Early American Imprint Series, presidential papers from the Library of Congress, and the papers of the Adamses, the Lees, Robert Morris, Nicholas Biddle, Timothy Pickering, and Winthrop Sargent. Bowling applauded the publication of these comprehensive microfilm editions because they enable scholars to know that they are missing no documents from the collection.[13] Such established historians as Alfred D. Chandler, Jr., and John A. DeNovo likewise commented that photocopy's great advantage was in reducing the length of research trips. As editor of the Eisenhower papers, Chandler said he has spent most of his life working with photoreproductions. Although tiring of reading photocopies, he thought it much better than traveling two thousand miles to see the originals. For him, photocopying is the "great hope of the future."[14]

While research with microforms can reduce time spent in travel, facsimiles, such as Xerox, photostat, and Thermofax, can greatly diminish time spent in the mechanical process of note taking. Frederick D. Kershner, Jr., urged his students to have extensive quotations duplicated unless they considered their time completely worthless.[15] When a researcher needs to take notes on large quantities of source material, he can save an enormous amount of time and ensure photographic accuracy by making facsimile copies. Thus, when William M. Leary, Jr., surveyed the four hundred boxes of H. Alexander Smith papers, he decided it would be too time consuming to take notes on the pertinent docu-

[12] Sharp, *ibid.*
[13] Bowling, *ibid.*
[14] Interviews, see Appendix C1.
[15] Kershner, *ibid.*

ments and had them Xeroxed, with "marvelous" results.[16] Further advantages of duplicated notes are that, as hard copies, they can be arranged in sequence and annotated.[17] They can also be dismembered for refinements in organization, but unless the worker carefully annotates each snippet, he may face difficulties with citations. Additionally, cutting and pasting removes information from its context and may therefore produce problems of analysis.[18] If a researcher wishes to study an entire roll of microfilm intensively, he can have facsimiles of each frame made with the Xerox Copyflo.

TECHNICAL PROBLEMS WITH PHOTOCOPY

Whatever the advantages of photocopy, its use nevertheless entails a variety of problems for researchers. One of the problems is esthetic. Wilfrid H. Callcott felt that for all the virtues of microfilm, "it has something of the quality of kissing a girl through a plate-glass window. You don't get the feel of the papers or the sense of the run of the material."[19] Not getting the feel of the papers makes microfilm "an antiseptic way of doing research."[20] Thus, many historians objected to the Eastman Recordak model MPE because the researcher has the sensation of sticking his head into a box.

The physical characteristics of some microform projectors have created various difficulties for researchers. Some contended that microfilm readers, in general, were mechanically inadequate,[21] while others said that age, inadequate maintenance, and unsuitable housing made the equipment unsatisfactory.[22] James P. Shenton saw in Columbia University's "hodgepodge" of unwieldy and antiquated machines a reflection of the changing technology of microfilm readers.[23] At many libraries improper room lighting,

[16] Interview, see Appendix C3.
[17] Interview with Richard S. Kirkendall, see Appendix C1.
[18] Interview with Fred Roach, Jr., see Appendix C3.
[19] Interview, see Appendix C1.
[20] Interview with Michael Wallace, see Appendix C3.
[21] Interview with Henry L. Swint, see Appendix C1.
[22] Interviews with James P. Shenton, *ibid.*; and James C. Curtis, see Appendix C3.
[23] Shenton, above.

tending most frequently toward darkness, hindered the effectiveness of microform readers. Librarians at Saint Louis University have experimented with lighting to obtain optimum results in the Vatican Film Library, which was equipped with readers for any microform. The experiments demonstrated that a moderate amount of light provided best reading conditions for their equipment.[24] A common complaint of mechanical deficiency concerned the microcard reader. The card's opacity often produced a blurred and gritty image, in contrast to the sharp image afforded by the translucent microfiche.[25] Many librarians and historians thought that costly reader-printers, which can produce a facsimile of an individual frame from a microfilm roll, were unsatisfactory. They complained that the black-on-white prints made from positive rolls were so dark as to be almost illegible. Prints made from negative rolls were more satisfactory.[26] Of course, different models of reader-printers produce results of varying quality, some quite good.[27]

Because of obvious problems produced by microform readers, researchers made specific suggestions concerning the mechanical equipment. Foremost was the need for a standardized reader for all types of microforms. Too often a new micropublication has entailed the purchase of a new reader, and the absurdity of having so many different microforms and readers is patent.[28] In addition

[24] Interview with James V. Jones, director of libraries; Rose Brady, Government Documents collection; Catherine E. Weidle, Rare Books librarian; Charles J. Ermatinger, Vatican Film librarian; Edward R. Vollmar, S.J., associate director; see Appendix C2a.
[25] Interviews with Ralph H. Parker, university librarian, University of Missouri, *ibid.*; Merrill Jensen, see Appendix C1; and Leslie W. Dunlap, director of the university library, Dale M. Bentz, associate director, Catharine J. Reynolds, head of Government Documents, Ronald Fingerson and Francis Paluka, Special Collections department, University of Iowa, see Appendix C2a. Cf. R. R. Dickison, "The Scholar and the Future of Microfilm," *American Documentation*, Vol. XVII, No. 4 (Oct., 1966), 178–79.
[26] Interviews with Earl E. Olson, Margaret Scriven, and Barbara Tyler, see Appendix C2b; Joseph Maizlish, see Appendix C3; Robert Thomson, see Appendix C1; Joseph E. Jeffs, see Appendix C2a.
[27] Interview with Albert H. Leisinger, Jr., see Appendix C2b.
[28] Interviews with Warren J. Haas, director; Neda M. Westlake, Rare Books librarian; Flora D. Colton, reference department, University of Pennsylvania library, see Appendix C2a; University of Kentucky library staff, see n. 32, Chap. V;

to the mindless variations in equipment, many models were mechanically inadequate. The University of Kentucky library staff complained about having to tear a machine apart just to replace a bulb.[29] Arthur Bestor commented on the "extraordinarily cumbersome" readers, which a little engineering could improve greatly. He suggested that Eastman develop an inexpensive microfilm cartridge that would slip into the Recordak and thus eliminate the awkward threading and winding of the film.[30] Jacob R. Marcus advocated that a national testing agency such as Consumers' Union study and rate microform equipment so that potential purchasers might have the benefit of impartial judgment.[31]

Historians commented that libraries frequently have given little thought to making research with microforms expedient. They often keep the equipment to be used with the microforms in areas with poor lighting and inconvenient or inadequate space, frequently without consideration for how the researcher can take notes, either manually or with a typewriter, while using the microfilm reader.[32] Sometimes the equipment itself, as in the case of the old Eastman Recordak Model C with the nearly perpendicular green frosted screen, made note taking difficult.[33]

An inherent problem in the use of microforms is the inability of the researcher to rearrange the sequence to suit his purposes. Nor can the image on the screen be filed with other notes. These frustrations caused Louis R. Harlan to speak of the agony of using microfilm. He liked to Xerox source materials so that he could arrange them in any sequence he desired.[34] Harold T. Parker also

---

Jack M. Sosin, see Appendix C1; questionnaire returned by W. S. Wallace, New Mexico Highlands University.

[29] Interview, above.

[30] Interview, see Appendix C1. Eastman developed such a cartridge for microfilms of Sears, Roebuck & Co. catalogs, but its high cost has prevented adaptation for scholarly use, a characteristic of too much of our technology.

[31] Interview, see Appendix C2a. The Library Technology Project, sponsored by the Council on Library Resources, has done this.

[32] Interviews with John K. Nelson, Michael McVaugh, Howard R. Lamar, and A. B. Erickson, see Appendix C1; Clyde E. Pitts and James L. Lancaster, see Appendix C3.

[33] Interview with Paul I. Chestnut, *ibid.*; Harold D. Langley, see Appendix C1.

[34] Harlan, *ibid.*

disliked working with a screen image rather than a hard copy, but he admitted belonging to an older generation.[35] That graduate students registered the same complaints indicated that the age of the researcher did not determine his reaction to microforms,[36] although David Kaser, director of the Joint University Libraries in Nashville, believed that the greatest resistance to microforms has come from those "quickly reaching the retirement age."[37] An obvious deterrent to doing research with microforms is the fact that the machines dictate where the work will be done. Unless one owns a portable reader and has access to film at any chosen time, his research is restricted to the time and place where readers are available.[38]

A criticism voiced with some frequency concerned the inadequate number of microform readers provided by universities. In some cases this was a matter of physical equipment not keeping pace with graduate enrollments, but in others the institutions simply have not been willing to recognize that technology has made a material difference in research techniques. Many libraries were built before photocopy had become an important aspect of scholarly research, and, as a consequence, the mechanical equipment has been housed in makeshift places. Too often, this has been in gloomy basements. Also, available space has limited the number of machines a library could hold. In some libraries, crowding and improvised housing have resulted in unsafe conditions. Whatever the reasons, professors and graduate students have commented on the shortage of microform readers at the following institutions: Tulane University, Texas Christian University, Michigan State University, University of Illinois, University of Nebraska, Indiana University, George Washington University, Georgetown University, University of Maryland, University of Southern California, Harvard University, George Peabody College for Teachers, University of Michigan, Vanderbilt University, Emory University, University of North Carolina, University of Texas, North-

[35] Parker, *ibid.*
[36] Interview with Eric Foner, see Appendix C3.
[37] Interview, see Appendix C2a.
[38] Interviews with James Zeidman, see Appendix C3; John W. Caughey and Alden T. Vaughan, see Appendix C1.

western University, University of Minnesota, University of Denver, Ohio State University, Columbia University, Yale University, Rutgers—The State University, the State University of New York at Albany, and the University of Mississippi.[39] Some departments attempted to alleviate their library's shortage of reading machines by purchasing their own readers and placing them in either the department or the library.

The effectiveness with which researchers can use original sources on microform frequently depended upon the way the library housed and administered them. When libraries allowed the form rather than the content to determine how the material was administered, the scholarly researcher usually suffered. Most libraries acquired newspapers as their first substantial amounts of microfilm, and many have decided that all microforms would be handled by the newspaper or periodical division, irrespective of the fact that the personnel in that division might know absolutely nothing about the contents of other types of microforms. The great danger in centralizing microforms is that librarians are tempted to put low-grade clerical help in charge of them. Such a clerk does well to find a given roll of microfilm, much less know anything of its contents. Among the libraries which administered microforms according to their content were those at the Universities of Illinois and Missouri. The University of Illinois archives treated its small amount of photocopy as manuscripts, preparing finding aids for it and including the information in the card catalog. The Missouri library also cataloged microfilmed manuscripts as if they were originals and tried to give researchers the same kind of help with film as with manuscripts.[40]

[39] Interviews with Thomas L. Karnes, Donald E. Worcester, Robert E. Brown, Raymond P. Stearns, James C. Olson, H. Trevor Colbourn, Peter P. Hill, Richard Walsh, David S. Sparks, Joseph Boskin, Frank Freidel, Kenneth S. Cooper, William B. Willcox, Paul H. Bergeron, R. Bingham Duncan, Harold A. Bierck, Francis B. Weisenburger, Robert A. Divine, Howard R. Lamar, and Richard W. Leopold, see Appendix C1; Edward B. Stanford, see Appendix C2a; Harold E. Van Horn, Thomas J. Archdeacon, and George W. Franz, see Appendix C3; questionnaires returned by Kendall Birr, State University of New York at Albany, and Joseph O. Baylen, University of Mississippi.

[40] Interviews with University of Illinois library staff, see n. 75, Chap. III; Ralph H. Parker, university librarian, University of Missouri, see Appendix C2a.

A problem many researchers complained about concerns delays by repositories in filling photocopy orders.[41] Scholars most frequently criticized the Library of Congress Photoduplication Service for its sluggish performance.[42] Those who did research regularly at the Library of Congress, as well as visiting scholars, also were frustrated with having to put up with the red tape and delays of the Photoduplication Service to obtain a single Xerox copy.[43]

While some historians commented that research was quicker with microfilm because of the savings in travel time, others contended that such work impeded them. John R. Alden, Fletcher M. Green, and Lewis E. Atherton lost a great deal of time working with microfilm.[44] A specific characteristic of microfilm that causes delays in research is the fact that it cannot be scanned easily. Merely locating desired information can take a long time if the reseacher has to wind the film back and forth, stopping to see if particular frames contain the needed data.[45] Microfilmed newspapers are particularly tedious since there is no way to flip through the pages.[46]

Practically every respondent to the survey's question on photocopy commented with varying degrees of intensity on the eyestrain caused by microfilm. As a result of their experiences, many historians had a positive aversion to microforms and dreaded having to use them.[47] Because of eyestrain, some could work with microfilm for only a limited period, sometimes as little as an hour. Anything beyond that at times produced violent headaches, dizzi-

[41] Interviews with J. Rogers Hollingsworth, see Appendix C1; John K. Alexander, see Appendix C3.

[42] Interviews with T. N. McMullan, director, Louisiana State University library, see Appendix C2a; Philip J. Funigiello and Roger Balt, see Appendix C3.

[43] Interview with William R. Hutchison, see Appendix C1; Larry D. Hill, see Appendix C3.

[44] Interviews, see Appendix C1.

[45] Interviews with William B. Willcox and Daniel W. Hollis, *ibid.*; Lynn Hales, see Appendix C3.

[46] Interview with Frank O. Gatell, see Appendix C1.

[47] Interviews with Paul C. Nagel, Richard S. Dunn, and Harold D. Langley, *ibid.*

ness, and temporary visual difficulties.[48] A few historians claimed that research with microforms resulted in a measure of permanent visual loss. Donald D. Johnson said that, as a consequence of his working with microfilm, his eyes had suffered.[49] Robert P. Hay had to start wearing glasses after he worked with microfilm,[50] and Lewis E. Atherton had to change to trifocals because of the strain microfilm put on his eyes.[51] Since microforms unquestionably produce eyestrain, which in turn slows research and creates various other physical discomforts, manufacturers of reading machines should investigate intensively means of eliminating optical hazards presently generated by their equipment.[52] Despite the overwhelming testimony of researchers that microforms cause eyestrain, medical opinion held that microfilmed books may be read for as long as six hours without causing any ill effects.[53] The physical discomforts of using microforms may be considered the price to be paid for having easy access to material that was often impossible to use before microphotography.

Not all the visual problems associated with microforms can be attributed to the reading equipment, for the quality of the film is sometimes substandard. This deficiency can result from the illegibility of the material being photographed or from deficiencies in the filming process. When microfilming was in its early days, many newspapers were copied, usually to relieve storage problems. Since the newspapers were often in bad shape and the filming techniques crude, the results were unsatisfactory. If the originals were destroyed, as they usually were, researchers have been obliged to use the inferior film. Unfortunately, bad filming has not been restricted to newspapers or early efforts, and any lapses in the mechanical process plague users of the film. Particularly

[48] Interviews with John Duffy, W. Stull Holt, George E. Mowry, and Allan Nevins, *ibid.*; Norman Crockett and Anne E. Hughs, see Appendix C3.
[49] Interview, see Appendix C1.
[50] Interview, see Appendix C3.
[51] Interview, see Appendix C1.
[52] Interviews with Ernest R. May and Richard A. Bartlett, *ibid.*
[53] Leonard Carmichael and Walter F. Dearborn, *Reading and Visual Fatigue*, 325–26.

troublesome are too-high reduction ratios.[54] The trouble produced by low-quality film is not just physical, for scholarly aspects can be involved. If a microform is illegible, a correct transcription becomes problematic. Kenneth W. Porter consistently had to employ a magnifying glass with microfilm and consequently considers its proper deciphering "a scholarly question."[55] Another technical lapse that affects accurate identification or interpretation of a document is the omission by the filmer of such things as envelopes, stamps, or endorsements.[56] In its comparatively brief history, microfilming often has been done with disregard for scholarly needs. If any microform is intended for researchers, it should be prepared by qualified technicians, according to standards established by the research community.[57]

While the omission of envelopes, stamps, and endorsements from filming might interfere with the interpretation of particular documents, researchers were even more leery of the omission of entire documents from a filmed series. Scholars dependent on the film are at the mercy of the photocopier.[58] Incomplete or poorly edited microfilm projects are unreliable and potentially treacherous.[59] When the Latter-day Saints Genealogical Society filmed some New England church and town records, they occasionally skipped pages lacking vital statistics without noting the omission. Any omissions from a putatively complete series should be called to the reader's attention on a separate picture or target.[60] To avoid de-

54 Interviews with Robert M. Sutton and William I. Hair, see Appendix C1; Charles O. Jackson, Edward L. Weldon, and John D. Unruh, Jr., see Appendix C3; Albert H. Leisinger, Jr., see Appendix C2b.

55 Interview, see Appendix C1.

56 Interview with George Mazaraki, see Appendix C3.

57 Interview with George C. Rogers, Jr., see Appendix C1. The National Archives, National Historical Publications Commission, and the Library of Congress have such standards, both technical and scholarly. Consequently, their micropublications are reliable additions to the body of research materials. Cf. Stephen R. Salmon, *Specifications for Library of Congress Microfilming*.

58 Interviews with John M. Bumsted, Edward C. Ezell, and Keith A. Winsell, see Appendix C3.

59 Interview with Kenneth R. Bowling, *ibid*.

60 Interview with William G. McLoughlin, Jr., see Appendix C1.

pendence on technicians of unknown capabilities, some historians do their own filming.[61]

Historians who do want to make their own film for reasons of accuracy, speed, or economy often have had roadblocks thrown in their way. Wood Gray, who has done extensive photocopying and has a wide knowledge of the equipment, said the great problem is with repositories that prohibit the researcher from making his own photocopies.[62] Donald L. Parman's experience at the National Archives bears this out. Even after he received permission from a division chief and an electrician to use a photocopier, the guards and assistants in the Central Research Room were officious about his using the machine.[63] Because the Colorado State Archives has complete facilities for photocopying, it has discouraged "itinerant historians" from using their own microfilming equipment. It is unwilling for historians to film its large records series.[64]

Many scholars, particularly graduate students, considered the cost of facsimile reproductions excessive. They appreciated the time saved by not having to take notes manually, but the expense of making copies prohibited their using that method for a large run of notes[65]—the usual cost of a Xerox copy, for example, is ten cents. The New York University library pioneered in providing the coin-operated machine, which has subsequently become common.[66] Another Xerox product, the Copyflo printer, was criticized as being too costly to use in reproducing large quantities of material—exactly what it was designed to do.[67] One professor commented that scholars have such a great need for facsimiles that

---

[61] Interview with Edward C. Ezell, above.

[62] Interview, see Appendix C1.

[63] Interview, see Appendix C3.

[64] Interview with Dolores C. Renze, state archivist, see Appendix C2b.

[65] Interviews with Michael Wallace, Robert C. Carriker, Howard L. Meredith, John L. Gaddis, John D. Holmfeld, and Bernard Axelrod, see Appendix C3; questionnaire returned by H. G. Jones, North Carolina Department of Archives and History.

[66] Interview with John E. Frost, librarian, see Appendix C2a.

[67] Interview with Herman H. Fussler, director; Robert Rosenthal, curator of Special Collections; Sabron Reynolds, Documents librarian, University of Chicago library, *ibid*.

Xerox patents should be shaken loose "so that Xerography could be used widely and inexpensively."[68]

Charges established by the Library of Congress Photoduplication Service for Xerox copies have been labeled "outrageous." When Edwin T. Layton ordered a copy of a seven-page journal article, the Photoduplication Service made two copies of the last three pages so that the order would come to ten pages. The charge was $3.50.[69] Lloyd C. Gardner termed the Photoduplication Service's sequence-change charge prohibitive.[70] Until this charge was suspended in October, 1965, it had cost twenty-five cents to remove a document from a collection. If a researcher wished to have a number of documents photocopied, he paid this charge for each piece taken out of sequence, plus the fee for reproduction. Gardner also called the cost of having material Xeroxed at the Library of Congress and the National Archives "a serious impediment to scholarship."[71] A graduate student from the University of Illinois shared his sentiment and noted that the Archives' charge of twenty cents a page was twice that of most university libraries.[72] A researcher who wishes to have the Library of Congress make Xerox copies of manuscripts in the same container must pay eighty-five cents for each of the first five sheets and eighteen cents apiece for subsequent sheets. Each time documents from a different container are copied, the charge again begins at eighty-five cents apiece for the first five pages.

Considering the expense of microfilm in relation to its frequency of use, some historians advocated that universities should put their money into travel fellowships instead of microfilm.[73] John C. Burnham questioned Ohio State University's purchase of microfilmed manuscripts when it is "overnight from every major research institution."[74] Howard H. Peckham explained that the University of Michigan's Clements Library, of which he was the

[68] Interview with Theodore R. Crane, see Appendix C1.
[69] Layton, *ibid.*
[70] Gardner, *ibid.*
[71] *Ibid.*
[72] Interview with Edmund J. Danziger, see Appendix C3.
[73] Interviews with Robert H. Ferrell and John C. Burnham, see Appendix C1.
[74] *Ibid.*

director, spent no money on photocopy, since photoreproductions were not additions to the body of original sources but merely copies that served the convenience of the researcher. "The necessity for convenience to scholars has decreased over the years with more travel and research money. It is now easy for professors and graduate students to travel."[75]

A condition that detracts from the utility of original sources on microfilm is imperfect or nonexistent indexing. Without an index, it can be extremely tedious trying to find a particular frame on a roll of film.[76] When major sets such as William Jenkins' *Early State Records* are badly indexed, their value to researchers is diminished.[77] It should be noted that one major microfilm program, the Library of Congress' presidential papers, carries thorough name indexes. Each is printed separately.[78] Indexes at the end of the roll, as in the case of the filmed *Congressional Record*, cause great frustration and loss of time.[79] To avoid this frustration, indexes should be on a separate roll so they can be used simultaneously with the sources, assuming the availability of a second reader. Of even greater use are printed indexes that can be consulted at the researcher's convenience.[80] Manufacturers should incorporate some device on microfilm readers that would enable a researcher to dial a desired frame rather than have to crank through an entire reel.[81] Despite the beliefs of many historians that having well-indexed microfilm is advantageous, Kenneth M. Stampp preferred no index at all. He feared that students would rely on an index and miss important things by not investigating the sources carefully. His reservation also applied to indexing original manuscripts.[82]

[75] Interview, see Appendix C2a.
[76] Interviews with Allan Nevins and H. Trevor Colbourn, see Appendix C1; Larry D. Hill, see Appendix C3.
[77] Interview with George E. Frakes, see Appendix C3.
[78] Cf. Fred Shelley, "The Presidential Papers Program of the Library of Congress," *American Archivist*, Vol. XXV, No. 4 (Oct., 1962), 429–33.
[79] Interview with Roy Bird, see Appendix C3.
[80] Interviews with Arthur Bestor and Robert E. Moody, see Appendix C1; Margaret L. Neustadt, see Appendix C3.
[81] Bestor, above.
[82] Interview, see Appendix C1.

However helpful elaborate indexing of microfilm might be to the researcher, L. H. Butterfield suggested that historians expect too much. Letterpress editions of documents deserve full indexes, but the rationale behind micropublication is to issue the material with as little delay as possible so that scholars may have quick access to it.[83]

PROBLEMS WITH CATALOGING PHOTOCOPY

Closely akin to the problem of indexing microforms is their cataloging. The obvious temptation of librarians is to catalog microforms "just like a book"; but when the material is not a book, such cataloging offers little aid to the researcher. To be of maximum assistance, microform catalogers should treat documents as if they were originals. This ideal, unhappily, can rarely be attained because of the expense entailed. But if catalogers cannot cope with discrete items on microforms, should they be content merely to list the name of a series or to copy the information off the label on a roll of microfilm? The efforts of university libraries to cope with this challenge of cataloging microforms so that researchers can get to the material with some facility were varied and too frequently unsuccessful.

A few institutions made a genuine effort to catalog microforms as thoroughly as they would originals. The Vatican Film Library, at Saint Louis University, had a full-time cataloger of filmed manuscripts, and the associate director of the university library maintained an item catalog for the Jesuitica on microfilm. This catalog contained an entry for each subject (but not frame) and listed its position on the roll.[84] The University of Rochester library tried "desperately" to describe the contents of microforms as fully as possible. If any descriptions of listings were prepared by the library or issued with the microforms, they were provided in the Microtext Room and in the Department of Special Collections.[85] Other libraries likewise purchased such guides or finding aids

[83] Interview, see Appendix C2b.
[84] Interview with staff, see n. 24, this chapter.
[85] Questionnaire returned by Margaret B. Andrews, assistant librarian in charge of Special Collections.

prepared by the filmer and noted their availability on the catalog card. The Trinity University archivist pointed out that the library's specific description of microfilm was to enable both students and librarians to know and use the material effectively.[86] The Wayne State University archives has cataloged microfilmed manuscripts just as if they were originals, since the librarians "want to do the cataloging once and not have to redo it." The university archives preferred to have Copyflo facsimiles prepared from the film, for they facilitated cataloging.[87] The process of describing all items on a reel of microfilm is inevitably slow, as the historians at Utah State University have discovered; yet they applauded the library's efforts to do analytics on all microfilmed material.[88] Similarly, historians appreciated the Georgetown University library's attempt to describe the contents of microforms rather than merely listing them.[89] Among the nonacademic repositories, the Kansas State Historical Society cataloged microfilmed manuscripts as if they were originals.[90]

Many university librarians were keenly aware of the need for descriptive cataloging of microforms and regretted its absence in their own institutions. The staff of the Stanford University library commented that they were greatly concerned that much of their microfilm did not show up in the catalog. Little more than a series title was given. The staff would like to provide a union list of its microforms next to the public catalog so that researchers could know the library's total microform holdings.[91] Historians at Stanford were aware of the dangers of uncataloged microforms being lost to researchers. For example, the library had *Travels in the Old*

---

[86] Questionnaire returned by Jay B. Clark.

[87] Interview with Philip P. Mason, see Appendix C1.

[88] Questionnaire returned by S. George Ellsworth.

[89] Interview with J. Joseph Huthmacher, see Appendix C1.

[90] Interview with Nyle H. Miller, secretary; Robert W. Richmond, state archivist; Joseph W. Snell, assistant state archivist; see Appendix C2b.

[91] Interview with Rutherford D. Rogers, director of university libraries; Ralph Hansen, university archivist and manuscript librarian; Mrs. Jeanne B. North, chief of Government Documents division; Julius P. Barclay, chief of Division of Special Collections; see Appendix C2a.

South in microform, but since it was not listed in the catalog, finding information about it was left to chance.[92]

Several university libraries intended to catalog microforms as if they were originals and did so slowly. During this painstaking process, libraries continued to acquire microforms and the cataloging arrearage mounted. In such cases, libraries usually shelved the material alphabetically so that researchers could investigate the uncataloged holdings.[93]

The Library of Congress' Manuscript Division faced the problem of cataloging microfilmed manuscripts a little differently. Rather than developing a backlog, it has not cataloged as meticulously as it would like. Theoretically, it tried describing microfilm as actual manuscripts but admitted that it did not achieve this kind of control.[94] When the division prepared a collection for filming, it automatically incorporated any related finding aid in the film publication.[95]

The intentions of some institutions to catalog microfilmed manuscripts have been thwarted through the years by budgetary and other problems. Rice University once had a full-time microfilm cataloger who prepared a calendar of American history manuscripts on film, but lack of personnel has prevented the library from maintaining this program.[96] Although this elaborate program was no longer possible, the library still analyzed manuscripts on film instead of merely listing the reels.[97] The Newberry Library planned to catalog microfilmed manuscripts as if they were orig-

[92] Interview with Don E. Fehrenbacher, see Appendix C1.

[93] Interviews with Dwight W. Hoover, Althea L. Stoeckel, Robert W. Johannsen, and Clark C. Spence, *ibid.*; Donald A. Sinclair and H. Gilbert Kelley, see Appendix C2a.

[94] Interview with John Knowlton, assistant head of Preparation Section, see Appendix C2b.

[95] Interview with John J. McDonough, Jr., specialist in the National Period, *ibid.*

[96] Interview with W. H. Masterson, see Appendix C1.

[97] Interview with Hardin Craig, Jr., librarian; Richard L. O'Keeffe, assistant director; Gilberta Zingler, Acquisitions librarian; Martha Bishop, cataloger; see Appendix C2a.

inals, but for fifteen years the practice has been merely to list the film.[98]

Many institutions made little or no pretense of cataloging microforms with enough description to enable researchers to understand something of the contents. In such cases, the utility of the material was restricted to those who had prior knowledge of it or stumbled upon it. When such institutions had large graduate programs, their cataloging policy could be a considerable handicap to graduate students seeking research material. For instance, the microfilm cataloging at the University of California at Berkeley was "either radically deficient or nonexistent."[99] Because of this very poor cataloging, it was "actually difficult to get information."[100] The director of the University of Oklahoma library realized that the microfilm collection had grown so that the staff could no longer rely on going to the shelf and checking labels and that a cataloging system had to be introduced.[101] A history professor there said that only the old-timers who used microfilms frequently had much notion of what was available.[102]

One difficulty with the "terribly cataloged" microfilm at the University of Notre Dame was that when the rolls are misshelved, "it's just too bad." There, the Evans Early American Imprint Series and other original sources on microfilm were stacked on unsupervised shelves and administered by persons who knew neither the collection nor the problems of scholars.[103] For the Evans Series, the Notre Dame library used only the catalog cards prepared by the Library of Congress. A drawback to these cards is that they do not enumerate the works of authors. For example, instead of listing all of John Eliot's works singly, it merely has an entry of "Works of John Eliot."[104] Professors admitted some bafflement about the microfilm situation at Notre Dame, where the library, archives, and mediaeval institute seemed not to co-

[98] Interview with Colton Storm, chief of Special Collections, see Appendix C2b.
[99] Interview with Charles G. Sellers, Jr., see Appendix C1.
[100] Interview with Henry F. May, *ibid.*
[101] Interview with Arthur M. McAnally, see Appendix C2a.
[102] Interview with John S. Ezell, see Appendix C1.
[103] Interview with Marshall Smelser, *ibid.*
[104] Interview with J. Philip Gleason, *ibid.*

ordinate their microfilm acquisitions or cataloging. The library employed a man to gather American Catholic material on film but it was not acquisitioned or cataloged.[105]

The problems encountered by libraries in cataloging microforms varied in intensity, according to the amount of cataloging undertaken. At Arizona State University the library's microforms were almost useless since they were not cataloged at all. Consequently, few people other than the librarians knew of their existence.[106] Except for microfilmed newspapers, the University of Kansas library cataloged microforms "fairly well." Since the library had newspapers no one knew about, John Clark asked a graduate student to track down and list all filmed newspapers in the library and in faculty hands.[107] Even without trying to describe the contents of microform sets, the library of the University of California at Riverside had such a cataloging backlog that users had difficulty knowing of its holdings.[108] In editing *The Papers of James Madison,* William T. Hutchinson worked entirely from photocopies. He found that the University of Chicago library's cataloging of microfilm rolls was insufficient for his purposes. Consequently he relied on each roll's label as the best indicator of the contents. Nevertheless, labels were often so general that the roll had to be studied frame by frame.[109] Hutchinson's dependence on photocopy typified that of the other great editorial projects in this country.[110]

Because cataloging microfilm was a major problem with the University of Iowa library, Lawrence E. Gelfand made an effort to alleviate it. When the library received microfilm he had requested from the National Archives, he gave the cataloging division a list of topics covered by the film. If a professor went through the film as a matter of course, there was no reason for

---

[105] *Ibid.*
[106] Questionnaire returned by Alan K. Lathrop, Arizona State University library.
[107] Interview, see Appendix C1.
[108] Interview with Standley W. Claussen, see Appendix C3.
[109] Interview, see Appendix C1.
[110] Interview with L. H. Butterfield, see Appendix C2b.

the cataloger's duplicating the effort.[111] The University of Iowa library has been reluctant to acquire portions of William Jenkins' *Early State Records* since reels contain more than one item and "that supposedly makes it hard to catalog."[112]

Unlike the Kansas State Historical Society, the Minnesota Historical Society and the Wyoming State Archives and Historical Department did not try to catalog microfilmed manuscripts as originals. The former included broad subject headings and authors but made no attempt to describe its microfilm in as much detail as its original manuscripts.[113] When the Wyoming State Archives acquired microfilm, it put on the catalog card just the information provided on the roll label.[114]

The manifest importance of microforms for research in United States history indicates that libraries should make the effort to identify this material in ways that will facilitate its use. Merely knowing what a library has on microform can be a considerable aid, and many historians have commented on the difficulty and inconvenience of locating microforms when they are interspersed in the public catalog. They suggested that libraries can render a genuine service by maintaining a separate microform catalog as well as continuing to include these materials in the public catalog, as the Princeton University library does. [115] A separate microform catalog cannot guarantee a full listing of these holdings, as the University of Pennsylvania library's experience illustrated. Since some of its microfilm was not even included in that special catalog, Richard S. Dunn suggested that the library needed to pay more attention to its handling of this material.[116]

COPYRIGHT PROBLEMS WITH PHOTOCOPY

The advent of quick, convenient photoduplication has raised

[111] Interview, see Appendix C1.

[112] Interview with Sydney V. James, Jr., *ibid.*

[113] Interview with Lucile M. Kane, see Appendix C2b.

[114] Interview with Neal E. Miller, director; Katherine Halverson, chief, Historical Division; Julia A. Yelvington, chief, Division of Archives and Records; Bonnie F. Svoboda, retiring chief, Division of Archives and Records, *ibid.*

[115] Interviews with Arthur S. Link, Richard P. McCormick, J. Philip Gleason, Don Higginbotham, and Aubrey C. Land, see Appendix C1.

[116] Dunn, *ibid.*

questions of copyright violation throughout the academic community. Quantitatively, the most serious questions deal with the wholesale copying of secondary works for teaching and learning purposes; but qualitatively, the prohibition of copying original sources through fear of copyright violation poses fundamental questions of the researcher's right of access to information. Most university librarians have taken the position that scholarly materials are intended for researchers and that researchers may photoreproduce them in lieu of manual copying. Under these guidelines, the photocopying machines run steadily. Some librarians admitted to a "quiet terror" concerning the copying within their institutions but permitted it in case of legitimate need.[117] With students Xeroxing materials "like mad" in the University of New Mexico library, the librarian feared being hauled into court at any time, but took comfort in the thought that he would enjoy the ample company of other university librarians.[118] The Georgetown University librarian saw no problems in continuing the *de facto* situation of common-law literary property: the aggrieved party having to prove injury as the result of violation of literary property rights. "Currently it seems that everyone is copying everything with no trouble." The library informed students with a sign on the copying machine that the responsibility of abiding by the copyright law is theirs, not the university's.[119] Many historians as well as librarians took a permissive view toward copying, since "everyone did it."[120] Librarians and historians alike could take courage in the fact that no library has been sued "for making copies for a scholar in lieu of his copying the material himself."[121]

In some instances where historians have had their research thwarted by families' refusing to donate literary rights to the

[117] Interview with John H. Berthel, librarian; J. Louis Kuethe, assistant librarian; Margaret E. Lough, Reference librarian; Johns Hopkins University, see Appendix C2a.
[118] Interview with David Otis Kelley, *ibid.*
[119] Interview with Joseph E. Jeffs, *ibid.*
[120] Interview with Sam B. Warner, Jr., see Appendix C1.
[121] Ralph R. Shaw, "Copyright in Relationship to Copying of Scholarly Materials," in *Reprography and Copyright Law*, edited by Lowell H. Hattery and George P. Bush, 95.

public after depositing the papers, they have assumed the risk of using the papers anyhow, with no adverse effects. When W. Stitt Robinson edited the J. E. B. Stuart diary, he faced the great difficulty of getting a decision from the widely scattered family, of which no member had assumed responsibility for the papers. Since monetary profits were not a consideration and since the material contained nothing defamatory, Robinson elected to publish the diary without clearing the literary rights. He experienced no repercussions.[122] Norman K. Risjord also researched a technically closed collection without arousing any protest.[123]

The most enlightened attitude of custodians of original sources —to which most historians would subscribe—is that they do not try to adjudicate possible cases of copyright violation. They let research scholars copy sources and be responsible for possible copyright violations. Dorman H. Winfrey has followed this policy at the Texas State Library and Archives and has had no problems.[124] Historians agreed that curators should honor restrictions placed by donors, but emphasized that curators must regard their original sources as being essentially in the public domain and therefore must allow photocopying for scholarly research.[125] The most forthright enunciation of this principle came from Seymour V. Connor, former Texas state archivist and director of the Southwest Collection at Texas Technological College. "No library or archival institution is a keeper of the public morals and it has no business preventing a researcher from using archival material. . . . The absurdity of the manuscript collection trying to protect literary property is patent. Does the librarian tell a reader he can't use a book because it's copyrighted? It is just so with a curator of manuscripts. . . . But as long as the institution does not own the literary property, it should not try to limit the use of the property. . . . The Library of Congress is the worst in the country on this score. Each institution should inform depositors that papers in that institution are to be used, subject to reasonable restrictions

[122] Interview, see Appendix C1.
[123] Risjord, *ibid.*
[124] Interview, see Appendix C2b.
[125] Interview with John A. Carroll, see Appendix C1.

that only the donor may wish to impose. Unless depositors are willing to grant free access to papers, including copying for research purposes, they shouldn't be left in the depository."[126]

Most curators of manuscripts and archives instruct researchers wanting to quote or publish documents to obtain written permission from the heirs who own the literary property if the property rights were not given to the depository along with the papers. This instruction is usually incorporated in the forms researchers sign when requesting manuscripts. In cases where depositories own all literary property rights, they often prescribe that scholars request permission to quote or publish documents.[127] Often depositories make an effort to get donors of manuscripts to assign literary property rights to the depository so that the question of permissions can be handled simply.[128] For the past decade or so, the Library of Congress Manuscript Division has asked donors to assign literary rights to the public at the time of the donation. If the rights are so assigned, the division allows photocopying of the manuscripts, no matter how recent. If the rights are not assigned, the division still requests the donor to permit photoreproduction of individual documents for research purposes.[129]

Since the major projects for publishing edited papers of famous Americans have employed photocopies extensively, they faced the question of literary property inhering in documents they copied and published. If any heirs of the great men are living, they usually have been happy to grant permission for the papers they own to be edited and published, but the rub has come with the heirs of the thousands of people who corresponded with the focal figures. Because these numerous heirs are so dispersed and would have difficulty proving monetary loss through publication of their ancestor's correspondence, most editors have proceeded without worrying about violation of literary property rights. None of the

[126] Connor, *ibid*. Cf. Seymour V. Connor, "The Problem of Literary Property in Archival Depositories," *American Archivist*, Vol. XXI, No. 2 (Apr., 1958), 143–52.

[127] Interviews with Elfrieda Lang, see Appendix C2a; Earl E. Olson and Enid T. Thompson, see Appendix C2b.

[128] Interview with William S. Dix and Alexander Clark, see Appendix C2a.

[129] Interview with John C. Broderick, assistant chief, see Appendix C2b.

editors interviewed reported having received any complaints from these heirs, although many hundreds of such letters have been published. Heirs with whom contact has been established often seem pleased to have their ancestors' connections with the "great men" established in this way. [130]

WILLINGNESS TO PHOTOCOPY

With the marked expansion of doctoral training in recent years, the availability of original sources has become a pressing issue. Usually the easiest way for universities to build up their research collections has been by acquiring sources on microforms. Their success in doing so depended upon the willingness of repositories to film and distribute their holdings. Before the National Archives began selling microfilm copies of its records in 1940, there was little inclination on the part of collecting agencies to share significant portions of their resources with other institutions, but the enthusiastic response of the academic community to the Archives' films established the program firmly.[131] Ernst Posner contended that the National Archives' microfilming program marked an important change in archival philosophy. "In preparing film negatives of series of outstanding research value and making copies of them available at nominal cost, the National Archives has abandoned monopoly of some of its most important holdings and has thrown them open to the use of scholars and searchers, regardless of personal merits and qualifications. This is basically a final break with the archivist's proprietary attitude toward his records, a democratization of the archival reference service that constitutes an entirely new departure."[132]

[130] Interviews with Arthur S. Link, editor, *The Papers of Woodrow Wilson*; Leonard W. Labaree, editor, *The Papers of Benjamin Franklin*; Julian P. Boyd, editor, *The Papers of Thomas Jefferson*; see Appendix C2a; L. H. Butterfield, editor, *The Adams Papers*; see Appendix C2b.

[131] Interviews with Norman A. Graebner and Malcolm J. Rohrbaugh, see Appendix C1; David Goodman, see Appendix C3. For a description of the genesis of the program, see Wayne C. Grover, "Toward Equal Opportunities for Scholarship," *Journal of American History*, Vol. LII, No. 4 (Mar., 1966), 715-24.

[132] "The National Archives and the Archival Theorist," *American Archivist*, Vol. XVIII, No. 3 (July, 1955), 211.

Before the National Archives was established, the Library of Congress pioneered in distributing photocopies of its holdings. Its foreign copying program began in 1905 and gained momentum in the 1920's with support from the Wilbur Fund and the Rockefeller Foundation. In 1965 the Council on Library Resources granted $75,300 to the Library of Congress to establish a Center for the Coordination of Foreign Manuscript Copying, which continues and amplifies the important work begun in 1905. Although the Library of Congress did not begin its systematic program of microfilm publication of presidential papers until 1959, as early as 1943 it had filmed the Jefferson papers. Through the 1940's and 1950's, it filmed and distributed the Lincoln, Madison, Polk, Van Buren, Theodore Roosevelt, and Jackson papers.[133]

When the State Historical Society of Wisconsin, in 1948, and the Massachusetts Historical Society, in 1954, offered filmed copies of their choicest treasures, the Draper Collection and the Adams family papers, respectively, the movement had matured. These publications went a long way to settling the old question of where such materials "should be": they can, and should, be everywhere needed. Then as the National Historical Publications Commission began awarding grants in 1965 to enable repositories across the country to publish collections of national significance on microfilm, the concept of sharing original sources gained even greater momentum.[134] This momentum did not mean that all repositories followed suit, for many were yet unwilling to share their resources in this manner. But it clearly indicated the firm establishment of the principle of replicating original holdings so that the greatest number of researchers might benefit.

Without question, the research community is increasingly aware of its interdependence. One token of this awareness is the growing willingness of repositories to make their holdings available to others through microfilm publication. Of 96 American institutions responding to a questionnaire on whether they would

[133] Letter, John C. Broderick, assistant chief, Manuscript Division, to author, July 7, 1967. Cf. Grover, *loc. cit.*, 719-20.

[134] See Appendix G for more details on this program. See also Grover, *loc. cit.*, 722-23.

photocopy entire series of their records for use by others, 79 said they would. "Particularly significant was the fact that a number of institutions that have had strong proprietary feelings toward their records in the past and had refused to film large blocks of records *in extenso* were now willing to do this."[135] The survey's findings likewise were encouraging. Of 139 depositories commenting on their willingness to microfilm an entire series, only 34 replied that they had restrictive policies. Clearly, preponderant support has developed for liberal and generous microfilming policies.

Naturally, those institutions offering doctoral programs without extensive collections of manuscripts or printed sources greatly appreciated the opportunity to enlarge their resources with microforms. They likewise were keenly aware of the need for co-operation among research institutions. Librarians and historians at such universities expressed great willingness to share their resources since they have long benefited from the co-operation of generous institutions.[136]

Those repositories which were not willing to sell or lend photo-duplicates of their sources to facilitate scholarly research elsewhere offered several reasons for their reluctance. Frequently, collecting institutions have had little or no funds for buying manuscripts. The growth of their collections depended upon gifts, either of manuscripts or of money. In the latter case, the usual pattern was for the institution to identify a set of papers it wished to add to its

[135] Albert H. Leisinger, Jr., "Microreproduction of Archives for Reference and Publication Purposes: Selected Aspects of Microreproduction in the United States," p. 7, paper presented May, 1966, at the Extraordinary Congress of the International Council on Archives and to be published in *Archivum.*

[136] Interviews with James W. Simonson, C.S.C., director, and George Sereiko, assistant director in charge of history area, University of Notre Dame library; Richard W. Boss, assistant director of libraries, Douglas Bush, Order librarian, Chizuko Ishimatsu, Documents librarian, Elva Dean, Reference librarian, University of Utah library; Henry C. Koch, assistant director of libraries, Francis X. Scannell, chief of Reference Services, Ronald S. Wilkinson, bibliographer in American history and literature, Michigan State University library; Reno W. Bupp, Social Science librarian, Florida State University; Robert D. Stevens, deputy director, University of Hawaii library; Benton L. Hatch, associate librarian for Special Collections, University of Massachusetts library; see Appendix C2a; Joe M. Richardson and Stow Persons, see Appendix C1.

collection and then to seek an affluent friend or "angel" to buy the papers and donate them. More often than not, such an angel was an alumnus or someone else who wanted a close identification with the institution. Presumably, such a person's generosity was narrowly channeled to redound to the glory of one institution, alma mater or whatever. A donor would be reluctant, the argument ran, for the recipient to make photocopies of donated material available to other depositories because this would somehow dilute his contribution. The recipient usually permitted a qualified visiting researcher to study these acquisitions but was unwilling to risk damaging whatever prestige possession of the unique material would bring by making photocopies available to other research institutions.

One type of restriction that no scholar could question was that imposed by donors of documents. If a depository accepted material upon which the donor placed certain restrictions, it was obliged to honor them. If papers were sealed for a number of years, they obviously could contribute nothing to historical knowledge during the period of restriction. The hope was that with the expiration of the restriction, the material would justify the efforts of the depository in collecting and maintaining it. When a donor specified that no reproduction be made of the papers he provided, such instructions had to be followed.

Another restriction on photoduplication which was beyond protest was that imposed by limited budgets, which implied limited staffs. Some institutions simply did not have the capital to furnish photocopying services, and filling a mail request for photocopies could involve a great deal of staff time in identifying and withdrawing documents for photoduplication and refiling the material afterward. Apparently few organizations allocated much staff time for such activity, with the result that what was done along this line became overload. Some institutions insisted that their staffs had more pressing and important duties than providing photocopy service.[137]

[137] Interviews with George W. Pierson, see Appendix C1; Mattie Russell and Thomas R. Adams, see Appendix C2a.

Occasionally, universities imposed restrictions on reproducing newly acquired collections of manuscripts. The position of the universities was that their own faculty and graduate students should have first call on the material. If no local scholar had staked out his claim within a stated time, the photocopying restriction was usually lifted from the collection.[138]

Some institutions were hesitant about photoduplicating parts of their collection because they contended that the researcher was unable to understand the full import of isolated documents. To do effective research, they argued, the individual needed to be immersed in the total content of a manuscript collection. In that way he could trace leads from one document to another and often from one collection to another. Being able to follow these clues enabled the researcher to get a full perspective on his subject, whereas if he were limited to using photocopies without access to the entire collection, his research was perforce canalized and he approached his topic wearing blinders.[139]

A reason institutions sometimes advanced for their reluctance to photocopy manuscripts—especially for other repositories—was that once copies were made, the institution lost control of the documents.[140] They evidently feared that researchers would reach irresponsible conclusions unless the documents were studied within the owning institution and, by implication, with staff supervision. Some repositories wanted not only to maintain control of

[138] Interviews with Alexander Moffit, librarian, Fred Folmer, assistant librarian, Chester V. Kielman, archivist, Ella Mae Bridges, Government Documents librarian, University of Texas; Thomas R. Buckman, director, university library, Michael Brodhead, director of the Kansas Room, Audrey Valaske, Documents librarian, Terrence Williams, Reference librarian, Alexandra Mason, Special Collections librarian, University of Kansas; Edward G. Holley, librarian, Virginia Murphy, Social Sciences librarian, University of Houston; Frederick H. Wagman, director, Janet White, Reference librarian, Harriet C. Jameson, Rare Books and Special Collections, Agnes N. Tysse, head of Reference Department, University of Michigan library; see Appendix C2a.

[139] Interviews with Charles E. Lee, see Appendix C2b; Dorothy Bridgwater and Thomas R. Adams, see Appendix C2a.

[140] Interviews with Howard H. Peckham, director, W. L. Clements Library, University of Michigan; W. H. Bond, director, Houghton Library, Harvard University; Vergil L. Bedsole, head, Department of Archives, Louisiana State University; Philip P. Mason, university archivist, Wayne State University; see Appendix C2a.

their documents but also to know of the research being conducted with their holdings and therefore kept a list of current projects. They reasoned that if they photocopied their material they would be unable to prevent duplicated research.[141] A related problem concerned the proper citation of photocopied material. Many institutions complained that writers did not give them credit for holding the originals of the photoduplicates used in research.[142]

Despite the magnitude of any university's primary sources, the doctoral candidate who did not travel in connection with his dissertation research in American history was in the distinct minority. According to the survey's findings, all universities granting the Ph.D. in United States history required most of their candidates to travel for research. The extent of travel that historians must undertake nowadays, however, is greatly modified by the willingness of most depositories to let researchers photocopy documents and by those micropublications already completed or in progress. If such photocopying were impossible, the cost of travel in time and money would significantly curtail historical research. Consequently, restrictive policies on photocopying have discouraged rather than promoted this scholarly activity.

The fact that departments of history throughout the country expected their graduate students to travel for research indicated that no university felt self-sufficient in original sources. Universities depended upon one another and upon nonacademic research institutions—to varying extents, to be sure—but still they were interdependent. Consequently, a policy of co-operation in photocopying was much more justifiable than one of restriction. A richly-endowed institution did not diminish its prestige through generosity, but gained the indebtedness of the research community for sharing its resources.

If there is to be a spirit of willing co-operation in photocopying among research institutions, it would be helpful to establish equitable arrangements. Since some institutions are more likely to be

[141] Peckham, above.
[142] Interviews with Clement Silvestro and Nyle H. Miller, see Appendix C2b; Vergil L. Bedsole, see Appendix C2a.

providers than receivers of photocopy, their interests need protection. When these providing institutions purchase a collection of manuscripts, they should not be expected to reproduce the entire collection immediately for the mere cost of filming.[143] If they wanted to be this generous, no one should complain; but, similarly, it would seem fair if the providing depository asked prospective institutional buyers to contribute something toward the cost of the collection. A logical variation of the foregoing arrangement is co-operative purchasing of original sources, either manuscripts or photocopies, by institutions within a region. Duke University and the University of North Carolina had such an agreement for buying microforms.[144] If a providing institution wished to amortize the very substantial cost of preparing papers for photoduplication, it could invite subscriptions to its film publications. The Massachusetts Historical Society used this device in its microfilm edition of the Adams papers and met with considerable success in the long run. Some institutions not wishing to vitiate the value of their unique material were willing to reproduce an entire collection only if they could exchange it for something of equal importance.[145] Although this was co-operation narrowly construed, the attitude did acknowledge the mutual dependence of the research community.

Within the last few years, two publications have made significant changes in the research patterns of historians. These were Philip M. Hamer's *A Guide to Archives and Manuscripts in the United States* and the Library of Congress' *National Union Catalog of Manuscript Collections*. The very nature of these volumes reinforced the notion of the corporateness and interdependence of the research community in the United States. By identifying

[143] Interviews with Winston Broadfoot, director, George Washington Flowers Collection, Duke University; E. L. Inabinett, director, South Caroliniana Library, see Appendix C2a; Daniel R. Porter, director, Ohio Historical Society, see Appendix C2b; William R. Hogan, see Appendix C1.

[144] Interview with Gertrude Merritt, chief, Processing Division, Duke University library, see Appendix C2a.

[145] Interviews with Judith Schiff, librarian of historical manuscripts and university archivist, Yale University library; Arthur M. McAnally, director, University of Oklahoma library; *ibid.*; University of Pennsylvania library staff, see n. 28, this chapter.

the location of various collections, these books have enabled researchers to plan their travel systematically and to make mail inquiries concerning specific items. The latter has led to some abuse, correctly and disparagingly labeled "mail-order research." Rather than requesting specific information, individuals have written to ask a depository to send reproductions of everything it had on a certain subject. If the staff complied with such requests, it would have entailed doing the writer's research for him.[146]

Historical research, because of the nature of the sources, must be a co-operative venture. Historians rely upon the depositories and no depository claims to be self-sufficient. Within this framework of interdependence, and to promote optimum service to scholarship, all institutions should seek to be as helpful as possible. Roadblocks to research should be cast aside, not perpetuated. The most significant advances that archivists, librarians, and historians could make would be to work together to bring manuscripts into repositories serving the public and to liberalize access to these manuscript collections through photoduplication.

[146] Interviews with Charles E. Lee, Margaret Scriven, and Nyle H. Miller, see Appendix C2b; Guy R. Lyle, director of libraries, Ruth Walling, chief Reference librarian and associate university librarian, David Estes, chief of Special Collections department, Mary Davis, reference archivist in the Special Collections Department, Emory University; Thomas T. McAvoy, C.S.C., university archivist, University of Notre Dame, Edward B. Stanford, director, University of Minnesota libraries; see Appendix C2a.

VIII. Finding Aids

TOWARD the beginning of research with manuscripts and archives, most students of history come to understand that their work is full of probabilities. They appreciate that chance may have played a large part in determining the availability of records related to their topics. Even when one feels confident that he has seen the extant sources, he cannot help wondering about those which may—for any number of reasons—have missed the collector's net. He should be open to doubts about the representativeness of his "sample." Considering these rather fundamental uncertainties inherent in historical research, which clearly underline an absence of scientific precision, historians are thankful to have some fortuitous elements removed from other areas of their activities. As a graduate student put it, "I feel at times overwhelmed by the imposing wilderness of original material before me and welcome any friendly guide."[1] Finding aids purport to minimize the chance in historical research. Their great contribution is in identifying the location and nature of original sources, as the contribution of bibliographies is in maintaining control over secondary works.

Graduate training in United States history was well along before

[1] Interview with Edward Weldon, see Appendix C3.

anyone made systematic attempts to direct researchers to original sources. As collecting institutions began to issue guides to their material, scholars could have some notion of what they might expect to find in the individual repositories. Among the notable finding aids were Justin Winsor's *Calendar of Sparks Manuscripts in Harvard College Library* (1889), Claude H. Van Tyne and Waldo G. Leland's *Guide to the Archives of the Government of the United States in Washington* (1904), Reuben Gold Thwaites's *Descriptive List of Manuscript Collections of the State Historical Society of Wisconsin* (1906), and the Library of Congress' *Handbook of Manuscripts* (1918). Since the turn of the century, the Library of Congress has issued a series of invaluable calendars, indexes, and registers of individual collections in the Manuscript Division.[2]

Concurrent with the publication of guides to individual collections was the appearance of general guides. Historians and curators understood the importance of the researcher having some overview of the sources relating to the subject, wherever their location. Winsor's *Narrative and Critical History of America* (Vol. VIII, pp. 413–68) dealt primarily with the location and nature of original materials related to the American Revolution. This landmark was the first attempt to inventory manuscripts throughout the nation. Winsor's achievement was so great that researchers can still use this work with profit, if they are mindful of its obsolescence. Subsequent publications intended as general guides include Edmund C. Burnett's "A List of Printed Guides to and Descriptions of Archives and Other Repositories of Historical Manuscript"[3] and the Library of Congress' *Check List of Collections of Personal Papers in Historical Societies, University and Public Libraries, and Other Learned Institutions in the United States* (1918), the revision of which was issued in 1924 as *Manuscripts in Public and Private Collections in the United States*. In the early decades of the century, J. Franklin Jameson was responsible for

[2] The classified bibliography contains a highly selected list of guides to individual collections.

[3] *Annual Report of the American Historical Association, Vol. I, Proceedings, 1896*, pp. 481–512.

the Carnegie Institution's issuing a series of guides to materials in foreign archives relating to American history. Also, his influence was evident in the reports of the AHA's Public Archives Commission. During the Great Depression, the Works Projects Administration's Historical Records Survey began studies that eventuated in the publication of its *Guides to Depositories of Manuscript Collections in the United States*. Another significant effort to apprise researchers of guides to original sources throughout the United States was Ray A. Billington's "Guides to American History Manuscript Collections in Libraries of the United States."[4]

By far the most comprehensive and ambitious attempt at an overview of archives and manuscripts in this country came in 1961: *A Guide to Archives and Manuscripts in the United States*, edited by Philip M. Hamer. The next year brought the first volume of the Library of Congress' *National Union Catalog of Manuscript Collections* (*NUCMC*), designed as a continuing publication with a cumulating index. (The sixth volume came late in 1968. Researchers should realize that whatever contribution *NUCMC* has made so far, its work has just begun. Countless collections remain unreported.) Before the appearance of these volumes, searches for original sources for a particular project were too much like stabs in the dark. Scholars wasted valuable time in locating sources and were frustrated by the feeling that they could have missed something important. While these volumes by no means solve all the problems of locating pertinent sources, they serve as a powerful magnet to find material that recently was like the proverbial needle in a haystack. The development of these general guides represents "one of the really important" contributions to research in the last decade.[5]

Since the appearance of the Hamer *Guide* and *NUCMC*, graduate students have commonly begun their search for original materials with these volumes, and many professors have specified

[4] *Mississippi Valley Historical Review*, Vol. XXXVIII, No. 3 (Dec., 1951), 467–96.
[5] Interview with William S. Dix, see Appendix C2a.

this procedure. Such quick, preliminary identification of sources related to a research project has established the great utility of these finding aids. As soon as students became immersed in their projects, their research usually suggested other leads to follow.[6]

THE HAMER *GUIDE*

From their experiences in using the Hamer *Guide* and *NUCMC*, professors and graduate students have assessed the strengths and weaknesses of each. As might be expected, historians sometimes disagreed on what the volumes should do. Some considered the Hamer *Guide* the most useful finding aid for United States historians. Its great advantage is that it enables searchers to identify appropriate collections quickly. Then if they need fuller information, they can write the depository.[7] Graduate students often found most of their dissertation sources through the Hamer *Guide*.[8] The feature identified as its greatest advantage is its geographical arrangement, which enables students to plan research trips.[9] This geographical arrangement was particularly helpful to one student because he knew where things happened but frequently not those persons involved.[10] Graduate students commented on further advantages of the Hamer *Guide*: the ease of finding material and the incorporation of small collections (fewer than fifty items) that *NUCMC* cannot report.[11]

While terming the Hamer *Guide* "a bible for all of us," John A. Carroll identified its foremost defect: the incorporation of erroneous information furnished by curators. "Hamer evidently accepted information . . . at face value and made no attempt to evaluate it." The *Guide*'s information, moreover, was almost a decade old.[12] Hamer depended on accurate reporting from reposi-

[6] Interviews with David Donald and William G. McLoughlin, Jr., see Appendix C1.
[7] Interview with Robert A. Divine, *ibid*.
[8] Interviews with Edward L. Gambill and Henry Feingold, see Appendix C3.
[9] Interviews with A. Hunter Dupree, Don E. Fehrenbacher, and Joe M. Richardson, see Appendix C1; Edward G. Holley, see Appendix C2a.
[10] Interview with Joseph M. Hawes, see Appendix C3.
[11] Interviews with Lisle A. Rose and James T. Kitson, *ibid*.
[12] Interview, see Appendix C1.

tories, and his project made no provision for verifying the reports. Consequently, the inaccurate information has resulted in some "wild goose chases."[13] Other complaints about the Hamer *Guide* were that the entries were too general to help much[14] and that the index was vague and abbreviated.[15] Opposing the geographical format of the Hamer *Guide*, Merrill D. Peterson thought the listings by repository were inadequate.[16] Whatever the limitations of the Hamer *Guide*, Herman H. Fussler, director of the University of Chicago library, favored expanding it as a single guide for locating manuscripts. He maintained that a researcher with different undefined problems needs a guide that will locate sources. Then the researcher can query the repositories about his problems. The Hamer *Guide*'s strength was in describing locations of sources simply.[17]

NUCMC

In its short existence, the *National Union Catalog of Manuscript Collections* has already won wide acclaim. Librarians and archivists have termed it "a tremendous step ahead,"[18] "the best possible approach to the problem of bringing our manuscript sources under bibliographical control,"[19] "a blessing . . . in enabling us to give reference service to students,"[20] "the most helpful and useful of the general guides,"[21] and "as good as it ought to be."[22] Some historians preferred *NUCMC* to the Hamer *Guide* on the bases of its comprehensiveness and organization.[23] Because *NUCMC* is a

[13] Questionnaire returned by James C. Cox, Loyola University library (Chicago).

[14] Interview with William Wheeler, see Appendix C3.

[15] Interviews with Merrill D. Peterson, see Appendix C1; John James, see Appendix C3.

[16] Peterson, above.

[17] Interview, see Appendix C2a.

[18] Interview with Robert W. Lovett, curator of manuscripts, Harvard Graduate School of Business Administration, see Appendix C2a.

[19] Interview with Clifford K. Shipton, Harvard University archivist, *ibid.*

[20] Interview with David Kaser, director, Joint University Libraries, Nashville, *ibid.*

[21] Interview with Leslie W. Dunlap, director, University of Iowa library, *ibid.*

[22] Interview with William S. Dix, Princeton University librarian, *ibid.*

[23] Interviews with Robert F. Berkhofer, Jr., and John L. Loos, see Appendix C1.

continuing publication with additional collections reported in each volume, it offers the hope of eventually achieving bibliographical control over this country's manuscripts. For those institutions that do not have the means for publishing guides to their collections, their reports to *NUCMC* in effect constitute such a guide.

One measure of the utility of *NUCMC* has been the correspondence it generated for a reporting depository. The Division of Manuscripts at the University of Oklahoma cannot keep reports current because of answering reference requests based on previous listings in *NUCMC*.[24] Most depositories stated that their listings in both the Hamer *Guide* and *NUCMC* have occasioned many mail inquiries, which attest to researchers' familiarity with these finding aids. Small depositories have had difficulty filling mail requests for photocopies from reported collections unless the collections were indexed.[25] Another practical gauge of *NUCMC*'s usefulness was that it has enabled an institution to judge the value of manuscripts offered for sale. When the Huntington Library was offered a collection of personal papers, the curator of manuscripts checked *NUCMC* for related manuscripts. He discovered that the great body of the individual's papers was in the East and that Huntington was offered only a splinter collection. By not buying, the library saved between ten and fifteen thousand dollars.[26] Furthermore, *NUCMC* enabled at least one depository to find manuscripts in its own collection. The library staff at the University of Illinois admitted embarrassment about having lost control over some of its holdings but was glad the material had been reported to *NUCMC* so that it could be relocated.[27]

Many repositories have encountered difficulty in making reports to *NUCMC* because of its rigid rules of not listing a collection of fewer than fifty pieces. Because the Cincinnati Historical Society thought it had valuable material in such collections, it tried to

[24] Interview with Arrell M. Gibson, *ibid.*
[25] Questionnaire returned by Harriet S. Lacy, New Hampshire Historical Society.
[26] Interview with Herbert C. Schulz, see Appendix C2b.
[27] Interview, see n. 75, Chap. III.

combine them to qualify for *NUCMC*; but the staff found it did not have sufficient time for the recataloging entailed.[28] James W. Patton, former director of the Southern Historical Collection (SHC) of the University of North Carolina, complained of *NUCMC*'s ironbound rules and the inadequacy of its library headings or tracings. Also, *NUCMC* changed the names of some of the SHC collections without consultation.[29]

In addition to posing some problems for reporting agencies, *NUCMC* has certain deficiencies that researchers should be aware of. Gene M. Gressley considered *NUCMC*'s indexing poor and its organization frustrating.[30] Mattie Russell, curator of manuscripts at Duke University, cautioned that consulting *NUCMC*, or any other guide of this nature, should not take the place of a visit to the repository. *NUCMC* is not sufficiently detailed to enable a researcher to know all he should about a collection.[31] Moreover, the spotty coverage of *NUCMC* has resulted from a lack of cooperation from manuscript repositories. Many such institutions have good intentions but simply have not had the resources to prepare the reports.[32]

NATIONAL ARCHIVES FINDING AIDS

Perhaps the most formidable body of research material in the United States is that in the National Archives. Students accustomed to tracking down information through a card catalog are unable to apply those techniques with archives, and having to employ unknown research methods to find material often results in apprehensiveness and frustration. Because of their great bulk, archival records are not susceptible to item cataloging or indexing. Whatever control is extended over them must be in more general terms. The efforts of the National Archives to identify and describe its holdings have resulted in a variety of finding aids, ranging from preliminary inventories to the meticulous *Guide to*

[28] Interview with Lee Jordan and Virginia Jergens, see Appendix C2b.
[29] Interview, see Appendix C2a.
[30] Interview, see Appendix C1.
[31] Interview, see Appendix C2a.
[32] Interview with Leonard W. Labaree, see Appendix C1.

Federal Archives Relating to the Civil War, by Kenneth W. Munden and Henry P. Beers.

Historians' reactions to the finding aids of the National Archives were as diverse as the finding aids themselves. Those who have consulted the Munden and Beers *Guide* expressed great enthusiasm for it, calling it a model.[33] Because this *Guide* is so good, its admirers wished that other National Archives finding aids could be of the same scope and quality. One of its most beneficial aspects is the listing of secondary works, both books and articles, based on Civil War records.[34] Even with the benefit of having studied this thorough *Guide* before going to Washington, however, a graduate student at the University of Illinois felt unprepared for the mass of records related to his subject in the National Archives.[35]

Researchers have singled out other National Archives finding aids as having been particularly beneficial. John A. DeNovo found Elizabeth Buck's reference information paper on Middle Eastern materials a great help.[36] According to Robert C. Davis, studying the Archives' finding aid for census records enabled him to accomplish in a two-day visit to the Archives what otherwise would have taken a week.[37] One of the leading benefits of these finding aids is that in describing federal records they reflect the administrative framework of the national government. Even the preliminary inventories help by providing first-level control over material that would otherwise be described only by an accession list.[38] Unfortunately, too little relation exists between various types of National Archives finding aids. Each finding aid should explain how it fits into the over-all scheme of Archives guides.[39] A considerable benefit of these finding aids is that they enable researchers to write intelligent letters to the Archives before making a trip.[40] Richard

[33] Interviews with Arthur Bestor, David Donald, David S. Sparks, and Barnes F. Lathrop, *ibid.*; David E. Meerse, see Appendix C3.

[34] Interview with Sparks, above.

[35] Interview with Meerse, above.

[36] Interview, see Appendix C1.

[37] Davis, *ibid.*

[38] Interview with A. Hunter Dupree, *ibid.*

[39] Interview with Barnes F. Lathrop, *ibid.*

[40] Interview with Robert V. Hine, Hal Bridges, and Edwin S. Gaustad, *ibid.*

W. Leopold, who termed the Archives finding aids "magnificent," encouraged students to write that repository for guides related to their topics.[41] Librarians from the Universities of Chicago and Florida reported that the National Archives guides have enabled them to build their ethnohistory and Latin American collections, respectively.[42]

The Archives' finding aid receiving the widest use (other than the *Guide to Genealogical Records in the National Archives*) was the annual *List of National Archives Microfilm Publications*. Librarians and historians were virtually unanimous in their preference for the 1961 *List*, for it itemized each reel. Subsequent publications have described only entire series in general terms and in some cases merely given titles. Librarians marked the 1961 *List* as a record of their holdings of Archives microfilm and employed the *List* as a guide to that film. All those expressing preference for the 1961 *List* advocated that the Archives return to that format in the future.[43] Only one library staff, at the University of Cincinnati, expressed satisfaction with the summary annotations in *Lists* published after 1961.[44] Those who lamented the absence of itemization in *Lists* after 1961 should know that the National Archives furnishes this itemization in processed form upon request.

Many institutions and individuals have used the *List* to identify and order material of particular importance to them.[45] The staff of the Nebraska State Historical Society was unaware of the exist-

[41] Leopold, *ibid.*

[42] Interview with University of Chicago library staff, see n. 66, Chap. VII; questionnaire returned by Margaret Knox Goggin, University of Florida library.

[43] Interviews with Nyle H. Miller and Katherine Halverson, see Appendix C2b; Andrew J. Eaton, librarian, William H. Kurth, assistant director, William Matheson, chief of the Rare Books Room, Jerry Ewing, Documents librarian, Marjorie Karlson, chief of the Reference Department, David Nevin, chief of the Audio-Visual Department, Washington University library; Arthur M. McAnally; Jo Kennedy, head, Documents-Maps Division, Florida State University library; see Appendix C2a; Richard P. McCormick, Lloyd C. Gardner, Richard M. Brown, and Noble E. Cunningham, Jr., see Appendix C1.

[44] Interview with Arthur T. Hamlin, university librarian, and Laszlo Velics, Reference librarian, see Appendix C2a.

[45] Interviews with Alfred Rawlinson, director of libraries, University of South Carolina; Francis X. Scannell, chief of Reference Services, Michigan State University library, *ibid.*; Arthur S. Link, see Appendix C1.

ence of the microfilmed state census of 1885 until they saw it in the *List*. This film proved "most valuable" to the society.[46] The University of Hawaii library found the *List* "extremely useful" for ordering material related to the Pacific and Asia.[47] When Edmund J. Danzinger, Jr., began investigating sources for a dissertation on "Problems in the Administration of Federal Indian Policy During the Civil War," the *List* proved to be "the most important key" to his material. The subsequent publication of the preliminary inventory of the records of the Bureau of Indian Affairs also helped immensely.[48]

In addition to the annual *List*, the National Archives publishes pamphlet guides to accompany some of its microfilm. Since these numerous guides greatly facilitate research with the film, the Archives should issue them collectively, or at least by subject-area groups. Also, the annual *List* should indicate clearly which microfilm publications have accompanying pamphlet guides.

However beneficial many researchers have found the Archives' finding aids, others maintained that these guides are not so effective as they should be. There is general criticism that the *Guide to the Records in the National Archives* (1948), its only comprehensive guide, is badly out of date.[49] Donald R. McCoy, who was employed in the Archives while a graduate student, diagnosed the problem with its finding aids thus: The aids have been designed on the assumption that users will spend three months a year at the Archives rather than the more usual one week every two or three years. In essence, then, these finding aids are more meaningful to the Archives staff than to visiting researchers.[50] James P. Shenton

---

[46] Interview with Donald F. Danker, see Appendix C2b.

[47] Interview with Robert D. Stevens, see Appendix C2a.

[48] Interview, see Appendix C3.

[49] Interviews with Hyman W. Kritzer, assistant director for Public Services; George Schoyer, in charge of the History Graduate Library; Mrs. Yvonne Wulff, former head of Government Documents; Joseph Placek, head of the Reference Department; Ruth Erlandson, consultant for Library Research, Ohio State University library, see Appendix C2a; Arthur Bestor and Barnes F. Lathrop, see Appendix C1; questionnaires returned by Joe W. Kraus, Kansas State University library; Francis Paul Prucha, S.J., Marquette University.

[50] Interview, see Appendix C1. As the forewords of many preliminary inventories indicate, they are prepared primarily for internal use.

agreed that the guides do not identify material sufficiently for the uninitiated researcher.[51]

The substance of these criticisms was reinforced by Morris Rieger's analysis of the Archives' finding aids: "Although the National Archives general guide is hopelessly dated, its content is fairly good in terms of its time of preparation. However, its organization, numerically by record group, means nothing to outside users; in fact, it imposes an unnecessary burden on them. While the record group basis of description should be retained in any revised version, the record group entries should be grouped meaningfully, regardless of number, under broad functional headings corresponding to the principal functions of the federal government: foreign affairs, financial affairs, military affairs, etc. [Recent specialized guides have been organized in this manner.]

"The next level of National Archives finding aids is the preliminary inventory. These vary greatly in quality. Some are excellent and provide realistic and balanced ideas of the contents of record groups. These are in the minority. Too often inadequately trained junior people prepare the preliminary inventories and their product [includes] much undigested data obscuring the essential subject-matter themes of the series described. . . . Record group inventories are essential, and all should be reviewed and, if necessary, revised to meet minimum quality standards. Among them should be a requirement that each series entry specify the core subjects dealt with. Some existing subject and area finding aids are quite good. Many more should be produced in accordance with a long-range plan developed in collaboration with the scholarly community and adapted to its needs."[52]

Regardless of the reasons for their shortcomings, many historians expressed emphatic dissatisfaction with National Archives finding aids. Dean Albertson called them a "mess." "I've never used one yet that I can make heads or tails of."[53] Daniel R. Beaver, who

[51] Shenton, *ibid.*
[52] Interview, see Appendix C2b. Currently Rieger directs the National Historical Publications Commission's National African Guide Project. For fifteen years he headed the Labor and Transportation Branch of the National Archives.
[53] Interview, see Appendix C1.

has used these guides extensively in connection with military records, said that they are "the hardest to use of any."[54] The files at the Archives are just too complex, Louis R. Harlan maintained, for its guides to be effective.[55] Historians who thought the guides described collections inadequately advocated reliance on Archives staff members for assistance in finding pertinent records. They also felt that personal trips to the Archives were necessary before a person could know much about the records.[56] In his research experience at the National Archives and elsewhere, Norman A. Graebner found it better to rely on the knowledge of curators than to study finding aids. He was never one "to pore over guides to materials."[57]

Whatever dissatisfaction with individual finding aids scholars expressed, most readily admitted that virtually any guide is better than none. The researcher consequently can profit from studying guides relating to his subject. Only when researchers are ignorant of pertinent finding aids do the finding aids become useless. Many archivists and librarians testified that the major faults were not with the quality of the guides but with professors who did not acquaint graduate students with these basic tools.[58]

TEACHING ABOUT FINDING AIDS

Recognizing that students' ignorance on the subject of finding aids reflects adversely on their training, some professors have taken concrete measures to counteract this deficiency. One of the problems in introducing finding aids involved the reluctance of stu-

[54] Beaver, *ibid.*
[55] Harlan, *ibid.*
[56] Interviews with Frank W. Klingberg, Oscar Handlin, Allan Nevins, and George C. Rogers, Jr., *ibid.*
[57] Graebner, *ibid.*
[58] Interviews with Charles E. Lee and Lucile M. Kane, see Appendix C2b; James Mink; T. N. McMullan; Edward B. Stanford, director of university libraries, John Parker, curator of James Ford Bell Collection, Richard F. Bernard, chief, Department of Special Collections, Maxine B. Clapp, head of Division of Manuscripts and Archives, William LaBissoniere, Government Documents librarian, University of Minnesota; Thomas R. Adams; see Appendix C2a; Brown University library staff, see n. 85, Chap. VI; questionnaire returned by Joe W. Kraus, Kansas State University library.

dents to study and master these tools. For one thing, many students felt insecure using original sources and guides, since they were more familiar with secondary works, which can be traced with comparative ease through a card catalog.[59] Too, some students preferred to "jump in and flounder around rather than do systematic before-hand work in guides."[60] To dispel any preference for floundering around, Roger H. Brown had specialists from the General Reference and Bibliography Division of the Library of Congress discuss guides and their utility with his seminarians at American University.[61]

In some seminars, professors assigned exercises requiring investigation of various finding aids, and students reported on their characteristics. Frequently, the guides were available in the seminar room for student perusal.[62] Although W. Frank Craven told his students in colonial history about such guides as Evans, Sabin, the *Harvard Guide to American History*, *Writings on American History*, union catalogs, and the list of serials, he considered it helpful to "turn students loose to fumble around to find the obvious things." Since the Princeton University library is well cataloged and has open stacks, students experienced little difficulty in locating material; and since a great number of colonial sources are printed and their bulk is much less than for later periods of American history, students had a fair chance of finding things on their own.[63]

The usefulness of finding aids depends on how teachers introduce them. In discussing guides with graduate students, Philip D. Jordan brought the volumes to class and pointed out how a particular guide enabled him to find specific sources for a research project. Concrete illustrations of the use of guides provided a better teaching device than abstract discussion of them.[64] For his bibliographical course at the University of Texas, Barnes F.

---

[59] Interview with Dorothy D. Gondos, see Appendix C1.
[60] Interview with Roger H. Brown, *ibid.*
[61] *Ibid.*
[62] Interviews with John R. Alden and Vincent P. De Santis, see Appendix C1.
[63] Craven, *ibid.*
[64] Jordan, *ibid.*

Lathrop said that the Hamer *Guide* and *NUCMC* have been immense pedagogical aids. Their compendiousness saved him detailed discussions of guides to individual repositories. In addition to thorough study of these two, he had students investigate a few institutional guides.[65] Not only should doctoral candidates learn about finding aids, but they also might profit from preparing them. The individual would enrich his understanding of a body of original sources and the profession would likewise benefit. Many master's candidates could probably make a greater contribution by preparing a descriptive and critical guide to primary sources than by writing an interpretative essay.[66]

Teaching students about finding aids represented only one dimension of training in new doctoral programs such as the one at the University of California at Santa Barbara. Far more important, the general finding aids and similar recent developments within the research community have made it possible for institutions like UCSB to offer doctoral work at all. "It is absolutely essential for a campus such as ours to make extensive use of the general finding aids. We couldn't even begin a graduate program without these guides. A place like Santa Barbara can offer graduate work because of the way the profession has changed—the existence of guides, original sources on microfilm, NHPC publications, and more travel funds."[67]

USES OF FINDING AIDS

The reactions of different institutions to finding aids often depended on their manuscript holdings and philosophy of collecting. Many universities with, or with aspirations toward, new doctoral programs and many which do not possess extensive original sources have made great efforts to collect all available bibliographies and finding aids. Their assumption was that if they did not have the material graduate students needed, they could at least provide the means for locating it.[68] One great advantage to a

[65] Lathrop, *ibid.*
[66] Interview with Joseph T. Durkin, S.J., *ibid.*
[67] Interview with Alexander DeConde, *ibid.*
[68] Interviews with Robert P. Lang, Edward G. Holley, John H. Berthel, and Alfred Rawlinson, see Appendix C2a.

depository in preparing guides to its material has been that they facilitated subsequent use of the sources by curators. Not only has this been the experience of the curator of special collections of the Rutgers—The State University library, but his 1964 guide has resulted in an increase of intelligent mail inquiries.[69] Unfortunately, excellent guides from individual repositories have not guaranteed such inquiries. Despite enthusiastic acclaim for the two-volume guide of the Minnesota Historical Society,[70] Lucile M. Kane, the society's manuscripts curator, reported amazement that mature scholars frequently did not investigate the guide before inquiring by mail.[71] Some depositories have not published guides because they do not want people to know about their manuscripts. Since the Hawaiian Mission Children's Society has been bothered with "irresponsible" researchers, the librarian thought that without a guide the society could prevent further knowledge of its manuscripts and therefore control them better.[72] The Northwestern University library staff admitted that it did not report some important collections because it wanted no notice of their existence.[73] While these lamentable attitudes were not normative, they nonetheless belied the rationale for a repository: serving scholarship.

As professors ordinarily recommended, many graduate students investigated finding aids systematically to locate research material. After Jay C. Thompson, Jr., selected "Technocracy During the Great Depression" as his master's topic, he began his search for original sources by consulting the *Harvard Guide*, the *Cumulative Book Index*, *Writings on American History*, and Besterman's *A World Bibliography of Bibliographies and of Bibliographical Catalogues, Calendars, Abstracts, Digests, Indexes, and the Like*.[74]

[69] Interview with Donald A. Sinclair, *ibid.*

[70] Interviews with Allan G. Bogue, see Appendix C1; Edmund J. Danziger, Jr., see Appendix C3; questionnaire returned by Francis Paul Prucha, S.J., Marquette University.

[71] Interview, see Appendix C2b.

[72] Interview with Mrs. E. C. Cluff, Jr., see Appendix C2b.

[73] Interview with David Jolly, assistant librarian; Noel A. S. Owens, chief of Reference and Special Services; Robert W. Baumgartner, Government Documents librarian; Richard D. Olson, curator of rare books and manuscripts, see Appendix C2a.

[74] Interview, see Appendix C3.

Clarke A. Chambers cautioned against undue reliance on the *Harvard Guide*, for its index can lead to blind alleys. For instance, the index entry on social welfare "actually leads to Billy the Kid. . . . the *Harvard Guide* is impossible for my field."[75] To determine whether anything had been written on the subject he was considering, Burton I. Kaufman consulted such bibliographical aids as *Writings on American History* and the American Historical Association's *List of Doctoral Dissertations in History in Progress or Completed at Colleges and Universities in the United States.*[76]

Because of the nature of some topics, finding aids may offer little assistance. In such cases, researchers frequently wrote numerous letters of inquiry to likely depositories. When John Clark began looking for sources, he "flooded" the country with such letters.[77] Similarly, David Goodman wrote six to seven hundred letters seeking information on J. Ross Browne. He made a list of Browne's correspondents and tried to locate their papers, hoping to get further information on his subject. From his letters, Goodman heard from thirty libraries with Browne material.[78]

Researchers have commented on the particular assistance of individual guides. Hugh F. Rankin declared, "I don't know what I would have done in England without Crick and Alman, *A Guide to Manuscripts Relating to America in Great Britain and Ireland.*"[79] For his dissertation, "The Catholic Press Reaction to Nativism, 1840–60," Robert Hueston made great use of the directory of Roman Catholic newspapers published by the Catholic University of America.[80] The Emory University library staff found Richard W. Hale's *Guide to Photocopied Historical Materials in the United States and Canada* extremely useful since it indicates the locations of photocopied materials.[81] The Oklahoma State University library staff commented that guides were most

[75] Interview, see Appendix C1.
[76] Interview, see Appendix C3.
[77] Interview, see Appendix C1.
[78] Interview, see Appendix C3.
[79] Interview, see Appendix C1.
[80] Interview, see Appendix C3.
[81] Interview, see n. 145, Chap. VII.

helpful when they give sufficient detail so that a researcher can request specific items for photocopying.[82]

RECOMMENDATIONS

Historians' involvement with and dependence on finding aids were signified by many and varied recommendations concerning them. These recommendations dealt with needs for improving existing guides, for new guides, and for better publicity of existing guides; with the most effective ways of preparation; and with desired characteristics. Because of the comparative difficulty of locating material in the National Archives, researchers away from the Archives have relied on its finding aids to a greater extent than they would those from other kinds of repositories. Consequently, they eagerly suggested ways of improving these guides. The most frequest suggestion was for a revision of the *Guide to the Records in the National Archives*. This 1948 volume remains the most recent general guide published by the Archives, but was being revised.[83] For greatest utility, the revision should be prepared along the lines of the Munden and Beers Civil War guide.[84] Other suggestions concerning National Archives finding aids included the following: publication of the State Department purport books, which contain brief descriptions of the diplomatic records;[85] greater detail and specificity about the records being described;[86] and regular distribution of the Archives' checklist of publications to seminar directors.[87]

Recommendations for other institutional finding aids and different types of guides were as follows: (1) repositories should give first priority to reporting to *NUCMC* so that informational

---

[82] Questionnaire returned by Marguerite S. Howland.

[83] Interviews with Barnes F. Lathrop, John Hope Franklin, and Allen J. Going, see Appendix C1; questionnaires returned by Geneva Kebler, Michigan Historical Commission Archives; Walter T. K. Nugent, Indiana University.

[84] Interview with Arthur Bestor, see Appendix C1.

[85] Interview with Ernest R. May, *ibid.*

[86] Interviews with John S. Ezell and Jack M. Sosin, *ibid.*; questionnaire returned by Philip S. Klein, Pennsylvania State University.

[87] Interview with Richard W. Leopold, see Appendix C1.

control over the nation's manuscripts may eventually be attained;[88] (2) a comprehensive guide to the collection of the Manuscript Division of the Library of Congress should be prepared;[89] (3) the 1904–1905 and 1941–47 gaps in *Writings on American History* should be filled, a cumulative index to the *Writings* should be prepared, and the annual volumes should be published more promptly; [90] (4) the "Sources" section in the *Harvard Guide to American History* should be expanded and the *Guide* should be revised;[91] (5) topical and chronological guides should be prepared;[92] (6) guides should be prepared by geographic regions;[93] (7) guides to state archives and state and private historical society collections should be compiled, using standardized formats;[94] (8) newspaper union lists and indexes, for both microfilmed and un-

[88] Interviews with Douglas W. Bryant, Alfred Rawlinson, Arthur M. McAnally, Howard H. Peckham, Robert M. Warner, and Frederick H. Wagman, see Appendix C2a; Charles A. Barker, Richard L. Watson, Jr., George E. Mowry, David S. Sparks, Richard S. Kirkendall, and Merrill Jensen, see Appendix C1; Daniel R. Porter, see Appendix C2b; questionnaire returned by Wilson Smith, University of California at Davis.

[89] Interviews with Kenneth M. Stampp and Frank Freidel, see Appendix C1; questionnaire returned by Elliott S. M. Gatner, Long Island University library.

[90] Interviews with David M. Potter, Wood Gray, Don E. Fehrenbacher, and I. B. Holley, Jr., see Appendix C1; Harold D. McDonald, chief of American History Division, New York Public Library, see Appendix C2b; questionnaire returned by Harold S. Snellgrove, Mississippi State University.

[91] Questionnaires returned by Lloyd Hooker, Pennsylvania State University library; Wayne S. Yenawine, University of Louisville library. The initial report from the Charles Warren Center for Studies in American History stated that Frank Freidel is editing such a revision.

[92] Interviews with John A. Schutz, Robert Dykstra, W. C. Nunn, and Alden T. Vaughan, see Appendix C1; Jane Smith, Julia B. Carroll, and John J. McDonough, Jr., see Appendix C2b; questionnaires returned by T. D. Seymour Bassett, curator, Special Collections, University of Vermont; Robert W. McCluggage, Loyola University (Chicago).

[93] Interviews with Thomas J. Pressly, Herbert Weaver, Ray A. Billington, Allen J. Going, and Bayrd Still, see Appendix C1; Margaret Scrivan, see Appendix C2b; questionnaire returned by Richard D. Goff, Eastern Michigan University.

[94] Interviews with John K. Nelson, William I. Hair, and Richard Walsh, see Appendix C1; University of Illinois library staff, see n. 75, Chap. III; Dolores Renze, see Appendix C2b; Jerome M. Clubb and Robert M. Warner, see Appendix C2a; questionnaires returned by H. G. Jones, North Carolina Department of Archives and History; Charlotte A. Smith, Stetson University library; James L. Hupp, West Virginia Department of Archives and History.

filmed papers, should be kept up to date;[95] and (9) a guide to finding aids for local sources, such as those published in France, should be compiled.[96]

While each of the foregoing recommendations reflected the thinking of several scholars, the following were individual suggestions for additions to or changes in finding aids and bibliographical tools: a cumulative listing of master's theses in history, similar to *Dissertations in History: An Index to Dissertations Completed in History Departments of United States and Canadian Universities, 1873–1960*, edited by Warren Kuehl;[97] a paperback supplement to update the Hamer *Guide*, which would be cheaper for the user than buying a completely revised edition;[98] a continuation of Frances G. Davenport's *European Treaties Bearing on the History of the United States*;[99] a cumulative calendar of manuscript collections at universities and other depositories without their own guides;[100] a guide to maps, down to the county level;[101] a comprehensive listing of holdings of presidential libraries;[102] finding aids for the papers of secondary figures in American history—the kind of papers graduate students are likely to use when they do not have access to major depositories in the East;[103] publication of the calendars H. B. Fant prepared for major collections, such as the Daniel Webster papers, housed in the Library of Congress Manuscript Division;[104] a usable guide and index to the microfilmed American Periodical Series;[105] a more coherent census guide;[106] a guide to edited documents published in historical jour-

[95] Interviews with University of Illinois library staff, see n. 75, Chap. III; Robert W. Johannsen, Carl H. Cramer, Madison Kuhn, and Paul C. Nagel, see Appendix C1.

[96] Interviews with Aubrey C. Land and Donald Meyer, see Appendix C1; questionnaire returned by Walter T. K. Nugent, Indiana University.

[97] Questionnaire returned by Wilson Smith, University of California at Davis.

[98] Interview with Lawrence E. Gelfand, see Appendix C1.

[99] *Ibid.*

[100] Questionnaire returned by Sigurd Johansen, New Mexico State University.

[101] Interview with John E. Frost, see Appendix C2a.

[102] Questionnaire returned by Homer L. Knight, Oklahoma State University.

[103] Interview with Earl Pomeroy, see Appendix C1.

[104] Interview with Maurice G. Baxter, *ibid.*

[105] Interview with Howard S. Miller, *ibid.*

[106] Interview with Philip L. White, *ibid.*

nals;[107] a finding aid for manuscripts related to Hawaii and the Pacific as well as a guide to National Archives materials on all Trust territories;[108] a guide to student publications—literary society magazines, fraternity publications, and alumni periodicals;[109] and a comprehensive guide to documents related to the United States which are kept in foreign archives.[110]

Since an obvious need exists for guides to manuscript collections in many important repositories that may never prepare the ideal finding aids they desire, these repositories should take advantage of the practical and commercially feasible method of reproducing card catalogs in book form. The two-volume reproduction by G. K. Hall and Company of the manuscripts catalog of the New York Public Library, whatever the shortcomings of the original catalog, is a genuine boon. The Massachusetts Historical Society plans a similar seven-volume publication. The lack in one's own library of *any* guide to many great collections severely handicaps scholarship and imposes penalties on the repositories. They risk being skipped entirely by researchers or overloaded with inquiries that would be obviated by a published catalog.

The proliferation of finding aids, coupled with the desires of the scholars for more, means that researchers and reference librarians may be unaware of a guide related to individual interests. To reduce the danger of missing any guide that could assist the scholar, a compendium should include information on printed guides as well as on any unpublished finding aids maintained by institutions. It should also contain statements on the research policies of the depositories, including information on photocopying.[111]

Closely related to the problem of a specialized guide's being unknown among the corpus of guides is the general problem of

[107] Interview with William S. Hanna, Jr., *ibid.*

[108] Interview with Robert D. Stevens, see Appendix C2a.

[109] Interview with Frederick D. Kershner, Jr., see Appendix C1.

[110] Interview with Joseph E. Jeffs, see Appendix C2a. The Library of Congress' Center for the Coordination of Foreign Manuscript Copying, directed by George O. Kent, is collecting such information. Until the publication of a comprehensive guide, information about such documents may be found in "News from the Center," a semiannual publication of the Library of Congress.

[111] Interviews with Russell L. Caldwell, Donald D. Johnson, and Charles G. Sellers, Jr., see Appendix C1; Sheldon Silverman, see Appendix C3.

publicity for finding aids. As a rule, the issuance of most finding aids is not accompanied with any significant fanfare, and consequently many tend to fall out of sight.This is especially true of finding aids from the National Archives, which has no budget for advertising its wares. Also, these finding aids are often salted away with government documents. To overcome this situation, historians suggested that the Archives and other depositories make a point of informing history departments, and each other, of new finding aids. Sometimes when such information goes to a university library, it does not get channeled to historians. Professional journals could also carry more publicity relating to finding aids and acquisitions.[112] To ensure close communication with historians, the Wayne State University archives had a staff member study its collections for possible thesis topics and then discuss them with members of the history department. According to Philip P. Mason, the university archivist and a professor of history, "Archivists need to sell and publicize what they've got."[113] One form of publicity that librarians can furnish for guides and finding aids is to shelve them in one location. If such a collection were kept up to date and intact, a student could study the material and have some assurance of having done as much bibliographical work as possible before beginning research.[114]

This problem of historians' knowledge of finding aids relates in large measure to their sense of the importance of bibliographical work. Historians obviously want the work done, but few think it worth their effort to do it. The rewards of the profession go to more exciting and glamorous projects. That these current values were not always held by the profession is amply attested to by the work of Winsor, Jameson, Leland, and Bemis. But where are their successors today? Those who expect that in the future machines will do all the bibliographic grubbing for historians must realize

---

[112] Interviews with Wood Gray, W. H. Masterson, Harold D. Langley, James A. Rawley, Richard W. Leopold, Philip P. Mason, and Arthur H. DeRosier, Jr., see Appendix C1; questionnaires returned by Paul L. Simon, Xavier University, and Bert Fireman, Arizona Historical Foundation.

[113] Interview, above.

[114] Interview with Shaw Livermore, Jr., see Appendix C1.

that someone has to know what should be fed into the computers. The idle expectation of a better research world through electronics currently impedes progress toward practical remedies for the information explosion. One way that historians can keep abreast of finding aids as they become available is by reading the review section of *The American Archivist*, which gives by far the most comprehensive coverage of this field. Manifestly, the knowledge practicing historians have of these keys that unlock original sources has a direct bearing on the effectiveness of their research.

The question of who should prepare finding aids deserves close attention. Ordinarily the preparation is done by manuscript librarians or archivists with varying degrees of historical training. Richard C. Berner, curator of manuscripts at the University of Washington, contended that historians are not equipped to do this work,[115] and Robert E. Burke agreed with him.[116] "Historians can do a great deal, though," Berner said, "to boost the morale of archivists engaged in this kind of project."[117] Some historians disagreed sharply with Berner's proposition. They complained that too often guides have been assembled by librarians and archivists ignorant of the questions historians would ask of the records. If those preparing the guides do not understand how historians approach their task, they cannot describe the records adequately. They frequently force material into artificial categories that make little sense to specialists in the subject. Consequently, historians should be involved in preparing finding aids.[118] Herman H. Fussler, director of libraries at the University of Chicago, concurred that the "ideal guide is the work of a combination of the subject-matter specialist and archivist-curator. This is so that a reasonable balance can be given to the substantive and technical considerations in an entry."[119]

When the question of who prepares finding aids is settled, the next important problem becomes how they are to be compiled.

115 Interview, see Appendix C2a.
116 Interview, see Appendix C1.
117 Interview, above.
118 Interviews with John A. Carroll and Robert E. Brown, see Appendix C1.
119 Interview, see Appendix C2a.

Several historians suggested that automatic data processing could be employed to great advantage, if sufficient funds were available.[120] Sanford W. Higginbotham suggested specifically that the published volumes of *NUCMC* and current reports to *NUCMC* be computerized so that this information could be disseminated quickly.[121] Frank G. Burke, formerly of the Library of Congress' Manuscript Division, has been investigating the application of machine techniques to National Archives finding aids. At the Library of Congress he pioneered in preparing indexes with automatic data processing. His paper, "Automation in Bibliographical Control of Archives and Manuscript Collections," was published in *Bibliography and the Historian*, the volume of proceedings from the AHA's bibliographical conference in May, 1967. The paper dealt with Higginbotham's exact proposal. The entire volume covered a matter of basic concern to historians.

A further answer to the question of how finding aids should be prepared is "in greater detail." Practically everyone familiar with the great bulk of twentieth-century records recognizes that these records cannot be described minutely and that only some more general control over them is feasible. Yet for older and less distended bodies of documents, many historians recommended as detailed an analysis as possible. Some scholars advocated the preparation of more calendars for clearer indications of the contents of collections.[122] Others espoused item cataloging, which is especially helpful for the researcher using a collection for its peripheral material.[123] An advantage is that with detailed cataloging, the finding aid is not likely to claim too much for the contents of a collection. If a collection is not complete, the finding aid should so state and should mention the location of related papers.[124] Researchers would also be aided if guides indicated both the

[120] Interviews with Oscar Handlin, Warren S. Tryon, Sanford W. Higginbotham, William R. Hogan, and Chase C. Mooney, see Appendix C1.
[121] Interview, above.
[122] Interviews with Henry L. Swint, John Duffy, and Clarence L. Ver Steeg, see Appendix C1.
[123] Interviews with George C. Rogers, Jr., *ibid.*; Mattie Russell and Eugene M. Johnson, see Appendix C2a.
[124] Interview with Barry D. Karl, see Appendix C1.

holders of literary property rights of the manuscripts described and any restrictions on collections, including those concerning photocopying.[125]

Since most depositories have limited budgets, they are unable to prepare the desired kinds of finding aids as quickly as they would like. Nor, because of the meticulous preparation necessarily involved, are most depositories able to report to *NUCMC* promptly and in adequate volume. Consequently, institutions should seek grants to assist their preparation of finding aids.[126] Also, foundation support could be sought to enable a team of manuscript specialists to visit depositories around the country, arranging, cataloging, and reporting collections to *NUCMC*.[127]

When repositories publish finding aids in bound volumes, they can include additional information only by issuing cumbersome supplements or expensive revised editions. Since most repositories constantly add collections that need reporting, this difficulty is genuine. To overcome it, the research community could take a page from the army's regulation books and adopt loose-leaf guides. As soon as any report on manuscripts became obsolete, it could be replaced by a revised, loose-leaf statement with a minimum of difficulty and expense.[128]

The growing amount of research done with photocopy has made many librarians and historians want to know if material listed in a finding aid is available in this medium.[129] Some suggested that *NUCMC* incorporate a listing of all such material and thus replace Richard W. Hale's *Guide to Photocopied Historical Materials in the United States and Canada*, which is frustrating to use.[130] Others recommended that all guides use asterisks to indicate material

[125] Interview with Leslie W. Dunlap, see Appendix C2a; questionnaire returned by Chester H. Linscheid, New Mexico State University library.

[126] Interview with Ruth Corry, see Appendix C2b.

[127] Interviews with Morris Rieger, *ibid.*; Robert E. Burke, see Appendix C1; Maxine B. Clapp, see Appendix C2a; questionnaire returned by Dean A. Fales, Essex Institute.

[128] Interviews with Charles E. Lee, see Appendix C2b; William N. Chambers, see Appendix C1.

[129] Questionnaires returned by Jack Scroggs, North Texas State University, and Donald H. Kent, Pennsylvania Historical and Museum Commission.

[130] Interview with Sanford W. Higginbotham, see Appendix C1.

available on microfilm.[131] Whether the incorporation of photo-copied collections in *NUCMC* will replace the Hale *Guide* is questionable, but *NUCMC*, as a matter of express policy, includes photocopy when the originals are not available for research in one location.

Among the most helpful finding aids for microfilmed material are the pamphlets issued by the projects supported by the National Historical Publications Commission (NHPC). The third edition of the *Catalog of Microfilm Publications*, complete to September, 1968, listed seventy-two publications, comprising 1,324 rolls of microfilm. These works have been produced by twenty-four repositories, and many more are in process. The NHPC specified that a finding aid accompany each publication. These publications, together with their finding aids, will facilitate historical research enormously.

As these NHPC microfilm publications accumulate, they assume increased significance. In terms of research value for American history, the corpus of these publications and guides becomes greater than the sum of the parts. Consequently, the historical journals should do more than relegate notice of their appearance to "News" sections. The reproduction of original sources on microfilm deserves as much notice as the publication of sources in any other form. Unless the journals pay more attention to this important scholarly development, they will be remiss. Only *The American Archivist* regularly reviews such microfilm projects, and regrettably few historians read that quarterly.

The thoughtfulness and variety of recommendations about finding aids indicated their essentiality and centrality to historical research. In some areas of investigation, students obviously can operate without using manuscript guides. Yet hardly any field can be imagined where the researcher would not need some bibliographical equipment. The object of graduate education in history should not be merely to equip a candidate to research and write his doctoral dissertation; it should also endeavor to acquaint the candidate with a variety of means historians employ to get at their

131 Interview with Sam B. Warner, Jr., *ibid.*

sources. One way for doctoral candidates to improve their knowledge of bibliographical tools outside their immediate specialty would be for those with undergraduate quiz sections to assume responsibility for discussing bibliography with their students.[132] If a historian acquires and maintains some appreciation and understanding of the tools of his craft, throughout his career he can benefit greatly by minimizing the difficulty of locating research material. And he may in turn transmit some of these benefits to another generation of graduate students. If professors neglect this responsibility, however, their students labor under some disadvantage—with possible detriment to individuals and the craft.

[132] Interview with Joseph R. Strayer, *ibid.*

IX. Documentary Editing

THE evolution of documentary editing from the time of
Ebenezer Hazard to the present has been as significant as any
other part of American historiography.[1] When Hazard began his
work, his thought was to collect and print original sources related
to the colonial period and the American Revolution, without any
attempt at critical evaluation. While his *Historical Collections*
(1792–94) and Peter Force's *American Archives* (1837–53) may
seem crude renderings by today's standards, their importance in
launching the publication of historical documents was immense.
The next to capitalize on the public's "apparently insatiable appe-
tite for solid documentary works relating to early America" was
the indefatigable Jared Sparks.[2] In 1829–30 the Department of
State published his twelve-volume edition of *The Diplomatic
Correspondence of the American Revolution*, and he issued a
three-volume *Life of Gouverneur Morris*, containing correspondence, in 1832. His greatest achievement was the twelve-volume
Writings of George Washington (1839–40), in which Sparks did

---

[1] Any time that "historical editing" appears in this chapter, it means documentary editing rather than the editing of secondary historical writing.

[2] Butterfield, "Archival and Editorial Enterprise in 1850 and in 1950," *loc. cit.*,
164.

not hestitate to tamper with the texts to save Washington from indelicacies and grammatical blunders.

Toward the turn of the century, standards generated by graduate history training began to be imposed on documentary editing. J. Franklin Jameson keenly realized the need for authoritative rendition of texts with critical annotation. He turned his own efforts toward editing letters of John C. Calhoun, which the American Historical Association published in its 1899 *Annual Report*. In addition he urged Frederick Jackson Turner, George P. Garrison, Worthington C. Ford, and others to undertake editorial assignments, the products of which were subsequently published in the AHA's *Annual Reports* and the *American Historical Review*. Jameson's influence can be traced directly to other major editorial enterprises of the twentieth century: Max Farrand's *Records of the Federal Convention*, Edmund C. Burnett's *Letters of Members of the Continental Congress*, John C. Fitzpatrick's *The Writings of George Washington from Original Manuscript Sources*, and Clarence E. Carter's *Territorial Papers of the United States*. (In 1964, John Porter Bloom began editing Volume XXVII of this series.) The editorial work of Reuben Gold Thwaites, Lyman C. Draper's successor as director of the State Historical Society of Wisconsin, stands with the best of its time. *The Jesuit Relations and Allied Documents, Original Journals of the Lewis and Clark Expedition*, and *Early Western Travels, 1748–1846* represent his great contribution to this field.

An important bridge between the documentary editing of the early years of this century (including that inspired by Jameson but published later) and the recent editions of papers of famous Americans that began with Julian P. Boyd's work on Jefferson is Wilmarth S. Lewis' *The Yale Edition of Horace Walpole's Correspondence*, begun in the mid-1930's. Although Lewis dealt with English literary, rather than American historical, documents, his editorial techniques have influenced the "new school." The publication in 1950 of Volume I of *The Papers of Thomas Jefferson* not only marked the debut of this distinctive genre of scholar-editors but also brought about the revivification of the National

Historical Publications Commission. When President Harry S Truman received Volume I, he was so impressed with its importance that he called for a national agency to promote and coordinate the editing and publishing of documents of famous Americans. Congress responded by appropriating money and providing the organizational structure of the commission. By neglecting these two items in 1934 when it established the NHPC, Congress had ensured the commission's inactivity. Since 1950 the NHPC has been directly involved in promoting documentary editing, an area of American scholarship of ever increasing significance. From 1950 to 1961, Philip M. Hamer was the commission's executive director, and his successor was Oliver W. Holmes.[3]

ATTITUDES TOWARD TRAINING IN DOCUMENTARY EDITING

Evidence in Chapter VI indicates the great importance that publications of edited documents have for graduate history training, and their usefulness in this training is in direct ratio to the quality of the editing. The attitudes of the profession toward documentary editing and the training it affords in this specialty have much to do with current and future use of such original sources.

Traditionally, academic historians have not held the function

[3] An extensive literature pertains to documentary editing. Cf. Butterfield, "Archival and Editorial Enterprise," *loc. cit.*; Walter Muir Whitehill, *et al.*, "Publishing the Papers of Great Men: A Session at the Sixty-Ninth Annual Meeting of the American Historical Association, 30 December 1954," *Daedalus*, Vol. LXXXVI, No. 1 (May, 1955), 47–79; Butterfield and Julian P. Boyd, *Historical Editing in the United States*; the NHPC's 1954 and 1963 *Reports to the President, op. cit.*; Leonard W. Labaree, "Scholarly Editing in Our Times," *Ventures*, Vol. III (Winter, 1964), 28–31; Waldo Gifford Leland, "The Prehistory and Origins of the National Historical Publications Commission," *American Archivist*, Vol. XXVII, No. 2 (Apr., 1964), 187–94; James C. Olson, "The Scholar and Documentary Publication," *American Archivist*, Vol. XXVIII, No. 2 (Apr., 1965), 187–93; Lester J. Cappon, "A Rationale for Historical Editing Past and Present," *William and Mary Quarterly*, 3rd Series, Vol. XXIII, No. 1 (Jan., 1966), 56–75; Richard B. Morris, "The Current Statesmen's Papers Publication Program: An Appraisal from the Point of View of the Legal Historian," *loc. cit.*; and Oliver W. Holmes, "Recent Writings Relevant to Documentary Publication Programs," *American Archivist*, Vol. XXVI, No. 1 (Jan., 1963), 137–42, which is a systematic listing of the literature through 1962.

of documentary editing in especially high regard, with the expected result that they have offered students scant opportunity for systematic instruction in this field.[4] That these traditional attitudes persist was amply attested by the following comments. "Historical editing is professionally like being on the outside looking in. I think that Julian Boyd's *Number Seven* represents a desire on his part to write some history. But God save the editors!"[5] "We tend to view editing as something that anybody can do, and we consider it not quite as respectable academically as other things. But a lot of people are writing books who would have even more trouble doing historical editing."[6] Editing tends to be a refuge for unambitious scholars and is less demanding intellectually than writing a good monograph, according to Robert H. Ferrell. Editing can be a humdrum, eight-to-five life.[7] Documentary editors may forfeit "their claim to being historians in the sense of producing interpretive . . . works of a broader nature."[8] The most jaundiced comment was that training in historical editing could produce "a profession similar to nurse's aide or medical technician."[9]

Such attitudes naturally influenced departmental deliberations on formal editorial training. For instance, Alexander DeConde, chairman of the department at the University of California at Santa Barbara, said graduate training should be concerned with analysis and literary presentation, not editing, and that these intellectual processes should not be mixed.[10] Many contended that editorial training had either no place or a low priority in the graduate history curriculum.[11] Some historians saw no necessity for formal training in documentary editing because an orthodox

[4] Cf. Butterfield and Boyd, *Historical Editing*, 35.
[5] Interview with Shaw Livermore, Jr., see Appendix C1.
[6] Interview with Donald F. Carmony, *ibid.*
[7] Interview, *ibid.*
[8] Interview with Raymond P. Stearns, *ibid.*
[9] Interview with Marshall Smelser, *ibid.*
[10] DeConde, *ibid.*
[11] Interviews with Paul W. Glad, Arthur Bestor, Donald Meyer, John Braeman, Robert H. Ferrell, Clarke A. Chambers, Malcolm J. Rohrbough, John K. Nelson, and Charles G. Sellers, Jr., *ibid.*

263

doctoral program sufficiently equipped an individual to pick up editorial techniques, if he was interested.[12]

If professors ever doubted their influence on students, they could take encouragement from knowing that some students shared their attitudes toward documentary editing. James Zeidman thought that editing did not call for the full extent of a historian's intellectual powers. He would "hire graduate students and supervising technicians to see that the documents are printed correctly. . . . Why should editors check typing errors of secretaries?"[13] James Lane believed that for the professional historian, editorial work was both insufficiently original and "a lower scale of endeavor than writing something of your own."[14]

The coolness of some academic historians toward documentary editing resulted from their concern that it removed men from the profession.[15] To them, the "profession" obviously consisted of teaching historians. Editors "should not be taken out of the profession permanently . . . but fed back in with experience in editing original sources."[16] Although George C. Rogers, Jr., conceded that scholars with formal historical training usually wanted to follow their own careers rather than have them channeled into editorial projects, he has taken the assignment as assistant editor of the Henry Laurens papers. His experience has made him wonder if academic historians involved with an editorial project are not "cutting themselves off from main career opportunities." He has felt that since he began working on the Laurens papers, his department does not know how his editorial activities fit into its over-all concerns.[17] William T. Hutchinson, editor of *The Papers of James Madison*, acknowledged that editorial work was still outside the main stream of the historical profession and commented on the type of situation Rogers described. "One explanation may be that editorial projects have not been fully integrated with depart-

[12] Interviews with John Duffy, Elisha P. Douglass, George B. Tindall, and John Clark, *ibid.*
[13] Interview, see Appendix C3.
[14] Lane, *ibid.*
[15] Interviews with Richard S. Dunn and Robert H. Ferrell, see Appendix C1.
[16] Interview with Wood Gray, *ibid.*
[17] Rogers, *ibid.*

mental work. I hope I'm not correct in believing that historical editing is seldom regarded as prestigious a branch of productive scholarship as writing an interpretive book. One consequence of this judgment is that a faculty member, aspiring to reputation in his profession, including promotion in rank, hesitates to make editing his career."[18] The growing pressure for academic staffs may make it harder to recruit editors. With the pattern of exhaustive editing set, historians may be unwilling to devote their lives to such work. "If editors would do just a reasonable amount of identification, if they would be more selective in the documents they publish, it would be much better for the entire profession."[19]

The feeling that editors were "outside the profession" was reinforced by the often stated opinion that training in documentary editing would not justify displacing another component of the already crowded doctoral program. Both professors and graduate students commented that despite the benefit and need of such training, it was less important than existing requirements.[20] Departments offering terminal master's degrees also reported that their crowded programs did not allow training in documentary editing.[21]

Further reason for offering no training in documentary editing was that graduate students expressed little interest in it. Professors explained that students looked on editing as "an old man's vocation"[22] and consequently did not envision careers in that field.[23] Some could not imagine having a good student wanting to do an editorial project for a dissertation.[24] At the University of Cin-

18 Hutchinson, *ibid.* Cf. Edmund S. Morgan's comments on the editor's vocation in "John Adams and the Puritan Tradition," *New England Quarterly*, Vol. XXXIV, No. 4 (Dec., 1961), 519.

19 Interview with Thomas D. Clark, *ibid.*

20 Interviews with Oscar Handlin, David M. Potter, J. Joseph Huthmacher, Daniel W. Hollis, and J. Philip Gleason, *ibid.*; Alan R. Havig, Jean Gould, Jeffrey P. Kimball, David R. Kobrin, Neil R. McMillan, Lisle A. Rose, and Warren F. Kimball, see Appendix C3; questionnaire returned by William S. Greever, University of Idaho.

21 Questionnaires returned by Francis Paul Prucha, S.J., Marquette University; Gilbert L. Lycan, Stetson University; Charlton Tebeau, University of Miami.

22 Interview with William T. Hutchinson, see Appendix C1.

23 Interview with Oscar Handlin, *ibid.*

24 Interview with Robert E. Burke, *ibid.*

cinnati, Daniel R. Beaver was even unsuccessful in interesting a student in editing a diary as a master's thesis.[25] Professors' suppositions about student interest in editorial training were confirmed by some students, although the sentiment was far from unanimous. A few agreed that only senior historians should do the documentary editing.[26]

Professional opinion on the status of documentary editing, as in virtually every other facet of graduate history training, diverged. Opposing the traditional, unenthusiastic reactions, many professors described documentary editing and its published fruits as "one of the best features of the profession,"[27] "one of the most important jobs in our profession,"[28] "absolutely essential,"[29] and "the developing thing. Editors are considered respected scholars. Julian Boyd has done more for historical editing than any other figure."[30] John A. Schutz forecast that documentary editing will become a field for doctoral training,[31] and Charles C. McLaughlin hoped to launch his students at American University on an editorial project.[32] In comparing the values of documentary editing with conventional research, Thomas D. Clark maintained, "It would be better if much of our talent were set to editing and analyzing our original sources rather than writing puerile articles."[33]

Although universities rarely offered formal editorial training, some departments had considered introducing it, while professors at other institutions acknowledged its need. Some graduate students at Yale University got on-the-job editorial training with Leonard W. Labaree on *The Papers of Benjamin Franklin*, and the history department contemplated a doctoral specialty in documentary editing.[34] Merrill D. Peterson, chairman of the depart-

[25] Beaver, *ibid.*

[26] Interviews with Lisle A. Rose, Joseph Maizlish, Thomas M. Davies, and Warren F. Kimball, see Appendix C3.

[27] Interview with Harold T. Parker, see Appendix C1.

[28] Interview with Hugh T. Lefler, *ibid.*

[29] Questionnaire returned by S. George Ellsworth, Utah State University.

[30] Interview with Norman K. Risjord, see Appendix C1.

[31] Schutz, *ibid.*

[32] McLaughlin, *ibid.*

[33] Clark, *ibid.*

[34] Interview with Howard R. Lamar, *ibid.*

ment at the University of Virginia, thought that "a solid two-year master's degree in editing might be good. Or this might be offered on the doctoral level."[35] The department at the University of Houston had not progressed enough in its planning for a Ph.D. to consider incorporating editorial training, but the chairman felt that it might be helpful. "We've gotten away from the idealistic notion of an original contribution to scholarship."[36] Some historians commented that although their departments offered no editorial experience, it should be available somewhere.[37] Several suggested that, although the profession should provide this training, it should be offered by only one or two universities because of its limited appeal.[38]

Many graduate students agreed that such training should be available and were conscious of its conspicuous absence.[39] One admitted to having had "a ridiculously snobbish attitude toward editorial projects," but developing an understanding of their great value.[40] Editorial training would be "tremendously good" for those in the history of American science and technology, for hardly any editing has been done in this field.[41] Graduate training gave one student "no idea where to begin" an editorial project,[42] and another admitted, "I wouldn't know how to edit documents if I wanted to, but I could at least find material on how to go about editing."[43] A student of Wilbur R. Jacobs explained that Jacobs' enthusiasm for editing "rubs off on his students." In the course of instruction, Jacobs discussed editorial needs and techniques, citing

[35] Peterson, *ibid.*

[36] Interview with Allen J. Going, *ibid.*

[37] Interviews with David Donald, Lawrence E. Gelfand, and Clifford S. Griffin, *ibid.*

[38] Interviews with Gabriel Kolko, John R. Alden, Lawrence L. Graves, and Thomas N. Bonner, *ibid.*; questionnaire returned by Philip Klein, Pennsylvania State University.

[39] Interviews with James C. Curtis, Richard A. Andrews, Lloyd E. Ambrosius, Marilee S. Clore, Ian Mugridge, Charles Peterson, Bruce Sinclair, and Barry A. Crouch, see Appendix C3.

[40] Interview with Clore, above.

[41] Interview with Sinclair, above.

[42] Interview with Andrews, above.

[43] Interview with Ambrosius, above.

examples from his own publications.[44] A graduate of the University of Chicago referred to his training in documentary editing as "one of the most valuable experiences in my graduate work." Later, in making editing assignments to undergraduates at Ottawa University, he excited their enthusiasm for working in original sources. One such student became a doctoral candidate at the University of Kansas.[45]

The value many graduate students saw in editorial training was that it would sharpen critical faculties and thereby improve research techniques.[46] The painstaking process of identifying documents and appraising their credibility arouses "a healthy, skeptical attitude toward original sources."[47] It similarly makes the researcher more careful about justifying conclusions.[48] Such training would also aid a researcher in extracting the essence from a document,[49] thereby enabling the individual to take notes effectively.[50] For the foregoing reasons, these students strongly advocated editorial training in the graduate program. The department at Loyola University in Chicago found that "the challenges posed by editing projects offer intensive experience in a great variety of research techniques and materials."[51]

EDITORIAL PROJECTS AS DISSERTATIONS

The issue of whether an editorial project could qualify as a dissertation crystallized the attitudes of academic historians toward the value of documentary editing. As usual, these attitudes diverged.

Statistically, professors responded to the survey's question of

[44] Interview with Yasuhide Kawashima, see Appendix C3. Variations within departments were obvious from the testimony of Kawashima and Ian Mugridge, who spoke of editorial training as "conspicuously lacking" at the University of California at Santa Barbara, where Jacobs taught.

[45] Interview with Keith Shumway, *ibid*.

[46] Interviews with Larry D. Hill, Gerald Waldera, Harold E. Van Horn, Marilyn A. Domer, James T. Kitson, Joseph M. Hawes, and Edmund J. Danziger, Jr., *ibid*.

[47] Interview with Stanley K. Schultz, *ibid*.

[48] Interview with Edward C. Ezell, *ibid*.

[49] Interview with Keith A. Winsell, *ibid*.

[50] Interview with James Breeden, *ibid*.

[51] Questionnaire returned by Robert W. McCluggage.

whether an editorial project was acceptable as a dissertation as follows:

Interviews:

Yes	85
No	81
Depends on the documents and editorial apparatus	43
Noncommittal	18

Questionnaires (One answer per department):

Yes	4
No	10
Depends on the documents and editorial apparatus	6
Not so far	5
Noncommittal	1

Questionnaire responses from departments offering terminal master's degree on an editorial project as a thesis:

Yes	27
No	15
Depends on the documents and editorial apparatus	11
Usually no	4
Not so far	6

Many professors thought that the original research and synthesis demanded by a monographic dissertation, but not by an editorial project, were essential for doctoral training.[52] "Elements of imagination, observation, and comprehension connected with a dissertation would not necessarily be involved in an editorial project."[53] W. Stull Holt said, "An editorial project is not good enough for a Ph.D. dissertation in my field. The editor is a lesser scholar preparing material for a greater scholar."[54] Robert H. Ferrell was "violently opposed" to an editorial project as a dissertation, for an editorial piece "allows a student to avoid the problems of writing

[52] Interviews with Arthur Bestor, Sanford W. Higginbotham, Norman K. Risjord, Francis P. Weisenburger, Madison Kuhn, and Chase C. Mooney, see Appendix C1.
[53] Interview with Henry L. Swint, *ibid.*
[54] Holt, *ibid.*

and organization which, presumably, a doctoral thesis is supposed to present."[55] Since the aim of the history department at Washington University was "to train students to undertake sophisticated analysis of historical problems," William N. Chambers opposed editorial projects as dissertations.[56] Stephen E. Ambrose stipulated that doctoral candidates should write a monograph because it poses a much wider range of problems than editing. "A student can move from a monograph to editing, but it would be difficult to move in the other direction."[57] Agreeing that an individual needed the training represented by a monographic dissertation to know what should be selected for editing, Alfred D. Chandler, Jr., would not entrust an editorial project to a doctoral candidate.[58] Louis R. Harlan contended that editorial projects usually ranged more widely than monographic dissertations. Because of this and his belief that typical graduate students did not have the ripened historical judgment to edit satisfactorily, he objected to editorial projects as dissertations. "My opinion is based on the belief that an editorial job in the Boyd tradition takes not less judgment than a monograph, but more."[59]

Some professors of history were willing for students to do editorial work for dissertations, believing that such work could demand more knowledge of history, involve a higher degree of scholarship, and contribute as much or more than monographic studies.[60] Although the survey did not ask graduate students what they thought about editorial projects as dissertations, two volunteered that editorial work should qualify, citing the lasting value of well-edited sources and the critical faculties required.[61]

Certain conditions should be met, several historians specified, before a doctoral candidate undertakes an editing assignment as a

[55] Ferrell, *ibid.*
[56] Chambers, *ibid.*
[57] Ambrose, *ibid.*
[58] Chandler, *ibid.*
[59] Harlan, *ibid.*
[60] Interviews with Hugh T. Lefler, H. Trevor Colbourn, Daniel R. Beaver, Dorothy D. Gondos, Merrill Jensen, Robert V. Haynes, and William B. Willcox, *ibid.*
[61] Interviews with Richard M. McMurray and Albert T. Klyberg, see Appendix C3.

dissertation: The document to be edited should have innate significance and the editing require substantial research.[62] Further, the
introductory essay must be of sufficient scope to indicate the editor's
ability to organize, synthesize, interpret, and write. Mere annotation of documents would not qualify as a dissertation.[63] Bernard
Bailyn would accept an editorial project as a dissertation only if
the edited and introductory material involved the reconstruction
and interpretation of historical events.[64] Many historians commented that they would examine each proposal for an editorial
project with a highly critical eye so that such a project would not
be an easy substitute for a monographic dissertation.[65] Unless
professors carefully investigated editorial proposals for dissertations, unworthy projects could easily be accepted. The profession
should guard against edited dissertations becoming "wide open
to abuse."[66] Indeed, the profession should similarly guard against
the abuses of unworthy monographic dissertations.

Irrespective of the scholarly merits and requirements of the
editorial project, some professors were reluctant to advise a candidate to attempt it.[67] From the realistic standpoint of the profession's dominant attitudes toward editing, a student is better off
writing a monograph. "A historian needs a book of his own,"[68]
and there is the practical consideration of the immediate rewards
of a conventional dissertation.[69]

TRAINING IN DOCUMENTARY EDITING

Through various means graduate students have had the opportunity to acquire training in documentary editing. Sometimes this
education has been on an individual basis gained as the student

[62] Interviews with Thomas D. Clark, W. Eugene Hollon, Merle Curti, and
Burl Noggle, see Appendix C1.
[63] Interviews with Allan Nevins, Leonard W. Labaree, David M. Pletcher,
Wilfrid H. Callcott, Allan G. Bogue, W. H. Masterson, and John A. Carroll, *ibid*.
[64] Bailyn, *ibid*.
[65] Interviews with George E. Mowry, J. Rogers Hollingsworth, and Paul H.
Bergeron, *ibid*.
[66] Interview with Frederick D. Kershner, Jr., *ibid*.
[67] Interviews with Maurice G. Baxter and Paul C. Nagel, *ibid*.
[68] Baxter, above.
[69] Nagel, above.

worked on an editorial project for a thesis or a dissertation. At some universities professors gave the training in methods courses or seminars, and a few students got on-the-job experience with the letterpress publication projects. Among the institutions which have actually accepted editorial projects as dissertations were Harvard University and the University of Chicago. At the former, Charles C. McLaughlin edited selections from the Frederick Law Olmsted papers,[70] and at Chicago, J. Harold Easterby edited the Robert F. W. Allston papers.[71] The department at the University of Texas has approved editorial work for both the thesis and the dissertation, despite some initial hesitancy.[72] Barnes F. Lathrop directed Dwight F. Henderson's thesis that involved editing the journal of the wife of a Confederate major. The Confederate Publishing Company published the thesis in 1963.[73] Master's candidates at the Universities of Oklahoma and Oregon have similarly used editorial projects as theses.[74] At Duke University, Harold T. Parker occasionally assigned editorial work as a thesis. He put one student on an editorial project because she did not have a sequential mind. "In the process of editing, she learned how to write. Her introduction was actually a monograph, and a very good one."[75] The departments of history at the University of Wyoming, Mississippi State University, and San Diego State College also reported that some students have received training in documentary editing through thesis projects.[76]

Courses in historical method have frequently incorporated training in documentary editing. At Wayne State University, the department offered a course in bibliography and research techniques that ran for three quarters. In the first quarter, the professor spent four to six weeks on editing. Then if a student wished, he

[70] Interview with Frank Freidel, *ibid.*
[71] Interview with Avery O. Craven, *ibid.*
[72] Interview with Barnes F. Lathrop, *ibid.*
[73] Interview with Henderson, see Appendix C3.
[74] Interviews with Howard L. Meredith, *ibid.*; Kenneth W. Porter, see Appendix C1.
[75] Interview, see Appendix C1.
[76] Interview with T. A. Larson, *ibid.*; questionnaires returned by Harold S. Snellgrove, Mississippi State University; William Hanchett, San Diego State College.

could devote his entire in-service project to documentary editing.[77] The methods course at the University of Denver allotted at least a week to editing,[78] and Noble E. Cunningham, Jr., incorporated this training in his methods course at the University of Missouri, exciting considerable interest.[79] At Vanderbilt University, Henry L. Swint's students often edited James K. Polk letters as exercises in the methods course. The letters came from the Polk editorial project, headed by Herbert Weaver.[80] Before the Universities of Illinois and Minnesota discontinued their methods courses, they offered some training in documentary editing. At Illinois, Donald Jackson, editor of the university press, gave one lecture on the subject.[81] His editions of the *Letters of the Lewis and Clark Expedition* and *The Journals of Zebulon Pike* eminently qualified him to do so. When Philip D. Jordan offered the bibliography and criticism course at Minnesota, he conducted a two-hour session on documentary editing in which students were given a three-page document to edit. Jordan was "disconsolate" over the discontinuation of this course.[82]

Many professors offered training in documentary editing in their seminars, and depending on their inclinations, the training was intensive or casual. Richard Walsh's seminar at Georgetown University was the only one the survey encountered that was devoted exclusively to documentary editing. The three seminarians he instructed worked on sources in the Library of Congress: the papers of Alexander Hamilton of Maryland and of the Galloways. One student's work was published in the *Maryland Historical Magazine*.[83] At Columbia University, Richard B. Morris gave some training in documentary editing, since he has done editorial work. Students also had this opportunity in the course in nonacademic history careers, taught by James Heslin, director of the New-York Historical Society. His predecessor, R. W. G. Vail,

[77] Interview with Philip P. Mason, see Appendix C1.
[78] Interview with Allen D. Breck, *ibid.*
[79] Cunningham, *ibid.*
[80] Weaver, *ibid.*
[81] Interview with Clark C. Spence, *ibid.*
[82] Jordan, *ibid.*
[83] Walsh, *ibid.*

taught such a course at Columbia, as did Clifford Lord when he was dean of the School of General Studies. Lord went to Columbia from the directorship of the State Historical Society of Wisconsin, which offered a similar program.[84]

In his seminar at Boston University, Robert E. Moody gave students documents to annotate. They discussed what should be explained and searched for appropriate references. Moody also had students compare an old edition of Jefferson and Franklin papers with the current work of Boyd and Labaree.[85] At the University of Southern California, Doyce Nunis provided interested members of his seminar in the history of the Far West with material to edit, and student response was enthusiastic.[86] Fletcher M. Green, Douglas E. Leach, and Merrill Jensen introduced editing in their seminars and usually assigned students a document to edit, just for the experience.[87] After New York University completes its microfilm edition of the Gallatin papers, it hopes to publish a selected letterpress edition and perhaps to co-ordinate a course in documentary editing with this publication.[88]

Some professors initiated students in documentary editing by having them study the appropriate section in the *Harvard Guide*.[89] Because of the great differences in editorial projects, many professors recommended that a student wishing to become involved should be instructed individually. So few students have chosen this type of research that the training almost had to be tutorial.[90] One student received documentary editorial training through her work on the *Indiana Magazine of History*. When the *Magazine* published documents, she checked the footnotes as well as the original sources. She considered this documentary editing more

[84] Interview with Robert D. Cross, *ibid.*; letter, Henry F. Graff to author, Sept. 21, 1967.

[85] Interview, see Appendix C1.

[86] Interview with Gloria Creutz, see Appendix C3.

[87] Interviews, see Appendix C1.

[88] Interview with Bayrd Still, *ibid.*

[89] Interviews with Robert V. Hine, Harold D. Langley, and W. Stitt Robinson, *ibid.*

[90] Interviews with W. Frank Craven and William R. Hogan, *ibid.*; questionnaire returned by Walter T. K. Nugent, Indiana University.

rewarding than the secondary editing entailed by her work on the *Magazine*.[91]

Surely one of the great anomalies of the historical profession was that departments at universities sponsoring the major documentary editorial publications were not seizing opportunities afforded by these projects for training graduate students. While unusual, this situation can be understood in light of the attitudes of academic historians toward documentary editing as a field of endeavor. If university teachers of history labeled documentary editing a second-rate pursuit, as many of them explicitly did, they obviously would make no effort to see that their graduate students were given such training, however convenient. And the editors were ordinarily too busy with their herculean tasks to promote editorial training as a normal part of the department's graduate offering—especially in light of the attitudes of the professors. The training students received in connection with the major editorial enterprises, then, was piecemeal and coincidental. Graduate students were employed as assistants on these projects as they might have been hired to work in the library or the laboratory or to grade papers. Without systematic attempts to expose students to editorial training, it was fortunate that at least some interested students benefited from the employment opportunities offered.

The opportunities included the following: at Brown University students have worked on the Isaac Backus papers;[92] at Columbia University, on the Hamilton and Jay papers;[93] at the University of South Carolina, on the Calhoun and Laurens papers;[94] at the University of Hawaii, on the Adlai Stevenson papers;[95] at the University of Kentucky, on the Clay papers;[96] and at Princeton University, on the Wilson papers.[97]

At Princeton, which has supported both the Jefferson and the Wilson editorial projects, students, realizing the great opportuni-

[91] Interview with Lorna Sylvester, see Appendix C3.
[92] Interview with William G. McLoughlin, see Appendix C1.
[93] Interview with James P. Shenton, *ibid*.
[94] Interview with Robert D. Ochs, *ibid*.
[95] Interview with Herbert F. Margulies, *ibid*.
[96] Interview with James F. Hopkins, *ibid*.
[97] Interview with Arthur S. Link, *ibid*.

ties afforded, requested that Arthur S. Link offer a course in documentary editing.[98] But Link did not have time to both edit the Wilson papers and run a school for editors. "No editor of a big project has enough hours to train students in historical editing."[99] Julian P. Boyd stated his position by saying: "The editor of one of these large-scale documentary publication projects in a university should feel an obligation to teach, to train graduate students as historical editors, and to hold seminars. But both he and the university should understand that this will add to both the cost and duration of the enterprise. This is a cost that the university, the editor, and the department of history should insist upon bearing, for the benefits in disciplinary instruction are too great for the opportunity to be missed. But the editor should insist that this expenditure of time and money be resisted until the conventional view of editorial scholarship gives way to the view that this is only another manner in which the historian must function and that it possesses unique values to assist him in his highest duty of analysis and interpretation. It was appropriate in Jameson's day to insist upon a sharp line of demarcation between the historian and biographer on the one hand and the historical editor on the other and to require of the latter only that he present the documents for the use of the former. Such an attitude today is no longer defensible: it begs too many questions and leaves too many graduate students quite unsophisticated in the handling of the sources which they must use."[100]

Boyd has stated elsewhere that as universities have come to assume the responsibility of collecting original sources, they have not assumed the concomitant responsibilities of editing and publishing them. When historical societies collected sources in the nineteenth century, they accepted these related obligations as a matter of course. One reason why universities have been slow to shoulder the full set of obligations is that their history faculties have not been sufficiently appreciative of documentary editing to

[98] Interview with James L. Lancaster, see Appendix C3.
[99] Interview, see Appendix C1.
[100] Boyd, *ibid.*; letter to author, Aug. 8, 1967.

insist upon it. Academic historians have placed premiums on monographic history and the barriers of the profession have grown "higher against those who are not writers of history in colleges and universities." Consequently, the profession has not produced the skilled editors who make it unnecessary for "graduate students and the public to depend upon documentary sources that are incomplete, fragmentary, and misleading—sources of the first importance for an understanding of our history."[101]

ROLE OF THE NHPC

History professors agreed substantially that in the absence of any other qualified body, the National Historical Publications Commission (NHPC) should actively promote training in documentary editing. Although most graduate students would not be interested in the training, it should be available and the NHPC seems to be the "only possible agent to offer the kind of leadership necessary."[102] Several benefits could derive from this training, including clarification of the possibilities for work in this field. "Imaginative leadership . . . could be most important."[103] NHPC training could promote general standards for documentary editing that would prevent new editorial undertakings from "bouncing around" as they settle on their techniques.[104] Moreover, the standards would inform the profession of what to expect with letterpress publications of edited documents and thereby eliminate criticisms by reviewers that documents are over- or underedited.[105] This training could make graduate students aware that editorial work is "one of the most feasible ways for the fledgling Ph.D. to get into print." Also, it would promote awareness of materials that could be edited and published.[106] Louis R. Harlan suggested that any such training be postdoctoral, for the scholar would know he

[101] *The First Duty, An Address Delivered at the Opening of an Exhibition of the Arthur H. and Mary Marden Dean Collection of Lafayette at Cornell University on April 17, 1964,* 12–13.
[102] Interview with John A. Carroll, see Appendix C1.
[103] Interview with Paul W. Glad, *ibid.*
[104] Interviews with Allan G. Bogue and J. Rogers Hollingsworth, *ibid.*
[105] Hollingsworth, above.
[106] Interview with William B. Willcox, see Appendix C1.

needed the training for a specific purpose, whereas a doctoral candidate might have no definite ideas about its use.[107] Hardly anyone opposed NHPC training in documentary editing, although professors had different ideas about how it should be handled.

The most effective way for the NHPC to provide this training, according to many professors, would be through a summer seminar at the National Archives.[108] Those brought together would realize their common interest and establish an *esprit de corps*, a quality too often lacking as editors work in isolation.[109] A great advantage of a seminar at the National Archives would be the opportunity to learn something of the Archives and perhaps to do some individual research.[110] At that repository, the NHPC could assemble a highly qualified staff of editors to discuss their methods —something a single university probably could not do.[111] It could also reach more interested people than could a seminar at any one university.[112] The NHPC should offer stipends to draw qualified students into the seminar.[113] The NHPC might also consider recruiting prospective editors from graduate library schools as well as history departments.[114] Graduate librarians may be keenly interested in the field and the training would "improve the tone of library schools."[115]

Many professors were so enthusiastic about the NHPC's conducting a summer seminar in documentary editing that they wished to participate themselves.[116] If the NHPC established an editing seminar for senior historians, they could then disseminate

[107] Harlan, *ibid.*
[108] Interviews with Donald E. Worcester, Roger H. Brown, Charles C. McLaughlin, Arthur S. Link, W. Frank Craven, and Donald R. McCoy, *ibid.*; questionnaire returned by Harris G. Warren, Miami University.
[109] Interviews with Philip P. Mason and Richard S. Kirkendall, *ibid.*
[110] Interviews with W. Eugene Hollon, James P. Shenton, John Hall Stewart, Marshall Smelser, and Richard W. Leopold, *ibid.*
[111] Interview with Robert A. Divine, *ibid.*
[112] Interview with Alden T. Vaughan, *ibid.*
[113] Interview with William T. Hutchinson, *ibid.*
[114] Interviews with Robert E. Burke and Frederick D. Kershner, Jr., *ibid.*
[115] Burke, *ibid.*
[116] Interviews with Robert V. Haynes, Marvin R. Zahniser, Stow Persons, Raymond P. Stearns, Robert M. Sutton, and David M. Pletcher, *ibid.*

their experience to students. Once students were interested in editing, they could profit greatly from the seminar.[117]

Rather than the NHPC-sponsored editing seminar, some professors recommended that the commission provide fellowships or assistantships with established editorial projects.[118] "Training with the masters such as Boyd and Butterfield would be valuable to those who want to pursue careers in historical editing."[119] Leonard W. Labaree, editor of the Franklin papers, advocated this internship program. The intern should have finished all his doctoral work except the dissertation. The NHPC could pay him an instructor's salary and assign him to an editorial staff for one year. At the end of that time, the individual could write his dissertation and then decide whether to go into teaching or editorial work.[120] Oscar Handlin approved the idea of such apprenticeships but considered it preferable for apprentices to have just finished the Ph.D. The editorial work would then be an outlet for someone who became acquainted with documents while writing his dissertation.[121]

With funds from its Ford Foundation grant, the NHPC has already established fellowships for training documentary editors. In July, 1967, it announced the appointment of five Fellows in Advanced Historical Editing to serve for one year on projects associated with the Commission. They were James B. Bell (Jefferson papers), Joan M. Corbett (John Marshall papers), Peter T. Harstad (Clay papers), Gaspare J. Saladino (Adams papers), and C. Edward Skeen (Calhoun papers). Their stipends were equivalent to junior academic salaries.

Two different suggestions were that the NHPC promote training in documentary editing by maintaining a roster of editors willing to consult on editorial projects or lecture to seminars, with

[117] Interview with Philip D. Jordan, *ibid.*

[118] Interviews with John K. Nelson, Richard L. Watson, Jr., John R. Alden, Howard S. Miller, Robert E. Moody, Arthur Bestor, David Alan Williams, and Waldo H. Heinrichs, Jr., *ibid.*; questionnaires returned by Nelson M. Blake, Syracuse University; Francis Paul Prucha, S.J., Marquette University.

[119] Interview with I. B. Holley, Jr., see Appendix C1.

[120] Labaree, *ibid.*

[121] Handlin, *ibid.*

the NHPC underwriting the expenses,[122] or that it might prepare a series of editorial problems with inexpensive reproductions of documents that could be distributed to professors wishing to give students this training.[123] Irvin G. Wyllie suggested that the NHPC make video tapes of training in an editorial workshop and distribute them to interested departments. Furthermore, video tapes could be prepared on the use of bibliographies and finding aids such as the Hamer *Guide*, *NUCMC*, the union list of newspapers, and card catalogs. Such tapes "could be sold to all graduate schools and could make a real contribution in methodological training."[124]

An excellent way for the NHPC to encourage documentary editing, while providing standards for it, would be the publication of a handbook on editing.[125] It was suggested that Julian P. Boyd and L. H. Butterfield publish their statements on editorial techniques as handbooks that could be easily distributed. H. Trevor Colbourn called Boyd's statement of editorial policy, published in Volume I of the Jefferson papers, "superb."[126] The NHPC could publish more pamphlets like Clarence E. Carter's *Historical Editing*, but written with different views.[127] Allan Nevins had serious reservations about the usefulness of Carter's prescriptions for pedantic, rather than broadly humane, editing. "Carter wanted to reproduce every flyspeck on the document; he gave minute attention to every letter and comma. This was too narrow an approach."[128] Other professors suggested that the NHPC sponsor a volume of essays that would recount the experiences of dis-

[122] Interviews with Bayrd Still and Warren S. Tryon, *ibid.*
[123] Interviews with David Donald and Douglas E. Leach, *ibid.*
[124] Wyllie, *ibid.*
[125] Interviews with Stephen E. Ambrose, Elisha P. Douglass, Henry L. Swint, Richard Walsh, Lawrence L. Graves, John S. Ezell, Hugh F. Rankin, Gene D. Lewis, Allen D. Breck, and Arthur H. DeRosier, Jr., *ibid.*; Paul A. Whelen, see Appendix C3; questionnaires returned by George A. Frykman, Washington State University; William D. Metz, University of Rhode Island; George B. Woolfolk, Prairie View A&M College; Philip W. Kennedy, University of Portland; George Lobdell, Ohio University; J. M. Helms, Longwood College; Henry S. Stroupe, Wake Forest College.
[126] Interviews with Colbourn, see Appendix C1; Kenneth R. Bowling, see Appendix C3.
[127] Interview with Stephen E. Ambrose, see Appendix C1.
[128] Nevins, *ibid.*

tinguished editors[129] and that any handbook should deal explicitly with ways to improve typographical appearances. When editors work with documents containing imperfect language, the printing devices for making the text intelligible often "barbarize" the page.[130]

The issue of training in documentary editing aroused many historians to think of other employment opportunities outside the classroom. The relationship between editing and archival work is sufficiently close for many to consider them allied. Several professors indicated that they favor training in these nonacademic areas since some students were not interested in or suited for teaching.[131] Many termed the profession negligent for not calling to students' attention opportunities for nonacademic employment.[132] The University of Wisconsin has recognized these opportunities by offering doctoral candidates a minor in the work of historical agencies (including editing, archival management, and exhibits), but no more than two or three students a year have chosen this field. The state historical society conducted these courses.[133] Other universities have given courses in archival administration, with mixed success. In the late 1930's, Harvard and Columbia universities and the University of Illinois inaugurated such training, but they discontinued the courses shortly. In 1938, Solon J. Buck began teaching the history and theory of archival administration at American University, and the following year Ernst Posner took over the course and taught it until his retirement in 1961. Understandably, American University has relied heavily upon the resources and co-operation of the National Archives in presenting this course, taught by Frank B. Evans after Posner's retirement.[134] Professors at Rutgers—The State University

129 Interview with Paul C. Nagel, *ibid.*
130 Interview with Harold D. Langley, *ibid.*
131 Interviews with David Alan Williams, Hugh F. Rankin, Lawrence E. Gelfand, and Richard L. Watson, Jr., *ibid.*
132 Interviews with Gene M. Gressley and Herbert F. Margulies, *ibid.*; David M. Katzman, see Appendix C3.
133 Interviews with Irvin G. Wyllie, Merle Curti, and John A. DeNovo, see Appendix C1.
134 Cf. H. G. Jones, "Archival Training in American Universities, 1938–68," *American Archivist*, Vol. XXXI, No. 2 (Apr., 1968), 135–54.

considered such archival training more crucial to historians than training in documentary editing.[135]

Many historians suggested that the NHPC could spend its funds more profitably than in promoting skillful documentary editing. Sydney Nathans proposed that the commission establish a summer institute for librarians and archivists on the standardization of cataloging and indexing manuscript collections. "Presently, some collections are listed chronologically, others by correspondent, and still others by occult private codes. For the traveling researcher, standardization would save time; and, looking to the future and possible IBM cross-checks of names and topics, regularization of procedures now would save inefficiency or a crash program later."[136] W. Stull Holt contended that the NHPC should not be diverted from its main objective of publishing papers of famous Americans, which are "more important than editorial workshops."[137] Arthur Bestor felt just as strongly that it was more important for the NHPC to publish government documents, such as the records of the ratification of the Constitution and the Bill of Rights than to support the big letterpress projects.[138] Others agreed that the NHPC should put first priority on publishing documents and leave editorial training to others.[139]

For two decades the involvement of the NHPC with the major editorial projects and most of the minor ones has made it the logical agency to exert leadership and promulgate standards for documentary editing. Despite some disagreement about how the commission could render maximum service, the profession obviously looked to it for leadership. To the extent its far too modest staff and budget allow, the NHPC should experiment with ways to promote better editorial training and more appreciation throughout the profession of the editorial function and accomplishments.

[135] Interviews with Richard P. McCormick, Lloyd C. Gardner, Richard M. Brown, and J. Joseph Huthmacher, *ibid*.
[136] Interview, see Appendix C3.
[137] Interview, see Appendix C1.
[138] Bestor, *ibid*.
[139] Interviews with Lewis Atherton, Robert W. Johannsen, and William G. McLoughlin, Jr., *ibid*.

As Adrienne Koch observed, recent documentary editing has wrought a bloodless revolution in American historiography.[140] Many academic historians appreciated the importance of documentary publications and recognized the field as being worthy of their interest and concern. They realized that the solid editorial monuments weather the storms that wash many insubstantial, unimportant monographs into oblivion; yet far too many professors regarded documentary editing as an inferior employment of the historian's talents. This attitude has been transmitted from one generation of graduate students to another, largely because the important editorial work originated outside the academies and only recently has been taken under their wings. Although universities now sponsor several of the major documentary publications, the fact that the universities have not integrated the editorial work with graduate history training indicates an uneasy alliance. History professors often regarded the editorial projects as an appendage unrelated to their activities, and one editor said that for all the communication he had with his academic colleagues, his office might just as well have been in the telephone building.

Without question, documentary editing has become one of the piers supporting the house of American history. The only way it can continue to flourish is through the recognition by academic historians of its vital importance. This recognition entails systematic training of graduate students in the art. Whether such training is handled by individual universities or through the NHPC is immaterial. Manifestly, without the training which will enable the continuation of important projects, the structure so imaginatively and soundly raised may begin to crumble.

[140] "The Historian as Scholar," *Nation*, Vol. CXCV, No. 17 (Nov. 24, 1962), 358.

X. Researcher-Custodian Relations

IN the last few decades historians have drifted somewhat apart from their librarian-archivist partners in research. This drifting has been the result of two factors—the development of the attitude among historians that writing interpretative studies is their most "professional" and rewarding activity, and, secondly, the increased attention among curators to technical aspects of their work. In the days when curators also performed as creative scholars, the profession held their curatorial activities in high regard. With the decline of their creative scholarship, however, the profession has often regarded curators as hod carriers. Younger historians should remember that many of the celebrated names in the profession have carried the curatorial and bibliographical hod while making great contributions with their masonry of interpretative works. Among them are Justin Winsor, J. Franklin Jameson, Worthington C. Ford, Charles M. Andrews, Lawrence C. Wroth, Samuel F. Bemis, Julian P. Boyd, and Clifford K. Shipton.

Even if the great tradition of curator-scholars is in eclipse, relationships between historical researchers and the librarians and archivists charged with the custody of research materials are generally excellent. Any researcher naturally encounters difficulties and frustrations, and a historian would be naïve to expect this phase

memo

of his work to be without hindrance. Perhaps the reason scholars expressed annoyance with obstacles to research is that they have usually chosen and pursued their profession because of deep commitments that transform their labor into intellectual pleasure and excitement. When this activity is beset with problems, scholars realize—as do their laboring brothers daily—that work is not play. Were scholars not following, or preparing for, an idealized vocation, they probably would take ordinary aggravations with less fret. Since scholarly research does intersect the workaday world, historians should be prepared for their relations with curators and clerical assistants to be something less than perfect. The encouraging fact is that these relations are strikingly cordial. This chapter's discussion of existing problems attempts to identify areas where custodians and historians can work together to facilitate scholarly research.

An indication of the close co-operation between historians and university library staffs was that the latter frequently commented that history professors and students were the library's most active users. The reference department of the Rutgers–The State University library sometimes felt that it worked for the department of history since it had more requests and users from that department than any other.[1] At Louisiana State University the library's relations with the history department were "the best . . . on campus."[2] The social science librarian at Florida State University thought excellent relations with historians resulted from the "library-minded people in the history department." He commented further on a condition the survey frequently encountered: the history department's spending "its share of the budget and more."[3] Library staffs at the Universities of Minnesota and Nebraska and at Washington University said that historians were among their heaviest users.[4] At the University of Utah and at Emory University, only the English

1 Interview with H. Gilbert Kelley, see Appendix C2a.
2 Interview with T. N. McMullan, director, *ibid.*
3 Interview with Reno W. Bupp, *ibid.*
4 Interviews with University of Minnesota library staff, see n. 58, Chap. VIII; Eugene M. Johnson, associate director for Public Services, and Kathryn R. Renfro, associate director for Technical Services, University of Nebraska library, see Appendix C2a; Washington University library staff, see n. 43, Chap. VIII.

departments were as interested as historians in building the library collections.[5]

Both university libraries and nonacademic repositories often ensured good working relations by having historians on their governing boards and as directors. At Washington University the chairman of the faculty library council was a historian;[6] and in Philadelphia, Roy Nichols and Thomas C. Cochran were on the board of the Historical Society of Pennsylvania, and Anthony N. B. Garvan was on the board of the Library Company of Philadelphia.[7] In some institutions, such as the Universities of Oklahoma and North Carolina, historians held joint appointments in the library. At the former, Arrell M. Gibson and Duane H. D. Roller were professors as well as curators of the Western History and DeGolyer collections, respectively.[8] At North Carolina, James W. Patton was both a professor and the director of the Southern Historical Collection until his retirement in 1967. His successor, J. Isaac Copeland, also held professorial rank. Similarly, at the University of Wyoming, Gene M. Gressley taught and directed the Western History Research Center. Some libraries cemented their relations with historians by having Ph. D.'s in history as directors. Among these men were Stuart Forth of the University of Kentucky, Lawrence W. Towner of the Newberry Library, and Dorman H. Winfrey of the Texas State Library. Boston University assured "intimate" relations with the Boston Athenaeum by owning two shares of its stock, thus providing professors and graduate students with free access to the Athenaeum's library.[9]

INTERLIBRARY LOAN

The willingness of libraries throughout the country to lend books to facilitate work elsewhere is an emphatic acknowledgment of the interdependence of the research community. Because

[5] Interviews with University of Utah library staff, see n. 136, Chap. VII; Emory University library staff, see n. 146, Chap. VII.

[6] Interview, above.

[7] Interview with Cochran, see Appendix C1.

[8] Interview with Arthur M. McAnally, see Appendix C2a.

[9] Interview with Robert E. Moody, see Appendix C1.

the system has proved so valuable and has worked so well, graduate students frequently begin their extramural research at the inter-library loan desks of the universities they attend. Despite the rich-ness of any university's holdings, its students often need books that are not in its collection. As the testimony from the following insti-tutions indicated, any university can benefit from the interlibrary loan service. Doctoral candidates at the University of California at Berkeley and the University of Kentucky have called the service a "godsend" and "superb."[10] Professors, graduate students, and librarians throughout the country speak of the great help their universities receive through interlibrary loans.

Although great universities can profit from interlibrary loans, smaller libraries are naturally the most frequent borrowers. Statis-tics from the University of Chicago library bore this out. In 1965–66, it lent 5,301 volumes to 743 libraries and borrowed 2,970 from 183 libraries. The history department led the borrowing with 664 books, political science followed with 546, and economists bor-rowed 164.[11] Of course, when large universities borrow, they probably receive many more books from other large libraries than they lend to their smaller borrowers.

While the interlibrary loan system has potentialities for immense service, its effectiveness usually depended on the initiative shown by the borrowing institution. Graduate students at some univer-sities had difficulty getting books on interlibrary loan because of a lack of co-operation from their library. Elsewhere professors reported unsatisfactory service because the university library al-ways tried to borrow first from the state library. If the state library did not have the book, considerable delay ensued in the process of querying another library.

Libraries apparently were less hesitant about lending than bor-rowing. Many librarians were reluctant to borrow extensively to support an individual research project. R. B. Downs, University of Illinois librarian, contended that a student who needs sources relating to a particular topic should enroll at a university whose

10 Interviews with James R. Sharp and John Storey, see Appendix C3.
11 Interview with Herman H. Fussler, see Appendix C2a.

library has the requisite material.[12] The University of Michigan library's policy stated that dissertation and seminar topics "will be chosen with regard to the resources at hand and not with the anticipation of borrowing large numbers of publications from other libraries."[13] At Florida State University the position was not so stringent, for the library borrowed extensively; but it did expect students to avoid selecting topics on which it had no information, since the library did not want to borrow everything a student needed.[14]

The interlibrary loan system is most effective for universities whose term of instruction is the semester. Several professors commented on difficulties imposed on graduate students by the quarter system. A ten-week period seems inadequate for students to write papers requiring research in borrowed original sources.[15]

Once library staffs decide to borrow materials for a researcher, they should make the procedure simple and speedy. Too many libraries encumber the borrowing process by requiring the requester to fill out multiple forms and often to pay postage and other fees. For faculty and graduate students, the interlibrary loan system ought to be free. Moreover, the borrowing library should be willing to locate a desired book if its whereabouts is unknown and not demand that the requester furnish this information, for library staffs have better ideas of how to go about finding these materials than researchers do. An institution seeking periodicals from a library that does not lend them should have research funds to cover the cost of photocopying an article. Any increased costs incurred in improving interlibrary loans might be borne by institutional research funds so as not to be a direct drain on library budgets. Better service naturally adds to operating costs, but research-oriented universities must be prepared to meet such necessary expenses.

[12] Downs, *ibid.*

[13] Interview with Agnes N. Tysse, head, Reference Department, *ibid.*

[14] Interview with Florence Bethea, assistant dinrector of libraries, *ibid.*

[15] Interviews with Joe M. Richardson, Don E. Fehrenbacher, Marvin R. Zahniser, Gilman M. Ostrander, and Richard W. Leopold, see Appendix C1.

PREPARATION FOR RESEARCH TRIPS

When conducting research away from their universities, graduate students frequently discovered that their professors had prepared the way for them. This preparation was not individual and specific but resulted from professors' having used repositories for years and having established amicable working relations with the curators. The students, in turn, profited from the cumulate good will. Doctoral candidates at several universities said that the reputations of their major professors paved the way and opened doors for them wherever they went for research.

Since many graduate students did little research at their home institutions, it was fortunate that, whether or not the reputations of their professors had preceded them, the students ordinarily enjoyed excellent relations with curators. Students' avoidance of the libraries at their home universities may have resulted from generally inadequate holdings there or from dissertation topics unrelated to the library's collections. When repositories formulated their collecting policy to support research in certain areas, they were naturally disappointed when students did not choose topics related to the local resources. For instance, the Arizona Pioneers' Historical Society (the state historical society), located in Tucson near the University of Arizona, reported that few faculty members and graduate students pursued Western (or even American) studies.[16]

Part of the preparation professors gave students before research trips was a discussion of what the students should expect and how they should behave at research institutions.[17] Acquainting students with finding aids from the repository to be visited also was particularly helpful.[18] A doctoral candidate at the University of California at Berkeley regretted that his professors had said nothing about protocol in visiting other libraries. "We were not told, for instance, that we should write ahead to tell the library of our project and what we would like to see."

[16] Questionnaire returned by Andrew Wallace.
[17] Interviews with Don Higginbotham and Hugh F. Rankin, see Appendix C1.
[18] Interview with Philip P. Mason, *ibid*.

Since many professors felt that letters of introduction have enhanced the relations of students with research institutions, they sent letters either before the visit[19] or with the student.[20] The department at Yale University has tried to introduce graduate students formally each time they visited another research institution.[21] Because New York City abounds in all sorts and conditions of students, Columbia University history professors felt the need for formal statements when sending students to other repositories. When a student went elsewhere for research, his professor gave him a letter of introduction, telling the nature of his research interest.[22] Eric Foner, a Columbia graduate student, found that such a letter eased any problems that arose,[23] and doctoral candidates at the University of Illinois and the University of California at Santa Barbara reported that letters from their professors had similar results.[24] When graduate students from the University of Kansas traveled overseas for research, they took a letter of identification from the chancellor and had no difficulty.[25]

CONSIDERATION OF RESEARCHERS' NEEDS

A sure sign of good relations between repositories and researchers is the willingness of repositories to make special accommodations for its users. Since special collections often close at five o'clock and since traveling researchers need to use their time as effectively as possible, it is a great help when the repository will permit the researcher to come in after hours or transfer the material to another unit in the building that keeps later hours. Frequently institutions initiated these special arrangements to aid their own researchers, and visitors subsequently benefited.

Some libraries make special lending arrangements for scholars needing to use materials for prolonged periods. The University of Texas library has made extended loans of books to graduate

[19] Interview with Merle Curti, *ibid*.
[20] Interview with Stephen E. Ambrose, *ibid*.
[21] Interview with Howard R. Lamar, *ibid*.
[22] Interview with Robert D. Cross, *ibid*.
[23] Interview, see Appendix C3.
[24] Interviews with Edmund J. Danzinger, Jr., and George E. Frakes, *ibid*.
[25] Interview with W. Stitt Robinson, see Appendix C1.

students from Texas Christian University,[26] and the Sam Rayburn Library in Bonham, Texas, let a graduate student from the University of Cincinnati take material back to Cincinnati. This student was virtually the only researcher at the library in the summer of 1965.[27] Any time that a scholar was the only researcher in a library, he could usually count on the full attention and co-operation of the staff. This was Gabriel Kolko's experience when he visited the Eisenhower Library in July, 1966.[28] If regulations permitted, staffs sometimes allowed mature researchers into the stacks and thereby saved time for all. The American Antiquarian Society did this for David L. Ammerman when he was working on his dissertation, "The First Continental Congress and the Coming of the American Revolution." He "could not have asked for better treatment."[29]

Another indication of an institution's consideration for the needs of its researchers is its provision for using microforms and for photocopying. Doctoral candidates at the Universities of Utah, California at Berkeley, and Notre Dame commented on the great assistance their libraries rendered with good microform collections and reading facilities.[30] A University of Illinois student praised his library for scattering Docustat machines throughout the building. He felt that the charge of ten cents per page was well worth the typing time saved.[31] Low photocopying fees were partly responsible for the cordial relations the Massachusetts Historical Society had with its researchers, according to Stephen T. Riley, the director.[32] The American Jewish Archives claimed—and no doubt rightly so—that it does for a researcher what no other archives in the world will do: it makes from fifty to seventy-five free Xerox copies.[33]

[26] Interview with Ben Procter, *ibid.*
[27] Interview with Thomas N. Bonner, *ibid.*
[28] Kolko, *ibid.*
[29] Interview, see Appendix C3.
[30] Interviews with William Dirk Raat, Lisle A. Rose, and Paul A. O'Rourke, *ibid.*
[31] Interview with Edmund J. Danziger, Jr., *ibid.*
[32] Interview, see Appendix C2b.
[33] Interview with Jacob R. Marcus, see Appendix C2a.

The staffs of some repositories have maintained close relations with prospective researchers by informing historians of holdings on which specific topics could be based. When Morris Rieger was chief of the Labor and Transportation Branch in the National Archives, he wrote scholars about unused records related to their research interests.[34] The Colorado State Historical Society and the state archives similarly informed professors at the Universities of Colorado and Denver of their resources and suggested lists of subjects these resources would support.[35] Library staffs at the University of Kentucky and Saint Louis University likewise notified their history departments of topics that could be developed from their original sources.[36]

Other institutions have taken specific steps to make their services consonant with the needs of researchers. The Massachusetts Historical Society believed in making its manuscripts easy to use and therefore gave a scholar a sufficient number to keep him occupied for several hours.[37] To improve communication with historians in Pennsylvania, the Pennsylvania Historical and Museum Commission and the Pennsylvania Historical Association sponsored an invitational conference to acquaint historians with their facilities and resources.[38] In planning its new library, Northwestern University based the design on the needs of the users. Clarence L. Ver Steeg, chairman of the committee on the new library, said: "We tried to determine how students use the library and to put the needs of students ahead of the needs of the books. . . . We did not start with a building, but with its functions."[39]

INTRAMURAL PROBLEMS

Many frustrations historians experienced in their research resulted from problems within their academic institutions. Some of

[34] Interview, see Appendix C2b.
[35] Interviews with Enid T. Thompson and Dolores Renze, *ibid.*
[36] Interviews with University of Kentucky library staff, see n. 32, Chap. V; Saint Louis University library staff, see n. 24, Chap. VII.
[37] Interview with Stephen T. Riley, see Appendix C2b.
[38] Questionnaire returned by Donald H. Kent, Pennsylvania Historical and Museum Commission.
[39] Interview, see Appendix C1.

these were attributable to shortcomings within the library, but others stemmed from imperfect communication between history professors and the library. In some instances this situation was not peculiar to the department of history but applied to all academic divisions of a university. At one university the librarian assumed that library-faculty relations would be improved considerably if the library staff had faculty status. Without qualifying for membership in the academic senate and not being able to attend its meetings, the librarians were not routinely apprised of faculty plans that involved the library. Consequently, the faculty sometimes made plans that depended upon the support of the library without so advising the library. Such situations no doubt prevailed in many universities. One way of ensuring closer liaison between teaching and library staffs, in addition to giving the latter faculty status, would be for the directors of libraries at research institutions to have ex officio membership on the graduate council.

The head of the reference department at a major university library noted that, although the library had generally good relations with the history department, these relations would be improved by better co-ordination between professors and librarians when assignments involved the library. Without consulting with the library, professors frequently made assignments involving much participation by the library staff. "Since a limited staff must serve the entire campus community, this sort of thing may put a strain on the relationship at times." The librarians sometimes thought that they had to spend more time with students in certain history courses than the professors did. At another university the library staff considered its relations with the history department among the best in the university, but these relations depended too much on the few professors using the library. "It's just that we don't know many of the history professors."

Unfortunately, in some instances intramural hostility impaired the aid graduate students received from research collections. When the department of history at one institution decided to de-emphasize the programs developed around an important research collection, relations deteriorated. The collection, which had a degree of autonomy, retaliated by making graduate students from that department feel unwelcome.

Aside from the basic problem of communication between librarians and historians, the physical accommodations of the libraries greatly influenced researchers' attitudes. Historians complained about libraries that either did not allow or did not provide adequately for typewriters to be used in carrels or with microform readers. Historians also commented negatively on crowded or nonexistent carrels at their libraries. In addition to having inadequate carrels, libraries deterred research by providing no place where materials could be locked up or left out undisturbed. Students wasted a great deal of time having to tidy up each time they left their work area. Libraries with limited physical facilities often not only were unable to supply carrels but also could not provide seminar rooms or space for departmental studies. In addition, libraries occasionally served as social centers, especially when the university had no student union.

Crowding in some libraries resulted in preferential treatment for the most-used items, and research materials got pushed into spaces inaccessible to students. Rather than being able to browse in government documents, for example, students had to call for them by number. Inadequate space forced many repositories to store the more infrequently used parts of their collections. When researchers needed this material, the results were frustrating. Limited space in one university library necessitated storing an appreciable portion of its holdings, and researchers sometimes had to wait two weeks to get material from storage. An important research collection maintained some records in an annex twenty-two miles away, and, because of this distance, the staff could service the records only once a week, with resulting inconveniences and delays for researchers.

Anyone using the manuscript collection of the University of California at Los Angeles had to realize that no manuscripts were available immediately. They were stored in a subbasement vault, and student help provided only once-a-day paging service. Even if a request were submitted just before three o'clock, when the paging service began, manuscripts probably would not be available before four-thirty. Since the collection closed at five, effective research could not begin until the following morning.[40] The special collections department of the University of Southern California library similarly required a researcher to request records a day before he needed them. Such requirements made it difficult to coordinate a research schedule.[41]

Graduate students frequently commented that the hours maintained by special collections made it difficult to use them. Ordinarily, the hours were from nine to five, with an hour for lunch. Working students and those at one institution who wanted to use the special collection at another were the persons most inconvenienced by this schedule. Both professors and students wished that their libraries would keep longer hours at night and stay open more on week ends and holidays. Libraries that closed during week ends and vacations seemed geared to undergraduates rather than graduate students and professors, who often could work in the library most effectively during these periods. At most research libraries the scarcity of trained librarians late at night and the inability of student assistants to give proper service also were problems.

The attitudes of librarians toward both ordering microforms and providing decent reading facilities for them greatly influenced relations with historians. Some major research libraries were reluctant to purchase microforms, despite faculty pressure to do so. On occasion this reluctance stemmed from a librarian's notion that research with microforms was undignified. Such a librarian preferred to buy manuscripts. Although one university librarian acceded to historians' wishes to acquire microforms, he was "reluctant to make the necessary arrangements for their easy use." In the university's main library, there were only two microfilm readers for general purposes. Because of widespread dissatisfaction with this university library, in March, 1966, graduate students and fac-

---

[40] Interview with James Mink, historical manuscript librarian, see Appendix C2a.

[41] Interview with Thomas F. Andrews, see Appendix C3.

ulty members circulated a petition calling for improvements. One historian termed the library service "miserable in almost all respects."

Putting an even greater strain on relations between libraries and departments of history than inadequate microform sources was a lack of standard secondary works, especially at universities which recently inaugurated doctoral programs in history. A student at such a university described its library facilities as "particularly limited, except for magazines. . . . The . . . library is wanting in basic books." Moreover, those books listed in the card catalog were hard to locate because of misshelving, and the library sometimes took more than a month to return books to the shelves after they had been checked in. One of the problems with this library, according to a professor, was its gross overuse by undergraduates. To get to the library's holdings, graduate students had to "elbow their way in through hordes of undergraduates." A doctoral candidate at another university complained similarly that the great influx of undergraduates made the library's service to graduate students inadequate. One consequence of this lack of basic books at universities in the Washington, D.C., area is that graduate students depended almost entirely on the Library of Congress, a condition David S. Sparks described as the "Library of Congress syndrome." "Students feel that they must go there to be respectable, even if it's to have lunch, read the newspaper, or chat with friends. There is a great deal of work that scholars could do at their own libraries, rather than going to the LC. It's just that they feel it's somehow more scholarly to read the same work in the LC than at another library."[42]

Both the University of Massachusetts and the City University of New York (CUNY) recently began doctoral programs in history without having developed research collections. Their doctoral candidates have therefore depended on other libraries for books. Those at CUNY relied on obtaining books from the libraries of the component colleges—Brooklyn, Queens, City College of New York, and Hunter—or using the New York Public

[42] Interview, see Appendix C1.

Library (NYPL). The attendant difficulties forced students "to scrounge to get books for graduate research at CUNY."[43] The institution made some effort to alleviate this problem by locating its graduate center directly across Forty-second Street from the New York Public Library. In addition to CUNY students who rely on the NYPL, dozens of institutions make similar demands on that library. As a result, its distinguished collections are being ground into dust by overuse, a problem which may well be insoluble. The NYPL is a national research institution, but unfortunately without national support. At the University of Massachusetts the library's "fair working relations" with the history department resulted partly from the fact that "we never have what they want. . . . In the department of history as a whole, professors of non-U.S. history seem more aggressive in building the library collections than those in U.S. history."[44] It should be noted that some of the pressure was removed from the University of Massachusetts library by its consortium arrangement with Amherst, Smith, and Mt. Holyoke colleges.

Even when a university has had a successful doctoral program for some years and its library has systematically tried to build research collections, professors sometimes remembered the library in terms of its holdings before graduate work began. At one rapidly growing institution, the library generally had excellent relations with historians, but protested that the university was "plagued with an inferiority complex." Too many faculty members often assumed that the library's holdings were commensurate with its onetime cow-college status.

At other universities the various problems and lapses in library service kept relations between historians and librarians somewhat strained. Professors at one university were outspoken about the shortcomings of their library and contended that the librarian was uninterested in research and provided inadequate facilities for it. There were also indications that the university administration sup-

[43] Interview with Selma C. Berrol, see Appendix C3.
[44] Interview with Benton L. Hatch, associate librarian for Special Collections, see Appendix C2a.

ported the library improperly and that the situation might be improved, given better support. At another university lack of co-ordination between one library staff and the department of history resulted in "a great battle" over newspapers. The librarian sent all the state newspapers to the state historical society without consulting the department, thereby "with one fell swoop" removing one of the "major research resources" of the historians. If the department wanted any of this material subsequently, it had to buy microfilmed copies.

Historians also expressed dissatisfaction with university libraries that were uninterested in developing manuscript collections. A few years ago one university not only refused to acquire manuscripts but actually transferred important collections to the efficient state library in the same city. Later, the university resumed collecting. Another constant frustration to historians and librarians at many universities was the great loss from pilferage and mutilation of library materials. Many of the foregoing problems can be understood in light of the experience of the department at the University of Virginia. Until 1961 the graduate history enrollment was 50 students, but by 1965 there were 150.[45] Similar conditions elsewhere explained some of the difficulties researchers had with university libraries whose facilities had not expanded commensurately with enrollments.

Possibly the most dramatic indication of the willingness of universities to face the challenges of increased enrollments and the accompanying increased demand for research facilities was the erection of new libraries. Although incomplete, the following list of both nonuniversity libraries that work closely with the academic community and universities planning or already building new libraries or expanding existing ones gives some indication of the rapid expansion of physical facilities: Ball State University, Boston College, Boston University, Bowling Green State University, Central Michigan University, University of Chicago, Duke University, Eastern Michigan University, Emory University, University of Florida, Georgetown University, Harvard University,

[45] Interview with Edward Younger, see Appendix C1.

University of Houston, Indiana University, University of Kansas, Massachusetts Historical Society, Miami University, University of Michigan, University of Minnesota, University of Missouri at Kansas City, University of New Mexico, State University of New York at Albany and Buffalo, New York University, North Carolina Department of Archives and History, Northern Michigan University, North Texas State University, Ohio Historical Society, University of Oregon, University of Pennsylvania, Pennsylvania State University, University of Pittsburgh, Rice University, Sam Houston State College, San Francisco State College, University of Southern Mississippi, Temple University, Tulane University, University of Utah, Vanderbilt University, State Historical Society of Wisconsin, Woman's College of Georgia, and Xavier University.

EXTRAMURAL PROBLEMS

While scholars experienced annoyance with conditions hampering research at their own universities, difficulties encountered while traveling became magnified, especially if the researcher did not want to travel from the outset. Some graduate students, according to their professors, were reluctant to travel. For example, many doctoral candidates at the University of Southern California were natives of the region and did not want to leave.[46] Perhaps they assumed, as did some students at Columbia University, that if the records were not in their area, they were not to be found anywhere.[47] Some graduate students at the University of Oklahoma were reluctant to travel because they wanted to work quickly "and in a cloistered area."[48] Professors at the Universities of Texas, Kansas, and Minnesota reported that students either could not afford travel or were unwilling to spend their own money on it.[49] When students with these attitudes were required to travel,

[46] Interview with Howard S. Miller., *ibid.*

[47] Interview with James P. Shenton, *ibid.* Shenton said that Columbia students included New England in their region.

[48] Interview with Arthur H. DeRosier, Jr., *ibid.*

[49] Interviews with Barnes F. Lathrop, Clark S. Griffin, and Robert F. Berkhofer, Jr., *ibid.*

they probably began their research expecting the worst. Problems encountered at other university libraries may have arisen because the curators felt that their first obligation was to resident scholars and that visitors should be satisfied with whatever they got.

Evidence from both academic and nonacademic repositories indicated that approximately half their researchers came from outside the locality.[50] The library of the American Philosophical Society has had even more out-of-town graduate students doing research than those from the University of Pennsylvania, located across town. Of those students who did come from the University of Pennsylvania, more were in the American civilization program than in American history.[51] With the fact of traveling researchers well established, custodians of original sources—particularly at universities—should recognize that while they were serving the sojourner, some distant custodian was likely dealing with a researcher from their institution.[52] The ethical implications should not go unrecognized.

Among the most common complaints of traveling scholars was the difficulty of gaining admission to certain private libraries. While some of these nonacademic institutions received young postdoctoral researchers with coolness, their response to graduate students could be glacial. Often the difficulty lay in getting beyond cloakroom attendants and the clerical staff. Once these defenses were breached and the researcher proved his serious interest, the libraries could be most helpful and hospitable. In some instances, however, scholars had written to obtain permission to see certain collections in advance of a visit only to find upon arrival that curators were still reluctant to grant access to the materials. Such cases naturally made researchers wonder whose interests curators were trying to serve.

Scholars frequently encountered difficulties when doing research in church libraries and archives, especially if the church had been involved in controversial issues. As long as the material

[50] Interviews with Harriett C. Owsley and Colton Storm, see Appendix C2b; E. L. Inabinett, Herman H. Fussler, and Howard H. Peckham, see Appendix C2a.
[51] Interview with Whitfield J. Bell., Jr., see Appendix C2b.
[52] See Appendix H for further information on graduate student travel.

300

desired did not touch on matters related to church practices or doctrine, researchers experienced little trouble; but when sensitive issues were involved, scholars were either denied access to records or had to submit their notes for clearance. Although such restrictions are irritating, scholars must recognize the essentially private nature of church records and be grateful for the opportunity to see them. For their part, churches should realize that they can make great contributions to scholarship by granting liberal access to their records.

Public research institutions such as the Library of Congress and the New York Public Library have made great efforts to satisfy the needs of their researchers. But with their tremendous volume of resources and users, service has often been uneven. Usually it was not the experienced researcher who received cavalier treatment but the person paying his first visit to the institution— the person who had not yet learned whom to ask for advice and assistance. Many researchers reported that their difficulties at these two libraries stemmed from their contacts with clerks at the front desk, who often gave ill-considered and casual advice that resulted in false starts for the researchers. Despite shortcomings in service in the Library of Congress' Manuscript Division, David C. Mearns said that the division's relations with historians were "one of our great joys."[53] Mearns was chief of the division until his retirement in December, 1967, after having been on the Library of Congress staff for forty-nine years. During his last years in the Manuscript Division, he inaugurated a seminar to acquaint university students with the conditions encountered in manuscript research.

Graduate students from the entire country did research at the New York Public Library, but those from New York City naturally used it most. Both students and library staff agreed that they have mutual problems. A doctoral candidate from Columbia University found using the NYPL was a bit harrying. His major complaint was that the American History Room closed at six o'clock, making it impossible to work there at night. While some graduate students at the City University of New York felt that they had

[53] Interview, see Appendix C2b.

poor relations with the NYPL, another said that despite any difficulties, the NYPL was a marvelous resource. She admitted that it was physically uncomfortable and that researchers had to contend with drunks who came in from the cold. Harold D. McDonald, chief of the American History Division of the NYPL, considered the library's relations with historians "rather negative, particularly with professors. They do not make suggestions on acquisitions, never let us see the reading lists they give their students, never ask how certain problems should be handled."[54]

Historians commented on several other conditions that produced unpleasant relations with repositories. These included having to pay fees to use manuscripts and having to spend unwarranted amounts of time getting permission to use certain records. Scholars condemned one institution's practice of parceling out only five pieces of material at one time. This involved researchers in filling out numerous forms requesting more manuscripts and then waiting for their delivery. Curators who gave slow service because of unfamiliarity with their materials also annoyed researchers. One graduate student was disgusted with ex post facto restrictions a military librarian tried to impose. The librarian told the researcher that he should not have been allowed to see some of the 1919 Graham Committee hearings on the conduct of World War I and asked him not to use his notes.

UNIVERSITY–HISTORICAL SOCIETY RELATIONS

Working relationships between departments of history and historical societies were often symbolized by their close physical proximity, as in Madison, Wisconsin, and Lincoln, Nebraska. In some instances, however, tension existed between researchers and the societies, with resulting loss to each. Such tension often occurred when the societies were staffed by political appointees or amateurs incapable of rendering professional service. Academic historians often had little patience with amateurism—either in the administration or in programs of historical societies—and were quick to show it. Unfortunately, this attitude, while legitimate in

[54] McDonald, *ibid.*

regard to amateur scholarship, often impeded the work of serious researchers by causing a historical society to react defensively by restricting access to manuscripts. Another reason for strains between universities and historical societies was competition in manuscript collecting. In such rivalry, departments of history usually supported the university. This condition has resulted in difficulties for graduate students using the research facilities of the historical society. Significantly, professors in universities which have prickly relations with their historical societies reported that their state archives received graduate students cordially.

The need is great for closer communication between academic historians and personnel in museums, archives, and historical societies. The American Association for State and Local History (AASLH) makes an excellent effort to provide the needed meeting ground, but too few academicians know of its work or are interested in it. Some look upon the AASLH with disdain.[55] Nonetheless, historians can only profit by establishing amicable relations with custodians of original sources necessary for their research.

RELATIONS WITH THE NATIONAL ARCHIVES

Of all the repositories where United States historians researched, the National Archives commanded the greatest respect and enjoyed the friendliest relations with its clientele. The warmth of the relationship was reflected in the following comments. William T. Hutchinson said he and his students regarded the research facilities at the National Archives as well as the co-operativeness of its staff as ideal.[56] Carl G. Anthon called the National Archives curators "the most valuable part" of its service.[57] "The staff at the Archives is superb," commented David A. Shannon. "I often marvel at the way they get researchers into useful bodies of records."[58] Clark C. Spence found correspondence with the Archives most helpful: "I have no complaints whatsoever about the Archives staff."[59]

[55] Cf. Walter Muir Whitehill, *Independent Historical Societies.*
[56] Interview, see Appendix C1.
[57] Anthon, *ibid.*
[58] Shannon, *ibid.*
[59] Spence, *ibid.*

Lewis E. Atherton commended the staff for its good suggestions and for having material available for researchers when they arrived. "Students praise the National Archives staff highly. The staff enables the students to save a great deal of time while doing research in the Archives."[60] Thomas L. Karnes considered the staff "extremely co-operative. They're helpful in correspondence as well as personally."[61] Marvin R. Zahniser received so much assistance from the staff at the Archives that he noticed no deficiencies in its finding aids.[62]

Although members of the National Archives staff thought that their relations with historians were sound, they suggested ways by which historians could improve these relations. Sometimes researchers have arrived at the Archives expecting to use classified records without having inquired in advance about their accessibility. Thus valuable time was wasted getting clearance to use the records. If professors would inform students of the need to write the Archives well in advance of their visit, giving specific information about their projects, the staff could then give optimum service.[63] Professors could also improve relations by having more firsthand knowledge of the Archives. If they would spend time at the Archives to learn what was available for students, they could assign dissertation topics more effectively. Frequently professors approved topics that "are questionable and demonstrate a lack of knowledge of our sources."[64] Jane Smith, chief of the Social and Economic Branch of the Archives, was encouraged that scholars who had done extensive work at the Archives, such as Dean Albertson, were bringing their seminars to the Archives for research.[65]

Although most historians commended the Archives' service, some expressed dissatisfaction with various aspects of its operations. Brigham Madsen noted that the divisions of the Archives seemed to have little idea of what each other had or did. He saw,

[60] Atherton, *ibid.*
[61] Karnes, *ibid.*
[62] Zahniser, *ibid.*
[63] Interview with Julia B. Carroll, see Appendix C2b.
[64] Interview with Sherrod East, *ibid.*
[65] Smith, *ibid.*

moreover, insufficient co-ordination between agencies retiring records and the Archives.[66] Chase C. Mooney and John T. Farrell said their students commented that the Archives staff no longer had adequate knowledge of their material.[67] A student at Catholic University was not allowed to see unclassified records that he requested. The staff told him that those records were not pertinent to his project and wanted him to use other material. The student's argument was that he did not want archivists to determine his choice of research data.[68]

Scholars who needed records bearing security classifications sometimes faulted the Archives' administration of such records. Richard Dalfiume's dissertation on "Desegregation of the Armed Forces, 1940–1953" required World War II records. He found the Archives staff handling these records inefficient and unhelpful. Despite his security clearance, the staff would not let him examine material pertaining to John J. McCloy's formulation of policy for Negro troops in World War II. Later, while doing research in the Office of the Chief of Military History, Dalfiume came across these records and used them. Disregarding a directive that material twelve years old was eligible for declassification, the Archives staff was reluctant to take that action. The staff told Dalfiume that the army's condition for his using classified documents was that he take only fifty notes on the documents, a restriction which he considered intentional harassment. The notes then had to be reviewed for security clearance, which took approximately six months. Dalfiume felt that the Archives staff purposely did not show him pertinent documents.[69]

Other historians complained about unreasonable restriction on the use of War Department records. Edwin Lieuwen commented on having to fill out an elaborate petition, giving five references who could vouch for his good citizenship, before he could use certain War Department records. After interminable delays he discovered that one of the five persons had not responded, but the

[66] Interview, see Appendix C1.
[67] Mooney and Farrell, *ibid.*
[68] Farrell, above.
[69] Interview, see Appendix C3.

army would not identify him so that Lieuwen could prod him. "This kind of red tape is insufferable."[70] Researchers must keep in mind that the National Archives does not establish restrictions on using records, for these are the policy of the retiring agency; the Archives merely carries out instructions. It is possible, however, as Dalfiume indicated, that within these guidelines archivists may not have been willing to show a researcher all he was entitled to see.

Along with the general enthusiasm for the National Archives' microfilming program, there was some criticism of the inconvenience caused by the filming. For instance, James H. Holmes chose "The Bering Sea Patrol" as the subject for his master's thesis only to learn, after researching the pertinent Coast Guard records for approximately one year, that the Archives was immediately withdrawing the series for microfilming. As a result, he had to change topics. Holmes acknowledged the need for filming these records, but protested that the Archives should plan its filming far enough in advance that it could inform researchers when a series would be removed for filming.[71] Scholars also suggested that the Archives should make its extensive collection of film available on interlibrary loan.[72] The University of Illinois library wished to buy some microfilmed captured German war documents but complained that the Archives would not even lend film so that the library could identify what it wanted to purchase.[73]

One aspect of service at the National Archives on which historians differed was the grouping of all researchers in the Central Research Room. Before March, 1966, most researchers used the branch search rooms nearest the records being investigated. An advantage of these rooms was that subject specialists on the staff were immediately accessible, "thus facilitating the initial and interim consultations between researcher and archivist so essential to efficient exploitation of archival materials."[74] Harold D. Langley

[70] Interview, see Appendix C1.
[71] Interview, see Appendix C3.
[72] Interview with Harold D. Langley, see Appendix C1. All repositories publishing microfilmed collections on grants from the NHPC must make copies available through interlibrary loan.
[73] Interview with University of Illinois library staff, see n. 75, Chap. III.
[74] Interview with Morris Rieger, see Appendix C2b.

and Allan G. Bogue commented that closing the branch search rooms resulted in poorer service, since the centralization divorced researchers from records specialists.[75] Langley asserted that service would be improved if the members of the staff were themselves more involved in research.

In August, 1966, the Archives revamped service in the Central Research Room and designated a co-ordinator of research to enable visitors to start work on their projects with minimal delay. An advantage of the Central Research Room service was that a researcher could work there without interruption until 10:00 P.M. When the branch search rooms were used, records had to be transferred to the Central Research Room if a person wanted to work after 5:00 P.M. Some time was always lost in the transfers.[76] Since centralization, more scholars were working at night, and the staff supposed that the lack of interruption induced them to do so.

When serious researchers planned to use material in the custody of the Social and Economic Records Division, Jane Smith, the division chief, and the appropriate subject specialist consulted with them, suggesting pertinent materials and the most profitable records to study first. Also, they mentioned any related records in the Archives or elsewhere applicable to the research project. Subject specialists furnished scholars with all the relevant finding aids and saw that requested records were delivered to the Central Research Room without delay.[77]

Included in the National Archives and Records Service are the presidential libraries and the Federal Records Centers. The staffs of these repositories eagerly upheld the reputation of the National Archives with researchers. The testimony of historians who worked in the presidential libraries indicated the most harmonious relationships between the libraries and scholars. Frank Freidel, "a firm believer in the presidential libraries," complimented their "good physical arrangements and staff—in the National Archives tradition." Because of their superior facilities for maintaining man-

---

[75] Interviews, see Appendix C1.
[76] Interview with Sherrod East, see Appendix C2b.
[77] Interview with Jane Smith, *ibid.*

uscripts and rendering service, Freidel has encouraged donors to place collections in presidential libraries.[78] John Braeman liked to assign topics related to the New Deal because the Roosevelt Library co-operated so well in supplying microfilmed copies of its holdings.[79] Also, Elizabeth B. Drewry, director of the Franklin D. Roosevelt Library, has been helpful in providing duplicated copies of documents.[80] Professors from the Universities of Kansas and Missouri spoke of their perfect relations with the Harry S Truman Library, directed by Philip C. Brooks.[81]

However helpful presidential libraries were to nearby universities, some historians had serious reservations about the proliferation of the libraries and the concomitant decentralization of manuscript collections.[82] Gabriel Kolko called this decentralization "the most serious problem" American historians face, saying, "The whole decentralization pattern of manuscript sources is a colossal mistake."[83] Of greater concern than the travel connected with using presidential libraries was their inclination toward "directed research." The libraries themselves were not involved in this, but their privately endowed institutes such as at the Truman Library were. "The step between directed research and controlled research might be a short one."[84]

Those scholars who feared the implications of the decentralization of research materials within the National Archives system should consider the alternatives. The really "colossal mistake" would have been to gather all these manuscripts in the Library of Congress or some other repository, where processing would have required decades. This has certainly been the case with the presidential papers already in the Library of Congress. In fact, some scholars commented that the Manuscript Division of the Library

[78] Interview, see Appendix C1.
[79] Interview, *ibid.*
[80] Interview with Barry A. Crouch, see Appendix C3.
[81] Interviews with Clifford S. Griffin, Donald R. McCoy, and Richard S. Kirkendall, see Appendix C1.
[82] Interviews with Frank W. Klingberg, Robert D. Ochs, Thomas C. Cochran, and Lloyd C. Gardner, *ibid.*
[83] Kolko, *ibid.*
[84] Interview with Lawrence E. Gelfand, *ibid.*

of Congress had more material than it could administer satisfactorily and that it did not give adequate service to the crowd it drew. The same allegations were made concerning many of the other older repositories. In the case of presidential libraries, historians can only hope that each successive occupant of the White House who creates a library will do so in conjunction with established research centers. The great error is for these libraries to be isolated and inaccessible by public transportation.

Most United States historians were unaware of the existence of the twelve Federal Records Centers containing archival material. Since their creation in 1950, the centers have received noncurrent records from operating agencies of the federal government and also have fallen heir to some records dating from the inception of the government and before. To the extent that historians have known of and used the Federal Records Centers, they have enjoyed excellent receptions. So few scholars have visited the centers that they usually received exceptional service. Dwight F. Henderson commented, "The Atlanta FRC treated me like a long-lost child, they were so happy to have someone there using their materials."[85] The Atlanta FRC was also very helpful to Marvin R. Zahniser in microfilming its legal records relating to Charles C. Pinckney.[86] Similarly, graduate students from the Universities of Utah and Houston have had good co-operation from the Denver and Fort Worth FRC's, which shipped records to the Salt Lake City post office and Houston federal court building for their perusal.[87] The department of history at Washington State University similarly reported excellent relations with the Seattle FRC,[88] and the department at the University of Kansas has actively worked with the Kansas City FRC in promoting use of its records and publication of its finding aids.[89]

Several of the Federal Records Centers, including those in Fort

[85] Interview with Dwight F. Henderson, see Appendix C3.
[86] Interview, see Appendix C1.
[87] Interviews with Floyd A. O'Neil, see Appendix C3; James A. Tinsley, see Appendix C1.
[88] Questionnaire returned by George A. Frykman.
[89] Interview with Donald R. McCoy, see Appendix C1.

Worth, San Francisco, and Kansas City, have held symposia to acquaint historians with their operations and research potentials. These have been on university campuses and at the centers.[90] To aid historians in their research, the San Francisco FRC established the post of research archivist. Operational pressures have sometimes prevented his functioning in this capacity, but his main assignment was to promote and facilitate serious research. Part of this work included preparing finding aids.[91] The pressure of routine operations has prevented the New York FRC from promoting its facilities for historical research, although it has given the best service it could to any visiting scholar. It did co-operate in one program designed to make graduate history students aware of its resources. Once a year James Heslin brought his students from Columbia University to the FRC for a session on federal depositories.[92]

Scholars, recognizing the essentialness of the National Archives and its related organizations to the study of American history, have suggested the following ways to promote closer co-operation: the National Archives might hold an annual meeting to acquaint the research community with its resources and procedures;[93] various learned societies should include sessions at their meetings on research possibilities at the National Archives, and the Archives should improve its public relations program;[94] the National Archives could appoint a council of historians to provide advice on finding aids and ways to improve searching activities for scholars;[95] and the Archives could formulate standard citations for archival materials, thereby aiding editorial work immensely.[96]

Historians should take satisfaction in the rapport they have established through the years with custodians of original sources.

[90] Interviews with Max W. Ulery, manager, Fort Worth FRC; James E. Cole, manager, San Francisco FRC; and Benjamin F. Cutcliffe, regional director, National Archives and Records Service; see Appendix C2b.

[91] Cole, above.

[92] Interview with Carlyle Bennett, manager, New York FRC, see Appendix C2b.

[93] Interview with Vincent P. Carosso, see Appendix C1.

[94] Interview with John Hope Franklin, *ibid.*

[95] Interview with Donald R. McCoy, *ibid.*

[96] Interview with Sanford W. Higginbotham, *ibid.*

One of the reasons for these good relations was that a significant number of custodians were themselves historians and understood the needs of researchers. Many of the difficulties historians experienced in their research arose from the inadequate physical facilities and staffs at the repositories—conditions susceptible to improvement, given requisite funds. It would behoove historians, therefore, to lend their support to efforts to meet the material needs of libraries, historical societies, and archives. The needs are particularly great with private agencies, for, by making their resources available for doctoral research, they are supporting the work of the universities but without financial aid from them. These older independent historical societies and libraries developed in the age of the amateur, for until the last quarter of the nineteenth century, there were no professional historians, and support for the institutions derived from collectors, antiquarians, and genealogists. Hence their problems in our own time: designed to serve a local constituency with modest demands, now they are overrun by platoons of graduate students and get more mail requests for Xerox copies of their records than they can possibly fill. They have no alumni, and the United States Office of Education never heard of them. How do they meet these new demands? Gladly, and without asking for cash compensation; but their underpaid and often superannuated staffs creak at the joints and are sometimes a bit crotchety in their manners—and no wonder!

Researchers can express appreciation to these repositories in several ways. They can mind their own manners and show respect for the unique materials placed in their hands; they might thank the librarian or director when they have been served well, or write him a letter; they should send reprints of their articles and copies of their books when the materials on which such publications were based came largely from a particular repository; if the membership of the organization is open, they could join and subscribe to its journal, thus manifesting their appreciation concretely. These things graduate students in our affluent age of fellowships and travel grants too seldom do. State and federal research agencies share this need for support by historians. Although they receive public monies, these agencies often are inadequately funded. Historians should ascertain that appropriations for public historical societies, libraries, and archives are sufficient, and they should be willing to lobby with legislatures when they are not.

While relationships between custodians and researchers have been predominantly satisfactory, both parties can take steps to improve them.[97] Historians and librarians on university campuses can recognize each other's needs and work to meet them. Also, both historians and custodians involved in extramural research should realize that problems always seem heightened to travelers, but that these problems are nonetheless real. Custodians should operate on the premise that their basic function is to serve scholarship, not impede it.

[97] Cf. Philip D. Jordan, "The Scholar and the Archivist—A Partnership," *American Archivist*, Vol. XXXI, No. 1 (Jan., 1968), 57–76.

XI. Research Needs

IN less than a century, the historical profession in this country has developed and dealt impressively with the American past. As in so many other areas of our national experience, the profession's growth since World War II has accelerated tremendously. This has been a period of rapidly expanding enrollments in graduate schools and of a significant increase in the number of universities awarding the Ph.D. in history. Because of the difficulty of obtaining precise information from institutions awarding this degree, it was impossible to determine exact numbers for any given year, but the following figures give the best available indication of the growth of graduate training in the profession. In 1941–42, 58 institutions offered the Ph.D. in history; in 1951–52, 65; in 1958–59, 82;[1] and in 1966–67, 114. This quick growth as well as other national changes since World War II has produced a variety of problems for students of American history.

The survey identified three major problems that prevented research in United States history from being as effective as possible: access to original sources is often difficult; communication between academic and nonacademic historians needs improvement; and more adequate training in historical methodology is necessary.

[1] Perkins and Snell, *op. cit.*, 17, 225–26.

In addition, there were several areas in which technical improvements would greatly facilitate research. If the profession solves these problems, the results could be impressive.

ACCESS TO ORIGINAL SOURCES

Possibly the greatest obstacle professors and graduate students faced in their research was getting access to needed materials. This obstacle had four dimensions—the unwillingness of repositories to photocopy their manuscripts for use elsewhere, the security and administrative restrictions placed upon documents by the federal government, conflicting or inadequate programs for collecting sources, and the great increase in scholarly traffic. This last condition entailed continually rising demands that usually prevent good service to researchers and proper processing and maintenance of collections. Many repositories faced serious shortages of personnel, apparatus, and space to cope with the requests of readers and correspondents on the one hand and the requirements of good library and curatorial practices on the other. These were problems that only large amounts of money would solve, but if the research community continues to demand these services—as it surely will —then the research community must find ways to pay for them. The historical profession, which is among the largest consumers of library services, must participate actively in raising funds to meet its research needs.

In evaluating the reasons depositories gave for not photocopying their manuscripts, one must assume that they acquired collections to further knowledge through research. A logical corollary is that this aim is fulfilled in direct ratio to the amount of research and publication based on the holdings. It follows, therefore, that if the scope and range of research can be extended by disseminating photocopies of the original sources, the service to scholarship is expanded. This willingness to serve distant scholars seems far worthier than the policy of collecting manuscripts for the pride of possession, as show pieces, as business investments, to bolster an institutional image, or to gratify institutional self-esteem.

In all fairness, one must acknowledge that private organizations are free to spend their money as they wish. Similarly, private institutions—universities, libraries, historical societies, or museums—are free to do what they want with the materials they buy, unless they are so restrictive that they forfeit their tax-exempt status as educational or cultural enterprises. If an individual collector buys and hoards original sources just for the joy and pride of ownership, he is likewise within his legal rights, but he can hardly pretend to serve scholarship.

Repositories that were unwilling to photocopy manuscripts that came as gifts sometimes supposed that donors did not want other institutions to benefit by receiving copies of the gift, for this would dilute the quality of the original contribution. But it is questionable whether the donors really were so particularistic in their generosity, for the scholarly value of their gift is not decreased but multiplied when photocopies are distributed. Certainly a depository's willingness to share its treasures with others through photocopy in no way diminished the income tax deduction the donor could take as a result of his contribution to an educational institution. Perhaps there were potential donors who felt such fierce loyalty to the single institution that they would be dissuaded from giving if they thought another would benefit from their largess. It seems, however, that those skilled enough to induce such gifts in the first place could easily extend their eloquence to convince a benefactor of the further service to scholarship that would be possible if the donated material could be photoduplicated, thereby benefiting even more scholars. Of course the possibility exists that some institutions regarded manuscript collecting as a branch of intercollegiate athletics and vigorously strove to beat the competition. The winners then jealously guarded their unique trophies. The issue is whether such attitudes stemmed from a desire to promote research or merely reflected institutional vanity.

If donors placed absolute restrictions on the reproduction of their gifts, repositories had no choice but to honor them; yet it would be well for receiving institutions to suggest to prospective donors that their gifts could serve scholarship more fully if the institution were free to photocopy the material for interested researchers. Possibly many donors were unaware of the great changes wrought in research by photocopying techniques and needed only to be informed of the aid they could render by allowing copies to be made. The Manuscript Division of the Library of Congress, as well as other repositories, has suggested to donors that they transfer literary rights to the public so that the papers may be copied without restriction.[2]

Even in the absence of prohibitions by donors against copying, timid curators have refused to photoduplicate manuscripts for fear of violating the common law regarding literary property inhering in the documents. In case of doubt, it was always safest for the curator to be restrictive, irrespective of the genuine disservice done to researchers. Once material has been placed in repositories to which the public has access, that material should be considered in the public domain unless depositors specify otherwise. Curators should not pass judgment on the way scholars use manuscripts except to ensure their physical safety.[3]

Budgetary limitations, which impose staff limitations, have prevented some repositories from making copies of their holdings. Since photocopying documents involved their being taken out of and returned to the files, a great deal of staff time could be consumed, and some institutions simply could not divert their staffs from more pressing work. While this situation cannot be gainsaid in its own terms, one has the uneasy feeling it was sometimes used to camouflage a basic aversion to photoduplicating. For those institutions willing to photocopy but hamstrung by lack of money, the easy solution would be to provide more funds. Such a solution may not be entirely wishful thinking, for with the growing interest of both the federal government and foundations in educational and research activities, funds may well become available for this purpose.

Understandably, some universities would not reproduce newly

[2] Interview with John C. Broderick, see Appendix C2b.
[3] Cf. Walter Rundell, Jr., "The Recent American Past v. H.R. 4347: Historians' Dilemma," *American Archivist*, Vol. XXIX, No. 2 (Apr., 1966), 209–15, for a discussion of the implications of the impending copyright bill for research in twentieth-century American history.

acquired collections because they wanted to give their professors and graduate students first chance at the manuscripts. Since most universities—both private and public—promoted staff research as a matter of policy, there should be no general dissatisfaction with a university's giving top priority to the needs of its faculty and students, provided that the term of restriction is kept short, perhaps one year.

A few repositories resisted photoduplicating parts of their collections because, they contended, a researcher needs to be immersed in an entire collection as well as in related material to derive maximum understanding. They held that researchers could not fathom the import of isolated documents and that they lost some perspective by not working with the full collection. Without question, there is merit in this position. If an individual were conducting research under optimum conditions, he would naturally desire access to the full range of information that would throw light on his subject. Sometimes, however, this "full range" is only part of a collection, one that the experienced researcher or even the tyro with a good finding aid can identify easily.[4] Since researchers often do not command optimum conditions, it would be more utilitarian for institutions to supply photocopies when requested than to resist because of the inadequacy of research done through this medium. The benefits of research with photocopy obviously outweigh the alternative of being unable to use the documents in any form.

Some distinct advantages accrue to depositories that will reproduce an entire collection for research elsewhere. Just to preserve the contextual nature of documents from a specific collection is a cogent reason for institutions to photocopy full series rather than random pieces upon request. Once the material is reproduced *in toto*, the originals are preserved from repeated wear and tear, and with the dispersal of photocopies, the danger of the material's being destroyed through some disaster is mitigated. As Thomas Jefferson wrote to Ebenezer Hazard in 1791, there should be "such a multiplication of copies as shall place them beyond the reach of

[4] Letter, Donald R. McCoy to author, Aug. 19, 1966.

317

accident." If documents are properly arranged for photoduplication, this organization is permanently preserved in the copy. Furthermore, when the institution has photocopied the entire collection, no further staff time need be spent filling requests for copies of individual documents. The requester simply can be told that the roll of microfilm is available at the given price, and if there is any dissatisfaction with having to buy an entire roll, the selling agency can defend its position easily. In buying the complete roll, the purchasing institution will be acquiring resources of value to more than one researcher.

Often curators refused to permit photoreproduction of their holdings for fear of losing control of them. They seemed to fear that without their help and guidance, researchers might come to conclusions at variance with their own. This position was highly suggestive of controlled research. A depository has no function in determining or influencing a researcher's investigations. Neither is there any reason to think a researcher working with reproductions would be any less conscientious than when using originals nor that actual documents would instill a sense of responsibility in a researcher otherwise predisposed. The depository cannot dictate and should not try to influence the use historians make of documents. Obviously, the Massachusetts Historical Society, the Library of Congress, and the National Archives, in making more and more of their choicest material available on film, have not been afflicted with the fear of losing control of their collections. It might be pointed out also that microfilm from these and other public-spirited institutions has found its way into communities throughout the United States and into some foreign countries. Historical scholarship in a democratic society demands both easy access to the records of the past and unfettered research.

Another type of control some curators feared losing was knowledge of research projects involving their records. To prevent duplication, they kept a list of such projects, and they believed that photocopying would undermine these efforts.[5] This clearinghouse service is commendable, for it can prevent a great deal of

[5] Interview with Howard H. Peckham, see Appendix C2a.

wasted effort; yet the fact that a depository wanted to know of research involving its holdings should not constitute a deterrent to research and therefore should not be used as an excuse for not photocopying. On the dissertation level, the American Historical Association has maintained a file of topics in progress and published a *List* of these topics triennially. If there was any danger that a submitted topic would conflict with one already registered, the AHA notified the candidate immediately. Consequently, this was one level of research for which depositories needed to assume no clearinghouse responsibility. Even on this level, the profession seemed to be less fearful of duplication than formerly. The assumption was that while it was desirable to avoid outright duplication, there were many ways to approach any given subject and that parallel investigations could be fruitful. Although some professors directing dissertations have stated flatly that they were unconcerned about duplicated research, implying that their graduate students would outshine the competition, this bravado was not yet typical of our conservatively inclined profession.

A further reason repositories advanced for reluctance to photocopy was that writers often did not credit them with holding originals of the photoreproductions used in research. Such oversights reflected ignorance, ingratitude, and/or poor research techniques—none justifiable under any circumstances. One way to help remedy this situation would be for each roll of film to include targets with clear explanations and examples of proper citation—desiderata often neglected in the casual and piecemeal photoduplication that has been practiced too long but very properly demanded in the large-scale microfilm publications sponsored by the National Archives, the Library of Congress, and the National Historical Publications Commission.

Several repositories not yet disposed to share their unique riches with any buyer would reproduce an entire collection if they could trade it for something of equal value. The very logic of events indicates that sooner or later institutions with holdings of national significance will practice this golden rule of photocopying. If they are to acquire photoduplications from other places to complement their own resources, they must be willing to reciprocate. Although the interlibrary loan system met with resistance from many quarters when it began, it flourishes today. The same comity should prevail with photoduplication.

Repositories were naturally reluctant to photocopy in response to letters requesting copies of "everything you've got on my subject." Manuscript staffs did not have time to research for a correspondent and, quite properly, disparaged "mail-order research." The willingness of an institution to photocopy materials should not be subjected to this abuse. One way to minimize such impositions is for depositories to photoduplicate entire collections of high research potential and to provide proper indexes or finding aids with the collections, on the pattern of the microfilm publications currently cosponsored by the NHPC.

Since historians have been apprised of institutional holdings through the Hamer *Guide* and *NUCMC*, many of them have traveled to the repositories hoping to identify their research material and photocopy it. With repositories making rules on in-house photoduplication that vary so greatly, students need a handbook explaining each institution's policies. The explanations should include information on access to collections, on photocopying rules for those with their own equipment, and on the institution's photoduplicating facilities. Such information should be collected from researchers as well as from the repositories, for the latter often are more generous in their policy statements than in actual practice. This is especially true of foreign institutions.[6]

SECURITY AND ADMINISTRATIVE RESTRICTIONS

The second dimension of the obstacle historical researchers faced in gaining access to original sources was the security and administrative restrictions on certain government records. In recent years doctoral candidates have shown a marked preference for dissertations dealing with the immediate past. In each successive triennial *List of Doctoral Dissertations* issued since World War II, the number of titles dealing with the period since the

[6] Interview with Wood Gray, see Appendix C1.

Great Depression seems to have grown geometrically. During these years the federal government has taken an increasingly more significant role in American life, especially in the areas of national defense and foreign affairs. Since records relating to these fields bear high security classifications, the research interests of historians have intersected the period with the greatest restrictions on military and diplomatic records.

Two questions may be asked by the researcher needing access to classified records. One concerns misapplications of the system; the other, what can be done about them.[7] The current security classification system has three categories: confidential, secret, and top secret. These classifications are created and maintained by specified government officials, military and civilian, according to executive orders.[8] The government, sustained by tax-paying citizens, creates and classifies the records yet is often unresponsive to the need and rights of citizens to obtain information from the past that is vitally important to their present and future welfare. No rational person denies the need for genuine security measures, but the system should not be abused by government officials with vested interests in it. The officials should be dissuaded from the temptation to overclassify and should be willing to downgrade materials with no further security value.[9]

Except under pressure, the executive branch of the government has shown little concern for the classification system that it created. Congress, however, has made some effort to redress the situation and in 1966 revised the Administrative Procedure Act of 1946 in an attempt to make available to the general public more of the administratively restricted records of the executive branch. Excepted, naturally, were those documents with security restrictions: national defense and foreign policy records that pertain to a vast

[7] For the discussion of security restrictions, I am indebted to Paul J. Scheips, "Government Records and Their Use by Students."

[8] Cf. U.S. Department of the Army, Memorandum No. 345-3, "Policies and Procedures Governing Processing of Applications for Unofficial Historical Research in Classified Army Records," 14 Jan. 1966.

[9] Cf. Herbert Feis, "The Shackled Historian," *Foreign Affairs*, Vol. XLV, No. 2 (Jan., 1967), 332-43.

segment of recent United States history.[10] Some of this material will automatically lose its classification after a period of years, but other records, while losing their once high classification, will yet retain restrictions on use. Moreover, included in the exemption of records pertaining to national defense and foreign policy are those of America's "intelligence community," notably the Central Intelligence Agency (CIA). Like other governmental agencies, the CIA has a records-management program and regularly retires files to the Federal Records Centers. None of this material is available for research, nor is there any provision for its ever being accessible. Because of the important role the CIA has played in international affairs, we shall be deprived of the full account of some vital aspects of our government's activities if researchers never have access to CIA records. Of course, the passage of years could result in some change of policy.[11]

Although Congress has been willing to liberalize restrictions on records of executive agencies, it could well give attention to problems within its own House. Exhibiting the characteristically European proprietary attitude toward archives, the House of Representatives since 1789 has made no provision for research in its records. An individual wishing to consult them must petition the Clerk of the House. If permission is granted, it is a matter of privilege rather than right. Historians with wide experience in the archives of foreign nations have pointed out that, since even today the restriction on House records applies all the way back to 1789, there may be no parallel in the free world. Even Soviet policy on access to archives is liberal by comparison.

If there is abuse or maladministration of the security classification system and administrative restrictions on public records, historians and all others who believe that a democratic society requires constant vigilance by an informed public can at least seek redress of the abuses.[12] We must be constant and unrelenting in requiring those who maintain the restrictions, in cases where any

[10] Cf. Public Law 89-487 of July 4, 1966, which became effective one year later. 80 Stat. 250 (1966).

[11] Cf. Henry Steele Commager, "Should Historians Write Contemporary History?" *Saturday Review* (Feb. 12, 1966), 18–20, 47.

doubt arises, to justify their classifications.[13] In fact, this require-ment will strengthen the basic purpose of security and administra-tive classification because overclassification may eventually degrade the entire system, if it has not already done so.

Ideally, classifications should be exact when records are created; but corrective action may be initiated after records come into the National Archives and Records Service, although the required procedure is complicated.

The passage of time automatically downgrades classified rec-ords, but researchers usually do not feel that they can wait for the years to pass, especially if there are indications that records are being withheld unjustifiably. The individual is limited in what he can do, even if he is a Herbert Feis, a Henry Steele Commager, or a Carl T. Rowan. Patience and pressure, however, can produce results. More important, professional organizations should be ever alert to the needs of scholars for access to original sources.

But what of the graduate student who has few professional connections and little time, reputation, or knowledge of the secur-ity system? While doing research for a dissertation, he is in no position to undertake any reformation of the system. Too often students arrive in Washington with little or no knowledge of the availability of records related to their topics and rarely have any inkling of the difficulties of research on topics that cross agency lines. They often have assumed that if they had access to army records, they could also see those of the Department of Defense, Joint Chiefs of Staff, or the Department of State. Some of these materials are altogether inaccessible and others require individual security clearances, which can take months. If graduate students contemplate topics for which records may be classified, they should begin investigating the feasibility of the topics and initiating a security clearance well in advance of a trip to Washington. They must also realize that after they have done their research in classi-fied records, their notes will be checked and some may be with-

12 Cf. U.S. Congress, House of Representatives, *Report No. 1497*, 89th Cong., 2nd sess. (1966), p. 12.

13 Cf. Carl T. Rowan, "State Dept. and Information Law," [Washington] *Evening Star*, Jan. 17, 1968, p. A17.

held, and that frequently the agency granting access to classified material will require that the final manuscript be checked for security information.[14]

Some measures may be taken to lessen the difficulties students encounter in working with recent records. First, professors whose students choose topics related to governmental activities since World War II should familiarize themselves with the problems of access to the records so that they can offer sound advice. Some, in fact, have tried to steer students away from recent diplomatic history since State Department records are closed from 1945 on.[15] Because these records are opened only when all the volumes of *Foreign Relations* for a given year are published, historians should insist that the State Department accelerate the production of the *Foreign Relations* series. Secondly, students should assume responsibility for making specific inquiries related to their research projects. This should be done by correspondence before a trip to Washington. Thirdly, there should be a central agency in Washington to handle inquiries by researchers about access to all government records. Such an agency, if located high within the executive department and invested with adequate authority, could greatly simplify and facilitate research in official documents. One would hope that it could promote uniform and liberal policies of access to these records and that it could standardize security clearances. Finally, historical agencies within the government should prepare guides to records created by their organizations and suggest topics that could be developed on the basis of these records.[16]

COLLECTING PATTERNS

A further aspect of the problem of researchers' access to original sources relates to programs and policies for collecting these sources. Many persons decried the decentralization of manuscript collections, but the day is long past when all important manuscripts could or should be found along the East Coast; and there

[14] DA Memo No. 345-3, *loc. cit.*
[15] Interview with Norman A. Graebner, see Appendix C1.
[16] Cf. U.S. *Naval History Sources in the Washington Area and Suggested Research Subjects.*

is every likelihood that the pattern of regional collecting will continue to flourish. Consequently, we must make the best of the situation. With the publication of annual volumes of *NUCMC*, it should not be too difficult to keep track of the location of manuscripts. Merely knowing where manuscripts are should not be the only concern of historians, however. They should make every effort to have manuscripts placed in logical repositories. If the state of Nebraska has facilities for the proper maintenance and service of manuscripts related to the state (which it does), then those papers belong there, not in Florida, for example. The research community needs clear-cut lines of responsibility for collecting original sources. If repositories within each region fulfill their responsibility, there should be no reason for collections going to illogical places. If a region has no repositories with adequate collecting programs, however, it can expect its manuscripts to be attracted elsewhere. Aggressive collectors have had no reluctance to move into "underdeveloped areas," witness the examples of Lyman C. Draper and J. G. de Roulhac Hamilton, who in different generations skimmed the cream of southern manuscripts. Obviously, competition in manuscript collecting serves useful purposes as long as it does not devolve into senseless rivalry. Among its benefits are the alertness repositories must maintain if they are to build their collections logically and the sense of the value of manuscripts, without which important collections may be—and have been—tragically destroyed.

The great benefit of a system whereby repositories collect and maintain records properly would be the elimination of senseless rivalry for manuscripts. Repositories could then devote their energies to more constructive matters such as the preparation of finding aids, service to researchers, and microfilm publication of their original sources to help equalize scholarly opportunities throughout the nation. Another kind of rivalry, which may or may not be geographic and which results in considerable ill will, is financial. Institutions which have come on the collecting scene with appreciable sums of money have inflated the manuscript market tremendously. By paying for manuscripts that once would have been donated, they have seriously jeopardized the collecting programs of institutions that must depend upon gifts. Moreover, except in rare instances, money would be better spent for the care of historical manuscripts than for their purchase.[17] Historians would be remiss if they left these matters of the collecting and maintenance of manuscripts entirely to curators. As users of original sources, historians should take an active interest in their preservation. They should support repositories in their collecting programs, and they should be familiar with material their students use, whether at the county courthouse or the National Archives. In short, historians should not abdicate to curators their responsibilities connected with the materials forming the basis of their research.

COMMUNICATION PROBLEMS

The second major problem affecting research in United States history is the poor communication between professors of history and persons with other historical and curatorial vocations. Much of this difficulty in communication results from the changing status of teaching historians. In plotting this change, we find that World War II seems to be the watershed. In the early days of the profession, before higher education became a popular commodity, teaching posts were relatively few, and the production of history Ph.D.'s was similarly small. Benefiting from the powerful leadership and example of J. Franklin Jameson, those historians who chose nonteaching careers enjoyed ample professional prestige. Academicians such as Charles M. Andrews, Herbert Levi Osgood, Herbert E. Bolton, Samuel F. Bemis, and Carl Russell Fish scoured the Old World and the New for original sources related to American history and thereby reminded their colleagues of valuable historical work to be done outside the classroom. The 1920's was a period of boom in higher education, as in virtually every other aspect of American life, but the depression erased memories of academic prosperity. Many scholars who earned their Ph.D.'s in the 1930's had little chance of finding teaching posts and conse-

[17] See Appendix I for the preferences of interviewees for spending money on original sources.

quently went into other types of work. The original professional staff of the National Archives consisted largely of such men. After World War II came a new and greater surge of higher education. As enrollments increased, the demand for professors grew. The outbreak of the Korean War in 1950 and the graduation of the G.I. Bill generation about the same time drastically, but only temporarily, curtailed the need for professors. As a result of the demand, professors enjoyed new-found prestige. True, the greatest kudos went to scientists, but all in the academic train prospered. Changing societal values and a great deal more money made the professor a man who counted.

From his own standpoint, the professor was in a favorable position. He could follow his research interests, not being tied to an office routine (as are most nonacademic historians), and he could spend long vacations as he wished. In short, the academic life, for one suited to it, appeared much more satisfactory and rewarding than following a more circumscribed type of historical work. Since teaching has been the main vocation for historians, professors naturally projected academic values in their contacts with students; and, not unnaturally, professors were flattered when their best students indicated a desire to follow in their footsteps. Most graduate history students pursued the doctorate with the thought of going into teaching, for it represented the kind of life they wanted to lead. They were excited by working with ideas and with students. Because higher education seemed to be the natural vocational goal for graduate history students, they usually did not understand or appreciate other vocational opportunities. They often could not fathom why a colleague chose to become an archivist or documentary editor or to work in a historical society or library. Persons who have chosen these paths, in the thinking of most historians, have "left the profession."

These academic attitudes largely explain professors' seeming lack of appreciation for the work of historians who did not teach. Not only is it unfortunate when academic historians underestimate the importance of these nonteaching tasks, but the underestimation also can seriously hamper the effectiveness of the professors. Un-

327

less the professor fully appreciates the importance of the archivist and the manuscript librarian to his and his students' research, that research may suffer. And unless professors appreciate the benefits of the current letterpress publications of edited documents, their students suffer. This appreciation should be expressed in far more systematic use of the major sets than is currently apparent. The editorial product certainly justifies the considerable expense involved, but unless professors are aware of the possibilities these sets offer for their teaching, they fail to capitalize on a significant asset.

As a result of poor communication between historians following different vocations, many professors pay insufficient attention to the welfare of repositories, the research roots of the profession. All historians must recognize their common interests and work together to promote mutual goals. Professors should actively support programs for collecting, processing, and reporting manuscripts, and curators should reciprocate by providing optimum conditions and accommodations for research. The lack of co-operation that has too often characterized relations between researchers and custodians does discredit to both. Probably the greatest contribution professors could make toward these good relations would be to emphasize in their teaching the ultimate dependence of researchers on custodians of original sources and to give better training in the use of primary materials.

METHODOLOGICAL TRAINING

The third great need of students carrying on research in United States history is more adequate training in methodology. A sizable percentage of graduate students felt this need, and the testimony of curators indicated that many professors shared it. Indeed, if professors became better acquainted with such basic tools as bibliographies, finding aids, and government documents, they would be more effective in transmitting information about them to their students.

In addition to dealing with the craft's basic tools, methodological training—either in a course or in connection with a research seminar—should apprise students of the research foundations of the profession. It should deal with the creation and maintenance of manuscript collections and archives and offer students experiences using each. Students should learn to evaluate evidence from such repositories as well as from newspapers or from any other source. Professors ought to discuss explicitly the amenities of research in different types of institutions and should inform students of what they may expect to encounter at various repositories. They should require students to write ahead to institutions where they plan to do research, for repositories appreciate advance notice and can render better service because of it. Professors should always be willing to write letters of introduction for students embarking on research trips.

Professors should make certain that students whose research entails the use of social or behavioral science techniques get the appropriate training; indeed, if students want to employ any type of nonliterary evidence, they deserve proper guidance. Individual professors may not be equipped to offer either type of specialized training, but they can at least direct students to someone who is knowledgeable or to the appropriate literature. It seems far more logical for students to equip themselves with the specific tools they need rather than try to master an entire range of techniques for which they may have little practical use.

The same principle applies to training in documentary editing, although such training would benefit any researcher dealing with documents. Those who wish to study this specialty should have the opportunity; and since very few doctoral programs offer this training, the National Historical Publications Commission should certainly do so. Enough students and professors expressed enthusiasm for a seminar in documentary editing to make such a project a mandate for the NHPC, the logical agency to sponsor it. If the NHPC offers leadership in editorial training, the profession could experience a dramatic and salutary change in its attitude toward this area of scholarship.

Surely the homely and pedestrian admonitions, cautions, and instructions comprising methodological training are not the most exciting part of graduate instruction. They are not the substance of historical research and writing, merely the mechanics. But because they have been neglected, the substantive quality of current historial research is less than it should be. The emphasis on changing historical interpretations in American history has led to a neglect of basic research in the primary documents, and inadequate methodological training has resulted in faulty interpretations of what documents actually said. If professors would realize that their "own work" includes training apprentices in the methods of the profession, we could expect graduate students to waste less time and produce better results in their research. Consequently, we could expect young Ph.D.'s to have more respect for their training than many now have. Such increased respect would probably brighten a man's entire professional outlook. If the young Ph.D. who feels that his own training has been thorough and inspiring goes into teaching, the benefits should be manifest.

SPECIFIC NEEDS

Aside from these major research needs of the profession, a number of specific problems require attention. With the publication of the Hamer *Guide* and the initiation of the *National Union Catalog of Manuscript Collections*, research in American history took forward strides, yet much remains to be done with finding aids. Probably the most pressing need in this category is for publication of a simplified guide to government documents. Both librarians and historians dealing with printed government documents acknowledged the complexity and unwieldiness of those materials. Their formidability has discouraged many scholars from even attempting to learn how to use them systematically. Historians frequently threw themselves on the mercy of documents librarians, hoping to get the information they needed. Similarly, they usually left any instruction regarding these documents to librarians, too often providing no formal occasion for supplying this information, but trusting that students would somehow make out. Because many professors were not well acquainted with the corpus of government documents, they could not inform their students of

330

the great variety of information contained therein. Since this information pertains to many aspects of American history other than the political and diplomatic, all students of the American past should be aware of the research potentials in government documents. Such awareness could best be promoted by a simplified guide to the documents. As long as the current complexities persist, historians and other researchers are not likely to mine this rich vein effectively. The federal government should undertake, or a foundation should subsidize, the preparation of a comprehensive, uniform guide to government publications. An acute need exists for a definitive bibliography of the documents of the first fourteen Congresses, with library locations indicated, and for the launching of a microfilm edition of the complete texts.

As many historians have indicated, the continuation of *NUCMC* should have top priority among finding aids. Consequently, the profession should exert its influence to see that repositories have sufficient resources to report currently to *NUCMC*. Since many libraries and historical societies operate with limited budgets, they find it difficult to process their manuscripts and prepare reports for *NUCMC* or to compile institutional finding aids; yet their collections may have considerable research potential for historians outside their region. So that the entire research community may be served, it would be well for foundations to grant funds to such repositories for processing their collections and compiling finding aids.

For all the aid *NUCMC* and the Hamer *Guide* have given, considerable need still exists for guides to individual repositories. Such guides should be standardized so that researchers would not have to cope with a series of unique systems for reporting manuscript holdings. Foundations should consider the demand for institutional finding aids, along with the obligation of these institutions to keep current their reports to *NUCMC* or to make reports for the proposed revision of the Hamer *Guide*. Like a graduate student who welcomed any friendly guide through the overwhelming wilderness of original sources, all researchers benefit from finding aids. They can save countless hours and help historians to be more systematic and thorough in their investigations. Therefore, to promote more effective research and to enable repositories to gain control over their manuscripts, foundations should give high priority to grants that would aid institutions in processing and reporting their holdings.

While some repositories were unwilling to make their manuscripts widely available through photocopying, the vast quantity of original sources available on microforms attested the impact of microphotography on research. So that research with this medium may be as effective as possible, several technical improvements are necessary. Despite medical evidence that permanent optical damage is unlikely to result from reading microforms, the overwhelming testimony of researchers was that working with microforms caused some combination of eyestrain, headaches, dizziness, or nausea. These conditions made such research unpleasant, even if no permanent eye damage ensued. Since increasing work obviously will be done with microforms, intensive medical and engineering research should be conducted to perfect filming and reading devices. A technology sufficiently developed to explore the universe should be adequate to cope with the mechanics of historical research. Should the cost of the latter be considered too high, it must be remembered that this amount could only be infinitesimal when compared to that of basic research in the applied sciences.

If microforms and reading machines were perfected to eliminate eyestrain, the benefits of this type of research still could not be enjoyed until libraries had replaced outmoded equipment. Even today, libraries make work with microforms unnecessarily difficult by providing either antiquated or too few reading machines. If technical improvements on reading equipment result in significant increases in cost, individual libraries should not be expected to bear the entire burden. The federal government, through its library grants, or foundations should underwrite part of the expense of improving the mechanics of research. Every library serving a Ph.D. program in history should have its own photographic laboratory, equipped with a microfilm camera, darkroom, and copying machine. Too few now have these facilities.

Part of the effectiveness of research with microforms depends on how the repository administers them. Libraries which lump all microforms together usually offer the lowest grade of service to researchers. Their great temptation is to put a clerk rather than a professional who knows something of the contents in charge of the collection. The clerk often handles the material in a routine, mechanical fashion, offering little assistance to the researcher who needs to know about its substance. Consequently, libraries are most helpful when they administer microforms according to their content, not their physical properties. Thus, microfilmed manuscripts should be handled by the manuscript division, and microfilmed newspapers by the newspaper room.

Indexes, catalogs, or finding aids are also needed to help researchers in their use of microforms. If a researcher begins working with only a bare identification of the microform, his progress is tedious. Any supplementary information that assists him in locating his material facilitates his research. There is little logic, however, in each repository's catalogers analyzing its microforms, for this would represent a tremendous duplication of effort. It would be far more sensible for agencies publishing their original sources in microform to catalog the material and issue the catalogs with the microforms, as the Library of Congress classifies current American books and offers its catalog cards for sale. Since the cost of preparing catalogs or finding aids is high—often equal to that of the filming—grants should be available for this aspect of the work. In fact, the NHPC grants for microfilm publication explicitly provide for finding aids to be issued with the film. They also specify that each frame in these publications be numbered so that location and citation of documents will be simple. Cataloging or indexing microforms so greatly increases their utility for researchers that money spent on this phase of microform publication is extremely well invested.

While the cost of having large quantities of documents microfilmed may seem high to researchers, the cost usually is modest in comparison with that of facsimile photoreproductions. Most university libraries charge ten cents for each Xeroxed page, which is approximately twice the amount it costs the library if the machine

333

produces as many as two thousand copies a month. Few researchers complain about such a fee, although it makes large-scale photocopying rather expensive. Yet when institutions, particularly those supported by public funds, charge more than ten cents a page for electrostatic reproductions, the price is unreasonable and the institutions have placed an unduly high tariff on scholarly research. Naturally, some staff time is spent in removing and refiling documents as well as in photoduplicating, and this must be taken into account. But it appears that public institutions should be willing to assume some of this cost as part of their service to the taxpayers who support them.

Many of the foregoing recommendations are predicated upon the assumption that adequate funds can solve a great number of the problems researchers face, and one can say facilely that the government or private philanthropy should undertake numerous projects designed to meet research needs. The survey contends that these needs are urgent and that their solution would benefit not only historians but all who conduct research in the humanities or social sciences. The assumption is, moreover, that the response of the government and foundations to these needs will to a large measure reflect the values of our society. Historians must not wait passively for this reflection. They must work actively to see that their research needs are met, for through their research and publication historians can inform society of whence it came and what it has done. Only through this knowledge do men have hope for understanding the present and meeting the future.

Appendices

Institutions Visited

American Jewish Archives
American Philosophical Soc.
American Univ.
Amon Carter Museum of Western Art
Ball State Univ.
Boston Univ.
Brown Univ.
California, Univ. of
    Berkeley
    Los Angeles
    Riverside
    Santa Barbara
California State Archives
Case Institute of Technology
Catholic Univ. of America
Center for Research Libraries
Chicago, Univ. of
Chicago Historical Soc.
Church of Jesus Christ of Latter-day Saints, Office of Church
    Historian
Cincinnati, Univ. of
Cincinnati Historical Soc.
City Univ. of New York
Colorado Division of State Archives and Public Records
Colorado State Historical Soc.
Columbia Univ.
Denver, Univ. of
Duke Univ.
Emory Univ.
Federal Records Centers

Atlanta
Boston
Chicago
Fort Worth
Kansas City, Missouri
New York City
San Francisco
Seattle
Florida State Univ.
George Peabody Coll. for Teachers
Georgetown Univ.
George Washington Univ.
Georgia State Archives
Harvard Univ.
    Harvard Graduate School of Business Administration
Hawaii, Univ. of
Hawaii State Archives
Hawaiian Mission Children's Soc.
Houston, Univ. of
Huntington Lib.
Illinois, Univ. of
Indiana Univ.
Inter-University Consortium for Political Research
Iowa, Univ. of
John Carter Brown Lib.
Johns Hopkins Univ.
Kansas, Univ. of
Kansas State Historical Soc.
Kentucky, Univ. of
Library Company of Philadelphia
Library of Congress
Louisiana State Univ.
Maryland, Univ. of
Massachusetts, Univ. of
Massachusetts Historical Soc.
Michigan, Univ. of
    Michigan Historical Collections
    William L. Clements Lib.

Michigan State Univ.
Minnesota, Univ. of
Minnesota Historical Soc.
Missouri, Univ. of
Montana Historical Soc.
National Archives and Records Service
Nebraska, Univ. of
Nebraska State Historical Soc.
Newberry Lib.
New Mexico, Univ. of
New York Public Lib.
New York Univ.
North Carolina, Univ. of
Northwestern Univ.
Notre Dame, Univ. of
Ohio Historical Soc.
Ohio State Univ.
Oklahoma, Univ. of
Oregon, Univ. of
Pacific, Univ. of the
Pennsylvania, Univ. of
Princeton Univ.
Rhode Island State Archives
Rice Univ.
Rutgers—The State Univ.
Saint Louis Univ.
South Carolina, Univ. of
South Carolina Archives Dept.
Southern California, Univ. of
Stanford Univ.
Tennessee State Lib. and Archives
Texas, Univ. of
Texas Christian Univ.
Texas State Lib.
Texas Technological Coll.
Harry S Truman Lib.
Tulane Univ.
Utah, Univ. of

Utah State Historical Soc.
Vanderbilt Univ.
    Joint Universities Lib.
Virginia, Univ. of
Washington, Univ. of
Washington Univ.
Western Reserve Univ.
Wisconsin, State Historical Soc. of
Wisconsin, Univ. of
Wyoming, Univ. of
Wyoming State Archives and Historical Dept.
Yale Univ.

APPENDIX B

Questionnaires and Interview Schedules

This "Questionnaire for Departments of History Offering the Ph.D." is the model for all the survey's questionnaires and interview schedules. Making revisions appropriate to each recipient group, the survey also sent the questionnaires to history departments offering a terminal M.A., historical societies, and librarians at universities offering both the Ph.D. and the M.A. in history. The survey sent these questionnaires to institutions it did not visit. In three cases, professors from visited universities filled them out. The survey had different interview schedules for the three groups of interviewees: professors supervising graduate research; graduate students; and librarians, archivists, and directors of historical societies.

Response to the questionnaires was most encouraging, reflecting concern with the problems identified by the survey. Twenty-seven departments of history offering the Ph.D. replied, giving the survey coverage of 97 of the 114 doctoral programs in American history (85 per cent). Sixty-two departments providing a terminal M.A. in history responded. Eighty-one libraries at universities with Ph.D. and M.A. programs in history returned questionnaires. From the nonacademic libraries, historical societies, and archives, there were 22 replies. Names of these institutions and respondents are in Appendix D.

SURVEY ON THE USE OF ORIGINAL SOURCES IN
GRADUATE HISTORY TRAINING

NATIONAL HISTORICAL PUBLICATIONS COMMISSION

Walter Rundell, Jr.
Survey Director

National Archives Building
Washington, D.C. 20408
202—962-5631

Questionnaire for Departments of History Offering the Ph.D.

1. What general types of original sources—manuscript, printed, or microcopy—are available for research at the university?

_____

_____

_____

_____

2. On what levels are original sources used?
   _____ a. Dissertation
   _____ b. Master's thesis
   _____ c. Seminar papers
   _____ d. Research papers for classes
   _____ e. Undergraduate training. If for undergraduate training, in what way? _____

3. Is there a course in historical method in which students are trained in the use of original sources, including microfilm reproduction and manuscripts? _____ If not, do students receive any separate methodological training? _____ If so, please explain.

_____

_____

_____

4. Please check which of these printed original sources graduate students use.
   _____ a. Papers of famous Americans (National Historical Publications Commission projects) or other letterpress publications of edited documents
   _____ b. *Foreign Relations* series
   _____ c. *Territorial Papers*
   _____ d. Congressional serial set (including the *Record* and the full series of the Senate and House documents)
   _____ e. *Official Records of the War of the Rebellion*
   _____ f. William Jenkins, ed., *Early State Records* (filmed)
   _____ g. James D. Richardson, ed., *Messages and Papers of the Presidents*
   _____ h. *Public Papers of the Presidents* (Harry S Truman on)
   _____ i. Navy publications, such as *Quasi-War with France, Barbary War*
   _____ j. Congressional committee hearings

_____ k. Other governmental documents

_____ l. Any others

Do you have any comment on the usefulness of any of these sources?

_____

_____

5. What kind of training do graduate students need to use printed original sources effectively? _____

_____

_____

_____

6. Local sources:
   a. Are such local sources as wills, tax records, newspapers, artistic and architectural evidence, deeds, church records, court records, voting records, business records, etc. used, and to what extent?

   _____

   _____

   b. Are students familiar with various social and behavioral science techniques (e.g., those listed below) so that they can extract meaningful data from such original sources?

   _____ (1) Sampling

   _____ (2) Career line analysis

   _____ (3) Reference group theory

   _____ (4) Guttman scale analysis

   _____ (5) Type, role, image, class, et al.

   _____ (6) Content analysis

   c. If students do not have or do not receive training in the above techniques, what is the attitude of the history faculty toward such techniques?

   _____

   _____

7. Do the physical arrangements of the research facilities in the library and the hours of access make it easy for graduate students to do research?

_____

_____

8. Does your department have good working relations with whatever libraries, historical societies, or state archives your graduate students have an opportunity to use? _____

_____

9. If original sources are not available at the university, please indicate where students are likely to go (please specify where appropriate):
   a. Library of Congress _____
   b. National Archives _____
   c. Other university libraries _____
   d. State libraries, archives, and historical societies _____

   e. Federal Records Centers _____
   f. Presidential libraries _____
   g. Smithsonian Institution _____
   h. Private research libraries—Huntington, Newberry, et al. _____

   i. Museums or art galleries _____
   j. Public libraries _____
10. Travel:
    a. Does the university have travel funds for students who must do extra-mural research? _____ How much? _____
    b. What percentage of graduate students have to travel to do research? _____
11. Guides to original sources:
    a. How useful and adequate are the general guides, finding aids, and indexes (those which purport to give an overview of manuscript collections throughout the country) in directing students to original sources? _____

    b. How useful are the National Archives guides in directing students to collections in the National Archives? _____

    c. What more is needed? What will be the most helpful, i.e., in what priority should finding aids—either in the National Archives or elsewhere—be produced? _____

    _____

344

    d. Is there a guide to your own manuscript collection ? _____ If not, is one planned? _____

    e. If you have a manuscript collection, is it being reported to the *National Union Catalog of Manuscript Collections*? _____

12. How much money is available in the library, graduate school, or departmental budget each year for acquisition of original sources? _____ How is the money spent?

    a. Manuscripts _____

    b. Photocopies (any form of photoduplication—microfilm, microcard, microfiche, Xerox, photostat, etc.) _____ When buying photocopy, which of the following are you more likely to get:

        (1) an entire set or series of papers? _____

        (2) documents selected from various sources to focus on a particular historical problem? _____

    c. Letterpress publications of edited documents _____

    d. Can a professor or graduate student usually depend on the institution to support his research project by purchasing the specific resources he needs? _____

13. Problems with the use of photocopied (any form of photoduplication) material:

    a. Mechanical _____

    b. Copyright _____

    c. Cataloging. When the library gets photocopied material, how is it cataloged? Is any attempt made to describe the contents, or is a roll of microfilm identified only by type?

_____

    In other words, does the library handle photocopy so that potential users can get at the material with some facility? _____

    d. Is your institution willing to make photocopies of manuscripts (if any) available to individuals or other institutions? _____ If willing, does this extend to a complete set of papers? _____ If to other institutions, do you expect them to contribute anything to help defray your cost of acquiring the manuscripts? _____

14. Assuming that large amounts of money were granted to make original sources readily available for graduate historical research (and assuming that the funds would go to a central agency for administration rather than being handled by individual universi-

ties), in what priority would you prefer to see the money spent so that the research dollar will do the most good? Your answer should consider over-all professional welfare, and not that of a particular institution.

_____ a. Photocopying original sources, with extensive finding aids provided?

_____ b. Letterpress publication of carefully edited documents?

_____ c. Acquiring and processing actual manuscripts?

15. What training is offered in historical (documentary) editing?

_____

_____

If none is offered, do you think this would be a helpful part of graduate training? _____

16. Can an editorial project qualify as a dissertation? _____

17. How might the National Historical Publications Commission assist in training historical editors?

_____

_____

_____

Signature of Respondent_____
Institution_____

APPENDIX C

List of Interviewees

1. *Professors*

Name	Institution	Date
Adelson, Howard L.	City Univ. of New York	7-21-66
Albertson, Dean	Univ. of Massachusetts	7-15-66
Alden, John R.	Duke Univ.	11-30-65
Allen, Jack	George Peabody Coll.	12-15-65
Ambrose, Stephen E.	Johns Hopkins Univ.	11-10-65
Anderson, George L.	Univ. of Kansas	4-22-66
Anthon, Carl G.	American Univ.	2-18-66
Atherton, Lewis E.	Univ. of Missouri	4-20-66
Bailyn, Bernard	Harvard Univ.	10-26-65
Bannon, John F., S.J.	Saint Louis Univ.	4-17-66
Barker, Charles A.	Johns Hopkins Univ.	11-9-65
Bartlett, Richard A.	Florida State Univ.	7-30-66
Bates, J. Leonard	Univ. of Illinois	5-26-66
Baxter, Maurice G.	Indiana Univ.	9-20-66
Beaver, Daniel R.	Univ. of Cincinnati	4-27-66
Bergeron, Paul H.	Vanderbilt Univ.	12-14-65
Berkhofer, Robert F., Jr.	Univ. of Minnesota	5-20-66
Bestor, Arthur	Univ. of Washington	10-20-65
Bierck, Harold A.	Univ. of North Carolina	12-3-65
Billington, Ray A.	Huntington Lib.	1-21-66
Bingham, Edwin R.	Univ. of Oregon	10-19-65
Bloch, Julius M.	City Univ. of New York	7-21-66
Blum, Jerome	Princeton Univ.	9-29-66
Blum, John Morton	Yale Univ.	1-17-67
Bogue, Allan G.	Univ. of Wisconsin	5-24-66
Bonner, Thomas N.	Univ. of Cincinnati	4-27-66
Boskin, Joseph	Univ. of Southern California	1-20-66

347

Boyd, Julian P.	Princeton Univ.	9-29-66
Bradley, Harold W.	Vanderbilt Univ.	12-13-65
Braeman, John	Univ. of Nebraska	5-16-66
Breck, Allen D.	Univ. of Denver	6-14-66
Bridges, Hal	Univ. of California, Riverside	1-31-66
Brown, Richard M.	Rutgers—The State Univ.	9-28-66
Brown, Robert E.	Michigan State Univ.	8-20-66
Brown, Roger H.	American Univ.	2-21-66
Buhite, Russell D.	Univ. of Oklahoma	3-7-66
Burke, Robert E.	Univ. of Washington	10-21-65
Burnham, John C.	Ohio State Univ.	8-16-66
Caldemeyer, Richard H.	Ball State Univ.	9-22-66
Caldwell, Russell L.	Univ. of Southern California	1-20-66
Callcott, Wilfrid H.	Univ. of South Carolina	12-7-65
Carmony, Donald F.	Indiana Univ.	9-20-66
Carosso, Vincent P.	New York Univ.	7-20-66
Carroll, John A.	Texas Christian Univ.	3-3-66
Caughey, John W.	Univ. of California, Los Angeles	1-19-66
Cave, Alfred A.	Univ. of Utah	6-21-66
Chambers, Clarke A.	Univ. of Minnesota	5-19-66
Chambers, William N.	Washington Univ.	4-19-66
Chandler, Alfred D., Jr.	Johns Hopkins Univ.	11-10-65
Clark, John	Univ. of Kansas	4-22-66
Clark, Thomas D.	Indiana Univ.	9-21-66
Clubb, Jerome M.	Inter-University Consortium for Political Research (Univ. of Michigan)	8-18-66
Cochran, Thomas C.	Univ. of Pennsylvania	8-25-66
Colbourn, H. Trevor	Indiana Univ.	9-21-66
Collins, Robert	Univ. of California, Santa Barbara	1-17-66
Connor, Seymour V.	Texas Technological Coll.	3-2-66
Cooper, Kenneth S.	George Peabody Coll.	12-15-65
Cotner, Robert C.	Univ. of Texas	3-11-66
Cowing, Cedric B.	Univ. of Hawaii	1-25-66
Cramer, Carl H.	Western Reserve Univ.	6-23-66
Crane, Theodore R.	Univ. of Denver	6-14-66
Craven, Avery O.	Univ. of Wisconsin	5-23-66
Craven, W. Frank	Princeton Univ.	9-29-66

Cross, Robert D.	Columbia Univ.	7-18-66
Cunningham, Noble E., Jr.	Univ. of Missouri	4-20-66
Curti, Merle	Univ. of Wisconsin	5-24-66
Dalgliesh, W. Harold	Univ. of Utah	6-21-66
Davis, Robert C.	Case Institute of Technology	6-24-66
DeConde, Alexander	Univ. of California, Santa Barbara	1-17-66
DeNovo, John A.	Univ. of Wisconsin	5-24-66
DeRosier, Arthur H., Jr.	Univ. of Oklahoma	3-7-66
De Santis, Vincent P.	Univ. of Notre Dame	9-23-66
Divine, Robert A.	Univ. of Texas	3-11-66
Donald, David	Johns Hopkins Univ.	11-10-65
Douglass, Elisha P.	Univ. of North Carolina	12-2-65
Duffy, John	Tulane Univ.	3-18-66
Duncan, R. Bingham	Emory Univ.	12-9-65
Dunn, Richard S.	Univ. of Pennsylvania	8-25-66
Dupree, A. Hunter	Univ. of California, Berkeley	1-11-66
Durkin, Joseph T., S.J.	Georgetown Univ.	2-16-66
Dykstra, Robert R.	Univ. of New Mexico	2-28-66
Eaton, Clement	Univ. of Kentucky	9-19-66
Erickson, A. B.	Western Reserve Univ.	6-23-66
Ezell, John S.	Univ. of Oklahoma	3-8-66
Farrell, John T.	Catholic Univ. of America	3-22-66
Fehrenbacher, Don E.	Stanford Univ.	1-14-66
Ferrell, Robert H.	Indiana Univ.	9-21-66
Fite, Gilbert C.	Univ. of Oklahoma	3-8-66
Fowler, Dorothy Ganfield	City Univ. of New York	7-21-66
Franklin, John Hope	Univ. of Chicago	8-22-66
Freidel, Frank	Harvard Univ.	10-26-65
Frost, Richard	Univ. of New Mexico	3-1-66
Gardner, Lloyd C.	Rutgers—The State Univ.	9-28-66
Gatell, Frank O.	Univ. of California, Los Angeles	1-19-66
Gaustad, Edwin S.	Univ. of California, Riverside	1-31-66
Gelfand, Lawrence E.	Univ. of Iowa	5-18-66
Gibson, Arrell M.	Univ. of Oklahoma	3-8-66
Glad, Paul W.	Univ. of Maryland	2-17-66
Gleason, J. Philip	Univ. of Notre Dame	9-23-66
Going, Allen J.	Univ. of Houston	3-15-66

Gondos, Dorothy D.	American Univ.	2-18-66
Graebner, Norman A.	Univ. of Illinois	5-27-66
Grantham, Dewey W., Jr.	Vanderbilt Univ.	12-14-65
Graves, Lawrence L.	Texas Technological Coll.	3-2-66
Gray, Wood	George Washington Univ.	2-23-66
Green, Fletcher M.	Univ. of North Carolina	12-2-65
Gressley, Gene M.	Univ. of Wyoming	6-13-66
Griffin, Clifford S.	Univ. of Kansas	4-22-66
Hair, William I.	Florida State Univ.	7-29-66
Handlin, Oscar	Harvard Univ.	10-25-65
Hanna, William S., Jr.	Univ. of Oregon	10-18-65
Harlan, Louis R.	Univ. of Cincinnati	4-29-66
Hasting, Martin F., S.J.	Saint Louis Univ.	4-18-66
Haynes, Robert V.	Univ. of Houston	3-15-66
Heinrichs, Waldo H., Jr.	Johns Hopkins Univ.	11-9-65
Hidy, Ralph W.	Harvard Graduate School of Business Administration	10-27-65
Higginbotham, Don	Louisiana State Univ.	3-16-66
Higginbotham, Sanford W.	Rice Univ.	3-14-66
Hill, Peter P.	George Washington Univ.	2-23-66
Hine, Robert V.	Univ. of California, Riverside	1-31-66
Hogan, William R.	Tulane Univ.	3-18-66
Holley, I. B., Jr.	Duke Univ.	11-30-65
Hollingsworth, J. Rogers	Univ. of Wisconsin	5-24-66
Hollis, Daniel W.	Univ. of South Carolina	12-7-65
Hollon, W. Eugene	Univ. of Oklahoma	3-7-66
Holt, W. Stull	Univ. of Washington	10-21-65
Hoover, Dwight W.	Ball State Univ.	9-22-66
Hopkins, James F.	Univ. of Kentucky	9-19-66
Hutchinson, William T.	Univ. of Chicago	8-22-66
Hutchison, William R.	American Univ.	2-25-66
Huthmacher, J. Joseph	Georgetown Univ.	2-16-66
James, Sydney V., Jr.	Univ. of Iowa	5-18-66
Jensen, Merrill	Univ. of Wisconsin	5-24-66
Johannsen, Robert W.	Univ. of Illinois	5-26-66
Johnson, Arthur M.	Harvard Graduate School of Business Administration	10-26-65
Johnson, Donald D.	Univ. of Hawaii	1-25-66

Jones, Robert H.	Western Reserve Univ.	6-23-66
Jordan, Philip D.	Univ. of Minnesota	5-20-66
Karl, Barry D.	Washington Univ.	4-19-66
Karnes, Thomas L.	Tulane Univ.	3-17-66
Kershner, Frederick D., Jr.	Columbia Univ. Teachers Coll.	7-18-66
Kirkendall, Richard S.	Univ. of Missouri	4-20-66
Klingberg, Frank W.	Univ. of North Carolina	12-2-65
Kolko, Gabriel	Univ. of Pennsylvania	8-25-66
Kranzberg, Melvin	Case Institute of Technology	6-24-66
Kuhn, Madison	Michigan State Univ.	8-19-66
Labaree, Leonard W.	Yale Univ.	7-12-66
Lamar, Howard R.	Yale Univ.	7-12-66
Land, Aubrey C.	Univ. of Maryland	2-15-66
Langley, Harold D.	Catholic Univ. of America	3-22-66
Larson, T. A.	Univ. of Wyoming	6-13-66
Lathrop, Barnes F.	Univ. of Texas	3-10-66
Layton, Edwin T.	Case Institute of Technology	6-24-66
Leach, Douglas E.	Vanderbilt Univ.	12-13-65
Lefler, Hugh T.	Univ. of North Carolina	12-2-65
Leopold, Richard W.	Northwestern Univ.	9-27-66
Lewis, Gene D.	Univ. of Cincinnati	4-27-66
Lieuwen, Edwin	Univ. of New Mexico	2-28-66
Link, Arthur S.	Princeton Univ.	9-29-66
Livermore, Shaw, Jr.	Univ. of Michigan	8-18-66
Loos, John L.	Louisiana State Univ.	3-16-66
McAvoy, Thomas T., C.S.C.	Univ. of Notre Dame	9-23-66
McCormick, Richard P.	Rutgers—The State Univ.	9-28-66
McCoy, Donald R.	Univ. of Kansas	4-22-66
McGiffert, Michael	Univ. of Denver	6-14-66
McLaughlin, Charles C.	American Univ.	2-21-66
McLoughlin, Wm. G., Jr.	Brown Univ.	7-13-66
McVaugh, Michael	Univ. of North Carolina	12-2-65
Madsen, Brigham	Univ. of Utah	6-21-66
Margulies, Herbert F.	Univ. of Hawaii	1-24-66
Mason, Philip P.	Wayne State Univ.	10-5-66
Masterson, W. H.	Rice Univ.	3-14-66

May, Ernest R.	Harvard Univ.	10-27-65
May, Henry F.	Univ. of California, Berkeley	1-12-66
Mayo, Bernard	Univ. of Virginia	11-17-65
Merrill, Horace S.	Univ. of Maryland	2-14-66
Merriman, Howard M.	George Washington Univ.	2-23-66
Meyer, Donald	Univ. of California, Los Angeles	1-18-66
Miller, Howard S.	Univ. of Southern California	1-20-66
Moody, Robert E.	Boston Univ.	10-28-65
Mooney, Chase C.	Indiana Univ.	9-20-66
Moule, Malcolm	Univ. of the Pacific	1-10-66
Mowry, George E.	Univ. of California, Los Angeles	1-18-66
Murphy, Paul L.	Univ. of Minnesota	5-20-66
Murrin, John M.	Washington Univ.	4-19-66
Nagel, Paul C.	Univ. of Kentucky	9-19-66
Nelson, John K.	Univ. of North Carolina	12-1-65
Nevins, Allan	Huntington Lib.	1-21-66
Noble, David W.	Univ. of Minnesota	5-19-66
Noggle, Burl	Louisiana State Univ.	3-16-66
Nunn, W. C.	Texas Christian Univ.	3-3-66
Ochs, Robert D.	Univ. of South Carolina	12-7-65
Olson, James C.	Univ. of Nebraska	5-16-66
Ostrander, Gilman M.	Michigan State Univ.	8-19-66
Parker, Harold T.	Duke Univ.	12-1-65
Persons, Stow	Univ. of Iowa	5-18-66
Peterson, Merrill D.	Univ. of Virginia	11-16-65
Peterson, Robert L.	Univ. of Oregon	10-19-65
Pierson, George W.	Yale Univ.	7-12-66
Pletcher, David M.	Indiana Univ.	9-21-66
Pomerantz, Sidney I.	City Univ. of New York	7-21-66
Pomeroy, Earl	Univ. of Oregon	10-18-65
Porter, Kenneth W.	Univ. of Oregon	10-18-65
Posey, Walter B.	Emory Univ.	12-9-65
Potter, David M.	Stanford Univ.	1-13-66
Pressly, Thomas J.	Univ. of Washington	10-21-65
Procter, Ben	Texas Christian Univ.	3-4-66
Rabun, James Z.	Emory Univ.	12-8-65
Rankin, Hugh F.	Tulane Univ.	3-18-66

Rawley, James A.	Univ. of Nebraska	5-16-66
Richardson, Joe M.	Florida State Univ.	7-28-66
Risjord, Norman K.	Univ. of Wisconsin	5-23-66
Robinson, W. Stitt	Univ. of Kansas	4-23-66
Rogers, George C., Jr.	Univ. of South Carolina	12-7-65
Rohrbough, Malcolm J.	Univ. of Iowa	5-18-66
Saloutos, Theodore	Univ. of California, Los Angeles	1-19-66
Saum, Lewis O.	Univ. of Washington	10-21-65
Savelle, Max	Univ. of Washington	10-20-65
Schutz, John A.	Univ. of Southern California	1-20-66
Sellers, Charles G., Jr.	Univ. of California, Berkeley	1-12-66
Shannon, David A.	Univ. of Maryland	2-15-66
Shenton, James P.	Columbia Univ.	7-19-66
Siney, Marion C.	Western Reserve Univ.	6-23-66
Smelser, Marshall	Univ. of Notre Dame	9-23-66
Sosin, Jack M.	Univ. of Nebraska	5-16-66
Sparks, David S.	Univ. of Maryland	2-14-66
Spear, Allan H.	Univ. of Minnesota	5-19-66
Spence, Clark C.	Univ. of Illinois	5-27-66
Stampp, Kenneth M.	Univ. of California, Berkeley	1-12-66
Stearns, Raymond P.	Univ. of Illinois	5-26-66
Stevens, Harry R.	Rutgers—The State Univ.	9-28-66
Stewart, John Hall	Western Reserve Univ.	6-23-66
Still, Bayrd	New York Univ.	7-20-66
Stoeckel, Althea L.	Ball State Univ.	9-22-66
Strayer, Joseph R.	Princeton Univ.	5-6-67
Sutton, Robert M.	Univ. of Illinois	5-27-66
Swint, Henry L.	Vanderbilt Univ.	12-13-65
Thomson, Robert Polk	George Peabody Coll.	12-15-65
Tindall, George B.	Univ. of North Carolina	12-3-65
Tinsley, James A.	Univ. of Houston	3-15-66
Tryon, Warren S.	Boston Univ.	10-28-65
Vandiver, Frank E.	Rice Univ.	3-14-66
Van Tassel, David D.	Univ. of Texas	3-10-66
Vaughan, Alden T.	Columbia Univ.	7-18-66
Ver Steeg, Clarence L.	Northwestern Univ.	9-27-66
Wallace, Ernest	Texas Technological Coll.	3-2-66

Walsh, Richard	Georgetown Univ.	2-16-66
Warner, Sam Bass, Jr.	Washington Univ.	4-19-66
Watson, Richard L., Jr.	Duke Univ.	11-29-65
Weaver, Herbert	Vanderbilt Univ.	12-13-65
Weisenburger, Francis P.	Ohio State Univ.	8-15-66
White, Philip L.	Univ. of Texas	3-10-66
Willcox, William B.	Univ. of Michigan	8-17-66
Williams, David Alan	Univ. of Virginia	11-17-65
Williams, T. Harry	Louisiana State Univ.	3-16-66
Wiltz, John E.	Indiana Univ.	9-20-66
Woody, Robert H.	Duke Univ.	11-30-65
Worcester, Donald E.	Texas Christian Univ.	3-4-66
Wright, Deil S.	Univ. of Iowa	9-14-65
Wyllie, Irvin G.	Univ. of Wisconsin	5-23-66
Young, James Harvey	Emory Univ.	12-8-65
Younger, Edward	Univ. of Virginia	11-16-65
Younger, Richard D.	Univ. of Houston	3-15-66
Zahniser, Marvin R.	Ohio State Univ.	8-15-66

2 a. *Academic Librarians and Archivists*

Adams, Thomas R.	John Carter Brown Lib.	7-13-66
Barclay, Julius P.	Stanford Univ. Lib.	1-14-66
Baughman, Roland	Columbia Univ. Lib.	7-18-66
Baumgartner, Robert W.	Northwestern Univ. Lib.	9-27-66
Bedsole, Vergil L.	Louisiana State Univ. Lib.	3-16-66
Bentz, Dale M.	Univ. of Iowa Lib.	5-18-66
Bernard, Richard F.	Univ. of Minnesota Lib.	5-19-66
Berner, Richard C.	Univ. of Washington Lib.	10-20-65
Berthel, John H.	Johns Hopkins Univ. Lib.	11-9-65
Bethea, Florence S.	Florida State Univ. Lib.	7-29-66
Bishop, Martha	Rice Univ. Lib.	3-14-66
Bond, W. H.	Houghton Lib., Harvard Univ.	10-26-65
Boss, Richard W.	Univ. of Utah Lib.	6-21-66
Brady, Rose M.	Saint Louis Univ. Lib.	4-18-66
Brichford, Maynard J.	Univ. of Illinois Lib.	5-26-66
Bridges, Ella Mae	Univ. of Texas Lib.	3-11-66

Bridgwater, Dorothy	Yale Univ. Lib.	7-21-66
Broadfoot, Winston	George Washington Flowers Collection, Duke Univ. Lib.	12-1-65
Brodhead, Michael	Univ. of Kansas Lib.	4-22-66
Bryant, Douglas W.	Harvard Univ. Lib.	10-27-65
Buckman, Thomas R.	Univ. of Kansas Lib.	4-22-66
Bull, Jacqueline	Univ. of Kentucky Lib.	9-19-66
Bupp, Reno W.	Florida State Univ. Lib.	7-29-66
Bush, Douglas	Univ. of Utah Lib.	6-21-66
Case, Leland D.	California Historical Foundation, Univ. of the Pacific Lib.	1-10-66
Clapp, Maxine B.	Univ. of Minnesota Lib.	5-19-66
Clark, Alexander	Princeton Univ. Lib.	9-30-66
Colton, Flora D.	Univ. of Pennsylvania Lib.	8-26-66
Craig, E. L.	Indiana Univ. Lib.	9-21-66
Craig, Hardin, Jr.,	Rice Univ. Lib.	3-14-66
Daly, Lowrie J., S.J.	Saint Louis Univ. Lib.	4-18-66
Davis, Mary	Emory Univ. Lib.	12-8-65
Day, Dorothy L.	Brown Univ. Lib.	7-13-66
Dean, Elva C.	Univ. of Utah Lib.	6-21-66
Dix, William S.	Princeton Univ. Lib.	9-30-66
Downs, R. B.	Univ. of Illinois Lib.	5-26-66
Dunlap, Leslie W.	Univ. of Iowa Lib.	5-18-66
Dunn, Roy Sylvan	Texas Technological Coll. Lib.	3-2-66
Eaton, Andrew J.	Washington Univ. Lib.	4-19-66
Erlandson, Ruth M.	Ohio State Univ. Lib.	8-16-66
Ermatinger, Charles J.	Saint Louis Univ. Lib.	4-18-66
Estes, David E.	Emory Univ. Lib.	12-8-65
Ewing, Jerry	Washington Univ. Lib.	4-19-66
Faris, Mary Charlotte	Texas Christian Univ. Lib.	3-4-66
Fingerson, Ronald	Univ. of Iowa Lib.	5-18-66
Folmer, Fred	Univ. of Texas Lib.	3-11-66
Forth, Stuart	Univ. of Kentucky Lib.	9-19-66
Frantz, Ray W., Jr.	Univ. of Wyoming Lib.	6-13-66
Freudenberg, Anne	Univ. of Virginia Lib.	11-17-65
Frost, John E.	New York Univ. Lib.	7-20-66

355

Fussler, Herman H.	Univ. of Chicago Lib.	8-23-66
Gosnell, Charles F.	New York Univ. Lib.	7-20-66
Gotlieb, Howard B.	Boston Univ. Lib.	10-28-65
Gracy, David B., II	Texas Technological Coll. Lib.	3-2-66
Grady, Marion B.	Ball State Univ. Lib.	9-22-66
Griffith, Connie G.	Tulane Univ. Lib.	3-18-66
Haas, Warren J.	Univ. of Pennsylvania Lib.	8-26-66
Hamlin, Arthur T.	Univ. of Cincinnati Lib.	4-27-66
Hansen, Ralph W.	Stanford Univ. Lib.	1-14-66
Harleston, Rebekah	Univ. of Kentucky Lib.	9-19-66
Hatch, Benton L.	Univ. of Massachusetts Lib.	7-15-66
Hathaway, Christine D.	Brown Univ. Lib.	7-13-66
Hayes, Isabella M.	Univ. of Maryland Lib.	2-17-66
Holley, Edward G.	Univ. of Houston Lib.	3-15-66
Inabinett, E. L.	South Caroliniana Lib., Univ. of South Carolina Lib.	12-6-65
Irvine, Kate T.	Univ. of Kentucky Lib.	9-19-66
Ishimatsu, Chizuko	Univ. of Utah Lib.	6-21-66
Jacobs, Claramae	Univ. of South Carolina Lib.	12-6-65
Jameson, Harriet C.	Univ. of Michigan Lib.	8-17-66
Jeffs, Joseph E.	Georgetown Univ. Lib.	2-16-66
Johns, Francis A.	Rutgers—The State Univ. Lib.	9-28-66
Johnson, Eugene M.	Univ. of Nebraska Lib.	5-17-66
Johnson, Ross S.	Ball State Univ. Lib.	9-22-66
Jolly, David	Northwestern Univ. Lib.	9-27-66
Jones, James V.	Saint Louis Univ. Lib.	4-18-66
Karlson, Marjorie E.	Washington Univ. Lib.	4-19-66
Kaser, David	Joint Univ. Libs. (Nashville, Tenn.)	12-13-65
Kelley, David Otis	Univ. of New Mexico Lib.	3-1-66
Kelley, H. Gilbert	Rutgers—The State Univ. Lib.	9-28-66
Kennedy, Jo	Florida State Univ. Lib.	7-29-66
Kielman, Chester V.	Univ. of Texas Lib.	3-10-66
Koch, Henry C.	Michigan State Univ. Lib.	8-19-66
Kritzer, Hyman W.	Ohio State Univ. Lib.	8-16-66
Kuethe, J. Louis	Johns Hopkins Univ. Lib.	11-9-65

Kurth, William H.	Washington Univ. Lib.	4-19-66
Kurtz, Helen G.	Brown Univ. Lib.	7-13-66
LaBissoniere, William	Univ. of Minnesota Lib.	5-19-66
Lang, Elfrieda	Indiana Univ. Lib.	9-21-66
Lang, Robert P.	Univ. of California, Riverside Lib.	1-31-66
Lightfoot, Helen M.	Indiana Univ. Lib.	9-21-66
Littlewood, John M.	Univ. of Illinois Lib.	5-26-66
Lohf, Kenneth	Columbia Univ. Lib.	7-18-66
Lough, Margaret E.	Johns Hopkins Univ. Lib.	11-9-65
Lovett, Robert W.	Harvard Graduate School of Business Administration, Baker Lib.	10-27-65
Lyle, Guy R.	Emory Univ. Lib.	12-8-65
McAnally, Arthur M.	Univ. of Oklahoma Lib.	3-9-66
McMullan, T. N.	Louisiana State Univ. Lib.	3-16-66
Marcus, Jacob R.	American Jewish Archives, Hebrew Union Coll.	4-27-66
Mason, Alexandra	Univ. of Kansas Lib.	4-22-66
Matheson, J. William	Washington Univ. Lib.	4-19-66
Maxwell, Norris K.	Univ. of New Mexico Lib.	3-1-66
Merritt, Gertrude	Duke Univ. Lib.	12-1-65
Miller, Robert A.	Indiana Univ. Lib.	9-21-66
Mink, James	Univ. of California, Los Angeles, Lib.	1-18-66
Moffett, Helen S.	Western Reserve Univ. Lib.	6-23-66
Moffit, Alexander	Univ. of Texas Lib.	3-11-66
Murphy, Virginia B.	Univ. of Houston Lib.	3-15-66
Natanson, Leo	Univ. of Denver Lib.	6-14-66
Nevin, David G.	Washington Univ. Lib.	4-19-66
North, Jeanne B.	Stanford Univ. Lib.	1-14-66
O'Keeffe, Richard L.	Rice Univ. Lib.	3-14-66
Olson, Richard D.	Northwestern Univ. Lib.	9-27-66
Owens, Noel A. S.	Northwestern Univ. Lib.	9-27-66
Palmer, Paul R.	Columbia Univ. Lib.	7-18-66
Paluka, Francis	Univ. of Iowa Lib.	5-18-66
Parham, Paul M.	Texas Christian Univ. Lib.	3-4-66

Parker, John	Univ. of Minnesota Lib.	5-19-66
Parker, Ralph H.	Univ. of Missouri Lib.	4-20-66
Patton, James W.	Southern Historical Collection, Univ. of North Carolina	12-1-65
Peckham, Howard H.	W. L. Clements Lib., Univ. of Michigan	8-17-66
Phillips, Virginia	Univ. of Maryland Lib.	2-17-66
Pinches, Mary Frances	Case Institute of Technology Lib.	6-24-66
Placek, Joseph	Ohio State Univ. Lib.	8-16-66
Popecki, Joseph T.	Catholic Univ. of America Lib.	3-22-66
Raeburn, Glorieux	Columbia Univ. Lib.	7-18-66
Ratcliffe, Thomas E., Jr.	Univ. of Illinois Lib.	5-26-66
Rawlinson, Alfred H.	Univ. of South Carolina Lib.	12-6-65
Renfro, Kathryn R.	Univ. of Nebraska Lib.	5-17-66
Reynolds, Catharine J.	Univ. of Iowa Lib.	5-18-66
Reynolds, Frances E.	Ball State Univ. Lib.	9-22-66
Reynolds, Sabron	Univ. of Chicago Lib.	8-23-66
Rogers, Rutherford D.	Stanford Univ. Lib.	1-14-66
Rosenthal, Robert	Univ. of Chicago Lib.	8-23-66
Rowell, Margaret K.	City Univ. of New York Lib.	7-21-66
Russell, Mattie	Duke Univ. Lib.	11-29-65
Scannell, Francis X.	Michigan State Univ. Lib.	8-19-66
Scherr, Jean W.	Ball State Univ. Lib.	9-22-66
Schiff, Judith	Yale Univ. Lib.	7-12-66
Schork, Francis W.	American Univ. Lib.	2-18-66
Schoyer, George P.	Ohio State Univ. Lib.	8-16-66
Sereiko, George E.	Univ. of Notre Dame Lib.	9-23-66
Sheehy, Eugene	Columbia Univ. Lib.	7-18-66
Shipton, Clifford K.	Harvard Univ. Lib.	10-26-65
Siefker, Donald L.	Ball State Univ. Lib.	9-22-66
Simonson, James W., C.S.C.	Univ. of Notre Dame Lib.	9-23-66
Sinclair, Donald A.	Rutgers—The State Univ. Lib.	9-20-66
Stanford, Edward B.	Univ. of Minnesota Lib.	5-19-66
Stevens, Robert D.	Univ. of Hawaii Lib.	1-24-66
Stevenson, Frances H.	Western Reserve Univ. Lib.	6-23-66
Suput, Ray R.	Western Reserve Univ. Lib.	6-23-66

Thomasson, Carol	Univ. of New Mexico Lib.	3-1-66
Todd, Julia	Univ. of Denver Lib.	6-14-66
Turnbull, Pender	Rice Univ. Lib.	3-14-66
Tysse, Agnes N.	Univ. of Michigan Lib.	8-17-66
Valaske, Audrey J.	Univ. of Kansas Lib.	4-22-66
Van Den Bogaerde, Mary	Western Reserve Univ. Lib.	6-23-66
Velics, Laszlo	Univ. of Cincinnati Lib.	4-27-66
Vollmar, Edward R., S.J.	Saint Louis Univ. Lib.	4-18-66
Wagman, Frederick H.	Univ. of Michigan Lib.	8-17-66
Walling, Ruth	Emory Univ. Lib.	12-8-65
Warner, Robert M.	Michigan Historical Collections, Univ. of Michigan	8-17-66
Weidle, Catherine E.	Saint Louis Univ. Lib.	4-18-66
Welsch, Irwin	Indiana Univ. Lib.	9-21-66
Wescott, Elizabeth	Brown Univ. Lib.	7-13-66
Westlake, Neda M.	Univ. of Pennsylvania Lib.	8-26-66
White, Janet	Univ. of Michigan Lib.	8-17-66
Wilkinson, Ronald S.	Michigan State Univ. Lib.	8-19-66
Williams, Terrence	Univ. of Kansas Lib.	4-22-66
Wolfe, Grace S.	Western Reserve Univ. Lib.	6-23-66
Wulff, Yvonne	Ohio State Univ. Lib.	8-16-66
Zingler, Gilberta H.	Rice Univ. Lib.	3-14-66

2 b. *Nonacademic Librarians, Archivists, and Directors of Historical Societies*

Beder, Elizabeth F.	New York Public Lib.	7-22-66
Bell, Whitfield J., Jr.	American Philosophical Soc. Lib.	8-26-66
Bennett, Carlyle	New York City FRC	7-19-66
Broderick, John C.	Lib. of Congress	12-12-66
Brooks, Philip C.	Truman Lib.	4-21-66
Brown, Beverley H.	Lib. of Congress	12-12-66
Butterfield, L. H.	Massachusetts Historical Soc.	7-10-67
Carroll, Julia B.	National Archives	12-9-66
Cluff, Sophie J.	Hawaiian Mission Children's Soc.	1-25-66
Cole, James E.	San Francisco FRC	1-11-66

Conrad, Agnes C.	State Archives of Hawaii	1-24-66
Cook, Frank	State Historical Soc. of Wisconsin	5-23-66
Cooley, Everett L.	Utah State Historical Soc.	6-22-66
Corry, Ruth	Georgia State Archives	12-10-65
Cutcliffe, Benjamin F.	Kansas City, Mo., FRC	4-21-66
Danker, Donald F.	Nebraska State Historical Soc.	5-17-66
Davis, Ruth H.	State Historical Soc. of Wisconsin	5-23-66
Davis, W. N., Jr.	California State Archives	1-10-66
Day, James M.	Texas State Lib.	3-9-66
Dempsey, Mary K.	Montana Historical Soc.	10-16-65
East, Sherrod E.	National Archives	12-9-66
Erney, Richard	State Historical Soc. of Wisconsin	5-23-66
Fielstra, Gerritt E.	New York Public Lib.	7-22-66
Fishel, Leslie H., Jr.	State Historical Soc. of Wisconsin	5-23-66
Frost, Mary C.	Atlanta FRC	12-10-65
Gorham, Alan	Boston FRC	10-29-65
Halverson, Katherine	Wyoming State Archives and Historical Dept.	6-13-66
Harper, Josephine L.	State Historical Soc. of Wisconsin	5-23-66
Heffron, Paul	Lib. of Congress	12-12-66
Hill, Robert W.	New York Public Lib.	7-22-66
Jergens, Virginia	Cincinnati Historical Soc.	4-26-66
Jordan, Lee	Cincinnati Historical Soc.	4-26-66
Kane, Lucile M.	Minnesota Historical Soc.	5-20-66
Knowlton, John	Lib. of Congress	12-12-66
Lagerquist, Philip	Truman Lib.	4-21-66
Lee, Charles E.	South Carolina Archives Dept.	12-6-65
Leisinger, Albert H., Jr.	National Archives	12-19-66
Lilly, Frank	Kansas City, Mo., FRC	4-21-66
Lindgard, Elmer	Seattle FRC	10-20-65
MacConomy, Edward N.	Lib. of Congress	12-12-66
McDonald, Harold D.	New York Public Lib.	7-22-66
McDonough, John J., Jr.	Lib. of Congress	12-12-66
Marshall, William E.	Colorado State Historical Soc.	6-15-66

Martin, Elizabeth R.	Ohio Historical Soc.	8-16-66
Mearns, David C.	Lib. of Congress	12-12-66
Miller, Neal E.	Wyoming State Archives and Historical Dept.	6-13-66
Miller, Nyle H.	Kansas State Historical Soc.	4-25-66
Motley, Archie	Chicago Historical Soc.	8-24-66
Nyholm, Amy Wood	Newberry Lib.	8-23-66
O'Brien, Paul J.	California State Archives	1-10-66
Olson, Earl E.	Office of Church Historian, Church of Jesus Christ of Latter-day Saints	6-22-66
Owsley, Harriet C.	Tennessee State Lib. and Archives	12-15-65
Polk, Ann	Georgia State Archives	12-10-65
Pomfret, John E.	Huntington Lib.	1-21-66
Porter, Daniel R.	Ohio Historical Soc.	8-16-66
Quinn, Mary T.	State Archives of Rhode Island	7-14-66
Renze, Dolores	Colorado Division of State Archives and Public Records	6-15-66
Richmond, Robert W.	Kansas State Historical Soc.	4-25-66
Rieger, Morris	National Archives	12-9-66
Riley, Stephen T.	Massachusetts Historical Soc.	10-25-65
Ross, Donald E.	Boston FRC	10-29-65
Schulz, Herbert C.	Huntington Lib.	1-21-66
Scriven, Margaret	Chicago Historical Soc.	8-24-66
Silvestro, Clement	Chicago Historical Soc.	8-24-66
Smith, Jane	National Archives	12-9-66
Smith, Murphy D.	American Philosophical Soc. Lib.	8-26-66
Smith, Sam B.	Tennessee State Lib. and Archives	12-15-65
Snell, Joseph W.	Kansas State Historical Soc.	4-25-66
Storm, Colton	Newberry Lib.	8-23-66
Svoboda, Bonnie F.	Wyoming State Archives and Historical Dept.	6-13-66
Thelen, Esther	State Historical Soc. of Wisconsin	5-23-66

361

Thompson, Enid T.	Colorado State Historical Soc.	6-15-66
Tonkin, Lillian	Library Company of Philadelphia	8-26-66
Tyler, Barbara	Amon Carter Museum of Western Art	3-4-66
Ulery, Max W.	Fort Worth FRC	3-4-66
Ulrich, John	Lib. of Congress	12-12-66
Wheeler, Robert C.	Minnesota Historical Soc.	5-20-66
Williams, Gordon	Center for Research Libs.	8-23-66
Wilson, Warren	Atlanta FRC	12-10-65
Winfrey, Dorman H.	Texas State Lib.	3-9-66
Wolfe, Robert	National Archives	7-12-67
Yelvington, Julia A.	Wyoming State Archives and Historical Dept.	6-13-66

3. Graduate Students

Alexander, John K.	Univ. of Chicago	8-22-66
Ambrosius, Lloyd E.	Univ. of Illinois	5-27-66
Ammerman, David L.	Cornell Univ.	7-29-66
Andrews, Richard A.	Northwestern Univ.	9-27-66
Andrews, Thomas F.	Univ. of Southern California	1-20-66
Archdeacon, Thomas J.	Columbia Univ.	7-19-66
Ashby, Darrel LeRoy	Univ. of Maryland	2-14-66
Axelrod, Bernard	Washington Univ.	4-19-66
Baker, Abner S.	Univ. of Oregon	10-19-65
Balt, Roger	New York Univ.	7-20-66
Baughin, William A.	Univ. of Cincinnati	4-27-66
Beltz, John S.	Ohio State Univ.	8-15-66
Berrol, Selma C.	City Univ. of New York	7-21-66
Bird, Roy	Univ. of California, Santa Barbara	1-17-66
Bledsoe, Wayne	Michigan State Univ.	8-19-66
Boatmon, Ellis G.	Univ. of South Carolina	12-6-65
Boughner, D. Terry	Catholic Univ. of America	3-22-66
Bowling, Kenneth R.	Univ. of Wisconsin	10-21-66
Breeden, James	Tulane Univ.	3-18-66
Brown, Katharine L.	Johns Hopkins Univ.	11-9-65
Buice, S. David	Univ. of Oklahoma	3-7-66

Bumsted, John M.	Brown Univ.	7-13-66
Calmes, Alan	Univ. of South Carolina	12-7-65
Carriker, Robert C.	Univ. of Oklahoma	3-8-66
Chalou, George	Indiana Univ.	9-21-66
Chestnut, Paul I.	Duke Univ.	11-29-65
Clanton, Orval G.	Univ. of Kansas	4-22-66
Claussen, Standley W.	Univ. of California, Riverside	1-31-66
Clore, Marilee S.	Univ. of Texas	3-11-66
Coe, Stephen	American Univ.	2-18-66
Creutz, Gloria	Univ. of Southern California	1-20-66
Crockett, Norman	Univ. of Missouri	4-20-66
Crouch, Barry A.	Univ. of New Mexico	2-28-66
Cuff, Robert	Princeton Univ.	9-30-66
Curry, Lawrence H., Jr.	Duke Univ.	12-1-65
Curtis, James C.	Northwestern Univ.	9-27-66
Cusack, John	Boston Univ.	10-28-65
Dalfiume, Richard	Univ. of Missouri	4-20-66
Danziger, Edmund J., Jr.	Univ. of Illinois	5-27-66
Davies, Thomas M.	Univ. of New Mexico	2-28-66
Domer, Marilyn A.	Ball State Univ.	9-22-66
Doolen, Richard M.	Univ. of Michigan	8-18-66
Dudley, John Bruce	Ball State Univ.	9-22-66
Edwards, Paul E.	American Univ.	2-18-66
Eisenman, Harry	Case Institute of Technology	6-24-66
Etulain, Richard W.	Univ. of Oregon	10-18-65
Ezell, Edward C.	Case Institute of Technology	6-24-66
Ezell, Macel D.	Texas Christian Univ.	3-3-66
Feingold, Henry	New York Univ.	7-20-66
Finney, John D.	Georgetown Univ.	2-16-66
Fitzgerald, Richard A.	Univ. of California, Riverside	1-31-66
Flanagan, Vincent J.	City Univ. of New York	7-21-66
Foner, Eric	Columbia Univ.	7-18-66
Frakes, George E.	Univ. of California, Santa Barbara	1-17-66
Franklin, Jimmie L.	Univ. of Oklahoma	3-7-66
Franz, George W.	Rutgers—The State Univ.	9-28-66
Funigiello, Philip J.	New York Univ.	7-20-66

363

Gaddis, John L.	Univ. of Texas	3-11-66
Gambill, Edward L.	Univ. of Iowa	5-18-66
Gardner, H. Warren	Univ. of Kansas	4-22-66
Gerstner, Patsy A.	Case Institute of Technology	6-24-66
Goodman, David	Texas Christian Univ.	3-3-66
Gould, Jean	Stanford Univ.	1-14-66
Gustafson, Milton O.	Univ. of Nebraska	5-16-66
Hales, Lynn	Stanford Univ.	1-14-66
Havig, Alan R.	Univ. of Missouri	4-20-66
Hawes, Joseph M.	Univ. of Texas	3-10-66
Hay, Robert P.	Univ. of Kentucky	9-19-66
Henderson, Dwight F.	Univ. of Texas	3-10-66
Hendrickson, Peter	Univ. of New Mexico	3-1-66
Hill, Larry D.	Louisiana State Univ.	3-16-66
Holman, Dale	Univ. of Pennsylvania	8-25-66
Holmes, James H.	George Washington Univ.	2-23-66
Holmfeld, John D.	Case Institute of Technology	6-24-66
Holstine, Jon	Indiana Univ.	9-20-66
Hopkins, Richard J.	Emory Univ.	12-9-65
Howe, Daniel	Univ. of California, Berkeley	1-12-66
Hueston, Robert F.	Univ. of Notre Dame	9-23-66
Hughs, Anne E.	Univ. of Hawaii	1-25-66
Ireland, Robert M.	Univ. of Nebraska	5-16-66
Jackson, Charles O.	Emory Univ.	12-9-65
James, John C.	Johns Hopkins Univ.	11-10-65
Johannesen, Stanley Karl	Univ. of Missouri	4-20-66
Jones, Ronald L.	Duke Univ.	11-29-65
Joyce, Davis D.	Univ. of Oklahoma	3-7-66
Katzman, David M.	Univ. of Michigan	8-17-66
Kaufman, Burton I.	Rice Univ.	3-14-66
Kawashima, Yasuhide	Univ. of California, Santa Barbara	1-17-66
Kimball, Jeffrey P.	Louisiana State Univ.	3-16-66
Kimball, Warren F.	Georgetown Univ.	2-16-66
Kitson, James T.	Western Reserve Univ.	6-23-66
Klyberg, Albert T.	Univ. of Michigan	8-17-66
Knight, Barry	Michigan State Univ.	8-19-66
Kobrin, David R.	Univ. of Pennsylvania	8-25-66

Kotynek, Roy A.	Northwestern Univ.	9-27-66
Kuehne, Raymond M.	Univ. of Virginia	11-16-65
Kurland, Gerald	City Univ. of New York	7-21-66
Lancaster, James L.	Princeton Univ.	9-30-66
Lane, James	Univ. of Hawaii	1-25-66
Leary, William M., Jr.	Princeton Univ.	9-30-66
Lyon, Elizabeth M.	Emory Univ.	12-9-65
McClellan, Keith	Univ. of Chicago	8-22-66
McMillen, Neil R.	Vanderbilt Univ.	12-14-65
McMurry, Richard M.	Emory Univ.	12-8-65
Maizlish, Joseph	Univ. of California, Los Angeles	1-18-66
Mazaraki, George	New York Univ.	7-20-66
Meerse, David E.	Univ. of Illinois	5-26-66
Meredith, Howard L.	Univ. of Oklahoma	3-8-66
Merriam, Paul G.	Univ. of Oregon	10-18-65
Morris, James M.	Univ. of Cincinnati	4-27-66
Mugridge, Ian	Univ. of California, Santa Barbara	1-17-66
Nathans, Sydney	Johns Hopkins Univ.	11-10-65
Neustadt, Margaret L.	Univ. of North Carolina	12-2-65
Nolan, Patrick B.	Univ. of Minnesota	5-19-66
Nutter, Glen L.	George Peabody Coll.	12-15-65
Olsen, Barton C.	Univ. of Utah	6-20-66
O'Neil, Floyd A.	Univ. of Utah	6-21-66
O'Rourke, Paul A.	Univ. of Notre Dame	9-23-66
Orr, Jane	Louisiana State Univ.	3-16-66
Parman, Donald L.	Univ. of Oklahoma	3-7-66
Peterson, Charles	Univ. of Utah	6-20-66
Pitts, Clyde E.	Univ. of North Carolina	12-2-65
Portuondo, Emma J.	Catholic Univ. of America	3-22-66
Pulley, Judith P.	Univ. of Virginia	11-16-65
Pulley, Raymond	Univ. of Virginia	11-16-65
Quitt, Martin H.	Washington Univ.	4-19-66
Raat, William Dirk	Univ. of Utah	6-21-66
Racine, Philip	Emory Univ.	12-8-65
Ready, Milton	Univ. of Houston	3-15-66

Roach, Fred, Jr.	Univ. of Oklahoma	3-7-66
Roberts, Richard C.	Univ. of Utah	6-21-66
Rose, Lisle A.	Univ. of California, Berkeley	1-12-66
Rowley, William D.	Univ. of Nebraska	5-16-66
Saucier, Bobby W.	Tulane Univ.	3-17-66
Schultz, Stanley K.	Univ. of Chicago	8-22-66
Schulz, Constance B.	Univ. of Cincinnati	4-27-66
Scott, Douglas A.	Univ. of Maryland	2-14-66
Sharp, James R.	Univ. of California, Berkeley	1-11-66
Shumway, Keith	Univ. of Chicago	8-22-66
Silverman, Sheldon	Univ. of California, Los Angeles	1-19-66
Simms, Lyman Moody, Jr.	Univ. of Virginia	11-17-65
Sinclair, Bruce	Case Institute of Technology	6-24-66
Skeen, Carl E.	Ohio State Univ.	8-15-66
Smith, Kenneth	Univ. of Southern California	1-20-66
Smith, W. Wayne	Univ. of Maryland	2-14-66
Sperling, Harvey	Washington Univ.	4-19-66
Stewart, James B.	Western Reserve Univ.	6-23-66
Storey, John	Univ. of Kentucky	9-19-66
Swails, Thomas W.	Univ. of Hawaii	1-25-66
Sylvester, Lorna	Indiana Univ.	9-21-66
Taylor, Graham D.	Univ. of Pennsylvania	8-25-66
Taylor, Sister Mary Christine	Saint Louis Univ.	4-18-66
Thompson, Jay C., Jr.	Ball State Univ.	9-22-66
Treon, John A.	Univ. of Virginia	11-17-65
Tyler, Ronnie	Texas Christian Univ.	3-3-66
Unruh, John D., Jr.	Univ. of Kansas	4-22-66
Van Horn, Harold E.	Univ. of Denver	6-14-66
Wakelyn, Jon	Rice Univ.	3-14-66
Waldera, Gerald	Univ. of Denver	6-14-66
Wallace, Michael	Columbia Univ.	7-19-66
Watts, Eugene	Emory Univ.	12-8-65
Wehr, Paul W.	Ball State Univ.	9-22-66
Weldon, Edward L.	Emory Univ.	12-9-65

Wheeler, William B.	Univ. of Virginia	11-17-65
Whelan, Paul A.	Saint Louis Univ.	4-18-66
Winsell, Keith A.	Univ. of California, Los Angeles	1-19-66
Zeidman, James	Univ. of California, Los Angeles	1-18-66

List of Respondents to Questionnaires

Ph.D. Institutions and Respondents

Brandeis Univ.–Morton Keller
Brigham Young Univ.–Eugene E. Campbell
California, Univ. of, Davis,–Wilson Smith
Claremont Graduate School and Univ. Center–John Niven
Colorado, Univ. of–Daniel M. Smith
Connecticut, Univ. of–Robert W. Lougee
Cornell Univ.–Paul W. Gates
Florida, Univ. of–John K. Mahon
Georgia, Univ. of–J. H. Parks
Howard Univ.–Elsie M. Lewis
Idaho, Univ. of–William S. Greever
Illinois, Univ. of–Harold M. Hyman (visited)
Indiana Univ.–Walter T. K. Nugent (visited)
Lehigh Univ.–John Cary
Loyola Univ. (Chicago)–Robert W. McCluggage
Maine, Univ. of–W. H. Jeffrey
Mississippi, Univ. of–Joseph O. Baylen
Mississippi State Univ.–Harold S. Snellgrove
Montana, Univ. of–M. E. Wren
New York, State Univ. of, Albany–Kendall Birr
New York, State Univ. of, Buffalo–John T. Horton
Northern Illinois Univ.–Emory G. Evans
Pennsylvania State Univ.–Philip S. Klein
Rochester, Univ. of–Loren Baritz
St. John's Univ.–Walter L. Willigan
Southern Mississippi, Univ. of–J. Treadwell Davis
Syracuse Univ.–Nelson M. Blake
Tufts Univ.–Freeland K. Abbott

Tulane Univ.–Bennett H. Wall (visited)
Washington State Univ.–George A. Frykman

M. A. Institutions and Respondents

Akron, Univ. of–Warren F. Kuehl
Albion Coll.–C. H. James
Andrews Univ.–Richard M. Schurz
Arizona State Univ.–Paul G. Hubbard
Bowling Green State Univ.–William R. Rock
Butler Univ.–G. M. Waller
California State Coll. at Los Angeles–David Lindsey
Canisius Coll.–William M. Harrigan
Central Connecticut State Coll.–Theodore Paullin
Central Michigan Univ.–Richard L. Wysong
Colgate Univ.–Raymond O. Rockwood
Creighton Univ.–Allan M. Schleich
Eastern Michigan Univ.–Richard D. Goff
Hardin-Simmons Univ.–Rupert N. Richardson
Longwood Coll.–J. M. Helms
Loyola Univ. of Los Angeles–Anthony F. Turhollow
Manhattanville Coll.–Clarence L. Hohl, Jr.
Mankato State Coll.–Cyril Allen
Marquette Univ.–Francis Paul Prucha, S.J.
Memphis State Univ.–Aaron M. Boom
Miami, Univ. of–Charlton Tebeau
Miami Univ.–Harris G. Warren
Midwestern Univ.–Kenneth F. Neighbours
Missouri, Univ. of, at Kansas City–Lawrence H. Larsen
Mt. Holyoke Coll.–Mary S. Benson
Nevada, Univ. of–Paul H. Smith
New Mexico Highlands Univ.–Lynn I. Perrigo
New Mexico State Univ.–Sigurd Johansen
North Texas State Univ.–Jack B. Scroggs
Ohio Univ.–R. L. Daniel, Bruce E. Steiner, John P. Finnegan, Robert
    P. Gilmore, Gifford B. Doxsee, P. Lindsay, and Harry R. Stevens
Oklahoma State Univ.–Homer L. Knight
Pepperdine Coll.–Howard A. White
Portland, Univ. of–Philip W. Kennedy

Prairie View A&M Coll.—George B. Woolfolk
Rhode Island, Univ. of—William D. Metz
Richmond, Univ. of—R. C. McDanel
Roosevelt Univ.—Jack J. Roth
Saint Rose, Coll. of—Sister Eileen Joseph Welch
Sam Houston State Coll.—Oliver M. Refsell
San Diego State Coll.—William Hanchett
San Francisco State Coll.—John L. Shover
Santa Clara Univ.—George F. Giacomini, Jr.
Scranton, Univ. of—Frank C. Brown
Stephen F. Austin State Coll.—C. K. Chamberlain
Stetson Univ.—Gilbert L. Lycan
Sul Ross State Coll.—Frances M. Phillips
Temple Univ.—Russell F. Weigley
Tennessee A&I State Univ.—Alonzo T. Stephens
Toledo, Univ. of—Noel L. Leathers
Trinity Coll. (Hartford)—Edward W. Sloan III
Trinity Univ. (San Antonio)—Donald E. Everett
Utah State Univ.—S. George Ellsworth
Vermont, Univ. of—Jeremy P. Felt
Villanova Univ.—Henry L. Rofinot
Virginia State Coll.—Edgar A. Toppin
Wake Forest Coll.—Henry S. Stroupe
Western Michigan Univ.—Alan S. Brown
West Texas State Univ.—Lowell H. Harrison
Wichita State Univ.—William E. Unrau
William and Mary, Coll. of—William W. Abbot
Woman's Coll. of Georgia, The—James C. Bonner
Xavier Univ. (Cincinnati)—Paul L. Simon

Historical Societies, Archives, and Libraries and Respondents

Alaska State Lib.—Helen Dirtadian
Arizona Dept. of Lib. and Archives—Marguerite B. Cooley
Arizona Historical Foundation—Bert M. Fireman
Arizona Pioneers' Historical Soc.—Andrew Wallace
Arkansas History Commission—John L. Ferguson
Essex Institute—Dean A. Fales, Jr.
Filson Club, The—Dorothy Thomas Cullen
Illinois State Historical Lib.—Paul Spence

Indiana Historical Soc. Lib.—Caroline Dunn
Maine Historical Soc.—Elizabeth Ring
Michigan Historical Commission Archives—Geneva Kebler
New Hampshire Historical Soc.—Harriet S. Lacy
New York State Lib.—Juliet Wolohan
North Carolina Dept. of Archives and History—H. G. Jones
North Dakota, State Historical Soc. of—Margaret Rose
Oklahoma Historical Soc.—Elmer L. Fraker
Oregon Historical Soc.—R. E. Fessenden
Pennsylvania Historical and Museum Commission—Donald H. Kent
South Carolina Historical Soc.—Mary B. Prior
Vermont Historical Soc.—Richard G. Wood
West Virginia Dept. of Archives and History—James L. Hupp
Wyoming State Archives and Historical Dept.—Katherine Halverson

Academic Libraries and Respondents

Akron, Univ. of—Ruth Clinefelter, social sciences librarian
Albion Coll. Lib.—Glen C. Stewart
Andrews Univ.—Mary Jane Mitchell
Arizona State Univ.—Alan K. Lathrop
Arkansas, Univ. of—Marvin A. Miller, director of libraries
Atlanta Univ.—Miles M. Jackson, Jr., chief librarian
Boston Coll.—Brendan Connolly, S.J.
Brigham Young Univ.—Donald T. Schmidt, reference librarian
Butler Univ., The Irwin Lib.—Harold L. Boisen, librarian
Central Connecticut State Coll., Elihu Burritt Lib.—Elizabeth H.
   Walden, special services librarian
Central Michigan Univ.—Orville L. Eaton, librarian
Colgate Univ. Lib.—Eric von Brockdorff, reference librarian
Colorado, Univ. of—John A. Brennan, Western Historical Collections
Eastern Michigan Univ.—Leona Berry, reference librarian
Florida, Univ. of, Libs.—Margaret Knox Goggin
Fresno State Coll. Lib.—L. S. Parker
Georgia, Univ. of, Libs.—W. P. Kellam
Hebrew Union Coll. (New York)—Edward Kiev
Howard Univ.—Joseph H. Reason
Idaho, Univ. of—Charles A. Webbert
John Carroll Univ., Grasselli Lib.—James A. Mackin, S.J., director
Kansas State Coll. of Pittsburg, Porter Lib.—Floyd R. Meyer, director

Kansas State Univ. Lib.—Joe W. Kraus
Lehigh Univ. Lib.—James D. Mack, librarian
Long Island Univ.—Elliott S. M. Gatner
Louisville, Univ. of—Wayne S. Yenawine
Loyola Univ. (Chicago)—James C. Cox
Maine, Univ. of—James C. MacCampbell
Manhattanville Coll. of The Sacred Heart—E. O. Connor
Marquette Univ., Memorial Lib.—Celia Hauck
Miami, Univ. of—A. L. McNeal, director
Miami Univ.—L. S. Dutton
Midwestern Univ.—J. P. Vagt
Minnesota, Univ. of, Center for Immigration Studies—William E. Wright
Mississippi Coll.—J. B. Howell
Mississippi State Univ., Mitchell Memorial Lib.—George Lewis, director
Missouri, Univ. of, at Kansas City—Bernice Miller, government documents librarian
Montana, Univ. of—Earle C. Thompson
Montana State Univ.—Lesley Muriel Heathcote
Mount Holyoke Coll.—Anne C. Edmonds, librarian
Nevada, Univ. of—Helen J. Poulton, reference librarian
New Mexico Highlands Univ.—W. S. Wallace
New Mexico State Univ.—Chester H. Linscheid, librarian
New York, State Univ. of, Albany—William Clarkin, bibliographer, social sciences
Niagara Univ. Lib.—Bernard H. Dollen, director
North Dakota, Univ. of, Chester Fritz Lib.—Ordean A. Hagen
Northeast Missouri State Teachers Coll.—George N. Hartje
Northern Michigan Univ.—Helvi E. Walkonen
North Texas State Univ. Lib.—Joe H. Bailey, associate librarian
Northwest Missouri State Coll., Wells Lib.—Barbara Palling
Ohio Univ.—Walter W. Wright, director
Oklahoma State Univ.—Marguerite S. Howland
Pennsylvania State Univ.—Lloyd Hooker
Pepperdine Coll. Lib.—Harry A. Butler
Pittsburgh, Univ. of—Glenora M. Edwards, asst. to director
Portland, Univ. of—Philip W. Kennedy, Dept. of History, for the lib.
Rhode Island, Univ. of, Lib.—Francis P. Allen

Rochester, Univ. of, Lib.—Margaret B. Andrews, asst. librarian in charge of special collections

St. Bonaventure Univ., Friedsam Memorial Lib.—Irenaeus Herscher, O.F.M., librarian

St. John's Univ. Lib.—William A. Gillard

St. Mary's Univ.—Paul Novosal

Saint Rose, Coll. of—Sister Anna Clare, librarian

Sam Houston State Coll., Estill Lib.—B. P. Simons

San Fernando Valley State Coll.—A. Greco, chief of public services

San Jose State Coll.—Robert L. Lauritzen, reference services librarian

Seton Hall Univ.—V. Rev. William Noé Field, director

Southern Illinois Univ.—Ferris S. Randall

Southwest Texas State Coll.—Selma W. Ottmers, reference librarian

Stephen F. Austin State Coll.—Mildred Wyatt, librarian

Stetson Univ.—Charlotte A. Smith

Sul Ross State Coll.—Wilbur D. Blackmon

Syracuse Univ.—Howard Applegate, manuscripts librarian

Trinity Univ.—Jay B. Clark, archivist

Tufts Univ.—Joseph S. Komidar

Vermont, Univ. of, Bailey Lib.—T. D. Seymour Bassett, curator, special collections

Virginia State Coll.—Wallace Van Jackson

Washington State Univ.—George J. Rausch, Jr.

Wayne State Coll.—Yale K. Kessler, librarian

Western Michigan Univ.—Donald R. Brown, reference librarian

West Virginia Univ.—C. Shetler, West Virginia Collection

Winthrop Coll.—H. Joanne Harrar

Woman's Coll. of Georgia, The—Barbara Ann Simons, public services librarian

APPENDIX E

David Donald Syllabus

THE JOHNS HOPKINS UNIVERSITY
BALTIMORE, MARYLAND
HISTORY 643–644
Professor David Donald

The purpose of this seminar is to give graduate students advanced training in the methods and techniques of historical research and writing, with special reference to the Civil War-Reconstruction era. A secondary purpose is to guide students in the selection and delimitation of their thesis topic in this field.

Part I

1st Meeting—The Nature and Purposes of a Seminar

2nd Meeting—The Historian and the Library

Reading assignment: Homer C. Hockett, *The Critical Method in Historical Research.*

Writing assignments: (1) Prepare a concise (not more than 2 pages), factual *vita*, giving your full name, addresses, telephone numbers, educational background, marital status, publications, previous occupations, etc.

(2) Prepare a brief autobiographical sketch (about 2500 words), which will both serve as an illustration of your best writing style and let me know more about your training and research interests.

Note. Both these papers (like all other papers submitted in this seminar) must be typewritten, double-spaced.

3rd Meeting—Matters of Form and Style

Reading assignments: W. J. Strunk, Jr., and E. B. White, *The Elements of Style*, and Kate L. Turabian, *A Manual for Writers of Term Papers, Theses, and Dissertations* (both available in paperback editions).

Writing assignments: (1) Using Turabian's *Manual* as a guide, bring to the seminar at least twenty correctly written footnotes, exemplifying as many different types of citations as possible.

(2) Using Turabian's *Manual* as a guide, prepare a correct, classified bibliography which includes all the items cited in your footnotes.

4th Meeting—Handling Controversial Evidence

Assignment: Read John H. Cramer, *Lincoln under Enemy Fire*, and prepare a narrative of Lincoln's experiences during Early's attack on Washington. Papers must be typed, double-spaced, and must not exceed 3,000 words. Papers are due at the beginning of the seminar.

Part II

5th Meeting—The Art of Biography

Reading assignments: John A. Garraty, *The Nature of Biography* (esp. Chapters 7–10) and Leon Edel, *Literary Biography* (available in paperback edition).

6th Meeting—Fashions in Biography

Individual Reading Assignments:

Dumas Malone, "Biography and History," in J. R. Strayer, ed., *The Interpretation of History*, pp. 121–148.

Frederick B. Tolles, "The Biographer's Craft," *South Atlantic Quarterly*, LIII (1954), 508–520.

Bernard DeVoto, "The Skeptical Biographer," *Harper's Magazine*, CLXVI (1933), 181–192.

Catherine Drinker Bowen, *The Writing of Biography*.

Alfred M. Tozzer, "Biography and Biology," *American Anthropologist*, XXXV (1933), 417–432.

Leon Edel, "The Biographer and Psycho-Analysis," in James L. Clifford, ed., *Biography as an Art*, pp. 226–239.

John A. Garraty, "The Interrelations of Psychology and Biography," *Psychological Bulletin*, LI (1954), 569–582.

Gamaliel Bradford, *A Naturalist of Souls*, pp. 3–25.

7th Meeting—Discussion of Problem Papers on Biography

Assignment: Prepare a character study of not more than 3,000 words on a figure who will play an important role in your dissertation. Typed, double-spaced. Footnotes and bibliography optional. Your essay may be in the form of physical description, formal character analysis, or anecdote—or all three combined.

8th Meeting—Discussion of Problem Papers on Biography (continued)

Part III

9th Meeting—Social Classes and Social Mobility
   Reading assignment: W. Lloyd Warner, *Social Class in America*
   (available in paperback edition) and Bernard Barber, *Social
   Stratification*, Chap. 16.
10th Meeting—The Study of Elites
   Individual reading assignments:
      William Miller, "American Historians and the Business Elite,"
      Journal of Economic History, IX (1949), 184-208.
      William Miller, "The Recruitment of the American Business
      Elite," *Quarterly Journal of Economics*, LXIV (1950), 242-253.
      William Miller, "American Lawyers in Business and Politics,"
      Yale Law Review, LX (1951), 66-76.
      William Miller, ed., *Men in Business*, Chap. 7.
      George E. Mowry, *The California Progressives*, Chap. 4.
      David Donald, *Lincoln Reconsidered*, Chap. 2.
      Stuart Adams, "Origins of American Occupational Elites, 1900-
      1955," *American Journal of Sociology*, LXII (1957), 361-368.
      Richard Bendix and Frank W. Howton, "Social Mobility and the
      American Business Elite," *British Journal of Sociology*, VIII
      (1957), 357-369, and IX (1958), 1-14.
      Ari A. Hoogenboom, "An Analysis of Civil Service Reformers,"
      The Historian, XXIII, 54-78.
      Grady McWhiney, "Were the Whigs a Class Party in Alabama?"
      Journal of Southern History, XXIII (1957), 510-522.
      Lee Benson, *The Concept of Jacksonian Democracy*, Chap. 4.
11th Meeting—Discussion of Problem Papers on Social History
   Assignment: Prepare a documented research paper upon an aspect
   of your dissertation topic which involves the concepts of social
   class, social mobility, or elite groups. Typed, double-spaced.
   Classified bibliography. Length of the paper itself (excluding annotations) not to exceed 5,000 words.
12th Meeting—Second Discussion of Problem Papers on Social History

Part IV

13th Meeting—Content Analysis
   Reading assignment: Bernard Berelson, *Content Analysis in Communications Research.*
14th Meeting—Content Analysis:—Some Case Studies

Individual reading assignments:
Leo Lowenthal, "Biographies in Popular Magazines," in William
Peterson, ed., *American Social Patterns* (paperback ed.), 63-
118.
Bernard Berelson and Patricia J. Salter, "Majority and Minority
Americans: An Analysis of Magazine Fiction," *Public Opinion
Quarterly*, X (1946), 168-190.
Norbert J. Gossman, "Political and Social Themes in the English
Popular Novel, 1815-1832," *Public Opinion Quarterly*, XX
(1956), 531-541.
Gerhart Saenger, "Male and Female Relations in the American
Comic Strip," *Public Opinion Quarterly*, XIX (1955), 195-205.
Daniel J. Lerner, et al., "Comparative Analysis of Political Ideol-
ogies," *Public Opinion Quarterly*, XV (1952), 715-733.
R. Richard Wohl, "The 'Rags to Riches Story': An Episode of
Secular Idealism," in Reinhard Bendix and Seymour Martin
Lipset, *Class, Status and Power*, pp. 388-395.
Robert W. Janes, "A Technique for Describing Community
Structure through Newspaper Analysis," *Social Forces*, XXX-
VII (1958), 102-109.
James W. Prothro, "Verbal Shifts in the American Presidency:
A Content Analysis," *American Political Science Review*, L
(1956), 726-739.
15th Meeting—Discussion of Problem Papers using Content Analysis
Assignment: Prepare a documented research paper upon an aspect
of your dissertation topic which involves the use of content anal-
ysis. Typed, double-spaced. Classified bibliography. Length not
to exceed 5,000 words.
16th Meeting—Second Discussion of Problem Papers using Content
Analysis

Part V

17th Meeting—The Study of Political Parties
Reading assignment: Robert Michels, *Political Parties* (available in
paperback edition).
18th Meeting—The Analysis of Political Parties
Reading assignment: *Either* Manning Dauer, *The Adams Federalists*
or David Truman, *The Congressional Party*.
19th Meeting—Discussion of Problem Papers on Political Parties

Assignment: Prepare a documented research paper upon an aspect of your dissertation topic which involves the analysis of the structure and behavior of a political party. Typed, double-spaced. Classified bibliography. Length not to exceed 5,000 words.

20th Meeting—Second Discussion of Problem Papers on Political Parties

21st Meeting—Election Analysis

Reading Assignment: Lee Benson, "Research Problems in American Political Historiography," in Mirra Komarovsky, ed., *Common Frontiers of the Social Sciences*, pp. 113-183.

Note: For this unit many students can profitably study V. O. Key, Jr., *A Primer of Statistics for Political Scientists*.

22nd Meeting—Elections: Some Case Studies

Individual reading assignments:

Seymour M. Lipset, *Political Man*, Chap. 11.

Lee Benson, *The Concept of Jacksonian Democracy*, Chap. 7.

V. O. Key, *Southern Politics*, Chap. 8.

Paul Lazarsfeld, et al., "The People's Choice," in William Peterson, *American Social Patterns*, pp. 119-169 (available in paperback edition).

H. F. Alderfer and R. M. Sigmond, *Presidential Elections by Pennsylvania Counties, 1920–1940*.

Harold F. Gosnell, *Grass Roots Politics*, Chap. 3.

W. A. Sullivan, *The Industrial Worker in Pennsylvania*, Chap. 8.

Eugene Pessen, "Did Labor Support Jackson: The Boston Story," *Political Science Quarterly*, XLIV (1949), 262-274, and R.T. Bower, "Note," *ibid.*, XLV, 441-444.

Aida D. Donald, "The Decline of Whiggery," *Rochester History*, XX (July, 1958), 1-19.

William Diamond, "Urban and Rural Voting in 1896," *American Historical Review*, XLVI (1941), 281-305.

23rd Meeting—Discussion of Problem Papers on Elections

Assignment: Prepare a documented research paper upon an aspect of your dissertation topic which involves an election analysis. Typed, double-spaced. Classified bibliography. Length not to exceed 5,000 words.

24th Meeting—Second Discussion of Problem Papers on Elections

Selected List of Microfilm Finding Aids

American Historical Association. *A Catalogue of Files and Microfilms of the German Foreign Ministry Archives, 1867–1920*, 1959.

Applebaum, Edmond L. "Implications of the *National Register of Microfilm Masters* as Part of a National Preservation Program," *Library Resources and Technical Services*, Vol. IX, No. 4 (Fall, 1965), 489–94.

Diaz, Albert James, ed., *Guide to Microforms in Print, 1966*. Washington, Microcard Editions, Inc., 1966.

Fisher, Mary Ann. *Preliminary Guide to Microfilm Collection in the Bancroft Library*. Berkeley, Univ. of California, 1955.

General Services Administration. *Copying Equipment: A GSA Handbook*. Washington, GSA, Oct., 1966.

Hale, Richard W., ed., *Guide to Photocopied Historical Materials in the United States and Canada*. Ithaca, Cornell Univ. Press for the American Historical Association, 1961.

Jenkins, William Sumner, comp., and Lillian A. Hamrick, ed. *A Guide to the Microfilm Collection of Early State Records*. Washington, Photoduplication Service, Library of Congress, 1950; Supplement, 1951.

Kent, George O., comp. *A Catalog of Files and Microfilms of the German Foreign Ministry Archives, 1920–1945*. Vols. I–III. Stanford, The Hoover Institution, 1962–66.

National Archives. *Guides to German Records Microfilmed at Alexandria, Virginia*. Vols. I–LV. Washington, GSA, 1959.

National Historical Publications Commission. *Catalog of Microfilm Publications*. 3rd ed. Washington, 1968.

National Register of Microform Masters. Washington, Library of Congress, 1965, irregular.

North Carolina Department of Archives and History. *North Carolina Newspapers on Microfilm, A Checklist*. 3rd ed. Raleigh, 1965.

Philadelphia Bibliographical Center and Union Library Catalogue, Eleanor Este Campion, ed. *Union List of Microfilms.* Ann Arbor, J. W. Edwards, Publisher, Inc., 1951.

Presidents' Papers Index Series. Washington, Library of Congress, 1960——.

Schwegmann, George A., Jr., *Newspapers on Microfilm.* 6th ed. Washington, Library of Congress, 1967.

Tennessee State Library and Archives (Archives Division). *Checklist of Microfilms in the Tennessee State Archives.* Nashville, 1960.

University Microfilms, Inc. *O-P Catalog* [Out of Print Books] Ann Arbor, University Microfilms, Inc., June, 1965.

Young, John. *Checklist of Microfilm Reproductions of Selected Archives of the Japanese Army, Navy, and Other Government Agencies, 1868–1945.* Washington, Georgetown Univ. Press, 1959.

National Historical Publications Commission Microfilm Program

Institutions which have received grants from the NHPC for micro-filming a body of papers in their collections are:

Academy of Natural Sciences of Philadelphia
Buffalo and Erie County Historical Soc.
Cornell Univ.
Dartmouth Coll.
Kansas State Historical Soc.
Massachusetts Historical Soc.
Minnesota Historical Soc.
Morristown National Historical Park
Mount Wilson Observatory—Carnegie Institution of Washington
Nebraska State Historical Soc.
New Jersey Historical Soc.
New Mexico State Records Center and Archives
New York Univ.
North Carolina, Univ. of
North Dakota, Univ. of
Notre Dame, Univ. of
Ohio Historical Soc.
Pennsylvania, Historical Soc. of
Pennsylvania Historical and Museum Commission
Stanford Univ.
Texas, Univ. of
Virginia, Univ. of
Washington, Univ. of
Wisconsin, State Historical Soc. of

Among the papers which have been filmed under these grants are: Minutes and correspondence of the Academy of Natural Sciences of Philadelphia; Richard A. Ballinger Papers; George Bancroft Papers; Bexar Archives of Texas; Thomas Bragg Diary; Orestes A. Brownson

Papers; Carter Family Papers; Records of the Territory of Dakota, 1861–89; Ignatius Donnelly Papers; Edward Droomgoole Papers; Millard Fillmore Papers; Albert Gallatin Papers; William Gaston Papers; Hamond Naval Papers; Warren G. Harding Papers; Ingram's Poe Collection; David Starr Jordan Papers; Claude Kitchin Papers; Lee Family Papers; Benjamin Lincoln Papers; Records of Diocese of Louisiana and the Floridas (New Orleans); William Lowndes Papers; Isaac McCoy Papers; Christopher G. Memminger Papers; J. Sterling Morton Papers; Nebraska Farmers' Alliance Papers; New England Emigrant Aid Company Papers; New Mexico Spanish Records; Oregon Improvement Company Records; Thomas Penn Papers; Minutes of the Provincial Council of Pennsylvania; Timothy Pickering Papers; John Rutledge Papers; Winthrop Sargent Papers; William T. Sherman Family Papers; Lawrence Taliaferro Papers; *Virginia Gazette* Daybooks; Artemas Ward Papers; Washington Territorial Government Records; and the Benjamin C. Yancey Papers.

For complete information on the NHPC microfilm program, write the National Historical Publications Commission, National Archives, Washington, D. C. 20408.

Travel

The following examples represent the types of support graduate students received for travel connected with dissertation research.

Funds administered by the department:

Cornell Univ.—grants of $100 to $300.[1]

Harvard Univ.—all doctoral candidates, as a matter of principle, traveled for dissertation research. "Even if there were no obvious need, we would find some reason to have a student travel to do research. . . . Students just go where they need to. It is as easy to find money for a long trip as a short one."[2]

Johns Hopkins Univ.—grants of as much as $100.

Indiana Univ.—grants of about $400 a summer. Little red tape was connected if the adviser pushed the request.[3]

Univ. of Michigan—summer grants of as much as $500, which could be divided between travel and photocopy as needed.[4]

Univ. of North Carolina—grants from the Smith Fund limited to $100 a student a year. These funds could also be used for photocopy.[5]

Princeton Univ.—funds for both graduate and undergraduate students. For graduate students, the amount depended on where they needed to go.[6]

Rice Univ.—funds for both graduate and undergraduate students. For graduate students, the amount depended on the itinerary and the intensity of research.[7]

---

[1] Questionnaire returned by Paul W. Gates; interview with David L. Ammerman, see Appendix C3.

[2] Interview with Oscar Handlin, see Appendix C1.

[3] Interviews with Maurice G. Baxter and Chase C. Mooney, *ibid.*

[4] Interviews with William B. Willcox, *ibid.*; Richard M. Doolen, see Appendix C3.

[5] Interview with George B. Tindall, see Appendix C1.

[6] Interview with Arthur S. Link, *ibid.*

[7] Interview with W. H. Masterson, *ibid.*

Univ. of Wisconsin—(1) The cost of round-trip transportation was paid by the graduate school, or (2) private grant money for research projects could be used for travel. In 1965–66 the department allocated NDEA overhead money for student research and travel.[8]

Yale Univ.—the department virtually promised to furnish money for needed travel. It came from foundations and individual donors.[9]

Funds administered outside the department:

Univ. of California at Berkeley—basic sources for travel funds, in addition to the department: Woodrow Wilson Fellowship money and the research committee of the academic senate. A doctoral candidate could count on round-trip transportation expenses to the East Coast.[10] James R. Sharp received $500 from the Woodrow Wilson fund and $300 from another university travel fund.[11]

Univ. of California at Los Angeles—the Regents' Patents Funds supported graduate student travel. This money was derived from patents developed by university professors. A maximum of $500 was available to a student who had the recommendation of his adviser and who had passed qualifying examinations.[12]

Univ. of Colorado—as much as $1,500 was available from outside the department.[13]

Univ. of Illinois—the graduate college furnished $500 a year for each of the department's University Fellows. The money was used for student travel and small amounts of photocopy.[14]

Univ. of Kentucky—beginning in 1967–68, income from grants supported graduate student travel.[15]

Louisiana State Univ.—the graduate school subsidized travel for doctoral candidates.[16]

Univ. of Maryland—no budgeted funds for graduate student travel, but in the summer of 1965 the department gave five students $400 apiece from surplus Woodrow Wilson Fellowship money.[17]

[8] Interview with Irvin G. Wyllie, *ibid*.
[9] Interview with Howard R. Lamar, *ibid*.
[10] Interview with A. Hunter Dupree, *ibid*.
[11] Interview, see Appendix C3.
[12] Interview with George E. Mowry, see Appendix C1.
[13] Questionnaire returned by Daniel M. Smith.
[14] Interview with Robert W. Johannsen, see Appendix C1.
[15] Interview with Paul C. Nagel, *ibid*.
[16] Interview with John L. Loos, *ibid*.
[17] Interview with Horace S. Merrill, *ibid*.

384

Univ. of Missouri—the graduate school furnished between $150 and $400, which could be used for travel or photocopy.[18]

Univ. of Nebraska—the graduate fellowship committee administered travel funds. Students submitted budgets for their research projects, and the committee tried to pay round-trip air fare and some per diem.[19]

Univ. of Oklahoma—the graduate school's travel grants averaged $400 a student a summer and came from surplus Woodrow Wilson scholarship funds.[20] A student who received a $300 allowance for travel in the summer of 1966 said that these funds "are not easy to locate, much less acquire."[21]

Fellowships

Graduate students frequently held fellowships that included money for travel connected with dissertation research. Among the fellowships were those awarded by the Danforth Foundation, the Fels Foundation, the Harry S Truman Library Institute, the Mershon Foundation, and various universities.[22] Four of the doctoral candidates interviewed held Woodrow Wilson dissertation-year fellowships.[23]

Indirect Travel Support

Many universities, including the following, did not have funds earmarked for graduate student travel but actually provided such funds under different labels.

Case Institute of Technology—underwrote travel by commissioning students to collect photocopied material for the Archive of Contemporary Science and Technology.[24]

Univ. of Chicago—labeled travel money as fellowship funds. Stanley K. Schultz received $500 in this manner.[25]

Ohio State Univ.—arranged schedules so that teaching assistants finished all their teaching in one quarter and had the rest of the year free for research.[26]

[18] Interviews with Richard S. Kirkendall, *ibid.*; Alan R. Havig, see Appendix C3.

[19] Interview with James C. Olson, see Appendix C1.

[20] Interview with W. Eugene Hollon, *ibid.*

[21] Interview with Robert C. Carriker, see Appendix C3.

[22] Interviews with James L. Lancaster, Philip J. Funigiello, Milton O. Gustafson, Richard Dalfiume, *ibid.*; Francis P. Weisenburger and Barry D. Karl, see Appendix C1.

[23] Interviews with Katharine L. Brown, Lisle A. Rose, Robert P. Hay, and Robert Cuff, see Appendix C3.

[24] Interview with Melvin Kranzberg, see Appendix C1.

[25] Interview, see Appendix C3.

[26] Interview with John C. Burnham, see Appendix C1.

Univ. of Pennsylvania—professors have used funds from their own research grants to finance students' travel.[27]

Texas Christian Univ.—a graduate student received $2,000 in grants from the Arizona Historical Foundation. While traveling for the foundation, he was able to do some of his own research.[28]

Univ. of Washington—students have been assigned as research assistants to professors. The "assistance" rendered has sometimes been related entirely to their own dissertation research.[29]

TABLES

A. The following Ph.D. departments reported that there were no travel funds available:[30]

Department	Percentage of Students Traveling
American Univ.	53*
Ball State Univ.	85*
Boston Univ.	64*
Brandeis Univ.	
Brigham Young Univ.	50
Claremont Graduate School	100
Connecticut, Univ. of	100
George Washington Univ.	75*
Georgia, Univ. of	75
Hawaii, Univ. of	10
Howard Univ.	.05
Idaho, Univ. of	100
Iowa, Univ. of	100
Lehigh Univ.	66
Loyola Univ. (Chicago)	
Maine, Univ. of	66
Mississippi State Univ.	90
Montana, Univ. of	40
New Mexico, Univ. of	100
New York, State Univ. of, at Albany	100

[27] Interview with Graham D. Taylor, see Appendix C3.
[28] Interview with David Goodman, *ibid.*
[29] Interview with Arthur Bestor, see Appendix C1.
[30] Asterisks denote percentages averaged from professors' reports.

Oregon, Univ. of	100
Pennsylvania State Univ.	95
Rutgers—The State Univ.	100
St. John's Univ.	90
Southern Mississippi, Univ. of	100
Syracuse Univ.	90
Texas Technological Coll.	100
Vanderbilt Univ.	82

B. Ph.D. departments reporting some form of assistance for travel, including departmental funds, fellowships, assistantships, university funds, etc.

University	Percentage of Student Travel	Range of Amounts Available
Brown Univ.	100	
California, Univ. of		
Berkeley	50	air coach fare
Davis	95	
Los Angeles	78*	up to $500/student
Riverside		
Santa Barbara	100	
Case Institute of Technology	95	
Catholic Univ. of America	50	
Cincinnati, Univ. of	100	
Colorado, Univ. of		up to $1,500
Columbia Univ.	77*	
Cornell Univ.	100	$100–$300/student
Denver, Univ. of	35*	
Duke Univ.	100	
Emory Univ.	100	
Florida, Univ. of	60	
Florida State Univ.	90*	
Georgetown Univ.	66*	
Harvard Univ.	75	
Illinois, Univ. of	86*	$100/year/student
Indiana Univ.	100	up to $500/student
Johns Hopkins Univ.	100	up to $100/student

Kansas, Univ. of	85*	$500–$600
Kentucky, Univ. of	75*	
Louisiana State Univ.	64*	$200–$300/trip
Maryland, Univ. of	100	
Massachusetts, Univ. of	100	
Michigan, Univ. of	100	up to $500
Michigan State Univ.	100	
Minnesota, Univ. of	40*	
Mississippi, Univ. of	95	
Missouri, Univ. of	90	$100–$400/trip
Nebraska, Univ. of	99	$6,000/year for department
New York, City Univ. of	50	
New York, State Univ. of, Buffalo	75	
New York Univ.	100	
North Carolina, Univ. of	95	up to $100/trip
Northern Illinois Univ.	75	
Northwestern Univ.	100	$2,500/year
Notre Dame, Univ. of	100	
Ohio State Univ.	100	
Oklahoma, Univ. of	100	
Pennsylvania, Univ. of	50	
Princeton Univ.	100	$500–$1,000/year/dept.
Rice Univ.	100	$200–$250/student
Rochester, Univ. of	65	
St. Louis Univ.	33	
South Carolina, Univ. of	72*	
Southern California, Univ. of		
Stanford Univ.	82*	
Texas, Univ. of	100	
Texas Christian Univ.	100	
Tulane Univ.	90	up to $600
Virginia, Univ. of	100	
Washington Univ.	90*	
Wayne State Univ.	75	up to $500
Western Reserve Univ.	100	
Wisconsin, Univ. of	90*	$4,500–$6,000/year/dept.
Yale Univ.	77*	

C. Institutions visited by graduate students while traveling on research projects (tabulated from interviews):

Institution	No. of times mentioned
Academy of Natural Science (Philadelphia)	1
AFL-CIO (D.C.)	3
Air Force Museum, Wright-Patterson AFB	1
Air Univ. Lib.	1
Alabama Historical Assoc.	3
Alabama State Dept. of Archives and History	9
American Antiquarian Soc.	10
American Institute of Architects (D.C.)	1
American Irish Historical Soc. (N.Y.C.)	1
American Jewish Archives	1
American Legion Lib. (Indianapolis)	1
American Philosophical Soc.	4
Amon Carter Museum of Western Art	4
Ann Arbor, Michigan, Chamber of Commerce	1
Arizona, Univ. of, Lib.	3
Arizona Pioneers' Historical Soc.	1
Arizona State Coll. Lib.	1
Arkansas Historical Commission	1
Atlanta Historical Soc.	1
Atlanta Public Lib.	1
Atlanta Univ. Lib.	2
Bancroft Lib.	18
Baptist Historical Collection (Wake Forest Coll.)	1
Baylor Univ. Lib.	1
Bishop Museum (Honolulu)	1
Boston Athenaeum	5
Boston Public Lib.	7
Bowdoin Coll. Lib.	1
Brandeis Univ. Lib.	1
Brigham Young Univ. Lib.	3
Brown Univ. Lib.	2
Bryn Mawr Coll. Lib.	2
California, Univ. of, Lib.	

Dayton Public Lib. — 1
Defense Documentation Center (Dayton) — 1
Denver Public Lib. — 4
Disciples of Christ Archives (Nashville) — 1
District of Columbia Public Lib. — 2
Duke Univ. Lib. — 46
Eastern Michigan Univ. Lib. — 1
East Washington Historical Soc. — 1
Eleutherian Mills Historical Lib. (Delaware) — 3
Emory Univ. Lib. — 1
Engineering Society Lib. (N.Y.C.) — 1
Enoch Pratt Lib. (Baltimore) — 3
Essex Institute — 1
Federal Records Centers
    Alexandria — 8
    Atlanta — 9
    Chicago — 1
    Denver — 4
    Fort Worth — 8
    Kansas City — 3
    Los Angeles — 1
    New York City — 1
    St. Louis — 4
    San Francisco — 1
    Seattle — 3
Federal Reserve Bank — 2
Filson Club Lib., The — 2
Fisk Univ. Lib. — 4
Florida, Univ. of, Lib. — 4
Florida State Lib. — 2
Food and Drug Administration — 2
Fordham Univ. Lib. — 1
Fort Lewis, Coll. of, Lib. — 1
Fort Worth Public Lib. — 1
Franklin Institute (Philadelphia) — 1
Free Lib. of Philadelphia — 2
Furman Coll. Lib. — 2
Garrett Theological Seminary (Evanston, Ill.) — 2
General Electric Lib. (Schenectady) — 1

George Peabody Coll. Lib. 1
Georgetown Univ. Lib. 6
George Washington Univ. Lib. 1
Georgia, State Dept. of Archives and History of 8
Georgia, Univ. of, Lib. 7
Georgia Historical Commission 3
Georgia Institute of Technology Lib. 1
Gilcrease Museum 5
Grand Lodge of Texas (Masonic) (Waco) 1
Harvard Univ. Lib. 35
Haverford Coll. Lib. 1
Hawaiian Historical Soc. 3
Hawaiian Mission Children's Soc. Lib. 2
Hawaii Public Archives Lib. 6
Hayes Memorial Lib. 7
Hebrew Union Coll. Lib. 1
Holy Cross Univ. Lib. 1
Hoover Institution on War, Revolution 2
  and Peace (Stanford, Calif.)
Houston, Univ. of, Lib. 1
Houston Public Lib. 2
Howard Univ. Lib. 3
Huntington Lib. 48
Idaho Historical Soc. 1
Idaho State Univ. Lib. 1
Illinois, Univ. of, Lib. 7
Illinois State Historical Soc. 9
Independence Hall Lib. 2
Indiana Historical Soc. 5
Indiana State Lib. 6
Indiana Univ. Lib. 8
Institute of Aeronautical Science (N.Y.C.) 1
Interior, Dept. of the 1
International Longshoremen's Union Records (Hawaii) 1
Iowa, State Historical Soc. of 3
Jackson State Coll. Lib. 1
Jewish Scientific Institute (YIVO) 1
Joslyn Art Museum (Omaha) 1
John Carter Brown Lib. 3

John Crerar Lib. (Chicago)	4
Kansas, Univ. of, Lib.	3
Kansas State Historical Soc.	15
Kentucky, Univ. of, Lib.	1
Kentucky State Archives and Records Service	1
Library Co. of Philadelphia	6
Lib. of Congress	254
Lincoln National Life Insurance Co. Archives	1
(Fort Wayne, Ind.)	
Los Angeles City Hall	1
Los Angeles County Museum	2
Los Angeles Public Lib.	1
Louisiana Historical Assoc.	4
Louisiana State Museum	1
Louisiana State Univ. Lib.	9
Loyola Univ. Lib. (New Orleans)	1
McCormick Theological Seminary	1
Marietta Coll. Lib.	1
Maryland, Univ. of, Lib.	2
Maryland Hall of Records	8
Maryland Historical Soc.	11
Massachusetts Historical Soc.	17
Massachusetts State Archives	7
Meadville Theological School (Chicago)	1
Mennonite Archives and Libs. (Lancaster, Pa.)	1
Mercantile Lib. (St. Louis)	2
Mexico City Archives	1
Miami Univ. Lib.	1
Michigan, Univ. of, Lib.	14
Michigan Historical Collections	3
Michigan Historical Soc.	1
Michigan State Lib.	4
Michigan State Univ. Lib.	3
Military History, Office of Chief of	1
Millikan Univ. Lib.	1
Milwaukee Public Lib.	1
Minnesota, Univ. of, Lib.	4
Minnesota Historical Soc.	15
Mississippi Dept. of Archives and History	3

393

Rosenberg Lib. (Galveston, Tex.)	4
Rutgers–The State Univ. Lib.	1
St. Augustine National Park Service	1
St. Louis Public Lib.	1
St. Louis Univ. Lib.	2
Salt Lake City Public Lib.	1
Sam Rayburn Lib.	1
San Jacinto Museum	3
Seattle Public Lib.	2
Smith Coll. Lib.	1
Smithsonian Institution	22
South, Univ. of the, Lib.	1
South Carolina, Univ. of, Lib.	9
South Carolina Archives Dept.	7
South Carolina Historical Soc.	10
South Dakota, Univ. of	1
South Dakota State Historical and Museum Library	2
Southern Baptist Theological Seminary	1
Southern California, Univ. of, Lib.	4
Southern California Jewish Historical Soc.	1
Southern Coll. of Pharmacy (Atlanta)	1
Southern Methodist Univ. Lib.	5
Southern Mississippi, Univ. of, Lib.	1
Southwest Museum (Los Angeles)	2
Springfield (Ohio) Armory Lib.	1
Standard Oil of Ohio Archives	1
Stovall Museum of Science and History (Univ. of Oklahoma)	1
Supreme Court Lib.	1
Tennessee, Univ. of, Lib.	5
Tennessee Historical Commission	6
Tennessee State Lib. and Archives	9
Texas, Univ. of, Lib.	21
Texas Dept. of Public Safety	1
Texas State Lib.	17
Texas State Museum	1
Texas Technological Coll., Southwest Collection	3
Theodore Roosevelt Assoc. Lib. (N.Y.C.)	1
Trinity Coll. Lib.	1

Tulane Univ. Lib.	3
United Nations Lib.	2
United States Dept. of Agriculture	2
United States Information Service	1
Utah State Historical Soc.	3
Utah State Univ. Lib.	1
Vanderbilt Univ. Lib.	1
Vermont, Univ. of, Lib.	1
Vermont Historical Soc.	1
Virginia, Univ. of, Lib.	15
Virginia State Lib.	10
Warren County (Pa.) Historical Soc.	1
Washington, Univ. of, Lib.	3
Washington State Historical Soc.	2
Washington State Univ. Lib.	2
Washington Univ. Lib.	5
Wayne State Univ. Lib.	3
Western Michigan Univ. Lib.	1
Western Reserve Historical Soc.	9
Western Reserve Univ. Lib.	2
West Virginia Univ. Lib.	1
William and Mary, Coll. of, Lib.	2
Williamsburg, Colonial, and Institute for Early American History and Culture	7
Will Rogers Museum	1
Wisconsin, State Historical Soc. of	18
Wisconsin, Univ. of, Lib.	11
W. L. Clements Lib.	21
Worcester (Mass.) Historical Soc.	1
Wyoming, Univ. of, Lib.	2
Wyoming State Archives and History Dept.	1
Yale Univ. Lib.	38

D. Questionnaire responses from M.A. and Ph.D. departments telling where students went for research materials: *

Institution Visited	M.A.	Ph.D.	Total
Lib. of Congress	25	20	45
National Archives	24	19	43
Other Univ. Libs.	63	24	87

State Libs. and Archives	61	25	86
Federal Records Centers	17	9	26
Presidential Libs.	15	12	27
Smithsonian Institution	8	6	14
Private Libs.	23	18	41
Museums and Art Galleries	20	12	32
Public Libs.	56	20	76

*Twenty-seven Ph.D.-granting departments responded to the questionnaire, and sixty-two departments offering a terminal M.A. responded.

Preferences for Spending Money on Original Sources

The appended tables show preferences of professors and custodians of research materials for spending money to make original sources available for graduate research in United States history. The survey specified that the responses were to be in terms of the profession's general needs rather than those of a particular institution.[1] The intent of the question was to determine how people thought money could best be spent to make sources generally available. Some respondents, however, were unable to divorce local needs from their thinking.

Since statistics cannot convey underlying thoughts, the following typical ideas furnish the context for a substantial number of responses. Practically everyone recognized that without basic manuscripts or archives there would be no opportunity for photocopying or publishing edited papers. Consequently, those giving first preference to acquiring and processing manuscripts did so with the thought that significant material must be brought into repositories—that it must be rescued from attics and basements or any hazardous conditions. Few were interested in spending money to enable repositories to outbid each other for material already under control. In fact, many respondents specified that great harm already has been done by competition in the manuscript market. When some institutions with considerable resources decided that they wanted to build manuscript collections, their bidding inflated the market tremendously. Repositories that depended on acquiring manuscripts by donation and that did not have funds to purchase them have been sorely disadvantaged when new competitors came into the field with ample money. One curator said that the people who traditionally donated family papers to his library would have been incensed with the idea of "selling granddaddy." When a well-heeled competitor in the same city offered fifteen thou-

---

[1] See Appendix B, No. 14.

sand dollars for granddaddy's papers, however, that was a different matter.

Competition in price was not the only critical factor in manuscript collecting, for regional competition could be similarly injurious. When a repository had clearly staked out a geographical area for collecting and was meeting its responsibilities, it resented poaching by another institution. If a manuscript collection in one state had traditionally received congressional papers and some outside agency began vying for them, friction was natural. The competition presented by presidential libraries has created growing concern on the part of state curators and professors.[2] Dorman H. Winfrey, head of the Texas State Library and Archives, saw "real danger" in the fact that presidential libraries are "scooping up material unrelated to the presidents. This often constitutes an illogical dispersion of materials."[3] The director of the State Historical Society of Wisconsin, Leslie H. Fishel, Jr., contended that presidential libraries should not collect in regions such as Wisconsin that "can take care of themselves." Nor did he think that the National Archives should solicit manuscripts for the presidential libraries, for the National Archives system presented tough competition. "We need responsible definitions of where federal collecting patterns end." Just as presidential terms end, the collecting programs of presidential libraries should end.[4]

Although the benefits of photocopying for graduate research were generally appreciated, several historians commented that it would be advisable to centralize microform resources. The central agency could establish uniform standards for the creation and distribution (by purchase or loan) of microforms. Some respondents suggested that such an agency could provide researchers with hard copies of any needed material.

Several librarians commented that the preparation of finding aids should take precedence over further photocopying projects, and some thought such preparation was more important than the duplication of microform copies in many depositories. While not giving them first place, other librarians put particular stress on finding aids accompanying photocopy projects.

Several librarians expressed first preference for letterpress publica-

[2] Interview with Barry D. Karl, see Appendix C1.
[3] Interview, see Appendix C2b.
[4] Fishel, *ibid*.

tions of edited documents because they liked the way volumes could be acquired by any library. They contended that original sources could have greater penetration in this form than in any other and liked their easy availability to undergraduates and laymen as well as to graduate students.

A number of respondents advocated that money be put into travel grants before being spent on original sources. One professor said that instead of the given options, he would prefer to spend money to computerize census manuscripts, for this "would have much more pay-off in understanding our national past."[5]

TABLES—(a=Photocopy; b=Letterpress; c=Manuscripts)
Professors' Priorities (in descending order):

	Interview	Questionnaire	Total
a, b, c:	82	30	112
a, c, b:	43	20	63
b, a, c:	32	8	40
c, a, b:	39	4	43
a:	0	22	22

The remaining 41 responses of the 321 who answered the question were divided widely among those expressing a preference for b and c alone and those who were undecided.

Librarians' Priorities (in descending order):

	Academic (Interview & Questionnaire)	Nonacademic (Interview & Questionnaire)	Total
a, b, c:	61	2	63
a, c, b:	32	7	39
c, a, b:	17	21	38
b, a, c:	26	3	29
a:	21	8	29
c, b, a:	5	9	14
undecided:		4	4
		Total	216

The survey asked graduate students in what form they would prefer

[5] Interview with J. Rogers Hollingsworth, see Appendix C1.

to use original sources rather than for their preference for spending money. Their responses follow:

Graduate Students' Preferences (in descending order):

c, a, b:	43
a, c, b:	23
c, b, a:	21
b, c, a:	17
a, b, c:	14
b, a, c:	11

Total 129

The survey asked professors, librarians, and graduate students if the university would purchase original sources directly related to dissertation topics. The responses follow:

Purchase of Original Sources Related to Doctoral Dissertations:

Questionnaire responses from twenty Ph.D. libraries and twenty-nine history departments:

Academic Libraries		*History Departments*	
Yes:	10	Yes:	9
Yes, depending on funds, topics, etc.:	9	Yes, depending on funds, topics, etc.:	14
Professors yes, graduate students no:	1	Professors yes, graduate students no:	4
No:	0	No:	2

Purchase of Original Sources Related to Master's Theses

Questionnaire responses from M.A. libraries and history departments:

Academic Libraries		*History Departments*	
Yes:	20	Yes:	21
Yes, depending on funds, topics, etc.:	24	Yes, depending on funds, topics, etc.:	20
Professors yes, graduate students no:	0	Professors yes, graduate students no:	4
No:	13	No:	11

Interview Responses:

Academic libraries reporting support for research projects (especially microfilm purchase) of history department professors and graduate students: 33 (of possible 66)

History departments reporting some support available (through the library, graduate school, private endowments, etc.) for individual research, by either professors or graduate students: 46 (of possible 68)

Professors reporting research support available for faculty only: 14 (from 9 departments)

Ten professors, in separate departments, disagreed markedly with their colleagues on the ease with which research materials could be purchased either through the library or from other sources.

BIBLIOGRAPHY

EDITED SOURCES

Adams, John. *Legal Papers of John Adams.* Ed. by L. Kinvin Wroth and Hiller B. Zobel. 3 vols. Cambridge, Belknap Press of Harvard Univ. Press, 1965.

Allston, Robert F. W. *The South Carolina Rice Plantation as Revealed in the Papers of Robert F. W. Allston.* Ed. by James Harold Easterby. Chicago, Univ. of Chicago Press, 1945.

American Archives. 9 vols. Washington, M. St. Clair Clarke and Peter Force, 1837–53.

Biddle, Nicholas. *The Correspondence of Nicholas Biddle.* Ed. by Reginald C. McGrane. Boston, Houghton Mifflin Co., 1919.

Burnett, Edmund C., ed. *Letters of Members of the Continental Congress.* 8 vols. Washington, Carnegie Institution of Washington, 1921–36.

Butterfield, L. H., ed. in chief. *The Adams Papers.* Cambridge, Harvard Univ. Press, 1961——.

Calhoun, John C. *The Papers of John C. Calhoun.* Ed. by Robert L. Meriwether. Columbia, Univ. of South Carolina Press, 1959——.

Cappon, Lester J., ed. "Correspondence between Charles Campbell and Lyman C. Draper, 1846–1872," *William and Mary Quarterly,* 3rd Series, Vol. III, No. 1 (Jan., 1946), 70–116.

Carter, Clarence E., comp. and ed. *Territorial Papers of the United States.* 26 vols. Washington, Government Printing Office, 1934–62.

Clark, William Bell, ed. *Naval Documents of the American Revolution, Vol. I, 1774–1775.* Washington, Dept. of the Navy, 1964.

Clay, Henry. *The Papers of Henry Clay.* Ed. by James F. Hopkins. Lexington, Univ. of Kentucky Press, 1959——.

Davenport, Frances G., ed. *European Treaties Bearing on the History of the United States and its Dependencies to 1648.* Washington, Carnegie Institution of Washington, 1917.

Farrand, Max, ed. *Records of the Federal Convention of 1787.* 3 vols. New Haven, Yale Univ. Press, 1911. 4 vols. rev. ed., 1966.

Franklin, Benjamin. *The Papers of Benjamin Franklin.* Ed. by Leonard W. Labaree. New Haven, Yale Univ. Press, 1959——.

Hamilton, Alexander. *The Papers of Alexander Hamilton.* Ed. by Harold C. Syrett. New York, Columbia Univ. Press, 1961——.

Hazard, Ebenezer, ed. *Historical Collections.* 2 vols. Philadelphia, T. Dobson, for the author, 1792–94.

Jackson, Donald, ed. *Letters of the Lewis and Clark Expedition.* Urbana, Univ. of Illinois Press, 1962.

Jameson, John Franklin. *An Historian's World: Selections from the Correspondence of John Franklin Jameson.* Ed. by Elizabeth Donnan and Leo F. Stock. Philadelphia, American Philosophical Society, 1956.

Jefferson, Thomas. *The Papers of Thomas Jefferson.* Ed. by Julian P. Boyd. Princeton, Princeton Univ. Press, 1950——.

——. *The Writings of Thomas Jefferson.* Ed. by Andrew A. Lipscomb and Albert E. Bergh. 20 vols. Washington, Thomas Jefferson Memorial Assn., 1905.

Lincoln, Abraham. *The Collected Works of Abraham Lincoln.* Ed. by Roy P. Basler. 9 vols. New Brunswick, N.J., Rutgers Univ. Press, 1953–55.

Madison, James. *The Papers of James Madison.* Ed. by William T. Hutchinson and William M. E. Rachal. Chicago, Univ. of Chicago Press, 1962——.

Manning, William R., ed. *Diplomatic Correspondence of the United States: Canadian Relations, 1784–1860.* 4 vols. Washington, Carnegie Endowment for International Peace, 1940–45.

——. *Diplomatic Correspondence of the United States: Inter-American Affairs, 1831–1860.* 12 vols. Washington, Carnegie Endowment for International Peace, 1932–39.

——. *Diplomatic Correspondence of the United States Concerning the Independence of the Latin-American Nations.* 3 vols. New York, Oxford Univ. Press, 1925.

Pike. Zebulon. *The Journals of Zebulon Pike.* Ed. by Donald Jackson. 2 vols. Norman, Univ. of Oklahoma Press, 1966.

Richardson, James D., ed. *Messages and Papers of the Presidents.* 10 vols. 53rd Cong., 2 sess., *House Misc. Doc. 210*, Pts. 1–10. Washington, Government Printing Office, 1907.

Roosevelt, Franklin D. *The Public Papers and Addresses of Franklin D. Roosevelt.* Comp. by Samuel I. Rosenman. 5 vols. New York, Random House, Inc., 1938.

Roosevelt, Theodore. *The Letters of Theodore Roosevelt.* Ed. by Elting E. Morison. 8 vols. Cambridge, Harvard Univ. Press, 1951–54.

Sparks, Jared, ed. *Correspondence of the American Revolution.* 4 vols. Boston, Little, Brown and Co., 1853.

——. *The Diplomatic Correspondence of the American Revolution.* 12 vols. Boston, Hale and Gray & Bowen, 1829–30.

Thwaites, Reuben Gold, ed. *Early Western Travels, 1748–1846.* 32 vols. Cleveland, The A. H. Clark Co., 1904–07.

——. *The Jesuit Relations and Allied Documents.* 73 vols. Cleveland, Burrows, 1896–1901.

——. *Original Journals of the Lewis and Clark Expedition.* 8 vols. New York, Dodd, Mead & Co., 1904–05.

Walpole, Horace. *The Yale Edition of Horace Walpole's Correspondence.* Ed. by Wilmarth S. Lewis. New Haven, Yale Univ. Press, 1937——.

Washington, George. *The Writings of George Washington.* Ed. by Jared Sparks. 12 vols. Boston, F. Andrews, 1839–40.

——. *The Writings of George Washington from the Original Manuscript Sources.* Ed. by John C. Fitzpatrick. 39 vols. Washington, Government Printing Office, 1931–44.

Wilson, Woodrow. *The Papers of Woodrow Wilson.* Ed. by Arthur S. Link. Princeton, Princeton Univ. Press, 1966——.

FINDING AIDS, GUIDES, AND BIBLIOGRAPHIES

Adcock, Lynette. *Guide to the Manuscript Collections of Colonial Williamsburg.* Williamsburg, Va., Colonial Williamsburg, Inc., 1954.

Besterman, Theodore. *A World Bibliography of Bibliographies and of Bibliographical Catalogues, Calendars, Abstracts, Digests, Indexes, and the Like.* 4th ed. Lausanne, Societa Bibliographica, 1965.

Billington, Ray A. "Guides to American History Manuscript Collections in Libraries of the United States," *Mississippi Valley Historical Review*, Vol. XXXVIII, No. 3 (Dec., 1951), 467–96.

Catalogue of the John Carter Brown Library in Brown University. Vol. I, 1569–99; Vol. II, 1600–58; Vol. III, 1659–74. Providence, Rhode Island, published by the John Carter Brown Library, 1919, 1922, 1931.

Channing, Edward, Albert B. Hart, and Frederick J. Turner. *Guide to the Study and Reading of American History.* Boston, Ginn and Co., 1912.

Crabtree, Beth G. *Guide to Private Manuscript Collections in the North Carolina State Archives.* Raleigh, State Dept. of Archives and History, 1964.

Crick, Bernard R., and Miriam Alman, eds. *A Guide to Manuscripts Relating to America in Great Britain and Ireland.* London, Oxford Univ. Press, 1961.

Cusack, Margaret R. *List of Business Manuscripts in Baker Library.* 2nd ed. Boston, 1932. Revised by Robert W. Lovett, Boston, Baker Library, 1951.

Cuthbert, Norma B., comp. *American Manuscript Collections in the Huntington Library for the History of the Seventeenth and Eighteenth Century.* San Marino, Calif., Huntington Library, 1941.

Gibson, Arrell M. *Guide to Regional Manuscript Collections in the Division of Manuscripts University of Oklahoma Library.* Norman, Univ. of Oklahoma Press, 1960.

Guide to the Manuscripts in the Southern Historical Collection of the University of North Carolina, WPA Project. Chapel Hill, Univ. of North Carolina Press, 1941.

Hale, Richard W., ed. *Guide to Photocopied Historical Materials in the United States and Canada.* Ithaca, Cornell Univ. Press for the American Historical Association, 1961.

Hamer, Philip M., ed. *A Guide to Archives and Manuscripts in the United States.* New Haven, Yale Univ. Press, 1961.

Handlin, Oscar, *et al. Harvard Guide to American History.* Cambridge, Belknap Press of the Harvard Univ. Press, 1954.

Haskell, Daniel C., comp. *Checklist of Newspapers and Official Gazettes in the New York Public Library.* New York, New York Public Library, 1915.

Historical Records Survey, *Guide to the Manuscript Collections of the Historical Society of Pennsylvania.* 2nd ed. Philadelphia, Historical Society of Pennsylvania, 1949.

Howe, George F., ed. *American Historical Association Guide to Historical Literature.* 2nd ed. New York, The Macmillan Co., 1961.

Kuehl, Warren, ed. *Dissertations in History: An Index to Dissertations Completed in History Departments of United States and Canadian Universities, 1873–1960.* Lexington, Univ. of Kentucky Press, 1965.

Larson, Henrietta M. *Guide to Business History.* Boston, Harvard Studies in Business History, 1948.

Lewinson, Paul. *A Guide to Documents in the National Archives for Negro Studies.* Washington, National Archives, 1947.

Library of Congress. *Calendar of the Papers of John Jordan Crittenden.* Prepared by C. N. Feamster. Washington, Government Printing Office, 1913.

List of Doctoral Dissertations in History in Progress or Completed at Colleges and Universities in the United States. Editor varies. Washington, American Historical Association, triennial.

Massachusetts Historical Society. "The Manuscript Collections of the Massachusetts Historical Society: A Brief Listing," *MHS Miscellany,* No. 5 (Dec., 1958).

Morgan, Dale L., and George P. Hammond, eds. *A Guide to the Manuscript Collections.* Berkeley, Univ. of California Press, for the Bancroft Library, 1963.

Munden, Kenneth W., and Henry P. Beers. *Guide to Federal Archives Relating to the Civil War.* Washington, National Archives and Records Service, 1962.

National Union Catalog of Manuscript Collections.
> Vol. I: Ann Arbor, J. W. Edwards, Publisher, Inc., 1962.
> Vol. II (in 2 parts): Hamden, Conn., The Shoe String Press, Inc., 1964.
> Vols. III–VI: Washington, Library of Congress, 1965, 1966, 1967, 1968.

Peckham, Howard H. *Guide to Manuscript Collections in the William L. Clements Library.* Ann Arbor, Univ. of Michigan Press, 1942. Second edition compiled by William S. Ewing, 1953.

Rhodes, James Ford. Introduction to *A List of Books and Newspapers,*

Maps, Music, and Miscellaneous Matter Printed in the South During the Confederacy, Now in the Boston Athenaeum. Boston, The Athenaeum, 1917.

Smith, Alice E., ed. *Guide to the Manuscripts of the Wisconsin Historical Society*. Madison, State Historical Society of Wisconsin, 1944. Supplement No. 1, Josephine L. Harper and Sharon C. Smith, eds., 1957; Supplement No. 2, Josephine L. Harper and Sharon C. Smith, eds., 1966.

Sowerby, E. Millicent. *Catalogue of the Library of Thomas Jefferson*. 5 vols. Washington, Library of Congress, 1952–59.

Stark, Lewis M. and Maud D. Cole. *Checklist of Additions to Evans' American Bibliography in the Rare Book Division of the New York Public Library*. New York, New York Public Library, 1960.

Thwaites, Reuben Gold. *Descriptive List of Manuscript Collections of the State Historical Society of Wisconsin; together with Reports on other Collections of Manuscript Material for American History in Adjacent States*. Madison, State Historical Society of Wisconsin, 1906.

Tilley, Nannie M., and Noma Lee Goodwin. *Guide to the Manuscript Collections in the Duke University Library*. North Carolina Historical Records Survey Project. Durham, Duke Univ. Press, 1947.

Van Tyne, Claude H., and Waldo Leland. *Guide to the Archives of the Government of the United States in Washington*. Washington, Carnegie Institution of Washington, 1904. Enlarged and revised by Waldo Leland, 1907.

Wagner, Henry R. *The Plains and the Rockies: A Bibliography of Original Narratives of Travel and Adventure, extended by Charles L. Camp*. San Francisco, Grabhorn Press, 1937.

Warner, Robert M., and Ida C. Brown. *Guide to Manuscripts in the Michigan Historical Collections of the University of Michigan*. Ann Arbor, Michigan Historical Collections, 1963.

Winchell, Constance. *Guide to Reference Books*. 8th ed. Chicago, American Library Assn., 1967.

Winsor, Justin. *Calendar of Sparks Manuscripts in Harvard College Library*. Republished from *Bulletin of Harvard Univ.*, No. 36–42, 1887–89. Cambridge, Library of Harvard Univ., 1889.

———. "Manuscript Sources of American History," *Papers of the American Historical Association.* New York, G. P. Putnam's Sons, 1889.

Winther, Oscar W. *A Classified Bibliography of the Periodical Literature of the Trans-Mississippi West, 1811–1957.* Bloomington, Indiana Univ. Press, 1961.

Work, Monroe N. *Bibliography of the Negro in Africa and America.* New York, H. W. Wilson Co., 1928.

Writings on American History. Imprint varies, 1902–03, 1906–40, 1948——.

SECONDARY WORKS (BOOKS AND PAMPHLETS)

Barzun, Jacques, and Henry Graff. *The Modern Researcher.* New York, Harcourt, Brace and World, Inc., 1957.

Baxter, Maurice G., Robert H. Ferrell, and John E. Wiltz. *The Teaching of American History in High Schools.* Bloomington, Indiana Univ. Press, 1964.

Beard, Charles A. *An Economic Interpretation of the Constitution of the United States.* New York, The Macmillan Co., 1913.

Becker, Carl. *Detachment and the Writing of History.* Edited by Phil L. Snyder. Ithaca, Cornell Univ. Press, 1958.

Bernheim, Ernst. *Lehrbuch der historischen Methode und der Geschichtsphilosophie.* 2 vols. Leipzig, Duncker & Humbolt, 1908.

Binkley, Robert C. *Manual on Methods of Reproducing Research Materials.* Ann Arbor, Edwards Brothers, Inc., 1936.

Boyd, Julian P. *The First Duty, An Address Delivered at the Opening of an Exhibition of the Arthur H. and Mary Marden Dean Collection of Lafayette at Cornell University on April 17, 1964.* Ithaca, Cornell Univ. Library, 1964.

———. *Number 7: Alexander Hamilton's Secret Attempts to Control American Foreign Policy.* Princeton, Princeton Univ. Press, 1964.

Brown, Wallace. *The King's Friends.* Providence, Brown Univ. Press, 1965.

Bruner, Jerome. *The Process of Education.* Cambridge, Harvard Univ. Press, 1960.

Butterfield, L. H., and Julian P. Boyd. *Historical Editing in the United States.* Worcester, Mass., American Antiquarian Society, 1963.

Cahnman, Werner J., and Alvin Boskoff, eds. *Sociology and History: Theory and Research*. New York, Free Press of Glencoe, Inc., 1964.

Cappon, Lester J. *Genealogy, Handmaid of History*. Special Publications of the National Genealogical Society, No. 17. Washington, National Genealogical Society, 1957.

Carmichael, Leonard, and Walter F. Dearborn. *Reading and Visual Fatigue*. Boston, Houghton Mifflin Co., 1947.

Carter, Clarence E. *Historical Editing*. Bulletins of the National Archives, No. 7. Washington, National Archives, 1952.

Cartter, Allan M. *An Assessment of Quality in Graduate Education*. Washington, American Council on Education, 1966.

Chambers, Clarke A. *Seedtime of Reform: American Social Service and Social Action*. Minneapolis, Univ. of Minnesota Press, 1963.

Clark, Thomas D. *Pills, Petticoats, and Plows: The Southern Country Store*. Indianapolis, Bobbs-Merrill Co., Inc., 1944; Norman, Univ. of Oklahoma Press, 1964.

Cochran, Thomas C. *The Inner Revolution*. Harper Torchbooks. New York, Harper & Row, Publishers, Inc., 1964.

Cremin, Lawrence A. *The Transformation of the School*. New York, Alfred A. Knopf, Inc., 1961.

Fowler, H. W. *A Dictionary of Modern English Usage*. 2d ed., revised by Sir Ernest Gowers. New York, Oxford Univ. Press, 1965.

Goodman, David. *A Western Panorama, 1849–1875: The Travels, the Writings, and the Influence of J. Ross Browne*. Glendale, Arthur H. Clark, 1966.

Gottschalk, Louis. *Understanding History*. New York, Alfred A. Knopf, Inc., 1951.

Gray, Wood. *Historian's Handbook*. 2nd ed. Boston, Houghton Mifflin Co., 1964.

Hamilton, J. G. de Roulhac. "The Southern Historical Collection," *Library Resources of the University of North Carolina*. Edited by Charles E. Rush. Chapel Hill, Univ. of North Carolina Press, 1945.

Hawken, William R. *Copying Methods Manual*. Chicago, Library Technology Program of the American Library Association, 1966.

Hesseltine, William B. *Pioneer's Mission*. Madison, State Historical Society of Wisconsin, 1954.

Higham, John, with Leonard Krieger and Felix Gilbert. *History*. Englewood Cliffs, N.J., Prentice-Hall, Inc., 1965.

Hockett, Homer C. *The Critical Method in Historical Research and Writing*. New York, The Macmillan Co., 1955.

———. *Introduction to Research in American History*. New York, The Macmillan Co., 1931.

Hosmer, Charles B. *Presence of the Past: A History of the Preservation Movement in the United States*. New York, G. P. Putnam's Sons, 1965.

Jones, Hugh. *The Present State of Virginia*. London, printed for J. Clarke, 1724.

Labaree, Benjamin W. *Patriots and Partisans: The Merchants of Newburyport, 1764–1815*. Cambridge, Harvard Univ. Press, 1962.

Langlois, Charles V., and Charles Seignobos. *Introduction aux études historiques*, published in the United States as *Introduction to the Study of History*. New York, Barnes and Noble, 1966.

Lindzey, Gardner, ed. *Handbook of Social Psychology*. Cambridge, Addison-Wesley Publishing Co., Inc., 1954.

McNeil, Donald R., ed. *The American Collector*. Madison, State Historical Society of Wisconsin, 1955.

Main, Jackson T. *Social Structure of Revolutionary America*. Princeton, Princeton Univ. Press, 1965.

A Manual of Style. 11th ed. Chicago, University of Chicago Press, 1949.

Nevins, Allan. *The Gateway to History*. Chicago, Quadrangle Books, Inc., 1963.

Perkins, Dexter, and John L. Snell. *The Education of Historians in the United States*. New York, McGraw-Hill Book Co., Inc., 1962.

Perman, Dagmar H., ed. *Bibliography and the Historian*. Santa Barbara, Clio Press, 1968.

Perrin, Porter G. *Writer's Guide and Index to English*. Chicago, Scott, Foresman and Co., 1950.

Posner, Ernst. *American State Archives*. Chicago, Univ. of Chicago Press, 1964.

———. *Archives and the Public Interest*. Washington, Public Affairs Press, 1967.

Potter, David M. *People of Plenty*. Chicago, Univ. of Chicago Press, 1954.

Powell, Sumner Chilton. *Puritan Village*. Middletown, Conn., Wesleyan Univ. Press, 1963.

Rhodes, James Ford. *History of the United States from the Compromise of 1850*. 7 vols. New York, The Macmillan Co., 1893–1906.

Salmon, Stephen R. *Specifications for Library of Congress Microfilming*. Washington, Library of Congress, 1964.

Saveth, Edward N., ed. *American History and the Social Sciences*. New York, Free Press of Glencoe, Inc., 1964.

Schlesinger, Arthur M., and Dixon R. Fox, eds. *A History of American Life*. 12 vols. New York, The Macmillan Co., 1927–44.

Schmeckebier, Laurence F., and Roy B. Eastin. *Government Publications and Their Use*. Washington, Brookings Institution, 1961.

Shaw, Ralph R. "Copyright in Relationship to Copying of Scholarly Materials," *Reprography and Copyright Law*. Edited by Lowell H. Hattery and George P. Bush. Washington, American Institute of Biological Sciences, 1965.

Social Science Research Council. *The Social Sciences in Historical Study*. Bulletin 64. New York, SSRC, 1954.

———. *Theory and Practice in Historical Study*. Bulletin 54. New York, SSRC, 1946.

Sparks, Jared. *The Life of Gouverneur Morris*. 3 vols. Boston, Gray & Bowen, 1832.

Stern, Fritz. *The Varieties of History*. New York, Meridian Books, 1957.

Strout, Cushing. *The Pragmatic Revolt in American History*. New Haven, Yale Univ. Press, 1958.

Taylor, William R. *Cavalier and Yankee*. New York, George Braziller, Inc., 1961.

Thernstrom, Stephan. *Poverty and Progress*. Cambridge, Harvard Univ. Press, 1964.

Thwaites, Reuben Gold. *Lyman Copeland Draper: A Memoir*. Madison, State Historical Society of Wisconsin, 1903.

Turabian, Kate L. *A Manual for Writers*. 3rd ed., rev. Chicago, Univ. of Chicago Press, 1967.

Van Tassel, David D. *Recording America's Past*. Chicago, Univ. of Chicago Press, 1960.

Whitehill, Walter Muir. *Independent Historical Societies*. Boston, The Athenaeum, 1962.

Winsor, Justin. *Narrative and Critical History of America*. 8 vols. Boston, Houghton Mifflin Co., 1884–89.

SERIAL LITERATURE

Alexander, John K. " 'American Privateersmen in the Mill Prison During 1772–1782': An Evaluation," *Essex Institute Historical Collections*, Vol. CII, No. 4 (Oct., 1966), 318–40.

Bailyn, Bernard, "Boyd's Jefferson: Notes for a Sketch," *New England Quarterly*, Vol. XXXIII, No. 3 (Sept., 1960), 380–400.

Beard, Charles A. "That Noble Dream," *American Historical Review*, Vol. XLI, No. 1 (Oct., 1935), 74–87.

———. "Written History as an Act of Faith," *American Historical Review*, Vol. XXXIX, No. 2 (Jan., 1934), 219–31.

———, and Alfred Vagts. "Currents of Thought in Historiography," *American Historical Review*, Vol. XLII, No. 3 (Apr., 1937), 460–83.

Binkley, Robert C. "New Tools for Men of Letters," *Yale Review*, Vol. XXIV, No. 3 (Mar., 1935), 519–37.

Bishop, William W., Jr., Robert H. Ferrell, Philip E. Mosley, Robert E. Osgood, Robert B. Stewart, Robert R. Wilson, and Richard W. Leopold. "Report of Advisory Committee on 'Foreign Relations,' 1964," *American Journal of International Law*, Vol. LIX, No. 4 (Oct., 1965), 914–18.

Bogue, Allan G. "United States: The 'New' Political History," *Journal of Contemporary History*, Vol. III, No. 1 (Jan., 1968), 5–27.

Boyd, Julian P. "Some Animadversions on Being Struck by Lightning," *Daedalus*, Vol. LXXXVI, No. 1 (May, 1955), 49–56.

Brubaker, Robert L. "The Publication of Historical Sources: Recent Projects in the United States," *Library Quarterly*, Vol. XXXVII, No. 2 (Apr., 1967), 193–225.

Butterfield, L. H. "Archival and Editorial Enterprise in 1850 and 1950: Some Comparisons and Contrasts," *Proceedings of the American Philosophical Society*, Vol. XCVIII, No. 3 (June, 1954), 159–70.

———. "Bostonians and Their Neighbors as Pack Rats," *American Archivist*, Vol. XXIV, No. 2 (Apr., 1961), 141–59.

Butterfield, Roger. "Henry Ford, the Wayside Inn, and the Problem of

'History is Bunk.' " *Massachusetts Historical Society Proceedings*, Vol. LXXVII (1965), 53–66.

Cappon, Lester J. "A Rationale for Historical Editing Past and Present," *William and Mary Quarterly*, 3rd Series, Vol. XXIII, No. 1 (Jan., 1966), 56–75.

Clubb, Jerome M., and Howard Allen. "Computers and Historical Studies," *Journal of American History*, Vol. LIV, No. 3 (Dec., 1967), 599–607.

Cochran, Thomas C. "The 'Presidential Synthesis' in American History," *American Historical Review*, Vol. LIII, No. 4 (July, 1948), 748–59.

Commager, Henry Steele. "Should Historians Write Contemporary History?" *Saturday Review* (Feb. 12, 1966), 18–20, 47.

Connor, Seymour V. "The Problem of Literary Property in Archival Depositories," *American Archivist*, Vol. XXI, No. 2 (Apr., 1958), 143–52.

Cotner, Robert C., and Peyton E. Cook. "Dudley Crawford Sharp— Secretary for Air," *East Texas Historical Journal*, Vol. II, No. 2 (Oct., 1964), 99–117.

Destler, Chester M. "Some Observations on Contemporary Historical Theory," *American Historical Review*, Vol. LV, No. 3 (Apr., 1950), 503–29.

Dickison, R. R. "The Scholar and the Future of Microfilm," *American Documentation*, Vol. XVII, No. 4 (Oct., 1966), 178–79.

Dunn, Roy Sylvan. "The Southwest Collection at 'Texas Tech,' " *American Archivist*, Vol. XXVII, No. 3 (July, 1965), 413–19.

Feis, Herbert. "The Shackled Historian," *Foreign Affairs*, Vol. XLV, No. 2 (Jan., 1967), 332–43.

Gambill, Edward L. "Who Were the Senate Radicals?" *Civil War History*, Vol. XI, No. 3 (Sept., 1965), 237–44.

Greven, Philip J., Jr. "Historical Demography and Colonial America," *William and Mary Quarterly*, 3rd Series, Vol. XXIV, No. 3 (July, 1967), 438–54.

Grover, Wayne C. "Toward Equal Opportunities for Scholarship," *Journal of American History*, Vol. LII, No. 4 (Mar., 1966), 715–24.

Harper, Josephine L. "Lyman C. Draper and Early American Archives," *American Archivist*, Vol. XV, No. 3 (July, 1952), 205–12.

Holmes, Oliver W. "Recent Writings Relevant to Documentary Publication Programs," *American Archivist*, Vol. XXVI, No. 1 (Jan., 1963), 137–42.

Holt, W. Stull. "The Idea of Scientific History in America," *Journal of the History of Ideas*, Vol. I, No. 3 (June, 1940), 352–62.

Jones, H. G. "Archival Training in American Universities, 1938–68," *American Archivist*, Vol. XXXI, No. 2 (Apr., 1968), 135–54.

Jordan, Philip D. "The Scholar and the Archivist—A Partnership," *American Archivist*, Vol. XXXI, No. 1 (Jan., 1968), 57–65.

Koch, Adrienne. "The Historian as Scholar," *Nation*, Vol. CXCV, No. 17 (Nov. 24, 1962), 357–61.

Labaree, Leonard W. "Scholarly Editing in Our Times," *Ventures*, Vol. III (Winter, 1964), 28–31.

Leland, Waldo Gifford. "The Prehistory and Origins of the National Historical Publications Commission," *American Archivist*, Vol. XXVII, No. 2 (Apr., 1964), 187–94.

Leopold, Richard W. "The *Foreign Relations* Series: A Centennial Estimate," *Mississippi Valley Historical Review*, Vol. XLIX, No. 4 (Mar., 1963), 595–612.

Marcus, Jacob R. "The American Jewish Archives," *American Archivist*, Vol. XXIII, No. 1 (Jan., 1960), 57–61.

Morgan, Edmund S. "John Adams and the Puritan Tradition," *New England Quarterly*, Vol. XXXIV, No. 4 (Dec., 1961), 518–29.

Morison, Samuel Eliot. "Faith of a Historian," *American Historical Review*, Vol. LVI, No. 2 (Jan., 1951), 261–75.

Morris, Richard B. "The Current Statesmen's Papers Publication Program: An Appraisal from the Point of View of the Legal Historian," *American Journal of Legal History*, Vol. XI, No. 2 (Apr., 1967), 95–106.

Nichols, Roy F. "History in a Self-Governing Culture," *American Historical Review*, Vol. LXXII, No. 2 (Jan., 1967), 411–24.

Olson, James C. "The Scholar and Documentary Publication," *American Archivist*, Vol. XXVIII, No. 2 (Apr., 1965), 187–93.

"Planning for Scholarly Photocopying," *Publications of the Modern Languages Association*, Vol. LXXIX, No. 4, pt. 2 (Sept., 1964), 77–90.

Posner, Ernst. "The National Archives and the Archival Theorist," *American Archivist*, Vol. XVIII, No. 3 (July, 1955), 207–16.

Rowan, Carl T. "State Dept. and Information Law," [Washington] *Evening Star*, Jan. 17, 1968, p. A17.

Rundell, Walter, Jr. "The Recent American Past v. H. R. 4347: Historians' Dilemma," *American Archivist*, Vol. XXIX, No. 2 (Apr., 1966), 209–15.

Shelley, Fred. "Ebenezer Hazard: America's First Historical Editor," *William and Mary Quarterly*, 3rd Series, Vol. XII, No. 1 (Jan., 1955), 44–73.

———. "Manuscripts in the Library of Congress: 1800–1900," *American Archivist*, Vol. XI, No. 1 (Jan., 1948), 3–19.

———. "The Presidential Papers Program of the Library of Congress," *American Archivist*, Vol. XXV, No. 4 (Oct., 1962), 429–33.

Silbey, Joel H. "The Civil War Synthesis in American Political History," *Civil War History*, Vol. X, No. 2 (June, 1964), 130–40.

Smith, Theodore Clarke. "The Writing of American History in America, from 1884–1934," *American Historical Review*, Vol. XL, No. 3 (Apr., 1935), 439–49.

Sorenson, Lloyd R. "Historical Currents in America," *American Quarterly*, Vol. VII, No. 3 (Fall, 1955), 234–46.

Webb, Walter Prescott. "The Historical Seminar: Its Outer Shell and Its Inner Spirit," *Mississippi Valley Historical Review*, Vol. XLII, No. 1 (June, 1955), 3–23.

———. "History as High Adventure," *American Historical Review*, Vol. LXIV, No. 2 (Jan., 1959), 265–81.

Whitehill, Walter Muir, Julian P. Boyd, Leonard W. Labaree, L. H. Butterfield, Wilmarth S. Lewis, and Waldo G. Leland. "Publishing the Papers of Great Men: A Session at the Sixty-Ninth Annual Meeting of the American Historical Association, 30 December, 1954," *Daedalus*, Vol. LXXXVI, No. 1 (May, 1955), 47–79.

Winfrey, Dorman H. "The Archive Wars in Texas," *American Archivist*, Vol. XXIII, No. 4 (Oct., 1960), 431–37.

Woodward, C. Vann. "History and the Third Culture," *Journal of Contemporary History*, Vol. III, No. 2 (Apr., 1968), 23–35.

Zagorin, Perez. "Historical Knowledge: A Review Article on the Philosophy of History," *Journal of Modern History*, Vol. XXXI, No. 3 (Sept., 1959), 243–55.

GOVERNMENT DOCUMENTS

U.S. *A National Program for the Publication of Historical Documents: A Report to the President by the National Historical Publications Commission.* Washington, [NHPC], 1954.

U.S. *A Report to the President Containing a Proposal by the National Historical Publications Commission.* Washington, [NHPC], 1963.

U.S. Bureau of Labor Statistics. *Negroes in the United States.* Washington, Government Printing Office, 1952.

U.S. Congress. House of Representatives. *Report No. 1497.* 89th Cong., 2nd sess., 1966.

U.S. Department of the Army, Memorandum No. 345-3, "Policies and Procedures Governing Processing of Applications for Unofficial Historical Research in Classified Army Records," 14 Jan. 1966.

U.S. Government. *The Children of Immigrants in the Schools.* 5 vols. (Reports of the Immigration Commission, Vols. XXIX-XXXIII). Washington, Government Printing Office, 1911.

U.S. *Military Operations of the Civil War: A Guide Index to the Official Records of the Union and Confederate Armies, 1861-1865.* Washington, Civil War Centennial Commission, 1966.

U.S. *Naval History Sources in the Washington Area and Suggested Research Subjects.* Rev. ed. Washington, Naval History Division, Navy Department, 1965.

U.S. *Official Records of the Union and Confederate Navies in the War of the Rebellion.* Washington, Government Printing Office, 1894-1927.

U.S. *Public Papers of the Presidents of the United States.* Washington, Office of the *Federal Register*, National Archives and Records Service, 1953——.

United States Statutes at Large, 1966, Vol. LXXX, Pt. 1. Washington, Government Printing Office, 1967.

U.S. *Style Manual.* Rev. ed. Washington, Government Printing Office, 1959.

U.S. *The War of the Rebellion: A Compilation of the Official Records of the Union and Confederate Armies.* Washington, Government Printing Office, 1880-1901.

PAPERS PRESENTED TO LEARNED SOCIETIES

Bogue, Allan G. "Fission or Fusion? Historians, Political Scientists and Quantification." Paper delivered to the American Political Science Association at the 1966 meeting.

Leisinger, Albert H., Jr. "Microreproduction of Archives for Reference and Publication Purposes: Selected Aspects of Microreproduction in the United States." Paper presented to the Extraordinary Congress of the International Council on Archives in May, 1966.

Storm, Colton. "Needs and Opportunities for Research at the Newberry Library." Paper delivered to the Western History Association at the 1966 meeting.

White, Gerald T. "Government Archives Afield: The Federal Records Centers and the Historian." Paper presented at the meeting of the Organization of American Historians, April 27, 1967.

MISCELLANEOUS

Annual Report of the American Historical Association, Vol. I, Proceedings, 1896, 1963, 1964, 1965. Washington, Government Printing Office, 1897, 1964, 1965, 1966.

Estrich, Willis A., George S. Gulick, William M. McKinney, *et al.*, eds. *American Jurisprudence.* San Francisco, Bancroft-Whitney, 1936——.

Mack, William, and William B. Hale, eds. *Corpus Juris.* 73 vols. New York, The American Law Book Co., 1914–37.

——, Donald J. Kiser, *et al.*, eds. *Corpus Juris Secundum.* 101 vols. Brooklyn, The American Law Book Co., 1936–58.

Scheips, Paul J. "Government Records and Their Use by Students," July 29, 1967. Processed.

INDEX

In Pursuit of American History was set on the Linotype in eleven-point Janson, a traditional typeface chosen for its condensed letter forms which harmonize well with the display type, Alternate Gothic No. 1, for an over-all "vertical" page design.

The paper on which this book is printed bears the watermark of the University of Oklahoma Press and has an effective life of at least three hundred years.

University of Oklahoma Press
Norman